Kershaw's Brigade

Volume 1

Kershaw's Brigade
Volume 1
South Carolina's Regiments
in the American Civil War:

Manassas, Seven Pines, Sharpsburg (Antietam),
Fredricksburg, Chancellorsville, Gettysburg,
Chickamauga, Chattanooga, Fort Sanders
and Bean Station

D. Augustus Dickert

LEONAUR

Kershaw's Brigade - Volume 1: South Carolina's Regiments
in the American Civil War: Manassas, Seven Pines, Sharpsburg (Antietam),
Fredricksburg, Chancellorsville, Gettysburg, Chickamauga, Chattanooga,
Fort Sanders and Bean Station
by D. Augustus Dickert

Originally published under the title
The History of Kershaw's Brigade

Published by Leonaur Ltd

ISBN (10 digit): 1-84677-105-6 (hardcover)
ISBN (13 digit): 978-1-84677-105-7 (hardcover)

ISBN (10 digit): 1-84677-104-8 (softcover)
ISBN (13 digit): 978-1-84677-104-0 (softcover)

http://www.leonaur.com

Contents

Introduction

The name of Kershaw's Brigade of South Carolinians is familiar to all who wore the gray and saw hard fighting on the fields of Virginia, in the swamps of Carolina and the mountains of Tennessee. This was "the First Brigade of the First Division of the First Corps of the Army of Northern Virginia," and many of its members volunteered for service before the first gun was fired at the Star of the West, while its ragged regimental remnants laid down their arms at Greensboro not till the 2d of May, 1865, nearly a month after the fateful day of Appomattox. Its history is a history of the war, for, as will he seen, there were few pitched battles in the East that did not call forth its valor.

The author of the book is D. Augustus Dickert, who, at the age of 15, ran away to fight and surrendered as captain in the Third South Carolina Volunteers. He was a gallant soldier all through, and he has written a good book, for the broader lines of history are interwoven with many slight anecdotes and incidents that illustrate the temper of the times and impart to the narrative a local coloring. The following is a good example of its style: "The writer was preparing to enter school in an adjoining county. But when on my way to school I boarded a train filled with enthusiasts, some tardy soldiers on their way to join their companions and others to see, and, if need be, to take old Anderson out of his den. Nothing could be heard on the train but war 'taking of Sumter,' 'old Anderson' and 'Star of the West.' Everyone was in high glee. Palmetto cockades, brass buttons, uniforms and gaudy epaulettes were seen in every direction. This was more than a youthful vision could withstand, so I directed myself toward the seat of war instead of schools." Although somewhat theatric, this is an accurate presentation of those early days.

The chief merit of Captain Dickert's book is that it presents the gay and bright, as well as the grave side of the Confederate soldier's experience. It is full of anecdote and incident and repartee. Such quips and jests kept the heart light and the blood warm beneath many a tattered coat.

The student of history may wish a more elaborate sketch. But the average man who wishes to snatch a moment for recreation will be repaid as he takes up this sketch. There are some faults of style and some of typography; but, all in all, this is a hearty, cheery, clean book. It extenuates some things, maybe; but it sets down naught in malice. As a local history it is an interesting contribution to the chronicle of the period.

R. Means Davis

Note to the 2006 Edition

We would ask readers to remember that this book necessarily reflects the attitudes of a sector of American society at the time in which it was written. We in no way endorse the views of the author when he expresses his beliefs regarding the nature and status of African Americans and in re-publishing this book we had to decide whether to amend such references to make them more palatable to modern readers. After much consideration our final decision was that historical accuracy would be best served by leaving them as originally published. We hope this decision does not cause offence.

The Leonaur Editors

Author's Announcement

Comrades: Years ago I was asked by the members of a local camp (James D. Nance Camp, United Confederate Veterans, Newberry, S.C.,) of Veterans to write a history of Kershaw's "Old First Brigade in the Civil War," in order that the part taken by you in that memorable struggle might be transmitted to posterity through the instrumentality of a proud and loving participant in all the events that went to make up the life of an organization second to none, that has ever stood face to face with an invading foe upon the face of earth.

This request was not based upon a supposition of superior educational qualifications on my part, for the parties who made it know that my school days ended at twelve, and that the time usually devoted to instruction of youth was spent by many of us, from '61 to '65, on the northern side of Richmond. Consequently, to the love that I treasure in my heart for the "Old First" is due whatever of distinction attaches to the position of recorder of actions which prove the worth and heroism of each constituent part of the brigade. In accepting this trust I shall repress all desire for rhetorical display. I will not even attempt to do that justice, which is beyond the power of mortals; but shall simply try to be your faithful chronicler or recorder of facts as they appeared to me and others, who have so kindly assisted me in the compilation of these records, and shall confine myself to the effort to attain my highest ambition—absolute correctness. It is true that inaccuracies may have crept in; but these will be found to be mostly among proper names—due in a great measure to the illegibility of the manuscripts furnished me by correspondents. Again, apparent errors will be explained, when it is recalled to your minds that no two men see the same circumstance from the same standpoint. Honest differences will appear, no matter how trivial the facts are upon which they are based.

I have endeavored to be fair and just, and in so doing have laid aside a soldier's pardonable pride in his own regiment, and have accorded "honor to whom honor was due." Despite all that maybe alleged to the contrary, ours was not a "War of the Roses," of brother against brother, struggling for supremacy; but partook more of the nature of the inhuman contest in the Netherlands, waged by the unscrupulous and crafty Duke of Alva at the instance Philip (the Good!), or rather like that in which the rich and fruitful Province of the Palatine was subjected to fire and rapine under the mailed hand of that monster of iniquity—Turenne.

How well the men of Kershaw's Brigade acted their part, how proudly they faced the foe, how grandly they fought, how nobly they died, I shall attempt not to depict; and yet—

> *Could heart and brain and hand and pen*
> *But bring to earth and life again*
> *The scenes of old,*
> *Then all the world might know and see;*
> *Your deeds on scrolls of fame would be*
> *Inscribed in gold*

I am indebted to many of the old comrades for their assistance, most notably Judge Y.J. Pope, of the Third South Carolina; Colonel Wm. Wallace, of the Second; Captain L.A. Waller, for the Seventh; Captains Malloy, Harllee, and McIntyre, of the Eighth; Captain D.J. Griffith and Private Charles Blair, of the Fifteenth; Colonel Rice and Captain Jennings, of the Third Battalion, and many others of the Twentieth. But should this volume prove of interest to any of the "Old Brigade," and should there be any virtue in it, remember it belongs to Y.J. Pope. Thrice have I laid down my pen, after meeting with so many rebuffs; but as often taken it up after the earnest solicitation of the former Adjutant of the Third, who it was that urged me on to its completion.

D. Augustus Dickert
Newberry, S.C.
August 15, 1899

CHAPTER 1

Secession

The secession bell rang out in South Carolina on the 20th of December, 1860, not to summon the men to arms, nor to prepare the State for war. There was no conquest that the State wished to make, no foe on her border, no enemy to punish. Like the liberty bell of the revolution that electrified the colonies from North to South, the bell of secession put the people of the State in a frenzy from the mountains to the sea. It announced to the world that South Carolina would be free—that her people had thrown off the yoke of the Union that bound the States together in an unholy alliance. For years the North had been making encroachments upon the South; the general government grasping, with a greedy hand, those rights and prerogatives, which belonged to the States alone, with a recklessness only equalled by Great Britain towards the colonies; began absorbing all of the rights guaranteed to the State by the constitution, and tending towards a strong and centralized government. They had made assaults upon our institutions, torn away the barriers that protected our sovereignty. So reckless and daring had become these assaults, that on more than one occasion the States of the South threatened dissolution of the Union. But with such master minds as Clay, Webster, and Calhoun in the councils of the nation, the calamity was averted for the time. The North had broken compact after compact, promises after promises, until South Carolina determined to act upon those rights she had retained for herself in the formation of the Union, and which the general government guaranteed to all, and withdrew when that Union no longer served the purposes for which it was formed.

Slavery, it has been said, was the cause of the war. Incidentally it may have been, but the real cause was far removed from the institution of slavery. That institution existed at the formation of the Union, or compact. It had existed for several hundred years, and in every State; the federation was fully cognizant of the fact when the agreement of the Union was reached. They promised not to disturb it, and allow each State to control it as it seemed best. Slavery was gradually but surely dying out. Among the border States it scarcely existed at all, and the mighty hand of an All-wise Ruler could be plainly seen in the gradual emancipation of all the slaves on the continent. It had begun in the New England States then. In the Caribbean Sea and South America emancipation had been gradually closing in upon the small compass of the Southern States, and that by peaceful measures, and of its own volition; so much so that it would have eventually died out, could not be denied by any who would look that far into the future, and judge that future by the past. The South looked with alarm and horror at a wholesale emancipation, when they viewed its havoc and destruction in Hayti and St. Domingo, where once existed beautiful homes and luxuriant fields, happy families and general progress; all this wealth, happiness, and prosperity had been swept away from those islands as by a deadly blight. Ruin, squalor, and beggary now stalks through those once fair lands.

A party sprang up at the North inimical to the South; at first only a speck upon the horizon, a single sail in a vast ocean; but it grew and spread like contagion. They were first called agitators, and consisted of a few fanatics, both women and men, whose avowed object was emancipation—to do by human hands that which an All-wise Providence was surely doing in His own wise way. At first the South did not look with any misgivings upon the fanatics. But when Governors of Northern States, leading statesmen in the councils of the nation; announced this as their creed and guide, then the South began to consider seriously the subject of secession. Seven Governors and their legislatures at the North had declared, by acts regularly passed and ratified, their determination "not to allow the laws of the land to be administered or carried out in their States." They made preparation to nullify the laws of Congress and the constitution. That party, which was first called "Agitators," but now took the name of "Republicans"—called at the South the "black Republicans"—had grown to such proportions that they put in the field candidates for President and Vice-President of the United States. Numbers increased with each succeeding campaign. In the campaign of 1860 they put Abraham Lincoln and Hannibal Hamlin forward as their standard bearers, and whose avowed purpose was the "the liberation of the slaves, regardless of the consequences." This party had spies all over the Southern States, and these emissaries incited insurrection, taught the slaves

12

"that by rising at night and murdering their old masters and their families, they would be doing God's will;" that "it was a duty they owed to their children;" this "butchery of the sleeping and innocent whites was the road to freedom." In Virginia they sent down armed bands of whites, roused the negroes at night, placed guns, pikes, and arms of every kind in the hands of the poor, deluded creatures, and in that one night they butchered, in cold blood, the families of some of the best men in the State. These cold blooded butcheries would have done credit to the most cruel and blood thirsty of the primeval savages of the forest. These deeds were heralded all over the North as "acts of God, done by the hands of men." The leader of this diabolical plan and his compeers were sainted by their followers and admirers, and praises sung over him all over the North, as if over the death of saints. By a stupendous blunder the people of the South, and the friends of the Union generally, allowed this party to elect Lincoln and Hamlin. The South now had no alternative. Now she must either remain in a Union, where our institutions were to be dragged down; where the laws were to be obeyed in one section, but not in another; where existed open resistance to laws in one State and quiet obedience in another; where servile insurrections were being threatened continuously; where the slaves were aided and abetted by whites at the North in the butcheries of their families; or secede and fight. These were the alternatives on the one part, or a severance from the Union and its consequences on the other. From the very formation of the government, two constructions were put upon this constitution—the South not viewing this compact with that fiery zeal, or fanatical adulation, as they did at the North. The South looked upon it more as a confederation of States for mutual protection in times of danger, and a general advancement of those interests where the whole were concerned. Then, again, the vast accumulation of wealth in the Southern States, caused by the overshadowing of all other commodities of commerce—cotton—created a jealousy at the North that nothing but the prostration of the South, the shattering of her commerce, the destruction of her homes, and the freedom of her slaves, could answer. The wealth of the South had become a proverb The "Wealthy Southern Planter" had become an eyesore to the North, and to humble her haughty pride, as the North saw it, was to free her slaves. As one of the first statesmen of the South has truly said, "The seeds of the Civil War were sown fifty years before they were born who fought her battles."

A convention was called to meet in Columbia, in December, 1860, to frame a new constitution, and to take such steps as were best suited to meet the new order of things that would be brought about by this fanatical party soon to be at the head of the government. Feeling ran high—people were excited—everywhere the voice of the people was for secession. The women of the South, who would naturally be the first sufferers if the programme of the "Agitators" were carried out, were loud in their cries for separation. Some few people were in favor of the South moving in a body, and a feeble opposition ticket for the delegates to the convention was put in the field. These were called "Co-operationists," i.e., in favor of secession, but to await a union with the other Southern States. These were dubbed by the most fiery zealots of secession, "Submissionists" in derision. The negroes, too, scented freedom from afar. The old cooks, mammas, house servants, and negro eavesdroppers gathered enough of "freedom of slaves," "war," "secession," to cause the negroes to think that a great measure was on foot somewhere, that had a direct bearing on their long looked for Messiah—"Freedom." Vigilance committees sprung up all over the South, to watch parties of Northern sentiment, or sympathy, and exercise a more guarded scrutiny over the acts of the negroes. Companies were organized in towns and cities, who styled themselves "Minute Men," and rosettes, or the letters "M.M.," adorned the lapels of the coats worn by those in favor of secession. The convention met in Columbia, but for some local cause it was removed to Charleston. After careful deliberation, a new constitution was framed and the ordinance of secession was passed without a dissenting voice, on the 20th of December, 1860, setting forth the State's grievances and acting upon her rights, declaring South Carolina's connection with the Union at an end. It has been truly said, that this body of men who passed the ordinance of secession was one of the most deliberate, representative, and talented that had ever assembled in the State of South Carolina. When the news flashed over the wires the people were in a frenzy of delight and excitement—bells tolled, cannons boomed, great parades took place, and orators from street corners and hotel balconies harangued the people. The ladies wore palmetto upon their hats or dresses, and showed by every way possible their earnestness in the great drama that was soon to be enacted upon the stage events. Drums beat, men marched through the streets, banners waved and dipped, ladies from the windows and from the housetops waved handkerchiefs or flags to the enthusiastic throng moving below. The bells from historic old St. Michael's, in Charleston, were never so musical to the ears of the people as when they pealed out the chimes that told of secession. The war was on.

Still with all this enthusiasm, the sober-headed, patriotic element of the South regretted the necessity of this dissolution. They, too, loved the Union their ancestors had helped to make—they loved the name, the glory, and the prestige won by their forefathers upon the bloody field of the revolution. While they did not view this Union as indispensable to their existence, they loved and reverenced the flag of their country. As a people, they loved the North; as a nation, they gloried in her past and future possibilities. The dust of their ancestors mingled in imperishable fame with those of the North. In the peaceful "Godsacre" or on the fields of carnage they were ever willing to share with them their greatness, and equally enjoyed those of their own, but denied to them the rights to infringe upon the South's possessions or rights of statehood. We all loved the Union, but we loved it as it was formed and made a compact by the blood of our ancestors. Not as contorted and misconstrued by demagogueism and fanaticism. We almost deified the flag of the Union, under whose folds it was made immortal by the Huguenots, the Roundheads, the Cavaliers, and men of every faith and conviction in the crowning days of the revolution. The deeds of her great men, the history of the past, were an equal heritage of all—we felt bound together by natural bonds equal to the ties of blood or kindred. We loved her towering mountains, her rolling prairies, her fertile fields, her enchanting scenery, her institutions, her literature and arts, all; all were equally the South's as well as the North's. Not for one moment would the South pluck a rose from the flowery wreath of our goddess of liberty and place it upon the brow of our Southland alone. The Mississippi, rising among the hills and lakes of the far North, flowing through the fertile valleys of the South, was to all our "Mother Nile." The great Rocky Mountains and Sierra Nevada chained our Western border together from Oregon to the Rio Grande. The Cumberland, the Allegheny, and the Blue Ridge, lifting their heads up from among the verdant fields of Vermont, stretching southward, until from their southern summit at "Lookout" could be viewed the borderland of the gulf. In the sceneries of these mountains, their legends and traditions, they were to all the people of the Union what Olympus was to the ancients. Where the Olympus was the haunts, the wooing places of the gods of the ancient Greeks, the Appalachian was the reveling grounds for the muses of song and story of the North and South alike. And while the glories of the virtues of Greece and Rome, the birthplace of republicanism and liberty, may have slept for centuries, or died out entirely, that spirit of national liberty and personal freedom was transplanted to the shores of the New World, and nowhere was the spirit of freedom more cherished and fostered than in the bright and sunny lands of the South. The flickering torch of freedom, borne by those sturdy sons of the old world to the new, nowhere took such strong and rapid growth as did that planted by the Huguenots on the soil of South Carolina. Is it any wonder, then, that a people with such high ideals, such lofty spirits, such love of freedom, would tamely submit to a Union where such ideals and spirits were so lightly considered as by those who were now in charge of the government—where our women and children were to be at the mercies of a brutal race, with all of their passions aroused for rapine and bloodshed; where we would be continually threatened or subjected to a racial war, one of supremacy; where promises were made to be broken, pledges given to be ignored; where laws made for all were to be binding only on those who chose to obey? Such were some of the conditions that confronted South Carolina and her sister States at this time, and forced them into measures that brought about the most stupendous civil war in modern or ancient times.

To sum up: It was not love for the Union, but jealousy of the South's wealth. It was not a spirit of humanity towards the slaves, but a hatred of the South, her chivalry, her honor, and her integrity. A quality wanting in the one is always hated in that of the other.

CHAPTER 2
Enrollment Of Troops

The Legislature, immediately after the passage of the ordinance of secession, authorized the Governor to organize ten regiments of infantry for State service. Some of these regiments were enlisted for twelve months, while Gregg's, the First, was for six, of, as it was understood at the time, its main duties were the taking of Sumter. The first regiments so formed were: First, Gregg's; Second, Kershaw's; Third, Williams'; Fourth, Sloan's; Fifth, Jenkins'; Sixth, Rion's; Seventh, Bacon's: Eighth, Cash's; Ninth, Blanding's; besides a regiment of regulars and some artillery and cavalry companies. There existed a nominal militia in the State, and numbered by battalions and regiments. These met every three months by companies and made some feeble attempts at drilling, or "mustering," as it was called. To the militia was intrusted the care of internal police of the State. Each company was divided into squads, with a captain, whose duties were to do the policing of the neighborhood, called "patrolling." They would patrol the country during Sundays, and occasionally at nights, to prevent illegal assemblies of negroes, and also to prevent them from being at large without permission of their masters. But this system had dwindled down to a farce, and was only engaged in by some of the youngsters, more in a spirit of fun and frolic than to keep order in the neighborhood. The real duties of the militia of the State consisted of an annual battalion and regimental parade, called "battalion muster" and "general muster." This occasioned a lively turn-out of the people, both ladies and gentlemen, not connected with the troops, to witness the display of officers' uniforms, and bright caparisoned steeds, the stately tread of the "muster men," listen to the rattle of the drums and inspiring strains of the fifes, and horns of the rural bands.

From each battalion a company was formed for State service. These companies elected their captains and field officers, the general officers being appointed by the Governor. Immediately after the call

17

of the Governor for troops, a great military spirit swept the country, volunteer companies sprang up like magic all over the land, each anxious to enter the service of the State and share the honor of going to war. Up to this time, few thought, there would be a conflict. Major Anderson, U.S.A., then on garrison duty at Fort Moultrie, heard of the secession of the State, and (whether by orders or his own volition, is not known and immaterial,) left Fort Moultrie, after spiking the guns and destroying the carriages; took possession of Fort Sumter. The State government looked with some apprehension upon this questionable act of Maj. Anderson's. Fort Sumter stood upon grounds of the State, ceded to the United States for purposes of defence. South Carolina now claimed the property, and made demands upon Maj. Anderson and the government at Washington for its restoration. This was refused.

Ten companies, under Col. Maxey Gregg, were called to Charleston for the purpose of retaking this fort by force of arms, if peaceful methods failed. These companies were raised mostly in towns and cities by officers who had been commissioned by the Governor. College professors formed companies of their classes, and hurried off to Charleston. Companies of town and city volunteers offered their services to the Governor—all for six months, or until the fall of Sumter.

On the 9th of January, 1861, the State was thrown into a greater paroxism of excitement by the "Star of the West," a Northern vessel, being fired on in the bay of Charleston by State troops. This steamer, laden with supplies for Sumter, had entered the channel with the evident intention of reinforcing Anderson, when the Citadel guards, under Captain Stevens, fired several shots across her bow, then she turned about and sped away to the sea. In the meantime the old battalions of militia had been called out at their respective "muster grounds," patriotic speeches made, and a call for volunteers made. Companies were easily formed and officers elected. Usually in selecting the material for officers, preference was given to soldiers of the Mexican war, graduates of the military schools and the old militia of officers. These companies met weekly, and were put through a course of instructions in the old Macomb's tactics. In this way the ten regiments were formed, but not called together until the commencement of the bombardment of Sumter, with the exception of those troops enlisted for six months, now under Gregg at Charleston, and a few volunteer companies of cavalry and artillery.

The writer was preparing to enter school in a neighboring county when the first wave of patriotism struck him. Captain Walker's Company, from Newberry, of which I was a member, had been ordered to Charleston with Gregg, and was stationed at Morris' Island before I could get off. Two of my brothers and myself had joined the company made, up from the Thirty-ninth Battalion of State militia, and which afterwards formed a part of the Third S.C. Volunteers (Colonel Williams). But at that time, to a young mind like mine, the war looked too remote for me to wait for this company to go, so when on my way to school I boarded a train filled with enthusiasts, some tardy soldiers on their way to join their companies, and others to see, and if need be, "take old Anderson out of his den." Nothing on the train could be heard but war, war—"taking of Sumter," "Old Anderson," and "Star of the West." Everyone was in a high glee—palmetto cockades, brass buttons, uniforms, and gaudy epaulettes were seen in every direction. This was more than a youthful vision could withstand, so I directed my steps towards the seat of war instead of school. By this time the city of Charleston may be said to have been in a state of siege—none could leave the islands or lands without a permit from the Governor or the Adjutant and Inspector General. The headquarters of Governor Pickens and staff were in the rooms of the Charleston Hotel, and to that place I immediately hied and presented myself before those "August dignitaries," and asked permission to join my company on Morris' Island, but was refused. First, on account of not having a permit of leave of absence from my captain; secondly, on account of my youth (I then being on the rise of 15); and thirdly, having no permission from my parents. What a contrast with later years, when boys of that age were pressed into service. The city of Charleston was ablaze with excitement, flags waved from the house tops, the heavy tread of the embryo soldiers could be heard in the streets, the corridors of hotels, and in all the public places. The beautiful park on the water front, called the "Battery," was thronged with people of every age and sex, straining their eyes or looking through glasses out at Sumter, whose bristling front was surmounted with cannon, her flags waving defiance. Small boats and steamers dotted the waters of the bay. Ordnance and ammunition were being hurried to the island. The one continual talk was "Anderson," "Fort Sumter," and "war." While there was no spirit of bravado, or of courting of war, there was no disposition to shirk it. A strict guard was kept at all the wharves, or boat landings, to prevent any espionage on our movements or works. It will be well to say here, that no moment from the day of secession to the day the first gun was fired at Sumter, had been allowed to pass without overtures being made to the government at Washington for a peaceful solution of the momentous question. Every effort that tact or diplomacy could invent was resorted to, to have an amicable adjustment. Commissioners had been sent to Washington, asking, urging, and almost begging to be allowed to leave the Union, now odious to the people of the State, without bloodshed. Commissioners of the North came to Charleston to treat for peace, but they demanded peace without any concessions, peace with submission, peace with all the chances of a servile war. Some few leaders at the North were willing to allow us the right, while none denied it. The leading journal at the North said: "Let the erring sisters depart in peace." But all of our overtures were rejected by the administration at Washington, and a policy of evasion, or dilly-dallying, was kept up by those in authority at the North. All the while active preparations were going on to coerce the State by force of arms. During this time other States seceded and joined South Carolina, and formed the "Confederate States of America," with Jefferson Davis as President, with the capital at Montgomery, Ala.

Being determined to reach my company, I boarded a steamer, bound for Morris' Island, intending, if possible, to avoid the guard. In this I was foiled. But after making several futile attempts, I fell in with an officer of the First South Carolina Regiment, who promised to pilot me over. On reaching the landing, at Cummings Point, I was to follow his lead, as he had a passport, but in going down the gang plank we were met by soldiers with crossed bayonets, demanding "passports." The officer, true to his word, passed me over, but then my trouble began. When I reached the shore I lost my sponsor, and began to make inquiries for my company. When it was discovered that there was a stranger in the camp without a passport, a corporal of the guards was called, I was placed under arrest, sent to the guardhouse, and remained in durance vile until Captain Walker came to release me. When I joined my company I found a few of my old school-mates, the others were strangers. Everything that met my eyes reminded me of war. Sentinels patrolled the beach; drums beat; soldiers marching and counter-marching; great cannons being drawn along the beach, hundreds of men pulling them by long ropes, or drawn by mule teams. Across the bay we could see on Sullivan's Island men and soldiers building and digging out foundations for forts. Morris' Island was lined from the lower point to the light house, with batteries of heavy guns. To the youthful eye of a Southerner, whose mind had been fired by Southern sentiment and literature of the day, by reading the stories of heroes and soldiers in our old "Southern Reader," of the thrilling romances of Marion and his men, by William Gilmore Simms, this sight of war was enough to dazzle and startle to an enthusiasm that scarcely knew any bounds. The South were "hero worshipers." The stories of Washington and Putnam, of Valley Forge, of Trenton, of Bunker Hill, and Lexington never grew old, while men, women, and children never tired of reading of the storming of Mexico, the siege of Vera Cruz, the daring of the Southern troops at Molino del Rey.

My first duty as a soldier, I will never forget. I went with a detail to Steven's Iron Battery to build embrasures for the forts there. This was done by filling cotton bags the size of 50 pound flour sacks with sand, placing them one upon the top of the other at the opening where the mouths of cannons projected, to prevent the loose earth from falling down and filling in the openings. The sand was first put upon common wheel-barrows and rolled up single planks in a zig-zag way to the top of the fort, then placed in the sacks and laid in position. My turn came to use a barrow, while a comrade used the shovel for filling up. I had never worked a wheel-barrow in my life, and like most of my companions, had done but little work of any kind. But up I went the narrow zig-zag gangway, with a heavy loaded barrow of loose sand. I made the first plank all right, and the second, but when I undertook to reach the third plank on the angles, and about fifteen feet from the ground, my barrow rolled off, and down came sand, barrow, and myself to the ground below. I could have cried with shame and mortification, for my misfortune created much merriment for the good natured workers. But it mortified me to death to think I was not man enough to fill a soldier's place. My good co-worker and brother soldier exchanged the shovel for the barrow with me, and then began the first day's work I had ever done of that kind. Hour after hour passed, and I used the shovel with a will. It looked as if night would never come. At times I thought I would have to sink to the earth from pure exhaustion, but my pride and youthful patriotism, animated by the acts of others, urged me on. Great blisters formed and bursted in my hand, beads of perspiration dripped from my brow, and towards night the blood began to show at the root of my fingers. But I was not by myself; there were many others as tender as myself. Young men with wealthy parents, school and college boys, clerks and men of leisure, some who had never done a lick of manual labor in their lives, and would not have used a spade or shovel for any consideration, would have scoffed at the idea of doing the laborious work of men, were now toiling away with the farmer boys, the overseers' sons, the mechanics—all with a will—and filled with enthusiasm that nothing short of the most disinterested patriotism could have endured. There were men in companies raised in Columbia, Charleston, and other towns, who were as ignorant and as much strangers to manual labor as though they had been infants, toiling away with pick and shovel with as much glee as if they had been reared upon the farm or had been laborers in a mine.

Over about midway in the harbor stood grim old Sumter, from whose parapets giant guns frowned down upon us; while around the battlements the sentinels walked to and fro upon their beats. All this preparation and labor were to reduce the fort or prevent a rein-forcement. Supplies had been cut off, only so much allowed as was needed for the garrison's daily consumption. With drill every two hours, guard duty, and working details, the soldiers had little time for rest or reflection. Bands of music enlivened the men while on drill, and cheered them while at work by martial and inspiring strains of "Lorena," "The Prairie Flower," "Dixie," and other Southern airs. Pickets walked the beach, every thirty paces, night and day; none were allowed to pass without a countersign or a permit. During the day small fishing smacks, their white sails bobbing up and down over the waves, dotted the bay; some going out over the bar at night with rockets and signals to watch for strangers coming from the seaward. Days and nights passed without cessation of active operations—all waiting anxiously the orders from Montgomery to reduce the fort.

General G.T. Beauregard, a citizen of Louisiana, resident of New Orleans, a veteran of the Mexican War, and a recent officer in the United States Engineering Corps, was appointed Brigadier General and placed in command of all the forces around Charleston. A great many troops from other States, which had also seceded and joined the Confederacy, had come to South Carolina to aid in the capture of Sumter. General Beauregard was a great favorite with all the people, and the greatest confidence felt in his skill and ability by the soldiers. The State officers and troops obeyed him cheerfully, and had implicit faith in his military skill. As he was destined to play an important part in the great role of war that was soon to follow, I will give here a short sketch of his life. General G.T. Beauregard was born near the city of New Orleans, May 18th, 1818. His first ancestors were from Wales, but engaging in an insurrection, they were forced to flee from their country, and sought an asylum in France. In the last of the thirteenth century one of them became attached to the Court of Philip the IV, surnamed the "Fair." He then married Mademoiselle de Lafayette, maid of honor to the sister of Philip. When Edward, King of England, married the sister of Philip, he followed with his wife the fortunes of the English King, and became a member at the Court of St. James. He was afterwards assigned to a British post on the continent. And again this family of the early Beauregards, then called Toutant-Beauregard, became citizens of France. Jacques Beauregard came to Louisiana from France with a colony sent out by Louis XIV. The grandson of this Jacques is the present Gustav Toutant Beauregard. At the early age of eleven years he was taken to New York and placed under a private tutor, an exile from France, and who had fled the Empire on the downfall of Napoleon. At sixteen he entered West Point as a cadet, and graduated July 1st, 1838, being second in a class of forty-five. He entered the service of the United States as Second Lieutenant of Engineers. He served with distinction through the Mexican War, under Major General Scott, in the engineer corps. For gallant and meritorious conduct he was twice promoted—first to the Captaincy and then to the position of Major. For a short time he was Superintendent of the West Point Military Academy, but owing to the stirring events just preceding the late war, he resigned on the first of March, 1861. He entered the service of the Confederate States; was appointed Brigadier General and assigned to the post of Charleston. Soon after the fall of Sumter he was made full General, and assigned to a command on the Potomac, and with J.E. Johnston fought the memorable battle of Bull Run. He was second in command at Shiloh with A.S. Johnston, then the "Department of South Carolina, Georgia, and Florida." With J.E. Johnston he commanded the last remnant of a once grand army that surrendered at Greensboro, N.C. He returned to his old home in New Orleans at the close of the war, to find it ruined, his fortune wrecked, his wife dead, and his country at the feet of a merciless foe. He took no further part in military or political affairs, and passed away gently and peacefully at a ripe old age, loved and admired by his many friends, and respected by his enemies. Such, in brief, was the life of the man who came to control the destinies of South Carolina at this most critical moment of her history.

On March 6th he placed Morris' Island under the immediate command of Brigadier General James Simonds, while the batteries were under the command of Lieutenant Colonel W.G. DeSaussure. Sullivan's Island was under the command of General R.G.M. Dunovant, and the batteries of this island were under Lieutenant Colonel Ripley. Captain Calhoun commanded at Fort Moultrie, and Captain Thomas at Fort Johnston. A floating battery had been constructed by Captain Hamilton, and moved out to the western extremity of Sullivan's Island. This was under command of its inventor and builder. It consisted of very heavy timbers; its roof overlaid with railroad iron in a slanting position, through which trap doors had been cut for the cannon to project. The Stevens' Battery, as it was called, was constructed on the same principle; was built at Cummings' Point, on Morris' Island, and commanded by Captain Stevens, of the Citadel Academy. It was feared at this time that the concussion caused by the heavy shells and solid shots striking the iron would cause death to those underneath, or so stun them as to render them unfit for further service; but both these batteries did excellent service in the coming bombardment. Batteries along the water fronts of the islands were manned by the volunteer companies of Colonel Gregg's Regiment, and other regiments that had artillery companies attached.

On the 8th of April a message was received at Montgomery to the effect that a fleet was then en route to reinforce Sumter, "peaceably if they could, but forcibly if necessary."

General Beauregard was instructed to demand the immediate evacuation of the fort; Anderson failing to comply with this demand, he was to proceed to reduce it. The demand was made upon Major Anderson, and was refused. General Beauregard had everything in readiness, only waiting the result of the negotiations for the surrender or evacuation, to give the command to fire. The night of the 11th was one of great excitement. It was known for a certainty that on to-morrow the long looked for battle was to take place. Diplomacy had done its work, now powder and ball must do what diplomacy had failed to accomplish. All working details had been called in, tools put aside, the heating furnaces fired, shells and red-hot solid shot piled in close proximity to the cannon and mortars. All the troops were under arms during the night, and a double picket line stretched along the beach, and while all seemed to be life and animation, a death-like stillness pervaded the air. There was some apprehension lest the fleet might come in during the night, land an army on Morris' Island in small boats, and take the forts by surprise. Men watched with breathless interest the hands on the dials as they slowly moved around to the hour of four, the time set to open the fire. At that hour gunners stood with lanyards in their hands. Men peered through the darkness in the direction of Sumter, as looking for some invisible object. At half past four Captain James, from Fort Johnston, pulled his lanyard; the great mortar belched forth, a bright flash, and the shell went curving over in a kind of semi-circle, the lit fuse trailing behind, showing a glimmering light, like the wings of a fire fly, bursting over the silent old Sumter. This was the signal gun that unchained the great bull-dogs of war around the whole circle of forts. Scarcely had the sound of the first gun died away, ere the dull report from Fort Moultrie came rumbling over the waters, like an echo, and another shell exploded over the deserted parade ground of the doomed fort. Scarcely had the fragments of this shell been scattered before General Stevens jerked the lanyard at the railroad battery, and over the water gracefully sped the lighted shell, its glimmering fuse lighting its course as it, too, sped on in its mission of destruction. Along the water fronts, and from all the forts, now a perfect sheet of flame flashed out, a deafening roar, a rumbling deadening sound, and the war was on. The men as a whole were alive to their work; shot after shot was fired. Now a red-hot solid shot, now a shell, goes capering through the air like a shower of meteors on a frolic. The city was aroused. Men, women, and children rush to the housetops, or crowd each other along the water front of the battery.

But Sumter remained silent, grim, defiant. All there seemed to be in peaceful, quiet slumber, while the solid shot battered against her walls, or the shells burst over their heads and in the court yard below. Round after round is fired. The gunners began to weary of their attempt to arouse the sleeping foe. Is the lion so far back in his lair as not to feel the prods of his tormentors? or is his apathy or contempt too great to be aroused from his slumber by such feeble blows? The grey streaks of morning came coursing from the east, and still the lion is not angry, or is loath to take up the struggle before he has had his morning meal. At seven o'clock, however, if there had been any real anxiety to rouse his temper, it was appeased. The stars and stripes ran up the flag staff, and from out the walls of the grim old stronghold burst a wreath of smoke—then a report, and a shot comes whizzing through the air, strikes the iron battery, and ricochets over in the sand banks. He then pays his respects to Moultrie. From the casements and barbette guns issue a flame and smoke, while the air is filled with flying shot. The battle is general and grand. Men spring upon ramparts and shout defiance at Sumter, to be answered by the crashing of shot against the walls of their bomb-proof forts. All day long the battle rages without intermission or material advantages to either side. As night approached, the fire slackened in all direction, and at dark Sumter ceased to return our fire at all. By a preconcerted arrangement, the fire from our batteries and forts kept up at fifteen-minute intervals only. The next morning the firing began with the same vigor and determination as the day before. Sumter, too, was not slow in showing her metal and paid particular attention to Moultrie. Early in the forenoon the smoke began to rise from within the walls of Sumter; "the tort was on fire." Shots now rain upon the walls of the burning fort with greater fury than ever. The flag was seen to waver, then slowly bend over the staff and fall. A shout of triumph rent the air from the thousands of spectators on the islands and the mainland. Flags and handkerchiefs waved from the hands of excited throngs in the city, as tokens of approval of eager watchers. Soldiers mount the ramparts and shout in exultation, throwing their caps in the air. Away to the seaward the whitened sails of the Federal fleet were seen moving up towards the bar. Anxiety and expectation are now on tip-toe. Will the fleet attempt the succor of their struggling comrades? Will they dare to run the gauntlet of the heavy dahlgreen guns that line the channel sides? From the burning fort the garrison was fighting for their existence. Through the fiery element and hail of shot and shell they see the near approach of the long expected relief. Will the fleet accept the gauge of battle? No. The ships falter and stop. They cast anchor and remain a passive spectator to the exciting scenes going on, without offering aid to their friends or battle to their enemies.

General Beauregard, with that chivalrous spirit that characterized all true Southerners, when he saw the dense curling smoke and the flames that now began to leap and lick the topmost walls of the fort, sent three of his aids to Major Anderson, offering aid and assistance in case of distress. But the brave commander, too proud to receive aid from a generous foe when his friends are at hand yet too cowardly to come to the rescue, politely refused the offer. But soon thereafter the white flag was waving from the parapets of Fort Sumter. Anderson had surrendered; the battle was over; a victory won by the gallant troops of the South, and one of the most miraculous instances of a bloodless victory, was the first battle fought and won. Thousands of shots given and taken, and no one hurt on either side.

A remarkable instance of Southern magnanimity was that of W.T. Wigfall, a volunteer aide to General Beauregard. As he stood watching the progress of the battle from Cummings' Point and saw the great volume of black smoke curling and twisting in the air—the storm of shot and shell plunging into the doomed walls of the fort, and the white flag flying from its burning parapets—his generous, noble, and sympathetic heart was fired to a pitch that brooked no consideration, "a brave foe in distress" is to him a friend in need. Before orders could be given to cease firing, or permission granted by the commanding general, he leaped into a small boat, and with a single companion rowed away to the burning fortress, shells shrieking over his head, the waves rocking his frail little craft like a shell in a vast ocean, but the undaunted spirit of the great man overcame all obstacles and danger, and reached the fort in safety. Here a hasty consultation was had. Anderson agreed to capitulate and Wigfall hastened to so inform General Beauregard.

It was agreed that Major Anderson should leave the fort—not as a prisoner of war, but as a brave foe, who had done all in human power to sustain the dignity of his country and the honor of his flag. He was allowed to salute his flag, by firing a number of guns, and with his officers and troops and all personal belongings placed upon a transport, was carried out to the fleet.

The only melancholy event of the memorable bombardment was the sudden death of one of the soldiers of the garrison, caused by the premature explosion of a shell while firing the salute to the flag.

The prominence given to Wigfall's exertion, and erratic conduct at the time, and his meritorious career during the existence of the Confederacy, prompt me to give a short sketch of this meteoric character. He was born in Edgefield County along in the first quarter of the century of good old South Carolina stock, and educated in the common schools and in South Carolina College. His large means, inherited from a long line of wealthy ancestors, afforded him opportunities to enjoy life at his pleasure. He was full of that fiery zeal for honor, hot headed and impulsive. His hasty and stubborn nature caused him many enemies; yet his charitable disposition and generous impulses gave him many friends. He could brook no differences; he was intolerant, proud of his many qualities, gifted, and brave to rashness. In early life he had differences with Whitfield Brooks, the father of Preston S. Brooks, Congressman from South Carolina, but at that time a student of South Carolina College. While the son was in college, Wigfall challenged the elder Brooks to a duel. Brooks, from his age and infirmities, refused. According to the rules of the code duello, Wigfall posted Brooks at Edgefield Court House, and guarded the fatal notice during the day with a loaded pistol. A relative of Brooks, a feeble, retiring, and unassuming young man, braved the vengeance of Wigfall, and tore the degrading challenge from the court house door in spite of the warning and threats of the Knight of the Code. A pistol shot rang out, and the young champion of Brooks fell dead at his feet. Preston Brooks, hearing of the indignity placed upon his father, the death of his kinsman and defender of his family honor, now entered the list, and challenged the slayer of his father's protector. Wigfall accepted the challenge with eagerness, for now the hot Southern blood was thoroughly aroused, and party feelings had sprung up and ran high. The gauge of battle was to be settled at Sand Bar Ferry, on the Savannah River near Augusta, Ga., the noted duelling ground of the high tempered sons of Georgia and the Carolinas. It was fought with dueling pistols of the old school, and at the first fire Brooks was severely wounded. Wigfall had kindled a feeling against himself in the State that his sensitive nature could not endure. He left for the rising and new born State of Texas. Years rolled by, and the next meeting of those fiery antagonists was at the Capital of the United States—Brooks in Congress, and Wigfall in the Senate.

CHAPTER 3
Incidents On The Way

There was much discussion at the time as to who really fired the first gun at Sumter. Great importance was attached to the episode, and as there were different opinions, and it was never satisfactorily settled, it is not expected that any new light can be thrown on it at this late day. It was first said to have been General Edmond Ruffin, a venerable octogenarian from Virginia, who at the secession of South Carolina came to this State and offered his services as a volunteer. He had at one time been a citizen of South Carolina, connected with a geological survey, and had written several works on the resources and possibilities of the State, which created quite an interest at that day and time. He was one of the noblest types of elderly men it has ever been my fortune to look upon. He could not be called venerable, but picturesque. His hair hung in long silvery locks, tied in a queue in the fashions of the past centuries. His height was very near six feet, slender and straight as an Indian brave, and his piercing black eyes seemed to flash fire and impressed one as being able to look into your very soul. He joined the "Palmetto Guards," donned the uniform of that company, and his pictures were sold all over the entire South, taken, as they were, in the habiliments of a soldier. These showed him in an easy pose, his rifle between his knees, coat adorned with palmetto buttons closely buttoned up to his chin, his hair combed straight from his brow and tied up with a bow of ribbon that streamed down his back, his cap placed upon his knee bearing the monogram "P.G.," the emblem of his company, worked in with palmetto.

The other aspirant for the honor of firing the first gun was Captain George S. James, afterwards the Colonel of James' Battalion, or "Third Battalion," as it was known in Kershaw's Brigade. It has been said that this honor was granted him, at his special request, by Captain Stephen D. Lee, on General Beauregard's staff (afterwards a Lieutenant General of the Confederate Army). Captain James' claim appears to be more valid than that of General Ruffin from the fact that it is positively known that James' company was on duty at Fort Johnston, on James' Island, while the Palmetto Guards, of which General Ruffin was a member, was at the railroad battery on Morris Island. However, this should not be taken as conclusive, as at that time discipline was, to a certain extent, not strictly enforced, and many independent volunteers belonged to the army over whom there was very little, if any control. So General Ruffin may have been at Fort Johnston while his company was at Cummings Point. However, little interest is attached to this incident after the lapse of so many years.

Perhaps never in the history of a State was there such a frenzy of excitement—not even in the days of Indian insurrections or the raids of the bloody Tarleton—as when the news flashed over the country that Sumter was being bombarded, and a call was made for all the volunteers to assemble in Charleston. There were not the facilities in those days as now for the spreading of news, there being but few telegraph lines in the State. Notwithstanding this, every method possible was put into practice for gathering in the troops. There were no assemblages of troops outside of Charleston. Men were following their daily vocations. Extra trains were put in motion; couriers dashed with rapid speed across the country. Private means, as well as public, were resorted to to arouse the men and bring them to the front. Officers warned the private, and he in turn rode with all the speed his horse, loosed from the plow, could command, to arouse his comrades. It was on Saturday when word was first sent out, but it was late the next day (Sunday) before men in the remote rural districts received the stirring notice. Men left their plows standing in the field, not to return under four years, and many of them never. Carpenters came down from the unfinished roof, or left their bench with work half finished. The student who had left his school on the Friday before never recited his Monday's lesson. The country doctor left his patients to the care of the good housewife. Many people had gone to church and in places the bells were still tolling, calling the worshippers together to listen to the good and faithful teachings of the Bible, but the sermon was never delivered or listened to. Hasty preparations were made everywhere. The loyal wives soon had the husband's clothes in the homemade knapsack; the mother buckled on the girdle of her son, while the gray haired father was burning with impatience, only sorrowing that he, too, could not go. Never before in the history of the world, not even in Carthage or Sparta, was there ever such a spontaneous outburst of patriotic feeling; never such a cheerful and willing answer to the call of a mother country. Not a regret, not a tear; no murmuring or reproaches—not one single complaint. Never did the faithful Scott give with better grace his sons for the defense of his beloved chief, "Eric," than did the fathers and mothers of South Carolina give their sons for the defense of the beloved Southland.

The soldiers gathered at the railroad stations, and as the trains that had been sent to the farthest limits of the State came along, the troops boarded them and hurried along to Charleston, then the seat of war. General M.L. Bonham had been appointed Major General of State troops and called his brigades together. Colonel Gregg was already in Charleston with the First Regiment. Col. Joseph B. Kershaw with the Second, Colonel James H. Williams with the Third, Colonel Thomas Bacon with the Seventh, and Colonel E.B.C. Cash with the Eighth, formed their regiments by gathering the different companies along at the various railroad stations. The Second, Seventh, and Eighth came on to Charleston, reaching there while the bombardment was still in progress, but not early enough to take active part in the battle. Colonel Williams with the Third, for want of transportation, was stopped in Columbia, and took up quarters in the Fair Grounds. The other regiments went into camp in the suburbs of Charleston and on the islands. After the surrender of Sumter the troops on the islands and mainland returned to their old quarters to talk upon the incidents of the battle, write home of the memorable events and to rejoice generally. Almost as many rumors were now afloat as there were men in the army. It was the generally conceded opinion of all that the war was at an end. A great many of the Southern leaders boasted of "drinking all the blood that would be shed in the war." The whole truth of the entire matter was, both sections underrated each other. The South, proud and haughty, looked with disdain upon the courage of the North; considered the people cowardly, and not being familiar with firearms would be poor soldiers; that the rank and file of the North, being of a foreign, or a mixture of foreign blood, would not remain loyal to the Union, as the leaders thought, and would not fight. While the North looked upon the South as a set of aristocratic blusterers, their affluence and wealth having made them effeminate; a nation of weaklings, who could not stand the fatigues and hardships of a campaign. Neither understood the other, overrating themselves and underrating the strength of their antagonists. When Lincoln first called for 50,000 troops and several millions of dollars for equipment and conduct of the war, the South would ask in derision, "Where would he get them?" When the South would talk of resistance, the North would ask, "Where are her soldiers?" "The rich planters' sons cannot fight." "The poor man will not do battle for the negroes of the rich." "The South has no arms, no money, no credit." So each mistook the strength, motives, spirits, and sentiments that actuated the other. A great change came over the feelings of the North after the fall of Sumter. They considered that their flag had been insulted, their country dishonored. Where there had been differences before at the North, there was harmony now. The conservative press of that section was now defiant and called for war; party differences were healed and the Democratic party of the North that had always affiliated in national affairs with the South, was now bitter against their erring sisters, and cried loudly for "Union or coercion." The common people of the North were taught to believe that the Nation had been irretrievably dishonored and disgraced, that the disruption of the Union was a death knell to Republican institutions and personal liberty. That the liberty and independence that their ancestors had won by their blood in the Revolution was now to be scattered to the four winds of heaven by a few fanatical slave holders at the South. But up to this time the question of slavery had not been brought into controversy on either side. It was not discussed and was only an after thought, a military necessity.

Virginia, three days after the fall of Sumter, joined her sister State. This act of the old commonwealth was hailed in the Gulf States with great rejoicing. Bells tolled and cannon boomed and men hurrahed. Until now it was not certain what stand would be taken by the Border States. They did not wish to leave the Union; neither would they be a party to a war upon their seceding sisters. They promised to be neutral. But President Lincoln soon dispelled all doubt and uncertainty by his proclamation, calling upon all States then remaining in the Union to furnish their quota of troops. They were then forced to take sides for or against and were not long in reaching a conclusion. As soon as conventions could be assembled, the States joined the Confederacy and began levying troops to resist invasion. Tennessee followed Virginia, then Arkansas, the Old North State being the last of the Atlantic and Gulf States to cross the Rubicon into the "plains of Southern independence." The troops that had been called for six months were now disbanded, and those who had enlisted for twelve months for State service were called upon to volunteer in the

Confederate Army for the unexpired time. They volunteered almost without a dissenting voice. Having left their homes so hurriedly, they were granted a furlough of a week or ten days to return to their families and put their houses in order. They then returned and went into a camp of instruction.

General Bonham had not gotten all of his regiments together up to this time. The Second, Seventh, and Eighth were around Charleston, while the Third was at Lightwood Knot Spring, four miles from Columbia. This camp was called "Camp Williams," in honor of their Colonel. That in Columbia was called "Camp Ruffin," in honor of General Ruffin. It was customary to give all the different camps a name during the first year's service, generally in honor of some favorite officer or statesman. Colonel Gregg's regiment remained on Morris Island until early in May, when it was sent to Norfolk, Va., to take charge of the large amount of government property there, now very valuable to the South.

At the reorganization of the First Regiment I came to Columbia and joined the company I had before enlisted in. I had two older brothers there, and I was given a place as Second Sergeant in the company.

At the secession of South Carolina, Colonel Williams was in Arkansas, where he had large estates, but on being notified of his election, he joined his regiment while at Lightwood Knot Springs. He was met at the railroad by his troops with great demonstrations of joy and pride. Stalwart men hoisted him upon their shoulders and carried him through the camp, followed by a throng of shouting and delighted soldiers. The regiment had been commanded up to that time by Lieutenant Colonel Foster, of Spartanburg, with James M. Baxter as Major, D.R. Rutherford as Adjutant, Dr. D.E. Ewart Surgeon, John McGowan Quartermaster.

Cadets were sent from the Citadel as drill masters to all the regiments, and for six hours daily the ears were greeted with "hep-hep" to designate the "left" foot "down" while on the drill. It took great patience, determination, and toil to bring the men under military discipline. Fresh from the fields, shops, and schools they had been accustomed to the freedom of home life, and with all their patriotism, it took time to break into the harness of military restraint and discipline these lovers of personal freedom. Many amusing incidents occurred while breaking these "wild colts," but all took it good humoredly, and the best of feelings existed between officers and men. Some few, however, were nettled by the restraint and forced obedience to those whom they had heretofore been accustomed to look upon as equals, but now suddenly made superiors. The great majority entered upon the duties of camp life with rare good will. All were waiting patiently the call to Virginia. Here I will give a short description of the regiments and their officers up to the time that all were brought together as a brigade. After that time we will treat them as a whole.

The regiments were uniformed by private donations, each neighborhood uniforming the company raised in its bounds. The tents were large and old fashioned—about 8 x 10 feet square, with a separate fly on top—one of these being allowed to every six or seven men. They were pitched in rows, about fifty feet apart, the front of one company facing the rear of the other. About the first of June all the regiments, except the Second, were ordered to Manassas, Va. The regiments were formed by companies from battalions of the militia from various counties, one company usually being formed from a battalion. These companies were organized into regiments, very much as at present, and like the old anti-bellum militia. At times some ambitious citizen would undertake to raise a volunteer company outside of those raised from battalions, and generally these were called "crack companies." Afterwards a few undertook to raise companies in this manner, i.e., selecting the officers first, and then proceeding to select the men, refusing such as would not make acceptable soldiers, thus forming exclusive organizations. These were mostly formed in towns and cities. At other times old volunteer companies, as they were called, of the militia would enlist in a body, with such recruits as were wanted to fill up the number. In the old militia service almost all the towns and cities had these companies as a kind of city organization, and they would be handsomely uniformed, well equipped, and in many cases were almost equal to regular soldiers. Columbia had at least three of these companies in our brigade—the Governor's Guards, Richland Rifles, and one more, I think, but on this point am not positive. Charleston had two or more, the Palmetto Guards and others; Greenville, the Butler Guards; Newberry, the Quitman Rifles; while the other counties, Abbeville, Anderson, Edgefield, Williamsburg, Darlington, Sumter, and almost all the counties represented in our brigade had one of these city volunteer companies. When all the companies called for had been organized, they were notified to what regiment they had been assigned, or what companies were to constitute a regiment, and were ordered to hold an election for field officers. Each company would hold its election, candidates in the meantime having offered their services to fill the respective places of Colonel, Lieutenant Colonel, and Major. After the elections thus held, the returns would be sent up to the Adjutant and Inspector General's office and there tabulated, and the result declared. The candidates for field officers were generally Mexican War Veterans, or some popular citizen, whom the old men thought "would take care of the boys." At first the qualification of a commander, be it Colonel or Captain, mostly required was clemency. His rules of discipline, bravery, or military ability were not so much taken into consideration.

SECOND SOUTH CAROLINA REGIMENT

Early in May or the last of April four companies of the Second Regiment, under Colonel Kershaw, volunteered for Confederate service, and were sent at once to Virginia. These companies were commanded by—

Captain John D. Kennedy, Kershaw County.
Captain W.H. Casson, Richland County.
Captain William Wallace, Richland County.
Captain John Richardson, Sumter County.

They were afterwards joined by companies under—

Captain Ferryman, of Abbeville County, (formerly of the Seventh Regiment).
Captain Cuthbert, Charleston.
Captain Rhett, Charleston.
Captain Haile, Kershaw.
Captain McManus, Lancaster.
Captain Hoke, Greenville.

These were among the first soldiers from the "Palmetto State" to go to Virginia, and the regiment when fully organized stood as follows:

J.B. Kershaw, Colonel, of Camden.
E.P. Jones, Lieutenant Colonel.
Fred Gaillard, Major.
A.D. Goodwin, Adjutant.

Company A—W.H. Casson, Richland.
Company B—A.D. Hoke, Greenville.

Company C—William Wallace, Richland.
Company D—T.S. Richardson.
Company E—John D. Kennedy, Kershaw.
Company F—W.W.Perryman, Anderson.
Company G—I. Haile, Kershaw.
Company H—H. McManus, Lancaster.
Company I—G.B. Cuthbert, Charleston.
Company K—R. Rhett, Charleston.
Surgeon—Dr. F. Salmond, Kershaw.
Quartermaster—W.S. Wood, Columbia.
Commissary—J.J. Villipigue.
Chaplain—A.J. McGruder.

Third South Carolina Regiment

The Third Regiment had originally twelve companies enlisted for State service, but in transferring to Confederate Army only ten were allowed by the army regulations. Two companies were left out, viz.: Captain J.C.S. Brown's, from Newberry, and Captain Mat. Jones', from Laurens. The privates, however, enlisted in the other companies as a general rule, for the companies were allowed a maximum number of 100. The Eighth and Third made no changes in their companies or officers from their first enlistment in the State service until their second enlistment in 1862, only as occasioned by resignations or the casualties of war. The two regiments remained as first organized, with few exceptions.

The Third stood, when ready for transportation to Virginia, the 7th of June, as follows:

James H. Williams, Colonel, Newberry.
B.B. Foster, Lieutenant Colonel, Spartanburg.
James M. Baxter, Major, Newberry.
W.D. Rutherford, Adjutant, Newberry.
Company A—B. Conway Garlington, Laurens.
Company B—S. Newton Davidson, Newberry.
Company C—R.C. Maffett, Newberry.
Company D—T.B. Furgerson, Spartanburg and Union.
Company E—James D. Nance, Newberry.
Company F—T. Walker, Newberry and Laurens.
Company G—R.P. Todd, Laurens.
Company H—D. Nunnamaker, Lexington.

Company I—Smith L. Jones, Laurens.

Company K—Benj. Kennedy, Spartanburg.

Surgeon—Dr. D.E. Ewart, Newberry.

Quartermaster—John McGowan, Laurens.

Commissary—Sergeant J.N. Martin, Newberry.

Chaplain—Rev. Mayfield.

SEVENTH SOUTH CAROLINA REGIMENT

Colonel, Thomas G. Bacon.

The following companies were from Abbeville:

Company A, Captain W.W. Perryman.

Company B, Captain G.M. Mattison.

Company C, Captain P.H. Bradley.

Company D, Captain S.J. Hester.

The following companies were from Edgefield:

Company E, Captain D. Dendy.

Company F, Captain John S. Hard.

Company G, Captain J. Hampden Brooks.

Company H, Captain Elbert Bland.

Company I, Captain W.E. Prescott.

Company K, Captain Bart Talbert.

Captain Perryman with his company, the "Secession Guards," volunteered for the Confederate service before the other companies, and left for Virginia on April 28th and joined the Second South Carolina Regiment. Captain Bland took his place with his company in the regiment as Company A.

The companies of the Seventh came together as a regiment at the Schutzenplatz, near Charleston, on the 16th of April. In about two weeks it was ordered to Edgefield District at a place called Montmorenci, in Aiken County. While here a company came from Edgefield County near Trenton, under Captain Coleman, and joined the regiment. But this company failed to enlist.

The Seventh Regiment elected as officers: Colonel, Thomas G. Bacon, of Edgefield District; lieutenant Colonel, Robert A. Fair, of Abbeville; Major, Emmet Seibles, of Edgefield; Adjutant, D. Wyatt Aiken, of Abbeville. All the staff officers were appointed by the Colonels until the transfer to the Confederate service; then the medical department was made a separate branch, and the Surgeons and

Assistant Surgeons were appointed by the Department. Colonel Bacon appointed on his staff: B.F. Lovelass, Quartermaster; Fred Smith, Commissary; afterwards A.F. Townsend.

Surgeon Joseph W. Hearst resigned, and A.R. Drogie was made Surgeon in his stead, with Dr. G.H. Waddell as Assistant Surgeon. A.C. Stallworth, Sergeant Major, left for Virginia about the first of June and joined the Second a few days afterwards.

Eighth South Carolina Regiment

The Eighth Regiment was organized early in the year 1861, but the companies were not called together until the 14th day of April, arriving in Charleston in the afternoon of that day, just after the fall of Fort Sumter. It was composed of ten companies, as follows: Three from Chesterfield, two from Marion, two from Marlborough, and three from Darlington, with Colonel, E.B.C. Cash; Lieutenant Colonel, John W. Henagan; Major, Thomas E. Lucas; Adjutant, C.B. Weatherly.

Companies first taken to Virginia:

Company A—A.I. Hoole, Darlington.
Company B—M.I. Hough, Chesterfield.
Company C—Wm. H. Coit, Chesterfield.
Company D—John S. Miller, Chesterfield.
Company E—W.E. Jay, Darlington.
Company F—W.H. Evans, Darlington.
Company G—John W. Harrington, Marlboro.
Company H—R.L. Singletary, Marion.
Company I—T.E. Stackhouse, Marion.
Company K—D. McD. McLeod, Marlboro.

After remaining in Charleston until the 4th of May it was moved to Florence. On the 1st of June the regiment re-enlisted for Confederate service. They were ordered to Richmond and arrived there on June 4th, and left on the 15th to join the Second then at Bull Run. On the 22nd of June they went into camp at Germantown, near Fairfax Court House, where all the regiments were soon joined together as Bonhams' Brigade.

The first real exciting incident connected with the Third South Carolina Regiment—the first panic and stampede—happened as the troops were returning from their ten days' furlough to their camp of instruction, near Columbia, just after their enlistment in the Confederate service. I record this occurrence to show what little incidents, and those of such little moment, are calculated to stampede an army, and to what foolish lengths men will go when excited. The train was rattling along at a good speed, something like ten or fifteen miles an hour, just above Columbia; a long string of box cars loaded with soldiers; the baggage of the troops scattered promiscuously around in the cars; trunks, valises, carpet bags, and boxes of all conceivable dimensions, holding the belongings of several neighborhoods of boys; spirits flowed without and within; congenial friends in a congenial cause; congenial topics made a congenial whole. When just below Littleton, with long stretches of lowlands on one side and the river on the other, the curling streaks of a little grey smoke made its appearance from under one of the forward cars. At first the merry good humor and enlivening effects of some amusing jest, the occasional round of a friendly bottle, prevented the men from noticing this danger signal of fire. However, a little later on this continuing and increasing volume of smoke caused an alarm to be given. Men ran to the doors on either side, shouted and called, waved hats, hands, and handkerchiefs, at the same time pointing at the smoke below. There being no communication between the cars, those in front and rear had to be guided by the wild gesticulations of those in the smoking car. The engineer did not notice anything amiss, and sat placidly upon his high seat, watching the fast receding rails as they flashed under and out of sight beneath the ponderous driving-wheels of the engine. At last someone in the forward car, not accustomed to, but familiar with the dangers of a railroad car by the wild rumors given currency in his rural district of railroad wrecks, made a desperate leap from the car. This was followed by another, now equally excited. Those in the front cars, clutching to the sides of the doors, craned their necks as far as possible outward, but could see nothing but leaping men. They fearing a catastrophe of some kind, leaped also, while those in the rear cars, as they saw along the sides of the railroad track men leaping, rolling, and tumbling on the ground, took it for granted that a desperate calamity had happened to a forward car. No time for questions, no time for meditation. The soldier's only care was to watch for a soft place to make his desperate leap, and in many cases there was little choice. Men leaped wildly in the air, some with their heels up, others falling on their heads and backs, some rolling over in a mad scramble to clear themselves from the threatening danger. The engineer not being aware of anything wrong with the train, glided serenely along, unconscious of the pandemonium, in the rear. But when all had about left the train, and the great driving-wheels began to spin around like mad, from the lightening of the load, the master of the throttle looked to the rear. There lay stretched prone upon the ground, or limping on one foot, or rolling over in the dirt, some bareheaded and coatless, boxes and trunks scattered as in an awful collision, upwards of one thousand men along the railroad track. Many of the men thinking, no doubt, the train hopelessly lost, or serious danger imminent, threw their baggage out before making the dangerous leap. At last the train was stopped and brought back to the scene of desolation. It terminated like the bombardment of Fort Sumter—"no one hurt," and all occasioned by a hot-box that could have been cooled in a very few minutes. Much swearing and good-humored jesting were now engaged in. Such is the result of the want of presence of mind. A wave of the hat at the proper moment as a signal to the engineer to stop, and all would have been well. It was told once of a young lady crossing a railroad track in front of a fast approaching train, that her shoe got fastened in the frog where the two rails join. She began to struggle, then to scream, and then fainted. A crowd rushed up, some grasping the lady's body attempted to pull her loose by force; others shouted to the train to stop; some called for crow-bars to take up the iron. At last one man pushed through the crowd, untied the lady's shoe, and she was loose. Presence of mind, and not force, did it.

Remaining in camp a few days, orders came to move, and cars were gotten in readiness and baggage packed preparatory to the trip to Virginia. To many, especially those reared in the back districts, and who, before their brief army life, had never been farther from their homes than their county seat, the trip to the old "Mother of Presidents," the grand old commonwealth, was quite a journey indeed. The old negroes, who had been brought South during the early days of the century, called the old State "Virginy" and mixing it with local dialect, in some parts had got the name so changed that it was called "Ferginey." The circus troops and negro comedians, in their annual trips through the Southern States, had songs already so catchy to our people, on account of their pathos and melody, of Old Virginia, that now it almost appeared as though we were going to our old home. Virginia had been endeared to us and closely connected with the people of South Carolina by many links, not the least being its many sentimental songs of that romantic land, and the stories of her great men.

The baggage of the common soldier at this stage of the war would have thrown an ordinary quartermaster of latter day service into an epileptic fit, it was so ponderous in size and enormous in quantities—a perfect household outfit. A few days before this the soldier had received his first two months' pay, all in new crisp bank notes, fresh from the State banks or banks of deposit. It can be easily imagined that there were lively times for the butcher, the baker and candlestick maker, with all this money afloat. The Third South Carolina was transported by way of Wilmington and Weldon, N.C. Had there ever existed any doubts in the country as to the feelings of the people of the South before this in regard to Secession, it was entirely dispelled by the enthusiastic cheers and good will of the people along the road. The conduct of the men and women through South Carolina, North Carolina, and Virginia, showed one long and continued ovation along the line of travel, looking like a general holiday. As the cars sped along through the fields, the little hamlets and towns, people of every kind, size, and complexion rushed to the railroad and gave us welcome and Godspeed. Hats went into the air as we passed, handkerchiefs fluttered, flags waved in the gentle summer breeze from almost every housetop. The ladies and old men pressed to the side of the cars when we halted, to shake the hands of the brave soldier boys, and gave them blessings, hope and encouragement. The ladies vied with the men in doing homage to the soldiers of the Palmetto State. Telegrams had been sent on asking of our coming, the hour of our passage through the little towns, and inviting us to stop and enjoy their hospitality and partake of refreshments. In those places where a stop was permitted, long tables were spread in some neighboring grove or park, bending under the weight of their bounties, laden down with everything tempting to the soldier's appetite. The purest and best of the women mingled freely with the troops, and by every device known to the fair sex showed their sympathy and encouragement in the cause we had espoused. At Wilmington, N.C., we crossed the Cape Fear River on a little river steamer, the roads not being connected with a bridge. At Petersburg and Richmond we had to march through portions of those cities in going from one depot to another, union sheds, not being in vogue at that time, and on our entry into these cities the population turned out en masse to welcome and extend to us their greeting. Every private house stood open to the soldiers and the greatest good will was everywhere manifested.

Much has been said in after years, since misfortune and ruin overtook the South, since the sad reverses of the army and the overthrow of our principles, about leaders plunging the nation into a bloody and uncalled for war. This, is all the height of folly. No man or combination of men could have stayed or avoided war. No human persuasion or earthly power could have stayed the great wave of revolution that had struck the land; and while, like a storm widening and gathering strength and fury as it goes, to have attempted it would have been but to court ruin and destruction. Few men living in that period of our country's history would have had the boldness or hardihood to counsel submission or inactivity. Differences there may have been and were as to methods, but to Secession, none. The voices of the women of the land were alone enough to have forced the measures upon the men in some shape or other. Then, as to the leaders being "shirkers" when the actual contest came, the history of the times gives contradictions sufficient without examples. Where the duties of the service called, they willingly obeyed. All could not fill departments or sit in the councils of the nation, but none shirked the responsibility the conditions called them to. Where fathers filled easy places their sons were in the ranks, and many of our leaders of Secession headed troops in the field. General Bonham, our Brigadier, had just resigned his seat in the United States Congress; so had L.M. Keitt, who fell at Cold Harbor at the head of our brigade, while Colonel of the Twentieth Regiment. James L. Orr, one of the original Secessionists and a member of Congress, raised the first regiment of rifles. The son of Governor Gist, the last Executive of South Carolina just previous to Secession, fell while leading his regiment, the Fifteenth, of our brigade, in the assault at Fort Loudon, at Knoxville. Scarcely was there a member of the convention that passed the Ordinance of Secession who had not a son or near kinsman in the ranks of the army. They showed by their deeds the truth and honesty of their convictions. They had trusted the North until trusting had ceased to be a virtue. They wished peace, but feared not war. All this idle talk, so common since the war, of a "rich man's war and a poor man's fight" is the merest twaddle and vilely untrue.

The men of the South had risked their all upon the cast, and were willing to abide by the hazard of the die. All the great men of South Carolina were for Secession, and they nobly entered the field. The Hamptons, Butlers, Haskells, Draytons, Bonhams, all readily grasped the sword or musket. The fire-eaters, like Bob Toombs, of Georgia, and Wigfall, of Texas, led brigades, and were as fiery upon the battlefield as they had been upon the floor of the United States Senate.

So with all the leaders of Secession, without exception; they contributed their lives, their services, and their wealth to the cause they had advocated and loved so well. I make this departure here to correct an opinion or belief, originated and propagated by the envious few who did not rise to distinction in the war, or who were too young to participate in its glories—those glories that were mutual and will ever surround the Confederate soldier, regardless of rank.

After stopping a few days in Richmond, we were carried on to Manassas and Bull Run, then to Fairfax, where we joined the other regiments. The Third Regiment camped first at Mitchell's Ford, remained at that point for a week or ten days, and from thence moved to the outpost just beyond Fairfax Court House. The Eighth and Second camped for a while at Germantown, and soon the whole brigade was between Fairfax and Bull Run.

CHAPTER 4

Camp at Fairfax—Battle of the 18th

General Bonham had gathered around him, as staff officers, a galaxy of gentlemen as cultured, talented, and patriotic as South Carolina could produce, and as gallant as ever followed a general upon the battlefield; all of whom won promotion and distinction as the war progressed in the different branches of service.

Colonel Samuel Melton, one of the staff, writing in a pleasant mood, thirty-five years afterwards, says: "That with universal acclamation it may be said, that the retinue gathered around the General of the old First Brigade was a gorgeous one. I am proud of it 'until yet.'"

This staff of General Bonham's was the one allowed by the State service, and the appointments were made under State laws. However, all followed him into the Confederate service, and, with a few exceptions, remained until after the battle of Manassas, serving without pay. The Confederate Government was much more modest in its appointment of staff officers, and only allowed a Brigadier General three or four members as his personal staff.

The following is a list of officers who followed General Bonham to Virginia, or joined him soon after his arrival:

W.C. Morayne, Assistant Adjutant General, with rank of Colonel

W.D. Simpson, Inspector General.

A.P. Aldrich, Quartermaster General.

R.B. Boylston, Commissary General.

J.N. Lipscomb, Paymaster General.

Aides, with rank of Major:

S.W. Melton, B.F. Withers, T.J. Davis, E.S. Hammond, S. Warren Nelson, Samuel Tompkins, W.P. Butler, M.B. Lipscomb. Colonel S. McGowan, Volunteer Aide.

Dr. Reeves, of Virginia, was Brigade Surgeon.

Colonels Morayne and Boylston remained only a few weeks. Captain George W. Say, an officer of the Confederate staff, succeeded Colonel Morayne, and remained a short while, when he was promoted and sent elsewhere. Colonel Lipscomb became the regular aide, with rank of First Lieutenant.

When Captain Say left, S.W. Melton was put in his place as Assistant Adjutant General, without appointment or without pay, and discharged the duties of that office until August, when he left on sick leave. When he returned he was appointed Major and Assistant Adjutant General, and assigned to duty upon the staff of Major General G.W. Smith, commanding Second Corps of the Army of the Potomac. In 1863 he was promoted to Lieutenant Colonel and assigned to duty in the war department.

William F. Nance, of Newberry, was appointed Captain and Assistant Adjutant General, and in September, 1861, was assigned to duty upon General Bonham's staff, where he remained until the General's resignation. In 1864 Nance was on duty in Charleston, where he remained on staff duty until the end.

S. McGowan and W.D. Simpson returned to South Carolina after the battle of Manassas, and assisted in raising the Fourteenth South Carolina Regiment of Volunteers, of which the former was elected Lieutenant Colonel and the latter Major. Colonel McGowan became Colonel of the regiment, and afterwards Brigadier of one of the most famous brigades (McGowan's) in the Confederate Army. Colonel Simpson served in the Confederate Congress after his retirement from the army.

All the others of the staff filled prominent positions, either as commanding or staff officers, or serving in the departments in Richmond. I have no data at hand to give sketches of their individual services.

Fairfax Court House was the extreme limit at which the infantry was posted on that side of the Blue Ridge. Cavalry was still in advance, and under the leadership of the indefatigable Stuart scouting the whole front between the Confederate and Federal armies. The Third South Carolina was encamped about a mile north of the little old fashioned hamlet, the county seat of the county of that name. In this section of the State lived the ancestors of most of the illustrious families of Virginia, Washington, Jefferson, Madison, Monroe, and Lee. It is a rather picturesque country; not so beautiful and productive, however, as the Shenandoah and Luray Valleys. The Seventh, Eighth, and Second Regiments were encamped several miles distant, but all in the hearing of one another's drums. Our main duties outside of our regular drills consisted in picketing the highways and block-ading all roads by felling the timber across for more than a hundred yards on either side of the roads. Large details armed with axes were sent out to blockade the thoroughfares leading to Washington and points across the Potomac. For miles out, in all directions, wherever the road led through wooded lands, large trees, chestnut, hickory, oak, and pine, were cut pell mell, creating a perfect abattis across the road—so much so as to cause our troops in their verdant ignorance to think it almost an impossibility for such obstructions to be cleared away in many days; whereas, as a fact, the pioneer corps of the Federal Army cleared it away as fast as the army marched, not causing as much as one hour's halt. Every morning at nine o'clock one company from a regiment would go out about two miles in the direction of Wash-ington Falls church or Annandale to do picket duty, and remain until nine o'clock next day, when it would be relieved by another compa-ny. The "Black Horse Cavalry," an old organization of Virginia, said to have remained intact since the Revolution, did vidette duty still beyond the infantry. Their duties were to ride through the country in every direction, and on every road and by-way to give warning of approaching danger to the infantry. These were bold riders in those days, some daring to ride even within view of the spires and domes of Washington itself. On our outposts we could plainly hear the sound of the drums of the Federalists in their preparation for the "on to Richmond" move. General Bonham had also some fearless scouts at this time. Even some of the boldest of the women dared to cross the Potomac in search of information for the Confederate Generals. It was here that the noted Miss Bell Boyd made herself famous by her daring rides, her many escapades and hair-breadth escapes, her bold acts of crossing the Potomac sometimes disguised and at other times not, even entering the City of Washington itself. In this way she gathered much valuable information for the Confederate Generals, and kept them posted on the movements of the enemy. She was one of the best horsewomen of that day; a fine specimen of womanhood, and as fearless and brave as a stout hearted cavalier. She generally carried a brace of Colt's revolvers around her waist, and was daring enough to meet any foe who was so bold as to cross her path. Bell Boyd was one of the many noble Virginia women who staked and dared all for the cause of the South. William Parley, of South Caro-lina, another bold scout, was invaluable to General Stuart and General

Bonham. It was he that John Esten Cooke immortalized in "Surry of Eagle's Nest" and was killed at the battle of Chancellorsville. He was a native of Laurens County.

The duties of picketing were the first features of our army life that looked really like war. The soldiers had become accustomed to guard duty, but to be placed out on picket or vidette posts alone, or in company with a comrade, to stand all day and during the dead hours of the night, expecting some lurking foe every moment to shoot you in the back, or from behind some bush to shoot your head off, was quite another matter. As a guard, we watched over our friends; as a picket, we watched for our foe. For a long time, being no nearer the enemy than the hearing of their drums, the soldiers had grown somewhat careless. But there was an uncanny feeling in standing alone in the still hours of the night, in a strange country, watching, waiting for an enemy to crawl up and shoot you unawares. This feeling was heightened, especially in my company, by an amusing incident that happened while on picket duty on the Annandale road. Up to this time there had been no prisoners captured on either side, and it was uncertain as to what would be the fate of any who would fall in the enemy's hands. As we were considered traitors and rebels, the penalty for that crime was, as we all knew, death. The Northern press had kept up quite a howl, picturing the long rows of traitors that would be hung side by side as soon as they had captured the Confederate Army. That there was a good deal of "squeamishness" felt at the idea of being captured, cannot be doubted. So videttes were stationed several hundred yards down the road with a picket post of four men, between the outside sentinels and the company, as reserve. A large pine thicket was to our right, while on the left was an old field with here and there a few wild cherry trees. The cherries being ripe, some of the men had gone up in the trees to treat themselves to this luscious little fruit. The other part of the company lay indolently about, sheltering themselves as best they could from the rays of the hot July sun, under the trees. Some lay on the tops of fences, and in corners, while not a few, with coats and vests off, enjoyed a heated game of "old sledge." All felt a perfect security, for with the pickets in front, the cavalry scouring the country, and the almost impassable barricades of the roads, seemed to render it impossible for an enemy to approach unobserved. The guns leaned carelessly against the fence or lay on the ground, trappings, etc., scattered promiscuously around. Not a dream of danger; no thought of a foe. While the men were thus pleasantly engaged, and the officers taking an afternoon nap, from out in the thicket on the right came "bang-bang," and a hail of bullets came whizzing over our heads. What a scramble! What an excitement! What terror depicted on the men's faces! Had a shower of meteors fallen in our midst, had a volcano burst from the top of the Blue Ridge, or had a thunder bolt fell at our feet out of the clear blue sky, the consternation could not have been greater. Excitement, demoralization, and panic ensued. Men tumbled off the fences, guns were reached for, haversacks and canteens hastily grabbed, and, as usual in such panics, no one could get hold of his own. Some started up the road, some down. Officers thus summarily aroused were equally demoralized. Some gave one order, some another. "Pandemonium reigned supreme." Those in the cherry trees came down, nor did the "cherry pickers" stand on the order of their coming. The whole Yankee army was thought to be over the hills. At last the officer commanding got the men halted some little distance up the road; a semblance of a line formed, men cocked their guns and peered anxiously through the cracks of the rail fence, expecting to see an enemy behind every tree. A great giant, a sergeant from the mountain section, who stood six feet, three inches in his stockings, and as brave as he was big, his face flushed with excitement, his whole frame trembling with emotion, in his shirt sleeves and bareheaded, rushed to the middle of the road, braced himself, as waiting for some desperate shock, and stood like Horatio Cockles at the Bridge, waving his gun in the air, calling out in defiant and stentorian voice, "Come on, I'll fight all of you; I'll fight old Lincoln from here to the sea." Such a laugh as was set up afterwards, at his expense! The amusing part of it was the parties who fired the shots at the time the stampeding was going on with us, were running for dear life's sake across the fields, worse scared, if possible, than we ourselves. They were three of a scouting party, who had eluded our pickets, and seeing our good, easy, and indifferent condition, took it into their heads to have a little amusement at our expense. But the sound of their guns in the quiet surrounding, no doubt excited the Yankees as much as it did the Confederates. This was an adventure not long in reaching home, for to be shot at by a real live Yankee was an event in every one's life at the time not soon to be forgotten. But it was so magnified, that by the time it reached home, had not the battle of Bull Run come in its heels so soon, this incident would no doubt have ever remained to those who were engaged in it as one of the battles of the war. The only casualty was a hole shot through a hat. I write this little incident to show the difference in raw and seasoned troops. One year later such an incident would not have disturbed those men any more than the buzzing of a bee. Picket duty after this incident was much more stringent. Two men were made to stand on post all night, without relief, only such as they gave each other. Half of the company's reserve were kept awake all night. Orders were given that the utmost silence should prevail, the men were not even to speak above a whisper, and on the approach of anyone they were to be hailed with the command, "Halt, who comes there?" If a satisfactory answer was given, they were allowed to pass. If not, to remain standing, and an officer of the guard called. At night they were to call "halt" three times, and if no answer, they were to fire and retreat to the reserve.

One night, shortly after this, one of the companies from Spartanburg had been sent out about three miles to the intersection of a country road leading off to the left. Down this country road, or lane, were two pickets. They concealed themselves during the day in the fence corners, but at night they crawled over into a piece of timber land, and crouched down behind a large oak. The shooting incident of a few days before made the two pickets feel somewhat tender at thus being alone in the forest, when at any moment an enemy might creep upon them sufficiently near as to shoot them in the dark. Everything was as quiet as the grave. The stars, peeping faintly out from behind the clouds, midnight came, and each began to nod, when a twig breaks some distance in front, then another, then the rustling of dry leaves. Their hearts leap to their throats and beat like sledge hammers. One whispers to the other, "Whist, some one is coming." They strain their ears to better catch the sound. Surely enough they hear the leaves rustling as if some one is approaching. "Click," "click," the two hammers of their trusty rifles spring back, fingers upon the triggers, while nearer the invisible comes. "Halt," rang out in the midnight air; "halt," once more, but still the steady tread keeps approaching. When the third "halt" was given it was accompanied by the crack of their rifles. A deafening report and frightful squeal, as an old female porker went charging through the underbrush like mad. The crack of the rifles alarmed the sleeping companions in reserve, who rushed to arms and awaited the attack. But after much good humored badgering of the two frightened sentinels, "peace reigned once more at Warsaw" till the break of day. The company returned next morning to camp, but the two sentinels who had fired on the old innocent porker were glad enough to seek the quietude of their quarters to escape the jests of their comrades.

A simple system of breastworks was thrown up just beyond our camp at Fairfax on a little eminence to the right of the road. This we thought sufficient to defeat quite an army, or at least keep them at bay. General Bonham had his headquarters at Fairfax Court House, but rode out daily to examine the work done on the entrenchments, or inspect the picket and outposts. General Bonham was one of the finest looking officers in the entire army. His tall, graceful figure, his commanding appearance, his noble bearing, and soldierly mien were all qualities to excite the confidence and admiration of his troops. He wore a broad-brimmed hat, with a waving plume floating out behind, and sat his horse as knightly as Charles the Bold, or Henry of Navarre. His soldiers were proud of him, and loved to do him homage. He endeared himself to his officers, and while he was a good disciplinarian as far as the volunteer service required, he did not treat his officers with that air of superiority, nor exact that rigid military courtesy that is required in the regular army. I will here give a short sketch of his life for the benefit of his old comrades in arms.

MILLEDGE LUKE BONHAM

Was born near Red Bank in that part of Edgefield District now included in Saluda County, South Carolina, on the 25th day of December, 1813. His father, Captain James Bonham, who had come from Virginia to South Carolina about the close of the last century, was the son of Major Absalom Bonham, who was a native of Maryland, but who enlisted for the war of the Revolution in a New Jersey regiment, and became a Major of the line on the establishment of that State. After the Revolution he moved to Virginia. Captain James Bonham was himself at the siege of Yorktown as a lad of fifteen, in a company whose captain was only twenty years old. He first settled in this State in the District of Colleton, and there married. After the death of his wife, he moved to Edgefield District, and there married Sophie Smith, who was the mother of the subject of this sketch. She was the daughter of Jacob Smith and his wife, Sallie Butler, who was a sister of that Captain James Butler who was the forefather of the illustrious family of that name in this State, and who with his young son, also named James, was cruelly massacred along with others at Cloud's Creek, in Edgefield District, by "Bloody Bill" Cunningham.

Milledge L. Bonham received his early education in the "old field" schools of the neighborhood, and his academic training under instructors at Abbeville and Edgefield. He entered the South Carolina College and graduated with second honor in 1834. Soon thereafter the Seminole or Florida war broke out, and he volunteered in the company from Edgefield, commanded by Captain James Jones, and was Orderly Sergeant of the company. During the progress of the war in Florida, he was appointed by General Bull, who commanded the South Carolina Brigade, to be Brigade Major, a position which corresponds with what is now known in military circles as Adjutant General of Brigade.

Returning from the war, he resumed the study of law and was admitted to the Bar and settled at Edgefield for the practice of his profession. In 1844 he was elected to the Legislature. He always took an ardent interest in the militia, and was first Brigadier General and afterwards Major General of militia. When the war with Mexico was declared, he was appointed lieutenant Colonel of the Twelfth United States Infantry, one of the new regiments added to the army for that war. With his regiment he went to Mexico and served with distinction throughout the war, being promoted to Colonel of the regiment, and having, by the way, for his Adjutant, Lieutenant Winfield Scott Hancock, afterwards a distinguished Major General of the Federal Army in the late war. After the cessation of hostilities, Colonel Bonham was retained in Mexico as Military Governor of one of the provinces for about a year. Being then honorably discharged, he returned to Edgefield and resumed the practice of law. In 1848 he was elected Solicitor of the Southern Circuit, composed of Edgefield, Barnwell, Orangeburg, Colleton, and Beaufort Districts. The Bars of the various Districts composing this Circuit counted among their members many of the ablest and most distinguished lawyers of the State, and hence it required the possession and industrious use of talents of no mean order to sustain one's self as prosecuting officer against such an array of ability. But General Bonham continued to hold the office until 1856, when, upon the death of Hon. Preston S. Brooks, he was elected to succeed that eminent gentleman in Congress, and again in 1858 was elected for the full term. Those were the stirring times preceding the bursting of the cloud of civil war, and the debates in Congress were hot and spicy. In all these he took his full part. When South Carolina seceded from the Union, he promptly resigned his seat in Congress, and was appointed by Governor Pickens Commander-in-Chief of all the forces of South Carolina with the rank of Major General. In this capacity, and waiving all question of rank and precedence, at the request of Governor Pickens, he served on the coast on Morris' Island with General Beauregard, who had been sent there by the Provisional Government of the Confederacy to take command of the operations around Charleston. On the permanent organization of the Confederate Government, General Bonham was appointed by President Davis a Brigadier General in the Army of the Confederate States. His brigade consisted of four South Carolina regiments, commanded respectively by Colonels Kershaw, Williams, Cash, and Bacon, and General Bonham used to love to say that no finer body of men were ever assembled together in one command. With this brigade he went to Virginia, and they were the first troops other than Virginia troops that landed in Richmond for its defense. With them he took part in the operations around Fairfax, Vienna, Centerville, and the first battle of Manassas.

Afterwards, in consequence of a disagreement with the Department of War, he resigned from the army. Soon thereafter he was elected to the Confederate Congress, in which body he served until he was elected Governor of this State in December, 1862. It was a trying time to fill that office, and President Davis, in letters, bears witness to the fact that no one of the Governors of the South gave him more efficient aid and support than did Governor Bonham. At the expiration of his term of office, in January, 1865, he was appointed to the command of a brigade of cavalry, and at once set to work to organize it, but the surrender of Johnston's army put an end to the war.

Returning from the war broken in fortune, as were all of his people, he remained for a year or more on his plantation on Saluda River, in Edgefield County. He then moved to Edgefield Court House, again to take up his practice, so often interrupted by calls to arms. He was elected to the Legislature in 1866, just preceding Reconstruction, but with the coming of that political era he, in common with all the white men of the State, was debarred from further participation in public affairs. In the movement known as the Taxpayers Convention, which had for its object the relief of the people from Republican oppression and corruption, he took part as one of the delegates sent by this convention to Washington to lay before President Grant the condition of the people of the "Prostrate State." He took an active interest and part in the political revolution of 1876 and warmly advocated what was known as "the straightout policy" and the nomination of Wade Hampton as Governor.

In 1878 Governor Simpson appointed him the first Railroad Commissioner under the Act just passed, and subsequently when the number of the Commissioners was increased to three, he was elected Chairman of the Commission, in which position he continued until his death, on the 27th day of August, 1890. He died suddenly from the rupture of a blood vessel while on a visit to Haywood White Sulphur Springs, N.C.

General Bonham married on November 13th, 1845, Ann Patience, a daughter of Nathan L. Griffin, Esq., a prominent lawyer of Edgefield. She survived him four years, and of their union there are living eight children.

Attached to Bonham's Brigade was Kemper's Battery of light artillery, commanded by Captain Dell Kemper. This company was from Alexandria, Va., just over the Potomac from Washington. This organization was part of the old State militia, known as volunteer companies, and had been in existence as such for many years. It being in such close proximity to Washington, the sentiment of the company was divided, like all companies on the border. Some of the company were in favor of joining the Union Army, while others wished to go with the State. Much discussion took place at this time among the members as to which side they would join, but Captain Kemper, with a great display of coolness and courage, cut the Gordian knot by taking those with him of Southern sentiment, like himself, and on one dark night he pulled out from Alexandria with his cannon and horses and made his way South to join the Southern Army. That was the last time any of that gallant band ever saw their native city for more than four years, and many of the poor fellows looked upon it that night for the last time. Between them and the South Carolinians sprang up a warm attachment that continued during the war. They remained with us as a part of the brigade for nearly two years, or until the artillery was made a separate branch of the service. While in winter quarters, when many troops were granted furloughs, those men having no home to which they could visit like the others, were invited by members of the brigade to visit their own homes in South Carolina and remain with their families the length of their leave of absence. Many availed themselves of these kind invitations, and spent a pleasant month in the hospitable homes of this State. The ladies of South Carolina, appreciating their isolated condition and forced separation from their homes, with no kind mother or sister with opportunities to cheer them with their delicate favors, made them all a handsome uniform and outfit of underwear, and sent to them as a Christmas gift. Never during the long years of the struggle did the hearts of South Carolinians fail to respond to those of the brave Virginians, when they heard the sound of Kemper's guns belching forth death and destruction to the enemy, or when the battle was raging loud and furious.

On the morning of the 16th of July, when all was still and quiet in camp, a puff of blue smoke from a hill about three miles off, followed by the roar of a cannon, the hissing noise of a shell overhead, its loud report, was the first intimation the troops had that the enemy had commenced the advance, it is needless to say excitement and consternation overwhelmed the camp. While all were expecting and anxiously awaiting it, still the idea of being now in the face of a real live enemy, on the eve of a great battle, where death and horrors of war, such as all had heard of but never realized, came upon them with no little feelings of dread and emotion. No man living, nor any who ever lived, retaining his natural faculties, ever faced death in battle without some feeling of dread or superstitious awe. The soldiers knew, too, the eyes of the world were upon them, that they were to make the history for their generation. Tents were hurriedly struck, baggage rolled and thrown into wagons, with which the excited teamsters were not long in getting into the pike road. Drums beat the assembly, troops formed in line and took position behind the breastwork; while the artillery galloped up to the front and unlimbered, ready for action. The enemy threw twenty-pound shells repeatedly over the camp, that did no further damage than add to the consternation of the already excited teamsters, who seemed to think the safety of the army depended on their getting out of the way. It was an exciting scene to see four-horse teams galloping down the pike at break-neck speed, urged forward by the frantic drivers.

It was the intention of McDowell, the Federal Chief, to surprise the advance at Fairfax Court House and cut off their retreat. Already a column was being hurried along the Germantown road, that intersected the main road four miles in our rear at the little hamlet of Germantown. But soon General Bonham had his forces, according to preconcerted arrangements, following the retreating trains along the pike towards Bull Run. Men overloaded with baggage, weighted down with excitement, went at a double quick down the road, panting and sweating in the noonday sun, while one of the field officers in the rear accelerated the pace by a continual shouting, "Hurry up, men, they are firing on our rear." This command was repeated so often and persistently that it became a by-word in our brigade, so much so that when anything was wanted to be done with speed the order was always accompanied with, "Hurry up, men, they are firing on our rear." The negro servants, evincing no disposition to be left behind, rushed along with the wagon train like men beset. While we were on the double-quick, some one noticed a small Confederate flag floating lazily in the breeze from a tall pine pole that some soldier had put up at his tent, but by the hurried departure neglected to take down. Its owner could not entertain the idea of leaving this piece of bunting as a trophy for the enemy, so risking the chance of capture, he ran back, cut the staff, and returned almost out of breath to his company with the coveted flag. We were none too precipitate in our movement, for as we were passing through Germantown we could see the long rows of glistening bayonets of the enemy crowning the hills to our right. We stopped in Centerville until midnight, then resumed the march, reaching Bull Run at Mitchell's Ford as the sun was just rising above the hill tops.

Colonel Kershaw and Colonel Cash were filing down the east bank to the left, while Colonels Williams and Bacon occupied some earthworks on the right. These had been erected by former troops, who had encamped there before us. General Beauregard had divided his troops into six brigades, putting regiments of the same State together, as far as possible, Bonham's being First Brigade. Beauregard was determined to make Bull Run his line of defense. This is a slow, sluggish stream, only fordable at certain points, its banks steep and rather rocky with a rough plateau reaching back from either side. The western being the more elevated, gave the enemy the advantage in artillery practice. In fact, the banks on the western side at some points came up to the stream in a bluff—especially so at Blackburn's Ford. In the rear and in the direction of the railroad was the now famous Manassas Plains. The Confederate line extended five miles, from Union Mills Ford to Stone Bridge. At the latter place was General Evans, of South Carolina, with two regiments and four pieces of artillery. On the extreme right, Ewell with his brigade and a battery of twelve-pounders was posted at Union Mills. McLean's Ford was guarded by D.R. Jones' brigade, with two brass six-pounders. Longstreet with two six-pounders, and Bonham with two batteries of artillery and a squadron of cavalry, guarded the fords at Blackburn's and Mitchell's respectively. Early's Brigade acted as reserve on the right. In rear of the other fords was Cooke's Brigade and one battery. The entire force on the roll on July 11th consisted of 27 pieces of light artillery and 534 men; cavalry, 1425; foot artillery, 265; infantry, 16,150—18,401, comprising the grand total of all arms of General Beauregard one week before the first battle. Now it must be understood that this includes the sick, guards, and those on outpost duty. McDowell had 37,300 of mostly seasoned troops.

The morning of the 18th opened bright and sunny. To our rear was all bustle and commotion, and it looked like a vast camp of wagon trains. From the surrounding country all wagons had been called in from the foraging expeditions laden with provisions. Herds of cattle were corralled to secure the troops fresh beef, while the little fires scattered over the vast plains showed that the cooking details were not idle. General Beauregard had his headquarters on the hill in our rear.

At eight o'clock on the 18th, McDowell pushed his leading division forward at Blackburn's Ford, where two old comrades, but now facing each other as foes, General Tyler and General Longstreet, were to measure strength and generalship. The Washington Artillery, under Captain Richardson, of New Orleans, a famous battery throughout the war, which claims the distinction of firing the first gun at Bull Run and the last at Appomattox, was with Longstreet to aid him with their brass six-pounders.

The enemy advanced over the plain and up to the very bluff overlooking the stream, and a very short distance from where Longstreet's force lay, but the Washington Artillery had been raking the field all the while, from an eminence in the rear, while the infantry now began to fire in earnest. The elevated position gave the enemy great advantage, and at one time General Longstreet had to call up his reserves, but the advantageous assault was speedily repulsed as soon as the Southern troops became more calm and better accustomed to the fire and tension of the battlefield. Several assaults were made, one immediately after the other, but each time Southern valor overcame Northern discipline. From our position at Mitchell's Ford, we could hear the fierce, continual roll of the infantry fire, mingled with the deafening thunder of the cannon. Bonham was under a continual shelling from long range, by twenty pounders, some reaching as far in the rear as the wagon yard. After the fourth repulse, and Longstreet had his reserves well in hand, he felt himself strong enough to take the initiative. Plunging through the marshes and lagoons that bordered the stream, the troops crossed over and up the bluff, but when on the heights they met another advance of the enemy, who were soon sent scampering from the field. Then was first heard the famous "Rebel yell." The Confederates finding themselves victorious in this their first engagement, gave vent to their feelings by uttering such a yell as suited each individual best, forming for all time the famous "Rebel Yell." Longstreet withdrew his forces to the east side, but a continual fusilade of artillery was kept up until night. Some of our soldiers visited the battlefield that night and next day, and brought in many trophies and mementoes of the day's fight, such as blankets, oilcloths, canteens, guns, etc.

The Battle of Manassas

Of the battle of the 18th, the enemy seemed to make little, and called it a "demonstration" at which General Tyler exceeded his orders, and pushed his troops too far. However, the Confederates were very well satisfied with the contest where the first blood was drawn. General Johnston, who at this time was up in the Shenandoah Valley, near Winchester, was asked by General Beauregard to come to his relief. He was confronted himself by General Patterson, an able Federal General, with a largely superior army. This General Johnston had assurance to believe was preparing to advance, and his own danger great. Still by a strategem, he succeeded in quietly withdrawing his troops, and began the hazardous undertaking of re-enforcing Beauregard. Some of his troops he placed upon the cars at Piedmont, and sped along o'er mountains and glens with lightning speed, while the others on foot came over and through the torturous mountain passes without halt or rest, bending all their energies to meet Beauregard upon the plains of Manassas. Couriers came on foaming steeds, their bloody sides showing the impress of the riders' spurs, bringing the glad tidings to the Army of the Potomac that succor was near. Beauregard was busy with the disposition of his troops, preparing to give battle, while the soldiers worked with a will erecting some hasty breastworks.

At this point I will digress for the moment to relate an incident of the Federal march, to show the brutal cowardice and baseness of the Federals in making war upon the non-combatants—women and children—and also the unyielding spirit and inflexible courage of our Southern people. Those dispositions were manifested on both sides throughout the whole war. It is unnecessary to say that feeling ran high on the border, as elsewhere, and everyone was anxious to display his colors in order to show to the world how his feelings ran. Confederate flags waved from many housetops along the border, and on the morning the Federals crossed the Potomac from Washington to Alexandria, many little pieces of bunting, displaying stars and bars, floated from the houses in that old sleeping city of Alexandria. Among that number was a violent Secessionist named Jackson. Colonel Ellsworth, commanding the New York Zouaves, the advance guard, ordered all flags with Confederate devices to be torn down by force. The soldiers thus engaged in the debasing acts of entering private dwellings, insulting the inmates with the vilest epithets, ruthlessly tore down the hated emblems of the South everywhere. When they came to Jackson's house they met the fiery defender of his home on the landing of the stairs, rifle in hand, who with determined air informed the Federal soldiers that whoever lowered his flag would meet instant death. Staggered and dazed by such a determined spirit, they lost no time in reporting the fact to Colonel Ellsworth. Enraged beyond all control by this cool impudence, Ellsworth rushed to Jackson's house, followed by a squad of soldiers. On reaching the landing he, too, met Jackson with his eyes flashing fire and determination, his whole frame trembling with the emotion he felt, his rifle cocked and to his shoulder, boldly declaring, "Whoever tears down that flag, dies in his tracks." Ellsworth and party thought this threat could not be real, and only Southern braggadocio. Brushing past the determined hero, Ellsworth snatched the hated flag from its fastening, but at that instant he fell dead at the feet of his adversary. The report of Jackson's rifle told too plainly that he had kept his word. The soldiers who had followed and witnessed the death of their commander, riddled the body of the Southern martyr with bullets, and not satisfied with his death, mutilated his body beyond recognition. Thus fell the first martyr to Southern principles. The South never showed this disposition of hatred on any occasion, for in after years while marching through Pennsylvania Union flags floated unmolested from housetops, over towns, and cities. The soldiers only laughed and ridiculed the stars and stripes. The South feared no display of sentiment, neither did they insult women and non-combatants.

A like occurrence happened in New Orleans a few years later, where General Butler commanded, and gained the unenviable sobriquet of "Beast" by his war upon the women and those not engaged in the struggle, and by trampling upon every right and liberty sacred to the people. He had issued some degrading order, which the citizens were bound in pain of death to obey. One brave man, Mumford, refused, preferring death to obeying this humiliating order. For this he was torn from the embrace of his devoted family, and, in sight of his wife and children, placed in a wagon, forced to ride upon his own coffin, and in the public square was hanged like a felon.

General Johnston, with a portion of his troops, reached the field on the 20th, and his forces were placed in rear of those of Beauregard as reserves. On the night of the 20th, both opposing generals, by a strange coincidence, had formed plans of the battle for the next day, and both plans were identical. Beauregard determined to advance his right by echelon of brigades, commencing with Ewell at Union Mills, then Jones and Longstreet were to cross Bull Run, with Bonham as a pivot, and attack McDowell in flank and rear. This was the identical plan conceived and carried out by the enemy, but with little success, as events afterwards showed. The only difference was McDowell got his blow in first by pushing his advance columns forward up the Warrenton Road on our left, in the direction of the Stone Bridge. He attacked General Evans, who had the Fourth South Carolina and Wheat's Battalion of Louisiana Tigers, on guard at this point, with great energy and zeal. But under cover of a dense forest, he moved his main body of troops still higher up the Run, crossed at Sudley's Ford, and came down on Evans' rear. Fighting "Shanks Evans," as he was afterwards called, met this overwhelming force with stubborn resistance and a reckless courage. The enemy from the opposite side of the Run was sending in a continued shower of shot and shell, which threatened the annihilation of the two little six-pounders and the handful of infantry that Evans had. But support soon reached him, the Brigade of Bee's coming up; still he was pressed back beyond a small stream in his rear. Bee, with his own and Bartow's Brigade, with a battery of artillery, were all soon engaged, but the whole column was forced back in the valley below. Jackson came upon the crest of the hill in their rear at this juncture, and on this column the demoralized troops were ordered to rally. It was here Jackson gained the name of "Stonewall," for Bee, to animate and reassure his own men, pointed to Jackson and said: "Look at Jackson, he stands like a stonewall." But the gallant South Carolinian who gave the illustrious chieftain the famous name of "Stonewall" did not live long enough to see the name applied, for in a short time he fell, pierced through with a shot, which proved fatal. Hampton, with his Legion, came like a whirlwind upon the field, and formed on the right, other batteries were brought into play, still the enemy pressed forward. Stone Bridge being uncovered, Tyler crossed his troops over, and joined those of

Hunter and Heintzelman coming from Sudley's Ford. This united the three divisions of the enemy, and they made a vigorous and pressing assault upon the demoralized Confederates. The roar of the cannon became continuous, the earth trembled from this storm of battle, sulphurous smoke obscures the sky, the air vibrates with shrieking shot and shell, men rush madly to the charge. Our small six-pounders against their twelve and twenty-pounders, manned by the best artillerists at the North, was quite an uneven combat. Johnston and Beauregard had now come upon the field and aided in giving order and confidence to the troops now badly disorganized by the fury of the charge. The battle raged in all its fierceness; the infantry and artillery, by their roaring and thunder-like tone, gave one the impression of a continued, protracted electrical storm, and to those at a distance it sounded like "worlds at war." On the plateau between the Lewis House and the Henry House the battle raged fast and furious with all the varying fortunes of battle. Now victorious—now defeated—the enemy advances over hill, across plateaus, to be met with stubborn resistance first, then driven flying from the field. Around the Henry House the battle was desperate and hand to hand. Here the Louisiana Battalion, under Major Wheat, immortalized itself by the fury of its assault. Again and again was the house taken and lost, retaken and lost again; the men, seeking cover, rushed up around and into it, only to be driven away by the storm of shot and shell sent hurling through it. Now our troops would be dislodged, but rallying they rushed again to the assault and retook it. Twelve o'clock came, and the battle was far from being decided. Bartow fell, then Bee. The wounded and dead lay strewn over the entire field from the Henry House to the bridge. Away to the left is seen the glitter of advancing bayonets, with flags waving, and the steady tread of long lines of soldiers marching through the open field. They are first thought to be the enemy, seeking to turn our left. Officers and men turned pale at the sight of the unexpected foe. Couriers were sent to Longstreet and Bonham to prepare to cover the retreat, for the day was now thought to be lost, and a retreat inevitable. The troops proved to be friends. Elzeys and Kirby Smith on the way from the Valley to Manassas, hearing the firing of the guns, left the cars and hurried to the scene of action. Cheer after cheer now rent the air, for relief was now at hand. They were put in on the left, but soon General Kirby Smith fell wounded, and had to be borne from the field. Other reinforcements were on the way to relieve the pressure that was convincing to the generals commanding, even, that the troops could not long endure. The Second and Eighth South Carolina Regiments, under the command of Colonels Kershaw and Cash, were taken from the line at Mitchell's Ford and hurried forward. When all the forces, were gotten well in hand, a general forward movement was made. But the enemy met it with a determined front. The shrieking and bursting of shells shook the very earth, while the constant roll of the infantry sounded like continual peals of heavy thunder. Here and there an explosion, like a volcanic eruption, told of a caisson being blown up by the bursting of a shell. The enemy graped the field right and left, and had a decided advantage in the forenoon when their long range twenty-pounders played havoc with our advancing and retreating columns, while our small four and six-pounders could not reach their batteries. But in the after part of the day, when the contending forces were nearer together, Rickett's and Griffin's Batteries, the most celebrated at that time in the Northern Army, could not stand the precision and impetuosity of Kemper's, the Washington, Stannard's, Pendleton's, and Pelham's Batteries as they graped the field. The Second and Eighth South Carolina coming up at a double quick, joined Hampton's Legion, with Early, Cox, and the troops from the Valley just in time to be of eminent service at a critical moment. The clear clarion voice of Kershaw gave the command, "Forward!" and when repeated in the stentorian voice of Cash, the men knew what was expected of them, answered the call, and leaped to the front with a will. The enemy could no longer withstand the desperate onslaught of the Confederate Volunteers, and McDowell now began to interest himself with the doubtful problem of withdrawing his troops at this critical juncture. With the rugged banks of the deep, sluggish stream in his rear, and only a few places it could be crossed, with a long sheet of flame blazing out from the compact lines of the Confederates into the faces of his men, his position was perilous in the extreme. His troops must have been of like opinion, for the ranks began to waver, then break away, and soon they found themselves in full retreat. Kershaw, Cash, and Hampton pressed them hard towards Stone Bridge. A retreat at first now became a panic, then a rout. Men threw away their baggage, then their guns, all in a mad rush to put the stream between themselves and the dreaded "gray-backs." Cannon were abandoned, men mounted the horses and fled in wild disorder, trampling underfoot those who came between them and safety, while others limbered up their pieces and went at headlong speed, only to be upset or tangled in an unrecognizable mass on Stone Bridge. The South Carolinians pressed them to the very crossing, capturing prisoners and guns; among the latter was the enemy's celebrated "Long Tom." All semblance of order was now cast aside, each trying to leave his less fortunate neighbor in the rear. Plunging headlong down the precipitous banks of the Run, the terror-stricken soldiers pushed over and out in the woods and the fields on the other side. The shells of our rifle and parrot guns accelerated their speed, and added to their demoralization by hissing and shrieking above their heads and bursting in the tree tops. Orders were sent to Generals Bonham, Longstreet, and Jones, who were holding the lower fords, to cross over and strike the flying fugitives in the rear near Centerville. Colonels Williams and Bacon, with their regiments, led by General Bonham, in person, crossed the stream at a double quick, and began the pursuit of the stampeded troops. When we reached the camps of the enemy, where they had bivouaced the night before, the scene beggared description. On either side of the road were piled as high as one could reach baggages of every description, which the men had discarded before going into action. Blankets rolled up, oilcloths, overcoats, tents, all of the very best material, piled up by the hundreds and thousands. Pots and camp kettles hung over fires, and from within came the savory smell of "rich viands with rare condiments," being prepared to appease the keen appetite of the battle-worn veterans after the day's victory. Great quarters of fresh beef hung temptingly from the limbs of the trees, wagons filled with arms and accoutrements, provisions, and army supplies, with not a few well-laden with all the delicacies, tidbits, and rarest old wines that Washington could afford, to assuage the thirst of officers and the men of note. Many of the high dignitaries and officials from the Capitol had come out to witness the fight from afar, and enjoy the exciting scene of battle. They were now fleeing through the woods like men demented, or crouched behind trees, perfectly paralyzed with uncertainty and fright. One old citizen of the North, captured by the boys, gave much merriment by the antics he cut, being frightened out of his wits with the thought of being summarily dealt with by the soldiers. Some would punch him in the back with their bayonets, then another would give him a thrust as he turned to ask quarters of the first tormentor. The crisis was reached, however, when one of the soldiers, in a spirit of mischief, called for a rope to hang him; he thought himself lost, and through his tears he begged for mercy, pleaded for compassion, and promised atonement. General Bonham riding up at this juncture of the soldiers' sport, and seeing the abject fear of the old Northern Abolitionist, took pity and showed his sympathy by telling the men to turn him loose, and not to interfere with non-combatants. He was told to run now, and if he kept the gait he started with through the woods, not many hours elapsed before he placed the placid waters of the Potomac between him and the blood-thirsty Rebels. Strict orders were given to "stay in ranks," but the sight of so much valuable plunder, and actual necessaries to the soldiers, was too much for the poorly provided Confederates; and not a few plucked from the pile a blanket, overcoat, canteen, or other article that his wants dictated. A joke the boys had on a major was that while riding along the line, waving his sword, giving orders not to molest the baggage, and crying out, "Stay in ranks, men, stay in ranks," then in an undertone he would call to his servant, "Get me another blanket, Harvy." The artillery that had been ordered to take part in the infantry's pursuit were just preparing to open fire upon the fleeing enemy, when by some unaccountable order, the pursuit was ordered to be abandoned. Had not this uncalled for order come at this juncture, it is not hard to conceive the results. The greater portion of the Federal Army would have been captured, for with the exception of General Sykes' Brigade of regulars and a battery of regular artillery, there was not an organization between our army and Washington City. All night long the roads through Centerville, and the next day all leading through Fairfax, Falls Church, and Anandale were one continual throng of fleeing fugitives. Guns and accoutrements, camp equipage, and ordnance strewed the sides of the road for miles; wagons, ambulances, cannon, and caissons had been abandoned, and terror-stricken animals galloped unbridled through the woods and fields. The great herds of cattle, now free from their keepers, went bellowing through the forest, seeking shelter in some secluded swamp.

At night, we were all very reluctantly ordered back to our old camp to talk, rejoice, and dream of the wonderful victory. Beauregard and Johnston had in this engagement of all arms 30,888, but 3,000 of Ewell's and part of Bonham's Brigade were not on the field on that day. The enemy had 50,000 and 117 cannon. Confederate loss in killed and wounded, 1,485. Federal loss in killed, wounded, and captured, 4,500. There being no enemy in our front and little danger of surprise, the soldiers were allowed to roam at will over the battlefield the next few days. Almost the entire army availed themselves of this their first opportunity of visiting a real battlefield and witnessing the real horrors and carnage of which they had often read and seen pictures but had never seen in reality.

Who is it that has ever looked upon a battlefield and could forget the sickening scene, or obliterate from his mind the memory of its dreaded sight? It was recorded of the great Napoleon, by one of his most intimate friends and historians, that after every great battle the first thing he did the next day was to ride over the field, where lay the dead and wounded, and when he would come to those points where the battle had been desperate and the dead lay thickest, he would sit as in a trance, and with silence and meditation never witnessed on other occasions, view the ghastly corpses as they lay strewn over the field. The field of carnage had a fascinating power over him he could not resist, and on which his eyes delighted to feast. With a comrade I went to visit the field of Manassas. Passing over the uneven and partly wooded country, we witnessed all the effect of the enemy's rifled guns. Trees were cut down, great holes dug in the ground where shells had exploded, broken wagons, upset ambulances, wounded and dead horses lining the whole way. The first real scene of carnage was on the plateau of the Lewis house. Here the Virginians lying behind the crest of the hill as the enemy emerged from the woods on the other side, gave them such a volley as to cause a momentary repulse, but only to renew their attack with renewed vigor. The battle here was desperate. Major Wheat with his Louisianians fought around the Henry house with a ferocity hardly equalled by any troops during the war. Their peculiar uniform, large flowing trousers with blue and white stripes coming only to the knees, colored stockings, and a loose bodice, made quite a picturesque appearance and a good target for the enemy. These lay around the house and in front in almost arm's length of each other. This position had been taken and lost twice during the day. Beyond the house and down the declivity on the other side, the enemy's dead told how destructive and deadly had been the Confederate fire. On the other plateau where Jackson had formed and where Bee and Bartow fell, the scene was sickening. There lay friend and foe face to face in the cold embrace of death. Only by the caps could one be distinguished from the other, for the ghouls of the battlefield had already been there to strip, rob, and plunder. Beyond the ravine to the left is where Hampton and his Legion fought, as well as the troops of Kirby Smith and Elzey, of Johnston's army, who had come upon the scene just in time to turn the tide of battle from defeat to victory. On the right of Hampton was the

Eighth and Second South Carolina under Kershaw. From the Lewis house to the Stone Bridge the dead lay in every direction. The enemy in their precipitate flight gave the Confederates ample opportunity to slay at will. The effects of artillery here were dreadful. Rickett's Battery, the best in the North, had pushed their guns far in advance of the infantry, and swept the field with grape and canister. Here was a caisson blown up by a shell from Kemper's Battery, and the havoc was frightful. Six beautiful horses, all well caparisoned and still attached to the caisson, all stretched as they had fallen, without so much as a struggle. The drivers lay by the side of the horses, one poor fellow underneath and badly mutilated. To one side and near by lay the officer in command and his horse, the noble animal lying as he had died in the beautiful poise he must have been in when the fatal shot struck him. His hind legs straightened as if in the act of rearing, his forefeet in the air, one before the other, the whole looking more like a dismantled statue than the result of a battlefield. Fragments of shells, broken guns, knapsacks, and baggage were scattered over the plains. Details were busy gathering up the wounded and burying the dead. But from the looks of the field the task seemed difficult. In the little clusters of bushes, behind trees, in gullies, and in every conceivable place that seemed to offer shelter, lay the dead. What a shudder thrills the whole frame when you stand and contemplate the gruesome faces of the battle's dead. In every posture and all positions, with every conceivable shade of countenance, the glaring, glassy eyes meet you. Some lay as they fell, stretched full length on the ground; others show a desperate struggle for the last few remaining breaths. There lay the beardless youth with a pleasant smile yet lingering on his face as though waiting for the maternal kiss; the cold stern features of the middle aged as he lay grasping his trusty rifle, some drawn up in a perfect knot of agony, others their faces prone upon the earth, all dead, dead. Great pools of blood here and there had saturated the earth, the victim perhaps crawling to a nearby shelter or some little glen, hoping to gain a mouthful of water to cool his parched lips, or perhaps some friendly hand had carried him away to a hospital. Few of our troops had been molested by the body snatchers of the battlefield, but the enemy had almost invariably been stripped of his outer clothing. On the incline of the far side of a little hill spots were pointed out where the gallant South Carolinian, Bee, had fallen, while rallying his men for the final assault, and also the brave Georgian, Colonel Bartow, in a like endeavor.

We came to the Henry house, on the opposite plateau from the

Lewis house, the former at this time almost as noted as the little log hut at Waterloo that stood half a century before as a landmark to the fall of Napoleon. They were common, old fashioned frame houses, occupied by some poor people on this frightful day. The battle came with such suddeness and unexpectancy, the unfortunate inmates could not get away, and there throughout the bloody day these three Henry women had endured all the dread, excitement, and dangers of a great battle, and forced to remain between the opposing armies. The house was perfectly riddled with minnie balls, while great openings were torn in the side and roofs by the shells shattering through. There was no escape or place of safety. They stretched themselves at full length upon the floor, calmly awaiting death, while a perfect storm of shot and shell raged without and within. As we went in the house two women sat around the few mouldering embers that had answered the purpose of cooking a hasty meal. It was a single room house, with two beds, some cheap furniture, and a few cooking utensils. These were torn into fragments. In one corner lay the dead sister, who had been shot the day before, with a sheet thrown over to shield her from the gaze of the curious. The two sisters were eating a morsel unconcernedly, unconscious of the surroundings, while the house was crowded during the day with sight seers and curious questioners. On the other side of the room were some wounded soldiers, carried in to be shielded from the rays of the July sun, while all without lay in heaps the mangled dead. The exceeding tension of excitement, fright, untold fear, that had been drawn around them during the continuous struggle of the day before, had rendered those women callous and indifferent to all surrounding appearance; but their haggard faces told but too plainly their mental anguish and bodily suffering of yesterday. The eyes tire of the sickening scene, and the mind turns from this revolting field of blood, and we return heartstricken to our camp. The poor crippled and deserted horses limp over the field nibbling a little bunch of grass left green in places after the day of mad galloping of horses. Everywhere we saw friends hunting friends. Relief corps had come up from Richmond and were working night and day relieving the suffering and moving the wounded away. Cars were run at short intervals from Manassas, carrying the disabled to Warrentown, Orange Court House, Culpepper, and Richmond. President Davis had come up just after the battle had gone in our favor, and the soldiers were delighted to get a glimpse at our illustrious chieftain. It was needless to say Beauregard's star was still in the ascendant.

CHAPTER 6
July to October.

Much discussion has taken place since the rout at Manassas as to reasons for not following up the victory so gloriously won, and for not pushing on to Washington at once. It is enough to say the two commanders at the time and on the field saw difficulties and dangers sufficient in the way to rest on their spoils. The President, who was in council with them, after due consideration was convinced of the impracticability of a forward movement. In the first place, no preparation had been made for such an event; that the spoils were so out of proportion to their most sanguine expectations; that the transportation for the troops had to be employed in its removal; that no thought of a forward movement or invasion had ever been contemplated; so there were no plans or specifications at hand. Then again, the dead and wounded of both armies had to be attended to, which crippled our medical department so as to render it powerless should another engagement take place. And again, a large portion of our people thought this total defeat of the enemy at the very outset of the war would render the design of coercion by force of arms impracticable. The South was conservative, and did not wish to inflame the minds of the people of the Union by entering their territory or destroying their capital. Knowing there was a large party at the North opposed to the war, some of our leaders had reason to think this shattering of their first grand army would so strengthen their feelings and party that the whole North would call for peace. They further hugged that fatal delusion to their breast, a delusion that eventually shattered the foundation of our government and betrayed the confidence of the troops, "foreign intervention." They reasoned that a great victory by the South would cause our government to be recognized by the foreign powers and the South given a footing as a distinct, separate, and independent nation among all other great nations of the earth. That the South would no longer be looked upon as an "Insurrectionary Faction," "Erring Sisters," or "Rebellious Children." Our ports had been ordered closed by the North, and an imaginary blockade, a nominal fleet, stood out in front of our harbors. Our people thought the world's desire for the South's cotton would so influence the commercial and laboring people of Europe that the powers would force the North to declare her blockade off. Such were some of the feelings and hopes of a large body of our troops, as well as the citizens of the country at large. But it all was a fallacy, a delusion, an *ignis fatuus*. The North was aroused to double her former fury, her energies renewed and strengthened, tensions drawn, her ardor largely increased, her feelings doubly embittered, and the whole spirit of the North on fire. Now the cry was in earnest, "On to Richmond," "Down with the rebellion," "Peace and unity." The Northern press was in a perfect blaze, the men wild with excitement, and every art and device was resorted to to arouse the people to arms. The stain of defeat must now be wiped out; a stigma had been put upon the nation, her flag disgraced, her people dishonored. Large bounties were offered for volunteers, and the recruiting was earnest and energetic. Lincoln called for 300,000 more troops, and the same question was asked at the South, "Where will he get them and how pay them?"

We were moved out near Centerville, and a few days afterwards took up camp at Vienna, a small station on the Baltimore and Ohio railroad. The day after our arrival all of the troops, with the exception of the ordinary detail, were put to work tearing up the railroad track. It being Sunday, loud complaints were made against this desecration of the Lord's Day, but we were told there was no difference in days in times of war. The railroad was a good one and well built on a roadbed of gravel and chips of granite, with solid heart pine or chestnut ties, laid with "T" rails. The cross-ties were piled in heaps, on these were laid the rails, and all set on fire; then for miles and miles up and down the road the crackling flames, the black smoke twining around the trees and curling upward, shrouded the whole earth with a canopy of black and blue, and told of the destruction that was going on. Here the troops suffered as seldom during the war for provisions, especially breadstuff. Loud murmurings were heard on all sides against the commissary department, and the commissary complained of the Quartermaster for not furnishing transportation. The troops on one occasion here had to go three days and at hard work without one mouthful of bread, except what little they could buy or beg of the citizens of the thinly settled country. Meat was plentiful, but no bread, and any one who has ever felt the tortures of bread hunger may imagine the sufferings of the men. For want of bread the meats became nauseating and repulsive. The whole fault lay in having too many bosses and red tape in the Department at Richmond. By order of these officials, all commissary supplies, even gathered in sight of the camps, had to be first sent to Richmond and issued out only on requisitions to the head of the departments. The railroad facilities were bad, irregular, and blocked, while our wagons and teams were limited to one for each one hundred men for all purposes. General Beauregard, now second in command, and directly in command of the First Army Corps of the Army of the Potomac, of which our brigade formed a part, wishing to concentrate his troops, ordered all to Flint Hill, three miles west of Fairfax Court House. General Johnston, Commander-in-Chief, directed the movements of the whole army, but more directly the Second Army Corps, or the Army of the Shenandoah. The army up to this time had not been put into divisions, commanded by Major Generals, nor corps, by Lieutenant Generals, but the two commanders divided nominally the army into two corps, each commanded by a full General—Brigadier General Beauregard having been raised to the rank of full General the day after his signal victory at Manassas by President Davis.

In the Confederate Army the grades of the Generals were different to those in the United States Army. A brigade consisted of a number of regiments joined together as one body and commanded by a Brigadier General, the lowest in rank. Four, more or less, brigades constituted a division, commanded by a Major General. Three or four divisions constituted a corps, commanded by a Lieutenant General, and a separate army, as two or more corps, was commanded by a General, the highest in rank. Their rank is the same, but the Seniors are those whose commissions had been granted first, and take precedence where two are together. So it is with all officers in the army—age is not taken into consideration, but the date of commission. Where a brigade, from any cause, temporarily loses its commander, the Colonel with the oldest commission takes the command; where a division loses its Major General, the Senior Brigadier in that division immediately assumes command; and the same way in the corps and the army. The Major General takes command of the corps where its commander is absent, and in case of absence, either temporary or permanent, of the Commander-in-Chief of an army, the ranking Lieutenant General takes command until a full General relieves him. In no case can an officer of inferior rank command one of superior rank. Rank gives command whether ordered or not. In any case of absence, whether in battle, march, or camp, whenever an officer finds himself Senior in his organization, he is commander and so held without further orders.

The soldiers had rather a good time at Flint Hill, doing a little drilling and occasional picket duty out in the direction of Munson and Mason Hill. The Commanding General wished to advance his pickets to Munson Hill, a few miles from Washington, and to do this it was necessary to dislodge the enemy, who had possession there. The Second Regiment, under Colonel Kershaw, was sent out, and after a considerable brush he succeeded in driving the enemy away. After this one regiment at a time was sent out to do picket duty. When our South Carolina regiments would go out orders were given to be quiet, and during our stay at Mason and Munson Hill the utmost secrecy prevailed, but when Wheat's Louisiana Battalion had to relieve a regiment we could hear the beating of their drums, the loud shouts of the men on their way out, and all would rush to the side of the road to see the "tigers" pass. Down the road they would come, banners waving, the swinging step of the men keeping time to the shrill notes of the fife and the rattle of the drums. Their large flowing pants, their gaudy striped long hose, made quite an imposing spectacle. This was a noted band of men for a time, but their brave commander, Wheat, and almost all of his men, were killed in the battles that followed around Richmond. Major Wheat had been in the Turkish Army when that nation was at war with Russia, and in several other foreign wars, as well as the Mexican War. When his State seceded he returned to Louisiana and raised a battalion of the hardest set of men in New Orleans. The soldiers called them "wharf rats," "sailors," "longshoremen," "cutthroats," and "gutter snipes." They knew no subordination and defied law and military discipline. While in camp here several of them were shot at the stake. Major Wheat had asked to be allowed to manage his men as he saw best, and had a law unto himself. For some mutiny and insubordination he had several of them shot. Afterwards, when the soldiers heard a volley fired, the word would go out, "Wheat is having another tiger shot."

The fields were green with the great waving corn, just in roasting ears, and it was a sight to see hundreds of men in these fields early in the morning plucking the fine ears for breakfast. In most cases the owners had abandoned their fields and homes, taking what was movable to other places in Virginia. What was left the soldiers were at liberty to "slay and eat." At first it was determined to protect the stock, but the soldiers agreed that what the Southern soldiers left the enemy would be sure to take. I remember the first theft I was engaged in during the war. I say "first" advisedly. Now soldiers have different views as to rights of property to that of the average citizen. What he finds that will add to his comfort or welfare, or his wants dictate, or a liability of the property falling into the hands of the enemy, he takes without compunction or disposition to rob—and more often he robs in a spirit of mischief. A few fine hogs had been left to roam at will through the fields by the refugee farmers, and orders were given not to kill or molest them, to eat as much corn as we wished, but to spare the hogs. When the regiments were sent on pickets, a detail was left in camp as guard, also to watch around the fields to prevent trespass. While our regiment was on its three days' picket, I was left as one of the detail to guard the camp. Some one reported a fine hog in the yard of a house some distance away. It was agreed to kill it, divide it up, and have a rare treat for the weary pickets when they returned. How to kill it without attracting the attention of the other guards was a question of importance, because the report of a rifle and the proverbial squeal of a hog would be sure to bring down upon us the guard. One of the men had a pistol, still we were afraid to trust this. A cellar door stood temptingly open. We tried to drive the hog into it, but with a hog's perverseness it refused to be driven, and after rushing around the yard several times with no results, it was decided to shoot it. The man claimed to be a good shot, and declared that no hog would squeal after being shot by him, but, as Burns says, "The best laid plans of mice and men aft' gang a glee." So with us. After shooting, the porker cut desperate antics, and set up a frightful noise, but the unexpected always happens, and the hog took refuge in the cellar, or rather the basement of the dwelling, to our great relief. We were proceeding finely, skinning away, the only method the soldiers had of cleaning a hog, when to our astonishment and dismay, in walked the much dreaded guard. Now there something peculiar about the soldier's idea of duty, the effects of military training, and the stern obedience to orders. The first lesson he learns is obedience, and the longer in service the more convinced he is of its necessity. While he may break ranks, pass guards, rob roosts, or pilfer fruits and vegetables himself, yet put a gun in his hand, place him on duty, order him to guard or protect men or property, and his integrity in that respect is as unyielding, inflexible, and stern as if his life depended upon his faithful performance. The Roman soldiers' obedience to orders made them immortal, and their nation the greatest on earth. But to resume the thread of my story. When the guard came in we thought ourselves lost. To be punished for hog stealing, and it published at home, was more than our patriotism could stand. The guard questioned us about the killing, said it was against orders to fire a gun within range of camp, and furthermore against orders to molest private property. We tried to convince the guard that it was contraband, that the owners had left it, and to crown the argument, insisted that if we did not take the hog the Yankees would. This was the argument always last resorted to to ease conscience and evade the law. In this case, strange to say, it had its effect. After some parleying, it was agreed to share the booty equally between the guard and ourselves. They helped us cut brush and cover it nicely, and after tattoo all were to return and divide up. We did not know the guards personally, but knew their command. And so we returned to the camp to await the return of our pickets and night. It was soon noised in camp that there was a fine fat porker to be distributed after tattoo, and no little eagerness and inquisitiveness were manifested, as all wished a piece. Armed with a crocus-sack, we returned to the house; all was dark and still. We whistled the signal, but no answer. It was repeated, but still no reply. The guard had not come. Sitting down on the door step, we began our long wait. Moments passed into minutes, minutes into hours, until at last we began to have some forebodings and misgivings. Had we been betrayed? Would we be reported and our tents searched next day? Hardly; a soldier could not be so treacherous. We entered the cellar and began to fumble around without results, a match was struck, and to our unspeakable dismay not a vestige of hog remained. Stuck against the side of the wall was a piece of paper, on which was written: "No mercy for the hog rogue." Such swearing, such stamping and beating the air with our fists, in imitation of the punishment that would be given the treacherous rascals if present; the atmosphere was perfectly sulphurous with the venom spit out against the foul party. Here was a true verification of the old adage, "Set a rogue to catch a rogue." Dejected and crestfallen, we returned to camp, but dared not tell of our misfortune, for fear of the jeers of our comrades.

Measles and jaundice began to scourge the camp; the green corn, it was said, did the army more damage than the enemy did in battle. Wagons and ambulances went out daily loaded with the sick; the hospitals were being crowded in Richmond and other cities; hotels, colleges, and churches were appropriated for hospital service, and the good people of Virginia can never be forgotten, nor amply rewarded for the self-sacrifices and aid rendered to the sick soldiers. Private houses were thrown open to the sick when their homes were far distant, or where they could not reach it. The soldier was never too dirty or ragged to be received into palatial homes; all found a ready welcome and the best attention.

Generals Johnston and Beauregard had now concentrated all their forces in supporting distance around Fairfax Court House, and were preparing for a movement across the Potomac. Bonham's Brigade was at Flint Hill, Cox's at Centerville, Jones's at Germantown, Hampton and Early on the Occoquon, the Louisiana Brigade at Bull Run, and Longstreet at Fairfax Court House. The troops were all in easy distance, and a gigantic plan of General Beauregard, with the doubtful approval of General Johnston and others, was for a formidable invasion of the North. General Johnston evinced that same disposition in military tactics that he followed during the war, "a purely defensive war." In none of his campaigns did he exhibit any desire to take advantage of the enemy by bold moves; his one idea seemed to be "defensive," and in that he was a genius—in retreat, his was a mastermind; in defense, masterly. In the end it may have proven the better policy to have remained on the defensive. But the quick, impulsive temperament of Beauregard was ever on the alert for some bold stroke or sudden attack upon the enemy's weaker points. His idea coincided with Longstreet's in this particular, that the North, Kentucky, Tennessee, or Maryland should be the theatre of war and the battleground of the Confederacy. General Lee, according to the ideas of one of his most trusted lieutenants, was more in accordance with the views of General Johnston, that is, "the South should fight a defensive war"—and it was only when in the immediate presence of the enemy, or when he observed a weak point in his opponent, or a strategic move, that he could not resist the temptation to strike a blow. In several of his great battles it is reported of Lee that he intended to await the attack of the enemy, but could not control his impatience when the enemy began to press him; then all the fire of his warlike nature came to the surface, and he sprang upon his adversary with the ferocity of a wild beast. But Lee in battle was not the Lee in camp.

The middle of summer the two commanding Generals called President Davis to Fairfax Court House to enter a conference in regard to the projected invasion. The plans were all carefully laid before him. First a demonstration was to be made above Washington; then with the whole army cross below, strike Washington on the east, crush the enemy in their camps, march through Maryland, hoist the standard of revolt in that State, make a call for all Southern sympathizers to flock to their banners, and to overawe the North by this sudden onslaught. But President Davis turned a deaf ear to all such overtures; pleaded the want of transportation and the necessary equipment for invasion. It was the feeling of the South even at this late day that much could yet be done by diplomacy and mild measures; that a great body of the North could be won over by fears of a prolonged war; and the South did not wish to exasperate the more conservative element by any overt act. We all naturally looked for peace; we fully expected the war would end during the fall and winter, and it was not too much to say that many of our leaders hugged this delusion to their breast.

While in camp here an incident occurred which showed that the men had not yet fully recognized the importance of military restraint and discipline. It is well known that private broils or feuds of any kind are strictly forbidden by army regulations. The French manner of settling disputes or vindicating personal honor according to code duello was not countenanced by our military laws; still the hot blood and fiery temper of the proud South Carolinians could brook no restraint at this time when an affront was given or his honor assailed. Captain Elbert Bland, of Edgefield, and Major Emett Seibles, both of the Seventh Regiment, were engaged in a friendly game of chess, a difference arose, then a dispute, hot words, and at last insult given that could not be recalled nor allowed to pass unnoticed. Challenge is offered and accepted, seconds appointed, pistols chosen; distance, twenty paces; time, sunrise next morning on a hillside near the outskirts of the camp. Early next morning a lone ambulance is seen moving out of camp, followed by two surgeons, then the principals with their seconds at a respectful distance. On reaching the spot chosen lots were cast for choice of stations. This fell to Captain Bland. The distance was measured with mechanical exactness, dueling pistols produced, each second loading that of his principal. The regular dueling pistol is a costly affair and of the very finest material. Long slim rifle barrel with hammer underneath, the stock finely chiseled and elaborately ornamented with silver or gold; the whole about ten inches in length and carrying a bullet of 22 calibre. The seconds took their places at an equal distance from each other and midway between the principals. Captain Bland takes his position at the west end of the field, and Major Seibles the east. Both stood confronting each other, not fierce nor glaring like two men roused in passion, or that either wished the blood of the other, but bold, calm, and defiant; an insult to be wiped out and honor to be sustained. They turned, facing the rear, hands down, with pistols in the right. The seconds call out in calm, deliberate tones: "Gentlemen, are you ready?" Then, "Ready, aim, fire!" "One, two, three, stop." The shooting must take place between the words "fire" and "stop," or during the count of one, two, three. If the principal fires before or after this command it is murder, and he is at once shot down by the second of his opponent. Or if in any case the principals fail to respond at the hour set, the second promptly takes his place. But no danger of such possibilities where two such men as Major Seibles and Captain Bland are interested. There was a matter at issue dearer than country, wife or child. It was honor, and a true South Carolinian of the old stock would make any sacrifice, give or take life, to uphold his name unsullied or the honor of his family untarnished. As the word fire was given the opponents wheeled and two pistol shots rang out on the stillness of the morning. Captain Bland stands still erect, commanding and motionless as a statue. Major Seibles remains steady for a moment, then sways a little to the left, staggers and falls into the arms of his second and surgeon. A hasty examination is made. "Blood," calls out the second of Major Seibles. A nod of satisfaction is given and acknowledged by both seconds. Captain Bland retires on the arm of his friend, while the Major, now bleeding profusely from a wound in the chest, is lifted in the ambulance and carried to his tent. It was many months before Major Seibles was sufficiently recovered from his wound to return to duty. The matter was kept quiet and no action taken. Major Seibles died the following year, while the gallant Bland was killed at Chickamauga while leading as Colonel the Seventh Regiment in battle.

While at Flint Hill, another stirring scene took place of quite a different nature. In front of the Third Regiment was a beautiful stretch of road, and this was selected as a course for a race to be run between the horse of Captain Mitchell of the Louisiana Tigers and that of the Colonel of a Virginia regiment of cavalry. The troops now so long inactive, nothing to break the monotony between drills, guard duty, and picketing, waited with no little anxiety the coming of the day that was to test the metal of the little grey from the Pelican State and the sorrel from the Old Dominion. Word had gone out among all the troopers that a race was up, and all lovers of the sport came in groups, companies, and regiments to the place of rendezvous. Men seemed to come from everywhere, captains, colonels, and even generals graced the occasion with their presence. Never before in our army had so many distinguished individuals congregated for so trivial an occasion. There was Wheat, fat, clean shaven, and jolly, his every feature indicating the man he was—bold as a lion, fearless, full of life and frolic as a school boy, but who had seen war in almost every clime under the sun. There was Turner Ashby, his eyes flashing fire from under his shaggy eyebrows, his long black beard and flowing locks, looking more like a brigand than one of the most daring cavaliers of the Confederate Army. Fitzhugh Lee, too, was there, with colonels, majors, and captains without number. Nothing seemed farther from the horizon of these jolly men than thoughts of the triumphs of war. Captain Mitchell's horse was more on the pony order than a racer, but it was said by those who knew that on more occasions than one the pony had thrown dirt into the eyes of the fastest horse in the Crescent City, and the Louisianans were betting on him to a man. The wiry sorrel was equally a favorite with the Virginians, while the South Carolinians were divided between the two. After a great amount of jockeying, usual on such occasions, judges were appointed, distance measured, horses and riders in their places, and hundreds of men stretched along the side of the road to witness the heated race. No little amount of Confederate money had been put upon the race, although it was understood to be merely a friendly one, and for amusement only. When the drum sounded, the two horses almost leaped into the air, and sped away like the wind, "little grey" shooting away from her larger adversary like a bullet, and came flying down the track like a streak, about a length ahead of the Virginia horse. The favorites on the Louisianan rent the air with their yells, hats went into the air, while the friends of the Virginian shouted like mad to the rider: "Let him out, let him out." When the distance was about half run he was "let out;" the rowels went into the side and the whip came down upon the flanks of the thoroughly aroused racer, and the Virginian began forging to the front, gaining at every leap. Now he is neck and neck, spur and whip are used without stint, he goes ahead and is leaving the "grey" far in the rear; Captain Mitchell is leaning far over on the withers of the faithful little pony, never sparing the whip for a moment, but all could see that he was running a losing race. When about the commencement of the last quarter the "grey" leaves the track, and off to the right he plunges through the trees, dashing head-long by the groups of men, till at last the Captain brings him up with one rein broken. A great crowd surround him, questioning, swearing, and jeering, but the Captain sat as silent, immovable, and inattentive as a statue, pointing to the broken rein. It had been cut with a knife. The Captain and his friends claimed that the friends of the Virginian had, unnoticed by him, cut the leather to a bare thread, while the friends of the other party, with equal persistency, charged the Captain with cutting it himself. That when he saw the race lost, he reached over and cut the rein about six inches from the bit, thus throwing the horse out of the track and saving its credit, if not the money. No one ever knew how it happened, but that there had been a trick played and foul means employed were evident. A great many had lost their money, and their curses were loud and deep, while the winners went away as merry as "marriage bells."

Winter Quarters at Bull Run

Sometime in October the brigade was withdrawn to the vicinity of Centerville for better facilities in the way of provisions, water, etc., and to be nearer the wooded section of the country. The water had been scarce at Flint Hill, a long distance from camp, and of inferior quality. The health of the troops was considerably impaired, a great many having been sent to the hospitals, or to their homes. The sickness was attributed, in a large measure, to the quality of green corn and fresh meat, salt being an object now with the Confederacy, and was issued in limited quantities. We fared sumptuously while at our camp near Centerville. Our wagon train going weekly up towards Warrenton and the mountains, returning laden with flour, meat, and the finest beef we had ever received. The teamsters acting as hucksters, brought in a lot of delicacies to sell on their own account—chickens, turkeys, and vegetables, and not unfrequently a keg of "Mountain Dew" would be packed in the wagon with the army supplies, and sold by the wagoners at an enormous profit. There being no revenue officers or "dispensary constables" in those days, whiskey could be handled with impunity, and not a little found its way into camp. The citizens, too, had an eye single to their own welfare, and would bring in loads of all kinds of country produce. Sometimes a wagon would drive into camp loaded with dressed chickens and turkeys to the number of one hundred or more. A large old-fashioned wagon-sheet would be spread over the bottom and side of the wagon body, and filled with as much as two horses could pull. I never knew until then how far a man's prejudice could overcome him. Our mess had concluded to treat itself to a turkey dinner on Christmas. Our boss of the mess was instructed to purchase a turkey of the next wagon that came in. Sure enough, the day came and a fine fat turkey bought, already dressed, and boiling away in the camp kettle, while all hands stood around and drank in the delightful aroma from turkey and condiments that so temptingly escaped from under the kettle lid. When all was ready, the feast spread, and the cook was in the act of sinking his fork into the breast of the rich brown turkey, some one said in the greatest astonishment: "Well, George Stuck, I'll be d——d if you haven't bought a goose instead of a turkey, look at its short legs." There was a go, our money gone, appetites whetted, and for a goose! Well up to that time and even now I cannot eat goose. A dispute arose, some said it was a goose, others held out with equal persistency that it was a turkey, and I not having discretion enough to judge by the color of the flesh, and so overcome by my prejudice, did not taste it, and a madder man was not often found. To this day I have never been convinced whether it was a turkey or a goose, but am rather inclined to give the benefit of the doubt to the goose.

We did not get into our regular winter quarters until after the first of January, 1862. These were established on the south Banks of Bull Run, near Blackburn's Ford, the place of the first battle of the name, where Longstreet fought on the 18th of July. Large details were sent out from camp every day to build foundations for these quarters. This was done by cutting pine poles or logs the right length of our tents, build up three or four feet, and over this pen the tent to be stretched. They were generally about ten feet square, but a man could only stand erect in the middle. The cracks between the logs were clinked with mud, a chimney built out of poles split in half and notched up in the ends of the log parts of the tent. An inside wall was made of plank or small round poles, with space between the two walls of five or six inches. This was filled with soft earth or mud, packed tightly, then a blazing fire started, the inner wall burned out, and the dirt baked hard and solid as a brick. In this way we had very good chimneys and comfortable quarters. From six to eight occupied one tent, and generally all the inmates messed together. Forks were driven into the ground, on which were placed strong and substantial cross-pieces, then round pipe poles, about the size of a man's arm, laid over all and thickly strewn with pine needles, on which the blankets are laid. There you have the winter quarters for the Southern soldiers the first year of the war.

But some of the men did not like so primitive an order of architecture and built huts entirely out of logs, and displayed as much originality as you would find in more pretentious cities. These were covered over with poles, on which straw and sand were tightly packed, enough so as to make them water-tight. Some would give names to their quarters, marked in large letters above their doors in charcoal, taxing their minds to give ingenious and unique names, such as "Uncle Tom's Cabin," "The House that Jack Built," "Park Row," "Devil's Inn," etc. To while away the long nights and cold days, the men had recourse to the soldier's game, "cards." Few ever played for the money that was in it, but more for an amusement and pastime. While almost all played cards, there were very few who could be considered gamblers, or who would take their comrades' money, if they even won it. There would be stakes played for, it is true, on the "credit system" generally, to be evened-up on pay-day. But when that time came around such good feeling existed that "poker debts," as they were called, were seldom ever thought of, and the game would continue with its varying successes without ever a thought of liquidation. You might often see a good old Methodist or a strict Presbyterian earnestly engaged in a "five cent antie" game, but never take his friend's money, even if honestly won. Something had to be done to pass away the time, and card-playing was considered an innocent amusement.

The long inactivity made men naturally think and dream of home. The soldiers had left home quite suddenly, and in many cases with little preparation, but the continual talk of "peace in the spring," and the daily vaporing of the press about England or France recognizing the South's belligerency—and the opening of her ports—buoyed up the spirits of the soldiers, and fanned the flame of hope. A great many of the old army officers of the United States, hailing from the South, had resigned their commissions on the Secession of the States, and tendered their services to the Confederacy. Of course it mattered not what was their former rank, or what service, if any they had seen, all expected places as generals. President Davis being a West Pointer himself, had great partiality for graduates of that institution. It was his weakness, this favoritism for West Pointers; and the persistency with which he appointed them above and over the generals of the volunteers, gave dissatisfaction. These appointments caused such resentment and dissatisfaction that some of our very best generals resigned their commissions, refusing to serve under men of no experience and doubtful qualifications. Longstreet, Van Dorn, McLaws, G.W. Smith, and a host of others, who had been captains and majors in the United States Army, were here or in Richmond waiting for some high grade, without first winning their spurs upon the field. McLaws, a Major in the regular army, was made a Major General, and Longstreet had been appointed over General Bonham, the latter having seen varied service in Mexico, commanding a regiment of regulars, doing staff duty, and Military Governor of one of the provinces after the war. At such injustice as this, gave General Bonham reason to resign his command and return to South Carolina, where he soon afterwards was elected to Congress, and later elected Governor of the State. This left the command to Colonel Kershaw as senior Colonel, but he was soon thereafter made Brigadier General. While the troops felt safe and confident under Kershaw, they parted with General Bonham with unfeigned reluctance and regret. Although none blamed him for the steps taken, for all felt keenly the injustice done, still they wished him to remain and lead them to victory, and share the glory they felt sure was in store for all connected with the old First Brigade.

In future we will call the brigade by the name of Kershaw, the name by which it was mostly known, and under whose leadership the troops did such deeds of prowess, endured so many hardships, fought so many battles, and gained so many victories, as to shed a halo around the heads of all who marched with him and fought under the banner of Joseph B. Kershaw. Here I will give a brief biography of General Kershaw.

JOSEPH BREVARD KERSHAW

Was born January 5th, 1822, at Camden, S.C. He was a son of John Kershaw and Harriet DuBose, his wife. Both of the families of Kershaws and DuBoses were represented by more than one member, either in the Continentals or the State troops, during the War of the Revolution, Joseph Kershaw, the most prominent of them, and the grandfather of the subject of this sketch, having lost his fortune in his efforts to maintain the patriot cause. John Kershaw died when his son, Joseph Brevard, was a child of seven years of age. He attended first a "dame school" in his native town. Afterwards he attended a school taught by a rigid disciplinarian, a Mr. Hatfield, who is still remembered by some of the pupils for his vigorous application of the rod on frequent occasions, with apparent enjoyment on his part, but with quite other sentiments on the part of the boys. He was sent at the age of fifteen to the Cokesbury Conference school, in Abbeville District, as it was then known, where he remained for only a brief time. Leaving this school, after a short sojourn at home, he went to Charleston, S.C., where he became a clerk in a dry goods house. This life not being congenial to him, he returned to Camden and entered as a student in the law office of the late John M. DeSaussure, Esq., from which, at the age of twenty-one, he was admitted to the Bar. He soon afterwards formed a copartnership with James Pope Dickinson, who was subsequently killed at the battle of Cherubusco, in the war with Mexico, gallantly leading the charge of the Palmetto Regiment. Both partners went to the Mexican War, young Kershaw as First Lieutenant of the Camden company, known as the DeKalb Rifle Guards. Struck down by fever contracted while in the service, he returned home a physical wreck, to be tenderly nursed back to health by his wife, Lucretia Douglass, whom he had married in 1844. Upon the recovery of his health, the war being over, he resumed the practice of law in Camden. But it was not long before his services were demanded in the State Legislature, which he entered as a member of the lower house in 1852. From this time on until the opening of hostilities in the war between the States, he practiced his profession with eminent success, and served also in the Legislature several terms, being handsomely re-elected when he stood for the place. He took a deep interest in the struggle then impending, and was a member of the Secession Convention from his native district. As it became more and more evident that there would be war, he ran for and was elected to the office of Colonel of the militia regiment composed of companies from Kershaw and adjacent districts, which, early in 1861, by command of Governor Pickens, he mobilized and led to Charleston and thence to Morris' Island, where the regiment remained until it volunteered and was called to go to Virginia to enter the service of the Confederacy. Several of the companies then in his regiment consented to go. These were supplemented by other companies which offered their services, and the new regiment, now known as the Second South Carolina Volunteers, proceeded to Richmond, thence to Manassas.

From this time until 1864 it is unnecessary to trace his personal history in this place, because the history of the brigade, to the command of which he was elected at the reorganization in 1862, and of its commander cannot be separated. In May, 1864, he was promoted to the rank of Major General and assigned to the command of a division, of which his brigade formed a part. His was the First Brigade of the First Division of the First Corps of the Army of Northern Virginia. On the retreat from Richmond his division, with other troops, numbering in all about 6,000 men, was surrounded and captured at the battle of Sailor's Creek, April 6th, 1865. In this disastrous battle Lieutenant General Ewell, Major Generals Kershaw and Custis Lee, Brigadier Generals D.M. DuBose, Semmes, Hunter, and Corse, and Commodores Hunter and Tucker, of the Confederate States' Navy, ranking on shore duty as Brigadiers, were captured, together with their respective commands, almost to a man, after a desperate and sanguinary struggle against immense odds. Those officers were all sent to Fort Warren, Boston Harbor, where they remained in prison until some time in August, 1865, when they were allowed to return to their respective homes.

General Kershaw resumed the profession of law in Camden immediately upon his return, and enjoyed a large and lucrative practice for many years, until called to serve his State as Circuit Judge in 1877, when the government was wrested from the hands of the Republicans. He took an active part in politics, having been elected to the State Senate in the fall of 1865. He ran for Congress from his district in 1874, but was counted out, as it was believed, at the election. He was also summoned to Columbia by Governor Hampton after his election in 1876, and rendered important service in securing the peaceable outcome of that most trying struggle. Upon the convening of the Legislature, he was at once elected Judge of the Fifth Circuit, a position which he held with distinguished honor for sixteen years, rendering it to Judge Ernest Gary in June, 1893, on which occasion there was tendered him a farewell probably unique in the judicial history of the State, by eminent representatives of the Bar of his Circuit. With impaired health, but with unwavering faith and carefulness that no adversity diminished, he once more returned to the practice of his profession. It was a gallant effort in the face of tremendous odds, but the splendid health that he had enjoyed for many years had been undermined slowly and insidiously by disease incident to a life that had ever borne the burdens of others, and that had spent itself freely and unselfishly for his country and his fellowman, and it was evident to all that his days were numbered. Devoted friends, the names of many of whom are unknown to me, offered him pecuniary help at this trying juncture, and these the writer would wish to hold, as he would have wished, "in everlasting remembrance." In his message to the General Assembly that year, 1893, Governor B.R. Tillman proposed him as the proper person to collect the records of the services of South Carolina soldiers in the Civil War, and to prepare suitable historical introduction to the volume. The Legislature promptly, and I believe unanimously, endorsed the nomination and made an appropriation for the work. To this he gave himself during the two succeeding mouths, collecting data, and even preparing in part the proposed introduction. But growing infirmities compelled him to lay it down, and in the latter part of March, 1894, he became alarmingly ill. All was done for his relief that the most competent skill and gentle care could do, but to no avail, and in the night of April 12th, just before midnight, be breathed his last. Among his last words to his son were these, spoken when he was perfectly conscious of what was before him: "My son, I have no doubts and no fears." On the occasion of his funeral there was a general outpouring of people from the town and vicinity for many miles, who sincerely mourned the departure of their friend. The State was represented by the Governor and seven members of his official family. On the modest monument that marks his last resting place is inscribed his name and the date of his birth and death. On the base the legend runs: "I have fought a good fight; I have kept the faith."

It may prove of interest to the surviving members of the old brigade to know that after the fight of Sailor's Creek, when General Kershaw and his companions were being taken back to Petersburg and thence to City Point to be shipped North, he spent a night at a farm house, then occupied as a field hospital and as quarters by the surgeons and attendants. They were South Carolinians, and were anxious to hear all about the fight. In telling of it the pride and love which he reposed in the old brigade received a wistful testimonial. It was then confronting Sherman somewhere in North Carolina. Its old commander said in a voice vibrant with feeling: "If I had only had my old brigade with me I believe we could have held these fellows in check until night gave us the opportunity to withdraw."

The roads in every direction near the army had become almost impassable—mud knee deep in the middle and ruts cut to the hubs on either side. The roads leading to Manassas were literally strewn with the carcasses of horses, some even sunk out of sight in the slough and mud. It would remind one of the passage of Napoleon across the Arabian desert, so graphically described by historians. The firewood had become scarce, and had to be carried on the men's shoulders the distance of a mile, the wagons being engaged in hauling supplies and the enormous private baggage sent to the soldiers from home. I remember once on my return from home on a short furlough, I had under my charge one whole carload of boxes for my company alone. Towards night every soldier would go out to the nearest woodland, which was usually a mile distant, cut a stick of wood the size he could easily carry, and bring into camp, this to do the night and next day. The weather being so severe, fires had to be kept up all during the night. Some constructed little boats and boated the wood across the stream, Bull Run, and a time they generally had of it, with the boat upsetting the men and the wood floundering and rolling about in the water, and it freezing cold.

The Department granted a thirty days' leave of absence to all individuals and companies that would re-enlist for the remaining two years or the war. Many officers were granted commissions to raise companies of cavalry and artillery out of the infantry commands, whose time was soon to expire. Lieutenant T.J. Lipscomb, of Company B, Third South Carolina Regiment, was given a commission as Captain, and he, with others, raised a company of cavalry and was given a thirty days' furlough. A great many companies volunteered in a body, not knowing at the time that the Conscript Act soon to be enacted would retain in service all between certain ages in the army, even after their time had expired.

About the middle of February President Davis called General Johnston to Richmond to confer with him upon the practicability of withdrawing the army to the south banks of the Rappahannock. It was generally understood at the time, and largely the impression since, that the army was withdrawn in consequence of McClellan's movements on the Peninsula. But such was not the case. This withdrawal was determined on long before it was known for certain that McClellan would adopt the Peninsula as his base of operations. The middle of February began the removal of the ordnance and commissary stores by railroad to the south of the rivers in our rear. These had been accumulated at Manassas out of all proportion to the needs of the army, and against the wishes of the commanding General. There seemed to be a want of harmony between the army officers and the officers of the Department in Richmond. This difference of feelings was kept up throughout the war, greatly to the embarassment at times of the Generals in the field, and often a great sacrifice to the service. The officials in Richmond, away from the seat of war, had a continual predilection to meddle with the internal affairs of the army. This meddling caused Jackson, who became immortal in after years, to tender his resignation, and but for the interference of General Johnston, the world would perhaps never have heard of the daring feats of "Stonewall Jackson." He asked to be returned to the professorship at the Military Institute, but General Johnston held his letter up and appealed to Jackson's patriotism and the cause for which all were fighting, to reconsider his action and to overlook this officious intermeddling and remain at his post. This he did under protest.

Our brigade, and, in fact, all regiments and brigades, had been put in different commands at different times to suit the caprice of the President or whims of the Department, and now we were Early's Division.

On the night of the 9th of March we broke up quarters at Bull Run and commenced our long and tiresome march for the Rappahannock. We were ordered by different routes to facilitate the movement, our wagon trains moving out in the morning along the dirt road and near the railroad. All baggage that the soldiers could not carry had been sent to the rear days before, and the greater part destroyed in the great wreck and conflagration that followed at Manassas on its evacuation. In passing through Manassas the stores, filled to the very tops with commissary stores, sutler's goods, clothing, shoes, private boxes, and whiskey, were thrown open for the soldiers to help themselves. What a feast for the troops! There seemed everything at hand to tempt him to eat, drink, or wear, but it was a verification of the adage, "When it rains mush you have no spoon." We had no way of transporting these goods, now piled high on every hand, but to carry them on our backs, and we were already overloaded for a march of any distance. Whiskey flowed like water. Barrels were knocked open and canteens filled. Kegs, jugs, and bottles seemed to be everywhere. One stalwart man of my company shouldered a ten gallon keg and proposed to hold on to it as long as possible, and it is a fact that a few men carried this keg by reliefs all night and next day. This was the case in other companies. When, we got out of the town and on the railroad, the men were completely overloaded. All night we marched along the railroad at a slow, steady gait, but all order and discipline were abandoned. About midnight we saw in our rear great sheets of flame shooting up from the burning buildings, that illuminated the country for miles around. Manassas was on fire! Some of the buildings had caught fire by accident or careless-ness of the soldiers, for the firing was not to begin until next day, after the withdrawal of the cavalry. The people in the surrounding country had been invited to come in and get whatever they wished, but I doubt if any came in time to save much from the burning mass. A great meat curing establishment at Thoroughfare Gap, that contained millions of pounds of beef and pork, was also destroyed. We could hear the burst-ing of bombs as the flames reached the magazines, as well as the explo-sion of thousands of small arm cartridges. The whole sounded like the raging of a great battle. Manassas had become endeared to the soldiers by its many memories, and when the word went along the line, "Ma-nassas is burning," it put a melancholy feeling upon all. Some of the happiest recollections of the soldiers that composed Kershaw's Brigade as well as all of Johnston's Army, were centred around Manassas. It was here they had experienced their first sensations of the soldier, Manassas was the field of their first victory, and there they had spent their first winter. It seemed to connect the soldiers of the Confederacy with those of Washington at Valley Forge and Trenton, the winter quarters of the army of the patriots. It gave the recollection of rest, a contrast with the many marches, the hard fought battles, trials, and hardships.

The next day it began to rain, and a continual down-pour continued for days and nights. Blankets were taken from knapsacks to cover over the men as they marched, but they soon filled with water, and had to be thrown aside. Both sides of the railroad were strewn with blankets, shawls, overcoats, and clothing of every description, the men finding it impossible to bear up under such loads. The slippery ground and the unevenness of the railroad track made marching very disagreeable to soldiers unaccustomed to it. Some took the dirt road, while others kept the railroad track, and in this way all organizations were lost sight of, but at night they collected together in regiments, joined the wagon trains, and bivouaced for the night. Sometimes it would be midnight before the last of the stragglers came up. We crossed the Rappahannock on the railroad bridge, which had been laid with plank to accommodate the passage of wagon trains, on the 11th and remained until the 19th. Up to this time it was not fully understood by the authorities in Richmond which route McClellan would take to reach Richmond, whether by way of Fredericksburg or Yorktown, but now scouts reported large transports, laden with soldiers, being shipped down the Potomac to the mouth of the James and York Rivers. This left no doubt in the minds of the authorities that the Peninsula was to be the base of operations. We continued our march on the 19th, crossed the Rapidan, and encamped around Orange Court House.

Beauregard, whom the soldiers loved dearly, and in whom they had every confidence as a leader, was transferred to the West, to join General A.S. Johnston, who had come from California and was organizing an army in Southern Tennessee.

Magruder, commanding at Yorktown, reporting large bodies disembarking in his front, Kershaw's Brigade, with several others, were placed upon cars and hurried on through Richmond to his support, leaving the other portion of the army to continue the march on foot, or on cars, wherever met. At Richmond we were put on board small sail boats and passed down the James River for the seat of war. This was a novel mode of transportation for most of the soldiers on board. It was a most bitter day and night. A cold east wind blowing from the sea, with a mist of sleet, the cold on the deck of the little vessel became almost unbearable. About two hundred were placed on board of each, and it being so cold we were forced to go below in the "hold," leaving only a little trap door of four feet square as our only means of ventilation. Down in the hold, where these two hundred men were packed like sardines in a box, caused us to almost suffocate, while to remain on deck five minutes would be to court death by freezing. Thus one would go up the little ladder, stick his head through the door a moment for a breath of fresh air, then drop back and allow another the pleasure of a fresh breathing spell. So we alternated between freezing and smothering all the way, a distance of one hundred and fifty miles or more. I had read of the tortures of the "middle passage" and the packing of the slave ships, but I do not think it could have exceeded our condition.

Now it must be remembered that for the most of the time on our march we were separated from our wagon trains that had our tents, cooking utensils, and other baggage. Many novel arrangements were resorted to for cooking. The flour was kneaded into dough on an oil cloth spread upon the ground, the dough pulled into thin cakes, pinned to boards or barrel heads by little twigs or wooden pegs, placed before the fire, and baked into very fair bread. Who would think of baking bread on a ram-rod? But it was often done. Long slices of dough would be rolled around the iron ram-rods, then held over the fire, turning it over continually to prevent burning, and in this way we made excellent bread, but by a tedious process. It is needless to say the meats were cooked by broiling. We parched corn when flour was scarce, and often guards had to be placed over the stock at feed time to prevent soldiers from robbing the horses of their corn.

At midnight the captain of the sloop notified us that we were now at our place of disembarkation, and we began to scramble up the ladder, a small lamp hanging near by and out on deck. The wooden wharfs were even with the deck, so we had no difficulty in stepping from one to the other. But the night was pitch dark, and our only mode of keeping direction was taken from the footsteps of the soldiers on the wharf and in front. Here we came very near losing one of our best soldiers. Jim George was an erratic, or some said "half witted" fellow, but was nevertheless a good soldier, and more will be said of him in future In going out of the hold on deck he became what is called in common parlance "wrong shipped," and instead of passing to the right, as the others did, he took the left, and in a moment he was floundering about in the cold black waves of the river below. The wind was shrieking, howling, and blowing—a perfect storm—so no one could hear his call for help. He struck out manfully and paddled wildly about in the chilly water, until fortunately a passing sailor, with the natural instinct of his calling, scented a "man overboard." A line was thrown Jim, and after a pull he was landed on shore, more dead than alive.

"How long were you in the water, Jim?" someone asked.

"Hell! more dan t'ree hours," was the laconic and good-natured reply.

Had we lost Jim here, the regiment would have lost a treat in after years, as time will show.

We went into camp a mile or so from the historic old York-town, if a few old tumbled down houses and a row of wooden wharfs could be called a town. The country around Yorktown was low and swampy, and the continual rains made the woods and fields a perfect marsh, not a dry foot of land to pitch a tent on, if we had had tents, and scarcely a comfortable place to stand upon. Fires were built, and around these men would stand during the day, and a pretense of sleep during the night. But the soldiers were far from being despondent; although some cursed our luck, others laughed and joked the growlers. The next day great numbers visited Yorktown through curiosity, and watched the Federal Fleet anchored off Old Point Comfort. Here happened a "wind fall" I could never account for. While walking along the beach with some comrades, we came upon a group of soldiers, who, like ourselves, were out sight-seeing. They appeared to be somewhat excited by the way they were gesticulating. When we came up, we found a barrel, supposed to be filled with whiskey, had been washed ashore. Some were swearing by all that was good and bad, that "it was a trick of the d——n Yankees on the fleet," who had poisoned the whiskey and thrown it overboard to catch the "Johnny Rebs." The crowd gathered, and with it the discussion and differences grew. Some swore they would not drink a drop of it for all the world, while others were shouting, "Open her up," "get into it," "not so much talking, but more drinking." But who was "to bell the cat?" Who would drink first? No one seemed to care for the first drink, but all were willing enough, if somebody else would just "try it." It was the first and only time I ever saw whiskey go begging among a lot of soldiers. At last a long, lank, lantern-jawed son of the "pitch and turpentine State" walked up and said:

"Burst her open and give me a drink, a man might as well die from a good fill of whiskey as to camp in this God-forsaken swamp and die of fever; I've got a chill now."

The barrel was opened. The "tar heel" took a long, a steady, and strong pull from a tin cup; then holding it to a comrade, he said: "Go for it, boys, she's all right; no poison thar, and she didn't come from them thar gun boats either. Yankees ain't such fools as to throw away truck like that. No, boys, that 'ar liquor just dropped from Heaven." The battle around the whiskey barrel now raged fast and furious; spirits flowed without and within; cups, canteens, hats, and caps were soused in the tempting fluid, and all drank with a relish. Unfortunately, many had left their canteens in camp, but after getting a drink they scurried away for that jewel of the soldier, the canteen. The news of the find spread like contagion, and in a few minutes hundreds of men were struggling around the barrel of "poison." Where it came from was never known, but it is supposed to have been dropped by accident from a Federal man-of-war. As the soldiers said, "All gifts thankfully received and no questions asked."

General J. Bankhead Magruder was in command of the Peninsula at the time of our arrival, and had established his lines behind the Warwick River, a sluggish stream rising near Yorktown and flowing southward to the James. Along this river light entrenchments had been thrown up. The river had been dammed in places to overflow the lowlands, and at these dams redoubts had been built and defended by our heaviest artillery.

In a few days all our division was in line, and soon thereafter was joined by Longstreet's, D.H. Hill's, and G.W. Smith's, with the cavalry under Stuart. General Johnston was Commander-in-Chief. We remained in camp around Yorktown about two weeks, when General Johnston decided to abandon this line of defense for one nearer Richmond. One of the worst marches our brigade ever had was the night before we evacuated our lines along the Warwick. Remember the troops had no intention of a retreat, for they were going down the river towards the enemy. It was to make a feint, however, to appear as if Johnston was making a general advance, thus to enable the wagon trains and artillery to get out of the way of the retreating army, and Kershaw was to cover this retreat.

At dark we began our march through long ponds and pools of water, and mud up to the knees, in the direction opposite Gloucester Point, and near a point opposite to the enemy's fleet of gunboats. Through mud and water we floundered and fell, the night being dark. Mile after mile we marched at a snail's gait until we came to a large opening, surrounded by a rail fence. This was about midnight. Here we were ordered to build great fires of the rails near by. This was done, and soon the heavens were lit up by this great stretch of roaring fires. Some had spread their blankets and lay down for a good sleep, while others sat around the good, warm, crackling blaze, wondering what next. Scarcely had we all became quiet than orders came to "fall in." Back over the same sloppy, muddy, and deep-rutted road we marched, retracing the steps made only an hour before, reaching our old camp at daylight, but we were not allowed to stop or rest. The retreat had begun. Magruder, with the other of his forces, was far on the road towards Williamsburg, and we had to fall in his rear and follow his footsteps over roads, now simply impassable to any but foot soldiers. We kept up the march until we had left Yorktown ten miles in our rear, after marching a distance of nearly thirty miles, and all night and day. A council of war had been held at Richmond, at which were present President Davis, Generals Lee, Smith, Longstreet, Johnston, and the Secretary of War, to determine upon the point at which our forces were to concentrate and give McClellan battle. Johnston favored Richmond as the most easy of concentration; thereto gather all the forces available in Virginia, North Carolina, and South Carolina around Richmond, and as the enemy approached fall upon and crush him. G.W. Smith coincided with Johnston. Longstreet favored reinforcing Jackson in the Valley, drive the enemy out, cross the Potomac, and threaten Washington, and force McClellan to look after his Capitol. The others favored Yorktown and the Peninsula as the point of concentration. But General Johnston found his position untenable, as the enemy could easily flank his right and left with his fleet.

On May 3rd began the long, toilsome march up the York River and the James. The enemy hovered on our rear and picked up our stragglers, and forced the rear guard at every step. At Williamsburg, the evening of the 4th of May, Johnston was forced to turn and fight. Breastworks and redoubts had been built some miles in front of the town, and it was here intended to give battle. The heavy down-pour of rain prevented Anderson, who was holding the rear and protecting the wagon trains, from moving, and the enemy began pressing him hard.

Kershaw and the other brigades had passed through Williamsburg when the fight began, but the continual roar of the cannon told of a battle in earnest going on in the rear and our troops hotly engaged. Kershaw and Simms, of our Division, were ordered back at double quick. As we passed through the town the citizens were greatly excited, the piazzas and balconies being filled with ladies and old men, who urged the men on with all the power and eloquence at their command. The woods had been felled for some distance in front of the earthworks and forts, and as we neared the former we could see the enemy's skirmishers pushing out of the woods in the clearing. The Second and Eighth South Carolina Regiments were ordered to occupy the forts and breastworks beyond Fort Magruder, and they had a perfect race to reach them before the enemy did. The battle was raging in all fierceness on the left, as well as in our front. More troops were put in action on both sides, and it seemed as if we were going to have the great battle there. D.R. Jones, Longstreet, and McLaws were more or less engaged along their whole lines. The Third Regiment did not have an opportunity to fire a gun that day, nor either the Seventh, but the other two had a considerable fight, but being mostly behind breastworks their casualties were light. The enemy withdrew at nightfall, and after remaining on the field for some hours, our army took up the line of march towards Richmond. It has been computed that McClellan had with him on the Peninsula, outside of his marines, 111,000 men of all arms.

As the term of first enlistment has expired, I will give a brief sketch of some of the field officers who led the regiments during the first twelve months of the war.

COLONEL JAMES H. WILLIAMS

OF THE THIRD SOUTH CAROLINA VOLUNTEERS

Colonel James H. Williams, the commander of the Third South Carolina Regiment, was born in Newberry County, October 4th, 1813. He was of Welsh descent, his ancestors immigrating to this country with Lord Baltimore. He was English by his maternal grandmother. The grandfather of Colonel Williams was a Revolutionary soldier, and was killed at the battle of Ninety-Six. The father of the subject of this sketch was also a soldier, and held the office of Captain in the war of 1812.

Colonel Williams, it would seem, inherited his love for the military service from his ancestors, and in early life joined a company of Nullifiers, in 1831. He also served in the Florida War. His ardor in military matters was such he gave little time for other attainments; he had no high school or college education. When only twenty-four years old he was elected Major of the Thirty-eighth Regiment of State Militia, and in 1843 took the Captaincy of the McDuffie Artillery, a crack volunteer company of Newberry. In 1846 he organized a company for the Mexican War, and was mustered into service in 1847 as Company L. Palmetto Regiment. He was in all the battles of that war, and, with the Palmetto Regiment, won distinction on every field. After his return from Mexico he was elected Brigadier General and then Major General of State Militia. He served as Mayor of his town, Commissioner in Equity, and in the State Legislature.

Before the breaking out of the Civil War, he had acquired some large estates in the West, and was there attending to some business connected therewith when South Carolina seceded. The companies that were to compose the Third Regiment elected him their Colonel, but in his absence, when the troops were called into service, they were commanded for the time by Lieutenant Colonel Foster, of Spartanburg. He joined the Regiment at "Lightwood Knot Springs," the 1st of May. He commanded the Third during the term of its first enlistment, and carried it through the first twelve months' campaign in Virginia.

At the reorganization of the regiment, the men composing it being almost wholly young men, desired new blood at the head of the volunteer service, and elected Captain James D. Nance in his stead. After his return to the State, he was placed at the head of the Fourth and Ninth Regiments of State Troops, and served as such until the close.

After the war, he returned to Arkansas and continued his planting operations until the time of his death, August 21st, 1892. He was a member of the Constitutional Convention of that State in 1874.

Colonel Williams was a born soldier, considerate of and kind to his men. He was cool and fearless to a fault. He understood tactics thoroughly, but was wanting in those elements of discipline—its sternness and rigidity that was required to govern troops in actual war. His age counted against him as a strict disciplinarian, but not as a soldier. He was elected to the Legislature of this State before Reconstruction, as well as a member of the Constitutional Convention of Arkansas in 1874.

LIEUTENANT COLONEL FOSTER

OF THE THIRD SOUTH CAROLINA VOLUNTEERS

Lieutenant Colonel C.B. Foster, of the Third South Carolina Regiment, was born in Spartanburg County, South Carolina, at the old Foster homestead, near Cedar Springs, in 1817. His father was Anthony Foster, a native of Virginia. Colonel Foster was a member of the Legislature before the war, and represented Spartanburg County in the Secession Convention, along with Simpson Bobo,

Dr. J.H. Carlisle, and others. After the Convention adjourned he returned to his home in Spartanburg and immediately began drilling a company for the war. He was elected Captain of the Blackstock Company, which was Company K, in the Third Regiment of South Carolina Volunteers. The Blackstock Company reported for duty as soon as volunteers were called for, and went immediately to the camp of instruction at Lightwood Knot Springs. Colonel Foster was elected Lieutenant Colonel of the regiment. After spending about three months at the camp of instruction, the Third Regiment was ordered to Virginia. Colonel Footer served until some time after the battle of First Manassas, having participated in that campaign. He remained in Virginia until the fall of 1861, when he was ordered to go home by the surgeon, his health having completely given way. It took long nursing to get him on his feet again. He was devoted to the Confederate cause, and was always willing and ready to help in any way its advancement. He gave two sons to his country. One, Captain Perrin Foster, also of the Third Regiment, was killed at Fredericksburg leading his command. His other son, James Anthony Foster, gave up his life in the front of his command during the frightful charge on Maryland Heights. He was a member of Company K, of the Third Regiment.

Colonel Foster was considered a wealthy man before the war, but when it ended he was left penniless. At that time he lived near Glenn Springs, Spartanburg County. In 1867 he moved to Union County and merchandised until 1884. He was also County Treasurer for a long time. He died on June 9th. 1897, at the residence of his daughter, Mrs. Benjamin Kennedy, at Jonesville, Union County. In early life Colonel Foster married Miss Mary Ann Perrin, a sister of Colonel Thomas C. Perrin, of Abbeville. She died in 1886. Three daughters survive Colonel Foster, Mrs. I.G. McKissick, Mrs. Benjamin Kennedy, and Mrs. J.A. Thompson. Colonel Foster was one of God's noblemen. He was true to his friends, his family, and his country. He never flinched from danger nor from his duty. He was faithful at all times and under all circumstances to the best principles of the Anglo-Saxon race.

COLONEL THOMAS G. BACON

OF THE SEVENTH SOUTH CAROLINA VOLUNTEERS

Thomas Glascock Bacon was born in Edgefield Village of English ancestry on the 24th of June, 1812. He was the youngest son of Major Edmund Bacon, the eloquent and distinguished member of the Edgefield Bar, and author of the humorous "Georgia Scenes," written under the nom de plume of Ned Brace. Colonel Bacon's mother was a sister of Brigadier General Thomas F. Glascock, of Georgia, a gallant and distinguished officer of the Revolutionary War, and after whom Colonel Bacon was named. He received the early rudiments of education at the Edgefield Academy, and when at the proper age he was sent for his classical education to the Pendleton English and Classical Institute, under the tutilage of that profound scholar and educator, Prof. S.M. Shuford. Colonel Bacon was fond of the classics, and had acquired rare literary attainments, and had he cultivated his tastes in that line assiduously, he no doubt would have become the foremost scholar of the State, if not the South. He was passionately fond of manly sports and out-door exercise. He was a devotee of the turf, and this disposition led him early in life to the development of fast horses and a breeder of blooded stock. He was a turfman of the old school, and there were but few courses in the South that had not tested the mettle of his stock. But like his brother in arms, Colonel Cash, of the Eighth, and brother turfman, he became disgusted with the thievery and trickery of later day sports and quit the turf, still owning at his death some of the most noted racers of the times, Granger Lynchburg, John Payne, Glengary, Father Ryan, Ned Brace, and others of lesser note.

He paid much attention to military matters, and held several offices in the State militia before the war. He, with his friend and superior, General M.L. Bonham, enlisted in the "Blues" and served in the Palmetto Regiment in the war with the Seminoles. At the breaking out of the Civil War he, with Elbert Bland, afterwards Colonel of the Seventh, organized the first company from Edgefield, and was elected Captain. The companies assigned to the Seventh Regiment unanimously elected him the Colonel, and in that capacity he led his regiment to Virginia, being among the first regiments from the State to reach the seat of war. He was at the battle of Manassas, and participated in the Peninsular campaign. At the reorganization of the regiment at the expiration of the term of enlistment, his failing health forced him to decline a re-election as Colonel. Returning home, and the State needing the services of trained soldiers to command the State troops, notwithstanding his failing health, he cheerfully accepted the command of the Seventh Regiment State troops. In 1863 he was elected to the State Senate. He died at his home, Pine Pond, in Edgefield County, September 25th, 1876, leaving a widow, but no children.

Strong in his friendship and earnest in his affection, but with a peaceable and forgiving temperament, pure in his motives, charitable in all things, generous to the needy, affectionate to his friends and relatives, chivalric and honorable in every relation of life, brave in action, and with that fortitude under adverse circumstances that makes heroes of men, just and impartial to the officers and men under his command, pleasant and sociable towards his equals in rank, obedient and courteous to his superiors, few men lived or died with so much respect and admiration, genuine friendship, and love from all as Colonel Thomas G. Bacon, of the Seventh South Carolina Volunteers.

COLONEL E.B.C. CASH

OF THE EIGHTH SOUTH CAROLINA VOLUNTEERS

Ellerbe Boggan Crawford Cash was born near Wadesboro, Anson County, North Carolina, on July 1st, 1823. His father was Boggan Cash, a Colonel in militia of that State, merchant, and member of Legislature. His mother was Miss Elizabeth Ellerbe, of Chesterfield County, S.C. He was the only child. His father died when he was near two years old, and his mother returned to her father's, in South Carolina. He was educated at Mt. Zion Institute, Winnsboro, S.C., and South Carolina College. He read law under General Blakeney, at Cheraw, S.C., and practiced in partnership a short while with Alexander McIver, Esq., the Solicitor of the Eastern Circuit, and father of Chief Justice Henry McIver, of South Carolina. But his mother owning a large landed estate, and several hundred negroes, he soon retired from the Bar to look after her affairs, and devoted himself to planting and raising fine horses and cattle. He married in 1847 his cousin, Miss Allan Ellerbe, of Kershaw, S.C. He was elected to the Legislature from his County, Chesterfield. He was elected Colonel, Brigadier General, and Major General of State militia.

When the war commenced he was one of the Major Generals of the State. He volunteered and was elected Colonel of the Eighth South Carolina Regiment. At the reorganization he did not offer for re-election, but came home and was made Colonel in State troops. He was kind to the poor the whole war, and gave away during the war over 50,000 bushels of corn and large quantities of other provisions to soldiers' families, or sold it in Confederate money at ante bellum prices. After the war all notes, claims, and mortgages he held on estates of old soldiers he cancelled and made a present of them to their families. In one case the amount he gave a widow, who had a family and small children, was over $5,000, her husband having been killed in his regiment.

After the war he continued to farm. In 1876 he took an active part in redeeming the State, and contributed his time, advice, and services, and a great deal of money. In 1881 he fought a duel with Colonel Wm. M. Shannon, in which he killed Colonel Shannon. Colonel Cash was the challenged party. His wife died in May, 1880. Colonel Cash died March 10, 1888, and was buried in the family burying ground at his residence, Cash's Depot, S.C.

Colonel Cash was a man of strong character, fearless, brave, generous and true, a good friend and patriot. He made no religious profession. He was charitable to the extreme, and was the soul of honor, and while he had many enemies, being a fearless man and a good hater, he had such qualities as inspired the respect and admiration of his fellow-men.

Chapter 8
Reorganized

On the 13th of April the term for which the twelve months' troops had enlisted was now soon to expire, the great number which had not re-enlisted were looking forward with longing anticipation for orders to disband and return to their homes. On the 14th, their obligations being at an end, officers and men were making rapid preparation to depart for home—not to quit the service, however, but more to enjoy a short leave of absence with their families, and to join other branches of the services, more especially cavalry. Some of the companies had actually left, and were a mile or two from camp when orders came to return. The Conscript Act had been passed, making it obligatory on all, between the ages of eighteen and thirty-five, to enter or remain in the army. The men took their sudden return in good humor, for really it was only the married men, who had left their families so unprepared twelve months before, who cared to return home; for some of the young men, who were under the conscript age, refused to leave. Those who had to return received a lot of good-natured badgering at their sudden return to the army. "Hello, boys, when did you get back? What's the news at home?" "How did you find all?" were some of the soothing jeers the "returned sinners" had to endure; and as so great a number had expressed a desire to join the cavalry, not a few were asked: "Did you bring your horses with you?" But all was soon forgotten, for in a few days a reorganization was ordered to take place, and new officers elected.

The Conscript Act was condemned in unmeasured terms in many places at the South, but its necessity and expediency was never doubted. To have allowed so great a number to absent themselves from the army at this time, in the face of an overwhelming enemy, and that enemy advancing upon our Capitol, was more than the morale of the army would admit. Not altogether would the absence of the soldiers themselves effect the army, but in the breaking up of organizations, for in some companies all had re-enlisted, while in others one-half, and in many cases none. New regiments would have had to be formed out of the re-enlisted companies, and new companies out of the large number of recruits, now in camps of instruction. So by keeping up the old organizations, and filling up the ranks by the conscripts at home, the army would be greatly benefited.

In some countries, to be called a conscript or drafted man was considered a stigma, but not so in the South. There is little doubt, had a call been made for volunteers, any number could have been had at a moment's notice, for there were hundreds and thousands at the South only awaiting an opportunity to enter the army. In fact, there were companies and regiments already organized and officered, only awaiting arms by the government, but these organizations were all raw men, and at this time it was believed to fill up the old companies with recruits, thus putting seasoned troops side by side with raw ones, would enhance the efficiency of the army, retain its discipline, and *esprit de corps*.

Then, again, the farms had to be managed, the slaves kept in subjection, and the army fed, and the older men were better qualified for this service than the young. In reality, all were in the service of the country, for while the younger men were fighting in the ranks, the older ones were working in the fields and factories to furnish them clothes, provisions, and munitions of war. Our government had no means at home, no ships on the ocean, little credit abroad, and our ports all blockaded. So all had to enter the service either as a fighter or a worker, and our wisest men thought it the better policy to allow the young men the glory upon the field, while the old men served at home. On the 13th of May all companies were allowed to elect their officers, both company and regimental, and enter the service for two more years. As I said in the commencement of this work, at the breaking out of the war men generally selected as officers the old militia officers for company officers and veterans of the Mexican War for field officers. General Bonham had been a Colonel in Mexico. Williams, of the Third, had led a company from Newberry to that far-off land. Kershaw went as First Lieutenant. Cash, of the Eighth, was a Major General of the militia at the breaking out of the war. The greatest number of the first Colonels of regiments under the first call were Mexican veterans. Another qualification that was considered at the first organization was popularity—gentle, clever, and kind-hearted. The qualification of courage or as a disciplinarian was seldom thought of; for a man to be wanting in the first could not be thought possible. Our men, who had known the proud feelings of personal freedom, dreaded discipline and restraint, naturally turned to those men for officers most conducive to their will and wishes. But twelve months' service in trying campaigns made quite a change. What they had once looked upon with dread and misgiving they now saw as a necessity. Strict discipline was the better for both men and the service. A greater number of the older officers, feeling their services could be better utilized at home than in the army, and also having done their duty and share by setting the example by enlistment and serving twelve months, relinquished these offices to the younger men and returned home. The younger, too, saw the advisability of infusing in the organizations young blood—men more of their own age and temperament—the stern necessity of military discipline, a closer attendance to tactics and drills, better regulations, and above all, courage. The organizations selected such men as in their opinions would better subserve the interests of the service, and who had the requisites for leadership. This is said with no disparagement to the old officers, for truer, more patriotic, nor a braver set of men ever drew a blade than those who constituted the old brigade during its first organization. In fact, some who had served during the first twelve months as officers, when they discovered their deficiency, or that the men had more confidence in others, after a short respite at home, returned and joined their old companies as privates. Was there ever greater patriotism and unselfishness and less ostentation shown as in the example of these men! It was but natural that men selected almost at random, and in many instances unacquainted with a majority of the men at enlistment unusual to military life, or the requirements of an officer in actual service, could possibly be as acceptable as those chosen after a year of service, and in close compact with the men.

SECOND REGIMENT

The Second Regiment chose as officers—
Colonel—Jno. D. Kennedy.
Lieutenant Colonel—A.S. Goodwin.
Major—Frank Gaillard.
Adjutant—E.E. Sill.
Quartermaster—W.D. Peck.
Commissary—J.J. Villipigue.

Chief Surgeon—Dr. F. Salmond.

Chaplains—Revs. McGruder and Smith.

I give below a list of the Captains, as well as the field officers, of the Second Regiment during the war. There were many changes from Lieutenants to Captains, and subsequent elections from the ranks to Lieutenants, caused by the casualties of war, but space forbids, and want of the facts prevents me from giving more than the company commanders and the field officers.

Colonels—J.B. Kershaw, E.P. Jones, Jno. D. Kennedy, and Wm. Wallace.

Lieutenant Colonels—E.P. Jones, A.D. Goodwin, F. Gaillard, Wm. Wallace, and J.D. Graham.

Majors—A.D. Goodwin, W.H. Casson, F. Gaillard, Wm. Wallace, I.D. Graham, B.F. Clyburn, G.L. Leaphart.

Adjutants—A.D. Goodwin, E.E. Sill, and A. McNeil.

Surgeons and Assistant Surgeons—J.A. Maxwell and J.H. Nott.

Some of them went from Captains and Majors through all the grades to Colonel. The following are the Captains, some elected at the first organization, some at the reorganization, and others rose by promotion from Lieutenant:

Company A—W.H. Casson, M.A. Shelton, G.L. Leaphart, M.M. Maddrey.

Company B—A.D. Hoke, Wm. Pulliam, W. Powell, J. Caigle.

Company C—Wm. Wallace, S. Lorick, J.T. Scott, A.P. Winson.

Company D—J.S. Richardson, J.D. Graham, W. Wilder.

Company E—John D. Kennedy, elected Colonel, Z. Leitner, J. Crackeford.

Company F—W.W. Ferryman, W.C. China, G. McDowell.

Company G—J. Hail, J. Friesdale, J.P. Cunningham.

Company H—H. McManus, D. Clyburn.

Company I—G.B. Cuthbreath, Ralph Elliott, R. Fishburn, B.F. Barlow.

Company K—R. Rhett, J. Moorer, K.D. Webb, J.D. Dutart,—Burton, G.T. Haltiwanger.

Many changes took place by death and resignation. Scarcely any of the field officers remained in the end. Many Captains of a low rank went all the way to Colonels of regiments, and Third Lieutenants rose by promotion to Captains. This shows the terrible mortality among the officers.

James D. Nance, of Newberry, Captain of Company E, elected Colonel.

Conway Garlington, of Laurens, Captain of Company A, elected Lieutenant Colonel.

W.D. Rutherford, of Newberry, formerly Adjutant, made Major.

Y.J. Pope, Newberry, formerly Orderly Sergeant of Company E, made Adjutant.

G.W. Shell, Laurens, Quartermaster.

J.N. Martin and R.N. Lowrance, Commissary.

Ed. Hicks, of Laurens, Sergeant Major.

All staff officers are appointed or recommended for appointment by the Colonel of the regiment. The offices of Regimental Quartermaster and Commissary, the encumbents heretofore ranking as Captains, were abolished during the year, having one Quartermaster and one Commissary for the brigade, the regiments having only Sergeants to act as such. I will state here that some of the companies from each regiment had reorganized and elected officers before the time of re-enlistment. This is one reason why rank was not accorded in the regular order. In the Third Regiment, Company E, Captain J.D. Nance, and perhaps several others, had reorganized, taken their thirty days' furlough, and had returned before the general order to reorganize and remain for two more years or the war. The new organizations stood in the Third as follows, by Captains:

Company A—Willie Hance, Laurens.

Company B—N. Davidson, Newberry.

Company C—R.C. Maffett, Newberry.

Company D—N.F. Walker, Spartanburg.

Company E—J.K.G. Nance—Newberry.

Company F—P. Williams, Laurens.

Company G—R.P. Todd—Laurens.

Company H—John C. Summer, Lexington.

Company I—D.M.H. Langston, Laurens.

Company K—S.M. Langford, Spartanburg.

Many changes took place in this regiment, some almost immediately after the election and others in the battle that followed in a few weeks.

Captain Davidson died in two weeks after his election from disease, and was succeeded by Lieutenant Thomas W. Gary, who had during the first twelve months been Captain Davidson's Orderly Sergeant. It seems the position of Orderly Sergeant was quite favorable to promotion, for nearly all the Orderlies during the first twelve months were made either Captains or Lieutenants.

Lieutenant Colonel Garlington being killed at Savage Station, Major Rutherford was promoted to that position, while Captain Maffett was made Major and Lieutenant Herbert Captain in his stead of Company C.

Captain Hance, of Company A, being killed at Fredericksburg, First Lieutenant Robert Richardson became Captain.

Lieutenant R.H. Wright became Captain of Company E after the promotion of Nance to Major in the latter part of the service.

Captain Williams, of Company F, was killed, and Lieutenant Wm. Deal made Captain and commanded at the surrender. There may have been other Captains of this company, but no data at hand.

John W. Watts became Captain of Company G after the promotion of Captain Todd to Major and Lieutenant Colonel.

Captain Summer being killed at Fredericksburg, Lieutenant G.S. Swygert became Captain, was disabled and resigned, and D.A. Dickert became Captain and commanded to the end.

Captain Langston, of Company I, being killed, Lieutenant Jarred Johnston became Captain, disabled at Chickamauga.

Company K was especially unfortunate in her commanders. Captain Langford was killed at Savage Station; then Lieutenant L.P. Foster, son of Lieutenant Colonel Foster, was promoted to Captain and killed at Fredericksburg. Then W.H. Young was made Captain and killed at Gettysburg. Then J.H. Cunningham became Captain and was killed at Chickamauga. J.P. Roebuck was promoted and soon after taken prisoner. First Lieutenant John W. Wofford commanded the company till the surrender, and after the war became State Senator from Spartanburg.

Captain N.F. Walker was permanently disabled at Savage Station, returned home, was appointed in the conscript bureau, and never returned to active duty. He still retained his rank and office as Captain of Company D, thereby preventing promotions in one of the most gallant companies in Kershaw's Brigade.

It was at the battle of Fredericksburg that the regiment lost so many officers, especially Captains, that caused the greatest changes. Captains Hance, Foster, Summer, with nearly a dozen Lieutenants, were killed there, making three new Captains, and a lot of new Lieutenants. It was by the death of Captain Summer that I received the rank of Captain, having been a Lieutenant up to that time. From December, 1862, to the end I commanded the company, with scarcely a change. It will be seen that at the reorganization the Third Regiment made quite a new deal, and almost a clean sweep of old officers—and with few exceptions the officers from Colonel to the Lieutenants of least rank were young men. I doubt very much if there was a regiment in the service that had such a proportion of young men for officers.

I will here relate an incident connected with the name of Captain Hance's family, that was spoken of freely in the regiment at the time, but little known outside of immediate surroundings—not about Captain Hance, however, but the name and connection that the incident recalled, that was often related by the old chroniclers of Laurens. Andrew Johnson, who was at the time I speak United States Senator from Tennessee, and was on the ticket with Lincoln, for Vice-President of the United States in his second race against McClellan, was elected, and afterwards became President. As the story goes, and it is vouched for as facts, Andrew Johnson in his younger days had a tailoring establishment at Laurens, and while there paid court to the mother of Captain Hance. So smitten was he with her charms and graces, he paid her special attention, and asked for her hand in marriage. Young Johnson was fine looking, in fact handsome, energetic, prosperous, and well-to-do young man, with no vices that were common to the young men of that day, but the great disparity in the social standing of the two caused his rejection. The family of Hance was too exclusive at the time to consent to a connection with the plebeian Johnson, yet that plebeian rose at last to the highest office in the gift of the American people, through the force of his own endowments.

Seventh South Carolina Regiment

The Seventh Regiment was reorganized by electing—

Colonel—D. Wyatt Aiken, Abbeville.
Lieutenant Colonel—Elbert Bland, Edgefield.
Major—W.C. White, Edgefield.
Adjutant—Thomas M. Childs.
Sergeant Major—Amos C. Stalworth.

Quartermaster—B.F. Lovelace.
Commissary—A.F. Townsend.
Company A—Stuart Harrison.
Company B—Thomas Huggins.
Company C—W.E. Cothran.
Company D—Warren H. Allen.
Company E—James Mitchell.
Company F—John S. Hard.
Company G—W.C. Clark.
Company H—H.W. Addison.
Company I—Benj. Roper.
Company K—Jno. L. Burris.
Company L—J.L. Litchfield.
Company M—Jerry Goggans.

I am indebted to Captain A.C. Waller, of Greenwood, for the following brief summary of the Seventh after reorganization, giving the different changes of regimental and company commanders, as well as the commanders of the regiment during battle:

Colonel Aiken commanded at Savage Station, Malvern Hill, and Antietam, till wounded at Gettysburg, after which he was ordered elsewhere.

Lieutenant Colonel Bland commanded at Fredericksburg, Chancellorsville, and Chickamauga; killed in latter battle.

Major White commanded at Antietam after the wounding of Aiken, and until he was himself killed at the enemy's battery, the farthest advance of the day. Captain Hard had command at the close. Captain Hard also led for a short while at Chickamauga after the death of Bland, and fell at the head of his regiment on top of Pea Ridge.

Captain Goggans was in command at Knoxville, Bean Station, and the Wilderness, until wounded.

Captain James Mitchell led the regiment in the charge at Cold Harbor, and was in command at Spottsylvania.

Lieutenant Colonel Maffett, of the Third, was placed in command of the Seventh during the Valley campaign under Early in 1864, and led at Fisher's Hill and Cedar Creek the 13th and 19th of September. Was captured in October.

Lieutenant Colonel Huggins commanded from October till the surrender, and at the battle of Averysboro and Bentonville.

Captain Goggans was promoted to Major after the battle of the Wilderness, but resigned.

Company E was divided into two companies, E and M. Company H took the place of Bland's, which became Company A.

Captain Stuart Harrison, Company A, resigned, being elected Clerk of Court of Edgefield, and Lieutenant Gus Bart was made Captain.

John Carwile, First Lieutenant of Company A, acted as Adjutant after the death of Adjutant Childs, and also on General Kershaw's staff.

Lieutenant James Townsend became Captain of Company B after the promotion of Huggins to Lieutenant Colonel.

After Captain Hard's promotion James Rearden was made Captain of Company E and was killed at Wilderness, and Lieutenant C.K. Henderson became Captain.

Captain Wm. E. Clark, Company G, was killed at Maryland heights. Lieutenant Jno. W. Kemp was made Captain and killed at the Wilderness.

Captain J.L. Burris, of Company K, was wounded at Antietam and resigned. First Lieutenant J.L. Talbert having been killed at Maryland Heights a few days before, Second Lieutenant Giles M. Berry became Captain; he resigned, and Lieutenant West A. Cheatham was made Captain by promotion.

Captain J.L. Litchfield, of Company I, was killed at Maryland Heights, and First Lieutenant Litchfield was made Captain.

First Lieutenant P. Bouknight became Captain of Company M after the promotion of Captain Goggans.

EIGHTH SOUTH CAROLINA REGIMENT

The Eighth South Carolina Regiment was reorganized by electing—

Colonel—Jno. W. Henagan, Marlboro.
Lieutenant Colonel—A.J. Hoole, Darlington.
Major—McD. McLeod, Marlboro.
Adjutant—C.M. Weatherly, Darlington.
Surgeon—Dr. Pearce.
Assistant Surgeon—Dr. Maxy.
Company A—John H. Muldrow, Darlington.
Company B—Richard T. Powell, Chesterfield.
Company C—Thomas E. Powe, Chesterfield.
Company D—Robt. P. Miller, Chesterfield.

Company E—M.E. Keith, Darlington.
Company F—T.E. Howle, Darlington.
Company G—C.P. Townsend, Marlboro.
Company H—Duncan McIntyre, Marion.
Company I—A.T. Harllee, Marion.
Company K—Frank Manning, Marlboro.
Company L—Thomas E. Stackhouse, Marion.
Company M—Thomas E. Howle, Darlington.

Company L was a new company, and T.E. Stackhouse was made Captain; also A.T. Harllee was made Captain of Company I. Company M was also a new company.

After the reorganization the Generals' staffs were reduced to more republican simplicity. General Kershaw was contented with—

Captain C.R. Holmes—Assistant Adjutant General.
Lieutenant W.M. Dwight—Adjutant and Inspector General.
Lieutenant D.A. Doby—Aide de Camp.
Lieutenant Jno. Myers—Ordnance Officer.
Major W.D. Peck—Quartermaster.
Major Kennedy—Commissary.

With a few privates for clerical service, General Kershaw had two fine-looking, noble lads as couriers, neither grown to manhood, but brave enough to follow their chief in the thickest of battle, or carry his orders through storms of battles, W.M. Crumby, of Georgia, and DeSaussure Burrows. The latter lost his life at Cedar Creek.

As I have thus shown the regiments and brigade in their second organization, under the name it is known, "Kershaw's," and as all were so closely connected and identified, I will continue to treat them as a whole. The same camps, marches, battles, scenes, and experiences were alike to all, so the history of one is the history of all. South Carolina may have had, and I have no doubt did have, as good troops in the field, as ably commanded as this brigade, but for undaunted courage, loyalty to their leaders and the cause, for self-denials and sacrifices, united spirits, and unflinching daring in the face of death, the world has never produced their superiors. There was much to animate their feelings and stimulate their courage. The older men had retired and left the field to the leadership of the young. Men were here, too, by circumstances of birth, education, and environment that could scarcely ever expect to occupy more than a secondary place in their country's history, who were destined to inferior stations in life, both social and political,—the prestige of wealth and a long family being denied them—still upon the battlefield they were any man's equal. On the march or the suffering in camp, they were the peers of the noblest, and when facing death or experiencing its pangs they knew no superiors. Such being the feelings and sentiments of those born in the humbler stations of life, what must have been the goal of those already fortune's favorites, with a high or aristocratic birth, wealth, education, and a long line of illustrious ancestors, all to stimulate them to deeds of prowess and unparalleled heroism? Such were the men to make the name of South Carolina glorious, and that of "Kershaw" immortal. How many of these noble souls died that their country might be free? the name of her people great? In the former they lost, as the ends for which they fought and died were never consummated. To-day, after nearly a half century has passed, when we look around among the young and see the decadence of chivalry and noble aspirations, the decline of homage to women, want of integrity to men, want of truth and honor, individually and politically, are we not inclined, at times, to think those men died in vain? We gained the shadow; have we the substance? We gained an unparalleled prestige for courage, but are the people to-day better morally, socially, and politically? Let the world answer. The days of knight-errantry had their decadence; may not the days of the South's chivalry have theirs?

CHAPTER 9

Battle of Seven Pines

It was the intention of General Johnston to fall back slowly before McClellan, drawing him away from his base, then when the Federal Corps become separated in their marches, to concentrate his forces, turn and crush him at one blow. The low, swampy, and wooded condition of the country from Yorktown up the Peninsula would not admit of the handling of the troops, nor was there any place for artillery practice to be effective. Now that he had his forces all on the South side of the Chickahominy, and the lands more rolling and firm, he began to contemplate a change in his tactics. Ewell, with several detached regiments under Whiting, had been sent in the Valley to re-enforce that fiery meteor, Stonewall Jackson, who was flying through the Shenandoah Valley and the gorges of the Blue Ridge like a cyclone, and General Johnston wished Jackson to so crush his enemy that his troops could be concentrated with his own before Richmond. But the authorities at Richmond thought otherwise. It is true Jackson had been worsted at Kernstown by Shields, but his masterly movements against Banks, Fremont, Siegle, and others, gave him such prestige as to make his name almost indispensable to our army. McDowell, with forty thousand men, lay at Fredericksburg, with nothing in his front but a few squadrons of cavalry and some infantry regiments. Johnston was thus apprehensive that he might undertake to come down upon his flanks and re-enforce "Little Mc." or the "Young Napoleon," as the commander of the Federal Army was now called. On the 20th of May, Johnston heard of two of the Federal Corps, Keyes' and Heintzleman's, being on the south side of the Chickahominy, while the others were scattered along the north banks at the different crossings. McClellan had his headquarters six miles away, towards the Pamunkey River. This was considered a good opportunity to strike, and had there been no miscarriages of plan, nor refusals to obey orders, and, instead, harmony and mutual understanding prevailed, the South might have gained one of its greatest victories, and had a different ending to the campaign entirely. G.W. Smith lay to the north of Richmond; Longstreet on the Williamsburg Road, immediately in front of the enemy; Huger on the James; Magruder, of which was Kershaw's Brigade (in a division under McLaws), stretched along the Chickahominy above New Bridge.

All these troops were to concentrate near Seven Pines and there fall upon the enemy's two corps, and beat them before succor could be rendered. No Lieutenant Generals had as yet been appointed, senior Major Generals generally commanding two divisions. The night before the attack, General Johnston called his generals together and gave them such instructions and orders as were necessary, and divided his army for the day's battle into two wings, G.W. Smith to command the left and Longstreet the right; the right wing to make the first assault (it being on the south side of the York River Railroad). G.W. Smith was to occupy the Nine Mile Road, running parallel with Longstreet's front and extending to the river, near New Bridge, on the Chickahominy. He was to watch the movements of the enemy on the other side, and prevent Sumner, whose corps were near the New Bridge, from crossing, and to follow up the fight as Longstreet and D.H. Hill progressed. Magruder, with his own and McLaws' Division, supported Smith, and was to act as emergencies required. Kershaw was now under McLaws. Huger was to march up on the Charles City Road and put in on Longstreet's left as it uncovered at White Oak Swamp, or to join his forces with Longstreet's and the two drive the enemy back from the railroad. Keyes' Federal Corps lay along the railroad to Fair Oaks; then Heintzleman's turned abruptly at a right angle in front of G.W. Smith. The whole was admirably planned, and what seemed to make success doubly sure, a very heavy rain had fallen that night, May 30th, accompanied by excessive peals of thunder and livid flashes of lightning, and the whole face of the country was flooded with water. The river was overflowing its banks, bridges washed away or inundated by the rapidly swelling stream, all going to make re-enforcement by McClellan from the north side out of the question. But the entire movement seemed to be one continual routine of blunders, misunderstandings, and perverseness; a continual wrangling among the senior Major Generals. The enemy had thrown up two lines of heavy earthworks for infantry and redoubts for the artillery, one near Fair Oaks, the other one-half mile in the rear. Longstreet and D.H. Hill assaulted the works with great vigor on the morning of the 31st of May, and drove the enemy from his first entrenched camp. But it seems G.W. Smith did not press to the front, as was expected, but understood his orders to remain and guard the crossing of the river. Huger lost his way and did not come up until the opportunity to grasp the key to the situation was lost, and then it was discovered there was a mistake or misunderstanding in regard to his and Longstreet's seniority. Still Huger waived his rank reluctantly and allowed Longstreet and Hill to still press the enemy back to his second line of entrenchments. From where we lay, inactive and idle, the steady roll of the musketry was grand and exciting. There was little opportunity for ability and little used, only by the enemy in their forts.

Several ineffectual attempts were made to storm these forts, and to dislodge the enemy at the point of the bayonet. Finally R.H. Anderson's Brigade of South Carolinians came up, and three regiments, led by Colonel Jenkins, made a flank movement, and by a desperate assault, took the redoubt on the left, with six pieces of artillery. When Rhodes' North Carolina Brigade got sufficiently through the tangle and undergrowth and near the opening as to see their way clear, they raised a yell, and with a mad rush, they took the fort with a bound. They were now within the strong fortress on the left and masters of the situation. Colonel Jenkins was highly complimented by the commanding General for his skill, and the energy and courage of his men. The enemy worked their guns faithfully and swept the ranks of Rhodes and Anderson with grape and canister, but Southern valor here, as elsewhere, overcame Northern discipline. Many of the enemy fell dead within the fort, while endeavoring to spike their guns.

Sumner, from the north side of the Chickahominy, was making frantic efforts to cross the stream and come to the relief of sorely pressed comrades. The bridges were two feet or more under water, swaying and creaking as if anxious to follow the rushing waters below. It is said the Federal General, Butler, called afterwards "Beast," covered himself with glory by rushing at the head of his troops, in and through the water, and succeeded in getting enough men on the bridge to hold it down, while the others crossed over. But the reinforcements came too late to aid their hard pressed friends. After the entrenchments were all taken, the enemy had no other alternative but to fall back in the dense forest and undergrowth, giving them shelter until night, with her sable curtains, hid friend and foe alike. Just as the last charge had been made, General Johnston, riding out in an opening, was first struck by a fragment of shell, thereby disabling him for further duty upon the field for a long time. The command of the army now fell upon General G.W. Smith, who ordered the troops to remain stationary for the night, and next morning, they were returned to their original quarters. Kershaw and the other Brigadiers of the division did not become engaged, as they were awaiting upon a contingency that did not arise. It is true, the enemy were driven from their strongly fortified position, and for more than a mile to the rear, still the fruits of the victory were swallowed up in the loss of so many good men, with no tangible or lasting results. From all the facts known at the time, and those developed since, it is the opinion that upon G.W. Smith rested the blame for the loss of the day. Had he been as active or energetic as the other Major Generals, or had he assumed responsibility, and taken advantage of events presenting themselves during the battle, that could not be known beforehand, nor counted in the plan of the battle, the day at Seven Pines might have loomed up on the side of the Confederate forces with those at Gaines' Mills or Second Manassas. But, as it was, it must be counted as one of the fruitless victories of the war.

General Smith left the army next day, never to return to active service. Here was a commentary on the question of the made soldier or the soldier born. At West Point General Smith stood almost at the very head of his class; at the commencement of the war, he was considered as one of our most brilliant officers, and stood head and shoulders above some of his cotemporaries in the estimation of our leaders and the Department at Richmond. But his actions and conduct on several momentous occasions will leave to posterity the necessity of voting him a failure; while others of his day, with no training nor experience in the science of war, have astonished the world with their achievements and soldierly conduct. The soldiers were sorrowful and sad when they learned of the fate of their beloved Commander-in-Chief. They had learned to love him as a father; he had their entire confidence. They were fearful at the time lest his place could never be filled; and, but for the splendid achievement of their new commander, R.E. Lee, with the troops drilled and disciplined by his predecessor, and who fought the battles on the plans laid down by him, it is doubtful whether their confidence could have ever been transferred to another.

General Lee took command the next day, June the 1st, 1862.

He did not come with any prestige of great victory to recommend him to the troops, but his bold face, manly features, distinguished bearing, soon inspired a considerable degree of confidence and esteem, to be soon permanently welded by the glorious victories won from the Chickahominy to the James. He called all his Lieutenants around him in a few days and had a friendly talk. He told none his plans—he left that to be surmised—but he gained the confidence of his Generals at once.

The troops were set to work fortifying their lines from the James to the Chickahominy, and up the latter stream to near Meadow Bridge. Engineer corps were established, and large details from each regiment, almost one-third of the number, were put to work under the engineers strengthening their camps on scientific principles. The troops thought they were to do their fighting behind these works, but strange to say, out of the hundred of fortifications built by Kershaw's men during the war, not one ever fired a gun from behind them.

On the 12th of June General Stuart started on his remarkable ride around the army of McClellan, and gained for himself the name of "Prince of Raiders." Starting out in the morning as if going away to our left at a leisurely gait, he rode as far as Hanover Court House. Before daylight next morning his troopers sprang into their saddles and swept down the country between the Chickahominy and the Pamunkey Rivers like a thunderbolt, capturing pickets, driving in outposts, overturning wagon trains, and destroying everything with fire and sword. He rides boldly across the enemy's line of communications, coming up at nightfall at the Chickahominy, with the whole of McClellan's army between him and Richmond. In this ride he came in contact with his old regiment in the United States Army, capturing its wagon trains, one laden with the finest delicacies and choicest of wines. After putting the enemy to rout Stuart and his men regaled themselves on these tempting viands, Stuart himself drinking a "bumper of choice old Burgundy," sending word to his former comrades that he "was sorry they did not stay and join him, but as it was, he would drink their health in their absence." Finding the bridges destroyed, he built a temporary one, over which the men walked and swam their horses, holding on to the bridles. When all were safely over Stuart sped like a whirlwind towards the James, leaving the enemy staring wildly in mute astonishment at the very audacity of his daring. That night he returned to his camps, having made in thirty-six hours the entire circuit of the Federal Army. Stuart was a rare character. Light hearted, merry, and good natured, he was the very idol of his cavaliers. His boldness, dash, and erratic mode of warfare made him a dreaded foe and dangerous enemy. One moment he was in their camps, on the plains, shouting and slashing, and before the frightened sleepers could be brought to the realization of their situation, he was far over the foothills of the Blue Ridge or across the swift waters of the Rappahannock.

During the first week after taking our position on the line, Magruder, with his divisions of eight brigades, was posted high up on the Chickahominy, nearly north of Richmond. McLaws, commanding Kershaw's, Cobb's, Semmes', and Barksdale's Brigades, was on the left, the first being South Carolinians, the next two Georgians, and the last Mississippians. General D.R. Jones, with his own, Toombs', G.T. Anderson's, and perhaps one other Brigade, constituted the right of the corps. The army was divided in wings. Huger, the senior Major General, commander on the right, next the James River, with Longstreet next; but before the great battle Magruder was given the centre and Longstreet the left with his divisions, and the two Hills', A.P. and D.H. But after the coming of Jackson A.P. Hill's, called the "Light Brigade," was placed under the command of the Valley chieftain.

While up on the Chickahominy, the enemy were continually watching our movements from lines of balloons floating high up in the air, anchored in place by stout ropes. They created quite a mystic and superstitious feeling among some of the most credulous. One night while a member of Company C, Third South Carolina, was on picket among some tangled brushwood on the crest of the hill overlooking the river, he created quite a stir by seeing a strange light in his front, just beyond the stream. He called for the officer of the guard with all his might and main. When the officer made his appearance with a strong reinforcement, he demanded the reason of the untimely call. With fear and trembling he pointed to the brilliant light and said:

"Don't you see 'em yonder? They are putting up a balloon."

"No," said the officer, "that's nothing but a star," which it really was.

"Star, hell! I tell you it's a balloon. Are the Yankees smart enough to catch the stars?" It is enough to say the man carried the name of "balloon" during the rest of his service.

A Federal battery was stationed immediately in our front, beyond the river, supported by infantry. Some one in authority suggested the idea of crossing over at night, break through the tangled morass on the other side, and capture the outfit by a sudden dash. The day before the Third South Carolina Regiment was formed in line and a call made for volunteers to undertake this hazardous enterprise. Only one hundred soldiers were required, and that number was easily obtained, a great number being officers. At least twenty-five Lieutenants and Captains had volunteered. The detachment was put under Captain Foster as chief of the storming party, and the next day was occupied in drilling the men and putting them in shape for the undertaking. We were formed in line about dark near the time and place allotted, and all were in high glee in anticipation of the novel assault. But just as all were ready, orders came countermanding the first order. So the officers and men returned to their quarters. Some appeared well satisfied at the turn of events, especially those who had volunteered more for the honor attached than the good to be performed. Others, however, were disappointed. An old man from Laurens was indignant. He said "the Third Regiment would never get anything. That he had been naked and barefooted for two months, and when a chance was offered to clothe and shoe himself some d——n fool had to countermand the order." Ere many days his ambition and lust for a fight were filled to overflowing.

The various grades and ranks of the Generals kept us continually moving from left to right, Generals being sometimes like a balky horse—will not pull out of his right place. We were stationed, as it appeared from the preparations made, permanently just in front of Richmond, or a little to the left of that place and the Williamsburg road, and began to fortify in earnest. About the middle of June Lee and his Lieutenants were planning that great campaign whereby McClellan was to be overthrown and his army sent flying back to Washington. Generals plan the moves of men like players their pieces upon the chess board—a demonstration here, a feint there, now a great battle, then a reconnoissance—without ever thinking of or considering the lives lost, the orphans made, the disconsolate widows, and broken homes that these moves make. They talk of attacks, of pressing or crushing, of long marches, the streams or obstacles encountered, as if it were only the movement of some vast machinery, where the slipping of a cog or the breaking of a wheel will cause the machine to stop. The General views in his mind his successes, his marches, his strategy, without ever thinking of the dead men that will mark his pathway, the victorious fields made glorious by the groans of the dying, or the blackened corpses of the dead. The most Christian and humane soldier, however, plans his battles without ever a thought of the consequences to his faithful followers.

On the 25th of June, orders came to be prepared to move at a moment's notice. This left no doubt in the minds of the men that stirring times were ahead. It had been whispered in camp that Jackson, the "ubiquitous," was on his way from the Valley to help Lee in his work of defeating McClellan.

About 4 o'clock, on the 26th of June, as the men lay lolling around in camp, the ominous sound of a cannon was heard away to our left and rear. Soon another and another, their dull rumbling roar telling too plainly the battle was about to begin. Men hasten hither and thither, gathering their effects, expecting every moment to be ordered away. Soon the roar of musketry filled the air; the regular and continual baying of the cannon beat time to the steady roll of small arms. Jackson had come down from the Valley, and was sweeping over the country away to our left like an avalanche. Fitz John Porter, one of the most accomplished soldiers in the Northern Army, was entrusted with the defense of the north side of the Chickahominy, and had erected formidable lines of breastworks along Beaver Dam Creek, already strong and unapproachable from its natural formations. Jackson was to have encountered Porter on the extreme right flank of the Union Army at an early hour in the day, and as soon as A.P. Hill heard the sound of his guns, he was to cross over on our left at Meadow Bridge and sweep down the river on Jackson's right. But after waiting for the opening of Jackson's guns until after 3 o'clock, without any information that he was on the field, Hill crossed over the river and attacked Porter in his strong position at Mechanicsville. His task was to beat back the enemy until the bridges below were uncovered, allowing re-enforcement to reach him. Jackson being unavoidably delayed, A.P. Hill assailed the whole right wing of the Federal Army, single-handed and alone, he only having five brigades, one being left some miles above on the river, but the brigade that was left was making rapid strides to join the fighting column. The strong earthworks, filled with fighting infantry and heavy field artillery in the forts, were too much for this light column, but undaunted by the weight of numbers and strength of arms, Hill threw himself headlong upon the entrenched positions with rare courage and determination. There were South Carolinians with him who were now engaging in their maiden effort, and were winning imperishable fame by their deeds of valor. Gregg, with the old First South Carolina Regiment of Veterans, with four new organizations, the Twelfth, Thirteenth, Fourteenth, and Orr's Rifles, went recklessly into the fray, and struck right and left with the courage and confidence of veteran troops. D.H. Hill, late in the evening, crossed over and placed himself on the right of those already engaged. The battle of Games' Mill was one continual slaughter on the side of the Confederates. The enemy being behind their protections, their loss was comparatively slight. The fight was kept up till 9 o'clock at night, with little material advantage to either, with his own and only a portion of Jackson's troops up. But the desperate onslaught of the day convinced Porter that he could not hold his ground against another such assault, so he fell back to a much stronger position around Gaines' Mill.

The next day, the 27th, will be remembered as long as history records the events of our Civil War as one of the most bloody and determined of any of the great battles of the war for the men engaged. For desperate and reckless charges, for brave and steady resistance, it stands second to none. Jackson, Ewell, Whiting, and D.H. Hill moved their divisions by daylight, aroused the enemy's right, intending to reach his rear, but at Cold Harbor they met the enemy in strong force. D.H. Hill attacked immediately, while A.P. Hill, who had been left in Porter's front, marched through the deserted camp, over his fortifications, and at Gaines' Mill, he met Porter posted on an eminence beyond the stream. This was only passable at few places, but Hill pushed his men over under a galling fire of musketry, while the enemy swept the plain and valley below with shell and grape from their batteries crowning the height beyond. A.P. Hill formed his lines beyond the stream, and advanced with a steady step and a bold front to the assault. Charge after charge was made, only to be met and repulsed with a courage equal to that of the Confederates. Hill did not know then that he was fighting the bulk of the Fifth Corps, for he heard the constant roll of Jackson and D. H. Hill's guns away to his left; Jackson thinking the Light Division under A.P. Hill would drive the enemy from his position, withdrew from Cold Harbor and sought to intercept the retreating foe in concealing his men for some hours on the line of retreat. But as the day wore on, and no diminution of the firing, at the point where A.P. Hill and his adversary had so long kept up, Jackson and D.H. Hill undertook to relieve him. Longstreet, too, near nightfall, who had been held in reserve all day, now broke from his place of inaction and rushed into the fray like an uncaged lion, and placed himself between A.P. Hill and the river. For a few moments the earth trembled with the tread of struggling thousands, and the dreadful recoil of the heavy batteries that lined the crest of the hill from right to left. The air was filled with the shrieking shells as they sizzled through the air or plowed their way through the ranks of the battling masses. Charges were met by charges, and the terrible "Rebel Yell" could be heard above the din and roar of battle, as the Confederates swept over field or through the forest, either to capture a battery or to force a line of infantry back by the point of the bayonet. While the battle was yet trembling in the balance, the Confederates making frantic efforts to pierce the enemy's lines, and they, with equal courage and persistency, determined on holding, Pickett and Anderson, of Longstreet's Division, and Hood and Whiting, of Jackson's, threw their strength and weight to the aid of Hill's depleted ranks. The enemy could stand no longer. The line is broken at one point, then another, and as the Confederates closed in on them from all sides, they break in disorder and leave the field. It looked at one time as if there would be a rout, but Porter in this emergency, put in practice one of Napoleon's favorite tactics. He called up his cavalry, and threatened the weakened ranks of the Confederates with a formidable front of his best troopers. These could not be of service in the weight of battle, but protected the broken columns and fleeing fugitives of Porter's Army.

South Carolina will be ever proud of the men whom she had on that memorable field who consecrated the earth at Gaines' Mill with their blood, as well as of such leaders as Gregg, McGowan, McCrady, Marshall, Simpson, Haskell, and Hamilton, and hosts of others, who have ever shed lustre and glory equal to those of any of the thousands who have made the Palmetto State renowned the world over.

McClellan was now in sore straits. He could not weaken his lines on the south side of the Chickahominy to re-enforce Fitz John Porter, for fear Magruder, Holmes, and Huger, who were watching his every movements in their front, should fall upon the line thus weakened and cut his army in twain. The next day McClellan commenced his retreat towards the James, having put his army over the Chickahominy the night after his defeat. His step was, no doubt, occasioned by the fact that Lee had sent Stuart with his cavalry and Ewell's Division of Infantry down the north side of the Chickahominy and destroyed McClellan's line of communication between his army and the York

River. However, the Confederate commander was equally as anxious to cut him off from the James as the York. He aimed to force him to battle between the two rivers, and there, cut off from his fleet, he would be utterly destroyed. Lee only wished McClellan to remain in his present position until he could reach the James with a part of his own troops, now on the north side of the Chickahominy.

On the evening of the 27th, Magruder made a feint with Kershaw's and some other brigades of this division, near Alens, as the troops in his front showed a disposition to retire. A line of battle was formed, skirmishers thrown out, and an advance ordered. Our skirmishers had not penetrated far into the thicket before they were met by a volley from the enemy's line of battle. The balls whistled over our heads and through the tops of the scrubby oaks, like a fall of hail. It put chills to creeping up our backs, the first time we had ever been under a musketry fire. For a moment we were thrown into a perfect fever of excitement and confusion. The opening in the rear looked temptingly inviting in comparison to the wooded grounds in front, from whence came the volley of bullets. Here the Third South Carolina lost her first soldier in battle, Dr. William Thompson, of the medical staff, who had followed too close on the heels of the fighting column in his anxiety to be near the battle.

Early in the morning of the 28th, Lee put the columns of Longstreet and A.P. Hill in motion in the direction of Richmond around our rear. After their meeting with Holmes and Huger on our extreme right, they were to press down the James River and prevent McClellan from reaching it. Jackson, D.H. Hill, and Magruder were to follow the retreating army. We left our quarters early in the day, and soon found ourselves in the enemy's deserted camp.

The country between the James and the Chickahominy is a very flat, swampy county, grown up in great forests, with now and then a cultivated field. The forests were over-run with a tangled mass of undergrowth. It was impossible for the army to keep up with the enemy while in line of battle. So sending our skirmishers ahead the army followed the roads in columns of fours. In each regiment the right or left company in the beginning of battle is always deployed at such distance between each soldier as to cover the front of the regiment, while in line of battle the regiments being from ten to fifty yards apart. In this way we marched all day, sometimes in line of battle, at others by the roads in columns. A great siege cannon had been erected on a platform car and pushed abreast of us along the railroad by an engine, and gave out thundering evidences of its presence by shelling the woods in our front. This was one of the most novel batteries of the war, a siege gun going in battle on board of cars. Near night at Savage Station Sumner and Franklin, of the Federal Army, who had been retreating all day, turned to give battle. Jackson was pressing on our left, and it became necessary that Sumner should hold Magruder in check until the army and trains of the Federals that were passing in his rear should cross White Oak Swamp to a place of safety. Our brigade was lying in a little declivity between two rises in the ground; that in our front, and more than one hundred yards distance, was thickly studded with briars, creepers, and underbrush with a sparse growth of heavy timber. We had passed numerous redoubts, where the field batteries of the enemy would occupy and shell our ranks while the infantry continued the retreat. Our brigade skirmishers, under command of Major Rutherford, had been halted in this thicket while the line of battle was resting. But hardly had the skirmishers been ordered forward than the enemy's line of battle, upon which they had come, poured a galling fire into them, the bullets whistling over our heads causing a momentary panic among the skirmishers, a part retreating to the main line. A battery of six guns stationed in a fort in our front, opened upon us with shell and grape. Being in the valley, between the two hills, the bullets rattled over our heads doing no damage, but threw us into some excitement. The Third being near the center of the brigade, General Kershaw, in person, was immediately in our rear on foot. As soon as the bullets had passed over he called out in a loud, clear tone the single word "charge." The troops bounded to the front with a yell, and made for the forest in front, while the batteries graped us as we rushed through the tangled morass. The topography of the country was such that our artillery could get no position to reply, but the heavy railroad siege gun made the welkin ring with its deafening reports. Semmes and Barksdale put in on our right; Cobb remaining as reserve, while the Division of D.R. Jones, which had been moving down on the left side of the railroad, soon became engaged. The enemy fought with great energy and vigor, while the Confederates pressed them hard. Much was at stake, and night was near. Stunner was fighting for the safety of the long trains of artillery and wagons seeking cover in his rear, as well as for the very life of the army itself. Soon after the first fire the settling smoke and dense shrubbery made the woods almost as dark as night in our front, but the long line of fire flashing from the enemy's guns revealed their position. The men became woefully tangled and disorganized, and in some places losing the organizations entirely, but under all these difficulties they steadily pressed to the front. When near the outer edge of the thicket, we could see the enemy lying down in some young growth of pines, with their batteries in the fort. The graping was simply dreadful, cutting and breaking through the bushes and striking against trees. I had not gone far into the thicket before I was struck by a minnie ball in the chest, which sent me reeling to the ground momentarily unconscious. Our men lost all semblance of a line, being scattered over a space of perhaps 50 yards, and those in front were in as much danger from friend as from foe. While I lay in a semi-unconscious state, I received another bullet in my thigh which I had every reason to believe came from some one in the rear. But I roused myself, and staggering to my feet made my way as well as I could out of the thicket. When I reached the place from whence we had first made the charge, our drummer was beating the assembly or long roll with all his might, and men collecting around General Kershaw and Colonel Nance. Here I first learned of the repulse. The balls were still flying overhead, but some of our batteries had got in position and were giving the enemy a raking fire. Nor was the railroad battery idle, for I could see the great black, grim monster puffing out heaps of gray smoke, then the red flash, then the report, sending the engine and car back along the track with a fearful recoil. The lines were speedily reformed and again put in motion. Jones, too, was forced by overwhelming numbers to give back, but Jackson coming up gave him renewed confidence, and a final advance was made along the whole line. The battle was kept up with varying success until after night, when Sumner withdrew over White Oak Swamp.

On the morning of the 30th, McClellan, like a quarry driven to bay, drew up his forces on the south side of White Oak Swamp and awaited the next shock of battle. Behind him were his trains of heavy siege guns, his army wagons, pontoons, and ordnance trains, all in bog and slush, seeking safety under the sheltering wings of his gunboats and ironclads on the James. Lee met him at every point with bristling bayonets of his victorious troops. At three o'clock A.M. Longstreet and A.P. Hill moved down the Darbytown road, leaving Jackson, D.H. Hill, and Magruder to press McClellan's retreating forces in the rear. Huger, with the two former, was to come down the James River and attack in the flank. Magruder, with his corps, was sent early in the day on a wild goose chase to support Longstreet's right, but by being led by guides who did not understand the roads or plan of battle, Magruder took the wrong road and did not get up in time to join in the battle of Frazier's Farm. Jackson for some cause did not press the rear, as anticipated, neither did Huger come in time, leaving the brunt of the battle on the shoulders of A.P. Hill and Longstreet. The battle was but a repetition of that of Gaines' Mill, the troops of Hill and Longstreet gaining imperishable glory by their stubborn and resistless attacks, lasting till nine o'clock at night, when the enemy finally withdrew.

Two incidents of these battles are worthy of record, showing the different dispositions of the people of the North and South. At night the division commanded by General McCall, who had been fighting Longstreet so desperately all day, was captured and brought to Longstreet's headquarters. General McCall had been Captain of a company in the United States Army, in which Longstreet had been a Lieutenant. When General Longstreet saw his old comrade brought to him as a prisoner of war, he sought to lighten the weight of his feelings as much as circumstances would admit. He dismounted, pulled his gloves, and offered his hand in true knightly fashion to his fallen foe. But his Federal antagonist, becoming incensed, drew himself up haughtily and waved Longstreet away, saying, "Excuse me, sir, I can stand defeat but not insult." Insult indeed! to shake the hand of one of the most illustrious chieftains of the century, one who had tendered the hand in friendly recognition of past associations, thus to smooth and soften the humiliation of his foe's present condition! Insult—was it?

When Bob Toombs, at the head of his brigade, was sweeping through the tangled underbrush at Savage Station, under a terrific hail of bullets from the retreating enemy, he was hailed by a fallen enemy, who had braced himself against a tree:

"Hello, Bob Toombs! Hello, Bob Toombs! Don't you know your old friend Webster?"

Dismounting, Toombs went to the son of his old friend but political adversary, Daniel Webster, one of the great trio at Washington of twenty years before, and found his life slowly ebbing away. Toombs rendered him all the assistance in his power—placed him in comfortable position that he might die at ease—and hastened on to rejoin his command, after promising to perform some last sad rites after his death. When the battle was ended for the day, the great fiery Secessionist hastened to return to the wounded enemy. But too late; his spirit had flown, and nothing was now left to Toombs but to fulfill the promises he made to his dying foe. He had his body carried through the lines that night under a flag of truce and delivered with the messages left to his friends. He had known young Webster at Washington when his illustrious father was at the zenith of his power and fame. The son and the great Southern States' Rights champion had become fast friends as the latter was just entering on his glorious career.

Our brigade lost heavily in the battle of Savage Station both in officers and men. Lieutenant Colonel Garlington, of the Third, was killed, and so was Captain Langford and several Lieutenants. Colonel Bland, of the Seventh, was wounded and disabled for a long time. The casualties in the battle of Savage Station caused changes in officers in almost every company in the brigade.

When I came to consciousness after being wounded the first thing that met my ears was the roar of musketry and the boom of cannon, with the continual swish, swash of the grape and canister striking the trees and ground. I placed my hand in my bosom, where I felt a dull, deadening sensation. There I found the warm blood, that filled my inner garments and now trickled down my side as I endeavored to stand upright. I had been shot through the left lung, and as I felt the great gaping wound in my chest, the blood gushing and spluttering out at every breath, I began to realize my situation. I tried to get off the field the best I could, the bullet in my leg not troubling me much, and as yet, I felt strong enough to walk. My brother, who was a surgeon, and served three years in the hospitals in Richmond, but now in the ranks, came to my aid and led me to the rear. We stopped near the railroad battery, which was belching away, the report of the great gun bringing upon us the concentrated fire of the enemy. As I sat upon the fallen trunk of a tree my brother made a hasty examination of my wound. All this while I was fully convinced I was near death's door. He pronounced my wound at first as fatal, a bit of very unpleasant information, but after probing my wound with his finger he gave me the flattering assurance that unless I bled to death quite soon my chances might be good! Gentle reader, were you ever, as you thought, at death's door, when the grim monster was facing you, when life looked indeed a very brief span? If so, you can understand my feelings—I was scared! As Goldsmith once said, "When you think you are about to die, this world looks mighty tempting and pretty." Everything in my front took on the hue of dark green, a pleasant sensation came over me, and I had the strangest feeling ever experienced in my life. I thought sure I was dying then and there and fell from the log in a death-like swoon. But I soon revived, having only fainted from loss of blood, and my brother insisted on my going back up the railroad to a farmhouse we had passed, and where our surgeons had established a hospital. The long stretch of wood we had to travel was lined with the wounded, each wounded soldier with two or three friends helping him off the field. We had no "litter bearers" or regular detail to care for the wounded at this time, and the friends who undertook this service voluntarily oftentimes depleted the ranks more than the loss in battle. Hundreds in this way absented themselves for a few days taking care of the wounded. But all this was changed soon afterwards. Regular details were made from each regiment, consisting of a non-commissioned officer and five privates, whose duty it was to follow close in rear of the line of battle with their "stretchers" and take off the disabled.

I will never forget the scene that met my eyes as I neared the house where the wounded had been gathered. There the torn and mangled lay, shot in every conceivable part of the body or limbs—some with wounds in the head, arms torn off at the shoulder or elbow, legs broken, fingers, toes, or foot shot away; some hobbling along on inverted muskets or crutches, but the great mass were stretched at full length upon the ground, uttering low, deep, and piteous moans, that told of the great sufferings, or a life passing away. The main hall of the deserted farm house, as well as the rooms, were filled to overflowing with those most seriously wounded. The stifling stench of blood was sickening in the extreme. The front and back yards, the fence corners, and even the out-buildings were filled with the dead and dying. Surgeons and their assistants were hurrying to and fro, relieving the distress as far as their limited means would allow, making such hasty examinations as time permitted. Here they would stop to probe a wound, there to set a broken limb, bind a wound, stop the flow of blood, or tie an artery.

But among all this deluge of blood, mangled bodies, and the groans of the wounded and dying, our ears were continually greeted by the awful, everlasting rattle of the musketry, the roar of the field batteries, and the booming, shaking, and trembling of the siege guns from friend and foe.

The peculiar odor of human blood, mingling with the settling smoke of the near by battlefield, became so oppressive I could not remain in the house. My brother helped me into the yard, but in passing out I fell, fainting for the third time; my loss of blood had

125

been so great I could stand only with difficulty. I thought the end was near now for a certainty, and was frightened accordingly. But still I nerved myself with all the will power I possessed, and was placed on an oil cloth under the spreading branches of an elm. From the front a continual stream of wounded kept coming in till late at night. Some were carried on shoulders of friends, others leaning their weight upon them and dragging their bodies along, while the slightly wounded were left to care for themselves. Oh, the horrors of the battlefield! So cruel, so sickening, so heart-rending to those even of the stoutest nerves!—once seen, is indelibly impressed upon your mind forever.

The firing ceased about 9 o'clock, and all became still as death, save the groaning of the wounded soldiers in the hospital, or the calls and cries of those left upon the battlefield. Oh, such a night, the night after the battle! The very remembrance of it is a vivid picture of Dante's "Inferno." To lie during the long and anxious watches of the night, surrounded by such scenes of suffering and woe, to continually hear the groans of the wounded, the whispered consultations of the surgeons over the case of some poor boy who was soon to be robbed of a leg or arm, the air filled with stifled groans, or the wild shout of some poor soldier, who, now delirious with pain, his voice sounding like the wail of a lost soul—all this, and more—and thinking your soul, too, is about to shake off its mortal coil and take its flight with the thousands that have just gone, are going, and the many more to follow before the rising of the next sun—all this is too much for a feeble pen like mine to portray.

The troops lay on the battlefield all night under arms. Here and there a soldier, singly or perhaps in twos, were scouring through the dense thicket or isolated places, seeking lost friends and comrades, whose names were unanswered to at the roll call, and who were not among the wounded and dead at the hospital. The pale moon looked down in sombre silence upon the ghastly upturned faces of the dead that lay strewn along the battle line. The next day was a true version of the lines—

Under the sod, under the clay,
Here lies the blue, there the grey.

for the blue and grey fell in great wind rows that day, and were buried side by side.

The Confederates being repulsed in the first charge, returned to the attack, broke the Federal lines in pieces, and by 9 o'clock they had fled the field, leaving all the fruits of victory in the hands of the Confederates.

No rest for the beaten enemy, no sleep for the hunted prey. McClellan was moving heaven and earth during the whole night to place "White Oak Swamp" (a tangled, swampy wilderness, of a half mile in width and six or eight miles in length,) between his army and Lee's. By morning he had the greater portion of his army and supply trains over, but had left several divisions on the north side of the swamp to guard the crossings. Jackson and Magruder began pressing him early on the 30th in his rear, while Longstreet, A.P. Hill, and others were marching with might and main to intercept him on the other side. After some desultory firing, Jackson found McClellan's rear guard too strong to assail, by direct assault, so his divisions, with Magruder's, were ordered around to join forces with Hill and Longstreet. The swamp was impassable, except at the few crossings, and they were strongly guarded, so they were considered not practicable of direct assault. But in the long winding roads that intervened between the two wings, Magruder and Jackson on the north and Longstreet and A.P. Hill on the south, Magruder was misled by taking the wrong road (the whole Peninsula being a veritable wilderness), and marched away from the field instead of towards it, and did not reach Longstreet during the day. But at 3 o'clock Longstreet, not hearing either Jackson's or Magruder's guns, as per agreement, and restless of the delays of the other portions of the army, feeling the danger of longer inactivity, boldly marched in and attacked the enemy in his front.

Here was Frazier's Farm, and here was fought as stubbornly contested battle, considering the numbers engaged, as any during the campaign. Near nightfall, after Longstreet had nearly exhausted the strength of his troops by hard fighting, A.P. Hill, ever watchful and on the alert, threw the weight of his columns on the depleted ranks of the enemy, and forced them from the field. The soldiers who had done such deeds of daring as to win everlasting renown at Gaines' Mill and Cold Harbor, did not fail their fearless commander at Frazier's Farm. When the signal for battle was given, they leaped to the front, like dogs unleashed, and sprang upon their old enemies, Porter, McCall, Heintzelman, Hooker, and Kearny. Here again the steady fire and discipline of the Federals had to yield to the impetuosity and valor of Southern troops. Hill and Longstreet swept the field, capturing several hundred prisoners, a whole battery of artillery, horses, and men.

McClellan brought up his beaten army on Malvern Hill, to make one last desperate effort to save his army from destruction or annihilation. This is a place of great natural defenses. Situated one mile from the James River, it rises suddenly on all sides from the surrounding marshy lowlands to several hundred feet in height, and environed on three sides by branches and by Turkey Creek. On the northern eminence McClellan planted eighty pieces of heavy ordnance, and on the eastern, field batteries in great numbers. Lee placed his troops in mass on the extreme east of the position occupied by the enemy, intending to park the greater number of his heaviest batteries against the northern front of the eminence, where McClellan had his artillery pointing to the east, and where the Confederates massed to sweep the field as Lee advanced his infantry. The object of Lee was to concentrate all his artillery on the flank of McClellan's artillery, then by an enfilade fire from his own, he could destroy that of his enemy, and advance his infantry through the broad sweep of lowlands, separating the forces, without subjecting them to the severe cannonading. He gave orders that as soon as the enemy's batteries were demolished or silenced, Armstead's Virginia Brigade, occupying the most advanced and favorable position for observation, was to advance to the assault, with a yell and a hurrah, as a signal for the advance of all the attacking columns. But the condition of the ground was such that the officers who were to put the cannon in position got only a few heavy pieces in play, and these were soon knocked in pieces by the numbers of the enemy's siege guns and rifled field pieces. Some of the brigade commanders, thinking the signal for combat had been given, rushed at the hill in front with ear piercing yells without further orders. They were mown down like grain before the sickle by the fierce artillery fire and the enemy's infantry on the crest of the hill. Kershaw following the lead of the brigade on his left, gave orders, "Forward, charge!" Down the incline, across the wide expanse, they rushed with a yell, their bayonets bristling and glittering in the sunlight, while the shells rained like hail stones through their ranks from the cannon crested hill in front. The gunboats and ironclad monitors in the James opened a fearful fusilade from their monster guns and huge mortars, the great three-hundred-pound shells from the latter rising high in the air, then curling in a beautiful bow to fall among the troops, with a crash and explosion that shook the ground like the trembling of the earth around a volcano. The whole face of the bluff front was veiled by the white smoke of the one hundred belching cannon, the flashing of the guns forming a perfect rain of fire around the sides of the hill. It was too far to fire and too dense and tangled to charge with any degree of progress or order, so, in broken and disconnected ranks, Kershaw had to advance and endure this storm of shot and shell, that by the time he reached the line of the enemy's infantry, his ranks were too much broken to offer a very formidable front. From the enemy's fortified position their deadly fire caused our already thinned ranks to melt like snow before the sun's warm rays. The result was a complete repulse along the whole line. But McClellan was only too glad to be allowed a breathing spell from his seven days of continual defeat, and availed himself of the opportunity of this respite to pull off his army under the protecting wings of his ironclad fleet.

The Confederates had won a glorious victory during the first six days. The enemy had been driven from the Chickahominy to the James, his army defeated and demoralized beyond months of recuperation. Lee and his followers should be satisfied. But had none of his orders miscarried, and all of his Lieutenants fulfilled what he had expected of them, yet greater results might have been accomplished—not too much to say McClellan's Army would have been entirely destroyed or captured, for had he been kept away from the natural defenses of Malvern Hill and forced to fight in the open field, his destruction would have followed beyond the cavil of a doubt. The Southern soldiers were as eager and as fresh on the last day as on the first, but a land army has a superstitious dread of one sheltered by gunboats and ironclads.

All the troops engaged in the Seven Days' Battle did extremely well, and won imperishable fame by their deeds of valor and prowess. Their commanders in the field were matchless, and showed military talents of high order, the courage of their troops invincible, and to particularize would be unjust. But truth will say, in after years, when impartial hands will record the events, and give blame where blame belongs, and justice where justice is due, that in this great Seven Days' Conflict, where so much heroism was displayed on both sides, individually and collectively, that to A.P. Hill and the brave men under him belongs the honor of first scotching at Gaines' Mill the great serpent that was surrounding the Capital with bristling bayonets, and were in at the breaking of its back at Frazier's Farm.

It was due to the daring and intrepidity of Hill's Light Division at Gaines' Mill, more than to any other, that made it possible for the stirring events and unprecedented results that followed.

Among the greater Generals, Lee was simply matchless and superb; Jackson, a mystic meteor or firey comet; Longstreet and the two Hills, the "Wild Huns" of the South, masterful in tactics, cyclones in battle. Huger, Magruder, and Holmes were rather slow, but the courage and endurance of their troops made up for the shortcomings of their commanders.

Among the lesser lights will stand Gregg, Jenkins, and Kershaw, of South Carolina, as foremost among the galaxy of immortal heroes who gave the battles around Richmond their place as "unparalleled in history."

CHAPTER 10
Capture of Harper's Ferry—Sharpsburg

The enemy lay quietly in his camps at Harrison's Landing for a few days, but to cover his meditated removal down the James, he advanced a large part of his army as far as Malvern Hill on the day of the 5th of August as if to press Lee back. Kershaw, with the rest of McLaw's Division, together with Jones and Longstreet, were sent to meet them. The troops were all placed in position by nightfall, bivouaced for the night on the field, and slept on their arms to guard against any night attack. The soldiers thought of to-morrow—that it perhaps might be yet more sanguinary than any of the others. Our ranks, already badly worn by the desperate conflicts at Savage Station, Frazier's Farm, Cold Harbor, etc., still showed a bold front for the coming day. Early in the morning the troops were put in motion, skirmishers thrown out, and all preparations for battle made, but to the surprise and relief of all, the "bird had flown," and instead of battle lines and bristling steel fronts we found nothing but deserted camps and evidences of a hasty flight. In a few days we were removed further back towards Richmond and sought camp on higher ground, to better guard against the ravages of disease and to be further removed from the enemy. The troops now had the pleasure of a month's rest, our only duties being guard and advance picket every ten or twelve days.

While McClellan had been pushing his army up on the Peninsula the Federals were actively engaged in organizing a second army in the vicinity of Manassas and Fredericksburg under General John Pope, to operate against Richmond by the flank. General Pope from his infamous orders greatly incensed the people of the South, and from his vain boasting gained for himself the sobriquet of "Pope the Braggart." He ordered every citizen within his lines or living near them to either take the oath of allegiance to the United States or to be driven out of the country as an enemy of the Union. No one was to have any communication with his friends within the Confederate lines, either by letter or otherwise, on the penalty of being shot as a spy and his property confiscated. Hundreds of homes were broken up by the order. Men and women were driven South, or placed in Federal prisons, there to linger for years, perhaps, with their homes abandoned to the malicious desecration of a merciless enemy, all for no other charges than their refusal to be a traitor to their principles and an enemy to their country. Pope boasted of "seeing nothing of the enemy but his back," and that "he had no headquarters but in the saddle." He was continually sending dispatches to his chief, General Halleck, who had been appointed Commander-in-Chief of all the Federal forces in the field, of the "victories gained over Lee," his "bloody repulses of Jackson," and "successful advances," and "the Confederates on the run," etc., etc., while the very opposites were the facts. On one occasion he telegraphed to Washington that he had defeated Lee, that the Confederate leader was in full retreat to Richmond, when, as a fact, before the dispatch had reached its destination his own army was overwhelmed, and with Pope at its head, flying the field in every direction, seeking safety under the guns at Washington. It is little wonder he bore the name he had so deservedly won by his manifestoes, "Pope the Braggart."

About the middle of July Jackson, with Ewell and A.P. Hill, was sent up to the Rapidan to look after Pope and his wonderful army, which had begun to be re-enforced by troops from the James. On the 9th of August Jackson came up with a part of Pope's army at Cedar Mountain, and a fierce battle was fought, very favorable to the Confederate side. A month after Jackson had left Richmond, Longstreet, with three divisions, headed by Lee in person, was ordered to re-enforce Jackson, and began the offensive. While the Federal commander was lying securely in his camp, between the Rappahannock and the Rapidan, unconscious of the near approach of the Confederate Army, his scouts intercepted an order written by General Lee to his cavalry leader, giving details of his intended advance and attack. Pope, being thus apprised, hurriedly recrossed the Rappahannock and concentrated his forces behind that stream. Lee followed his movements closely, and while watching in front, with a portion of his army, he started Jackson on his famous march around the enemy's rear. Pulling up at night, Jackson marched to the left, crossed the Rappahannock on the 25th, and by the night of the 26th he had reached the railroad immediately in Pope's rear, capturing trains of cars, prisoners, etc. On learning that large quantities of provisions and munitions of war were stored at Manassas Junction, feebly guarded, General Trimble, with a small number of brave Alabamians, Georgians, and North Carolinians, not five hundred all told, volunteered to march still further to that point, a distance of some miles, notwithstanding they had marched with Jackson thirty miles during the day, and capture the place. This was done in good time, defeating a brigade doing guard duty, and capturing a large number of prisoners, one entire battery of artillery, and untold quantities of provisions. Jackson now appeared to retreat, but only withdrew in order to give Longstreet time to come up, which he was doing hard upon Jackson's track, but more than twenty-four hours behind. This was one of the most hazardous feats accomplished by Lee during the war, with the possible exception of Chancellorsville, "dividing his army in the face of superior numbers," a movement denounced by all successful Generals and scientists of war. But Lee attempted this on more occasions than one, and always successfully.

Jackson concealed his forces among the hills of Bull Run, giving time for Longstreet, who was fighting his way through Thoroughfare Gap at the very point of the bayonet, to come up, while Pope was racing around the plains of Manassas, trying to intercept Jackson's imaginary retreat. It seems as if the one single idea impressed itself upon the Federal commander, and that was that Jackson was trying to get away from him. But before many days Pope found the wily "Stonewall," and when in his embrace endeavoring to hold him, Pope found himself in the predicament of the man who had essayed to wrestle with a bear. When the man had downed his antagonist he had to call lustily for friends. So Pope had to call for help to turn Jackson loose—to pull him loose. On the 29th the forces of Pope, the "Braggart," came upon those of Jackson hidden behind a railroad embankment on the plains of Manassas, and a stubborn battle ensued, which lasted until late at night. Longstreet came upon the field, but took no further part in the battle than a heavy demonstration on the right to relieve the pressure from Jackson. Longstreet's left, however, turned the tide of battle. Lee turned some prisoners loose at night that had been captured during the day, leaving the impression on their minds that he was beating a hasty retreat. Reporting to their chief that night, the prisoners confirmed the opinion that Pope was fooled in believing all day, that "Lee was in full retreat," trying to avoid a battle. Pope sent flaming messages to that effect to the authorities at

Washington, and so anxious was he lest his prey should escape, he gave orders for his troops to be in motion early in the morning. On the 30th was fought the decisive battle of Second Manassas, and the plains above Bull Run were again the scene of a glorious Confederate victory, by Lee almost annihilating the army of John Pope, "the Braggart." Had it not been for the steady discipline, extraordinary coolness, and soldierly behavior of Sykes and his regulars at Stone Bridge, the rout of the Federal Army at Second Manassas would have been but little less complete than on the fatal day just a little more than one year before.

At Ox Hill, 1st September, Pope had to adopt the tactics of McClellan at Malvern Hill, face about and fight for the safety of his great ordnance and supply trains, and to allow his army a safe passage over the Potomac. At Ox Hill, the enemy under Stephens and Kearny, displayed extraordinary tenacity and courage, these two division commanders throwing their columns headlong upon those of Jackson without a thought of the danger and risks such rash acts incurred. Both were killed in the battle. Phil. Kearney had gained a national reputation for his enterprising warfare in California and Mexico during the troublesome times of the Mexican War, and it was with unfeigned sorrow and regret the two armies heard of the sad death of this veteran hero.

During the time that all these stirring events were taking place and just before Magruder, with McLaw's and Walker's divisions, was either quietly lying in front of Richmond watching the army of McClellan dwindle away, leaving by transports down the James and up the Potomac, or was marching at a killing gait to overtake their comrades under Lee to share with them their trials, their battles and their victories in Maryland. Lee could not leave the Capital with all his force so long as there was a semblance of an army threatening it.

As soon as it was discovered that Manassas was to be the real battle ground of the campaign, and Washington instead of Richmond the objective point, Lee lost no time in concentrating his army north of the Rappahannock. About the middle of August McLaws, with Kershaw's, Semmes's, Cobb's, and Barksdale's Brigades, with two brigades under Walker and the Hampton Legion Cavalry, turned their footsteps Northward, and bent all their energies to reach the scene of action before the culminating events above mentioned.

At Orange C.H., on the 26th, we hastened our march, as news began to reach us of Jackson's extraordinary movements and the excitement in the Federal Army, occasioned by their ludicrous hunt for the "lost Confederate." Jackson's name had reached its meridian in the minds of the troops, and they were ever expecting to hear of some new achievement or brilliant victory by this strange, silent, and mysterious man. The very mystery of his movements, his unexplainable absence and sudden reappearance at unexpected points, his audacity in the face of the enemy, his seeming recklessness, gave unbounded confidence to the army. The men began to feel safe at the very idea of his disappearance and absence. While the thunder of his guns and those of Longstreet's were sounding along the valleys of Bull Run, and reverberating down to the Potomac or up to Washington, McLaws with his South Carolinians, Georgians, and Mississippians was swinging along with an elastic step between Orange C.H. and Manassas.

McClellan himself had already reached Alexandria with the last of his troops, but by the acts of the ubiquitous Jackson his lines of communication were cut and the Federal commander had to grope his way in the dark for fear of running foul of his erratic enemy.

When we began nearing Manassas, we learned of the awful effect of the two preceding days' battle by meeting the wounded. They came singly and in groups, men marching with arms in slings, heads bandaged, or hopping along on improvised crutches, while the wagons and ambulances were laden with the severely wounded. In that barren country no hospital could be established, for it was as destitute of sustenance as the arid plains of the Arabian Desert when the great Napoleon undertook to cross it with his beaten army. All, with the exception of water; we had plenty of that. Passing over a part of the battlefield about the 5th of September, the harrowing sights that were met with were in places too sickening to admit of description. The enemy's dead, in many places, had been left unburied, it being a veritable instance of "leaving the dead to bury the dead." Horses in a rapid state of decomposition literally covered the field. The air was so impregnated with the foul stench arising from the plains where the battle had raged fiercest, that the troops were forced to close their nostrils while passing. Here and there lay a dead enemy overlooked in the night of the general burial, stripped of his outer clothing, his blackened features and glassy eyes staring upturned to the hot September sun, while our soldiers hurried past, leaving them unburied and unnoticed. Some lay in the beaten track of our wagon trains, and had been run over ruthlessly by the teamsters, they not having the time, if the inclination, to remove them. The hot sun made decomposition rapid, and the dead that had fallen on the steep incline their heads had left the body and rolled several paces away. All the dead had become as black as Africans, the hot rays of the sun changing the features quite prematurely. In the opening where the Washington Battalion of Artillery from New Orleans had played such havoc on the 30th with the enemy's retreating columns, it resembled some great railroad wreck—cannon and broken caissons piled in great heaps; horses lying swollen and stiff, some harnessed, others not; broken rammers, smashed wheels, dismounted pieces told of the desperate struggle that had taken place. One of the strange features of a battlefield is the absence of the carrion crow or buzzard—it matters little as to the number of dead soldiers or horses, no vultures ever venture near—it being a fact that a buzzard was never seen in that part of Virginia during the war.

All was still, save the rumble of the wagon trains and the steady tread of the soldiers. Across Bull Run and out towards Washington McLaws followed with hasty step the track of Longstreet and Jackson.

On the 5th or 6th we rejoined at last, after a two months' separation from the other portion of the army. Lee was now preparing to invade Maryland and other States North, as the course of events dictated. Pope's Army had joined that of McClellan, and the authorities at Washington had to call on the latter to "save their Capital." When the troops began the crossing of the now classic Potomac, a name on every tongue since the commencement of hostilities, their enthusiasm knew no bounds. Bands played "Maryland, My Maryland," men sang and cheered, hats filled the air, flags waved, and shouts from fifty thousand throats reverberated up and down the banks of the river, to be echoed back from the mountains and die away among the hills and highlands of Maryland. Men stopped midway in the stream and sang loudly the cheering strains of Randall's, "Maryland, My Maryland." We were overjoyed at rejoining the army, and the troops of Jackson, Longstreet, and the two Hills were proud to feel the elbow touch of such chivalrous spirits as McLaws, Kershaw, Hampton, and others in the conflicts that were soon to take place. Never before had an occurrence so excited and enlivened the spirits of the troops as the crossing of the Potomac into the land of our sister, Maryland. It is said the Crusaders, after months of toil, marching, and fighting, on their way through the plains of Asia Minor, wept when they saw the towering spires of Jerusalem, the Holy City, in the distance; and if ever Lee's troops could have wept for joy, it was at the crossing of the Potomac. But we paid dearly for this pleasure in the death of so many thousands of brave men and the loss of so many valuable officers. General Winder fell at Cedar Mountain, and Jackson's right hand, the brave Ewell, lost his leg at Manassas.

The army went into camp around Frederick City, Md. From here, on the 8th, Lee issued his celebrated address to the people of Maryland, and to those of the North generally, telling them of his entry into their country, its cause and purpose; that it was not as a conqueror, or an enemy, but to demand and enforce a peace between the two countries. He clothed his language in the most conservative and entreating terms, professing friendship for those who would assist him, and protection to life and the property of all. He enjoined the people, without regard to past differences, to flock to his standard and aid in the defeat of the party and people who were now drenching the country in blood and putting in mourning the people of two nations. The young men he asked to join his ranks as soldiers of a just and honorable cause. Of the old he asked their sympathies and prayers. To the President of the Confederate States he also wrote a letter, proposing to him that he should head his armies, and, as the chieftain of the nation, propose a peace to the authorities at Washington from the very threshold of their Capital. But both failed of the desired effect. The people of the South had been led to believe that Maryland was anxious to cast her destinies with those of her sister States, that all her sympathies were with the people of the South, and that her young men were anxious and only awaiting the opportunity to join the ranks as soldiers under Lee. But these ideas and promises were all delusions, for the people we saw along the route remained passive spectators and disinterested witnesses to the great evolutions now taking place. What the people felt on the "eastern shore" is not known; but the acts of those between the Potomac and Pennsylvania above Washington indicated but little sympathy with the Southern cause; and what enlistments were made lacked the proportions needed to swell Lee's army to its desired limits. Lee promised protection and he gave it. The soldiers to a man seemed to feel the importance of obeying the orders to respect and protect the person and property of those with whom we came in contact. It was said of this, as well as other campaigns in the North, that "it was conducted with kid gloves on."

While lying at Frederick City, Lee conceived the bold and perilous project of again dividing his army in the face of his enemy, and that enemy McClellan. Swinging back with a part of his army, he captured the stronghold of Harper's Ferry, with its 11,000 defenders, while with the other he held McClellan at bay in front. The undertaking was dangerous in the extreme, and with a leader less bold and Lieutenants less prompt and skillful, its final consummation would have been more than problematical. But Lee was the one to propose his subalterns to act. Harper's Ferry, on the Virginia side of the Potomac, where that river is intersected by the Shenandoah, both cutting their way through the cliffs and crags of the Blue Ridge, was the seat of the United States Arsenal, and had immense stores of arms and ammunition, as well as army supplies of every description. The Baltimore and Ohio Railroad and the canal cross the mountains here on the Maryland side, both hugging the precipitous side of the mountain and at the very edge of the water. The approaches to the place were few, and they so defended that capture seemed impossible, unless the heights surrounding could be obtained, and this appeared impossible from a military point of view. On the south side are the Loudon and Bolivar Heights. On the other side the mountains divide into two distinct ranges and gradually bear away from each other until they reach a distance of three miles from crest to crest. Between the two mountains is the beautiful and picturesque Pleasant Valley. The eastern ridge, called South Mountain, commencing from the rugged cliff at Rivertoria, a little hamlet nestled down between the mountains and the Potomac, runs northwards, while the western ridge, called Elk Mountain, starts from the bluff called Maryland Heights, overlooking the town of Harper's Ferry, and runs nearly parallel to the other. Jackson passed on up the river with his division, Ewell's, and A.P. Hill's, recrossed the Potomac into Virginia, captured Martinsburg, where a number of prisoners and great supplies were taken, and came up and took possession of Bolivar Heights, above Harper's Ferry. Walker's Division marched back across the Potomac and took possession of Loudon Heights, a neck of high land between the Shenandoah and Potomac overlooking Harper's Ferry from below, the Shenandoah being between his army and the latter place. On the 11th McLaws moved out of Frederick City, strengthened by the brigades of Wilcox, Featherstone, and Pryor, making seven brigades that were to undertake the capture of the stronghold by the mountain passes and ridges on the north. Kershaw, it will be seen, was given the most difficult position of passage and more formidable to attack than any of the other routes of approach. Some time after Jackson and Walker had left on their long march, McLaws followed. Longstreet and other portions of the army and wagon trains kept the straight road towards Hagerstown, while Kershaw and the rest of the troops under McLaws took the road leading southwest, on through the town of Burkettville, and camped at the foothills of the mountain, on the east side. Next morning Kershaw, commanding his own brigade and that of Barksdale, took the lead, passed over South Mountain, through Pleasant Valley, and to Elk Ridge, three miles distance, thence along the top of Elk Ridge by a dull cattle path. The width of the crest was not more than fifty yards in places, and along this Kershaw had to move in line of battle, Barksdale's Brigade in reserve. Wright's Brigade moved along a similar path on the crest of South Mountain, he taking with him two mountain howitzers, drawn by one horse each. McLaws, as Commander-in-Chief, with some of the other brigades, marched by the road at the base of the mountain below Wright, while Cobb was to keep abreast of Kershaw and Barksdale at the base of Elk Ridge. Over such obstacles as were encountered and the difficulties and dangers separating the different troops, a line of battle never before made headway as did those of Kershaw and the troops under McLaws.

We met the enemy's skirmishers soon after turning to the left on Elk Ridge, and all along the whole distance of five miles we were more or less harassed by them. During the march of the 12th the men had to pull themselves up precipitous inclines by the twigs and undergrowth that lined the mountain side, or hold themselves in position by the trees in front. At night we bivouaced on the mountain. We could see the fires all along the mountain side and gorges through Pleasant Valley and up on South Mountain, where the troops of Wright had camped opposite. Early next morning as we advanced we again met the enemy's skirmishers, and had to be continually driving them back. Away to the south and beyond the Potomac we could hear the sound of Jackson's guns as he was beating his way up to meet us. By noon we encountered the enemy's breastworks, built of great stones and logs, in front of which was an abattis of felled timber and brushwood. The Third, under Nance, and the Seventh, under Aiken, were ordered to the charge on the right. Having no artillery up, it was with great difficulty we approached the fortifications. Men had to cling to bushes while they loaded and fired. But with their usual gallantry they came down to their work. Through the tangled undergrowth, through the abattis, and over the breastworks they leaped with a yell.

The fighting was short but very severe. The Third did not lose any field officers, but the line suffered considerably. The Third lost some of her most promising officers. Of the Seventh, Captain Litchfield, of Company L, Captain Wm. Clark, of Company G, and lieutenant J.L. Talbert fell dead, and many others wounded.

The Second and Eighth had climbed the mountains, and advanced on Harper's Ferry from the east. The Second was commanded by Colonel Kennedy and the Eighth by Colonel Henagan. The enemy was posted behind works, constructed the same as those assaulted by the Third and Seventh, of cliffs of rocks, trunks of trees, covered by an abattis. The regiments advanced in splendid style, and through the tangled underbrush and over boulders they rushed for the enemy's works. Colonel Kennedy was wounded in the early part of the engagement, but did not leave the field. The Second lost some gallant line officers. When the order was given to charge the color bearer of the Eighth, Sergeant Strother, of Chesterfield, a tall, handsome man of six feet three in height, carrying the beautiful banner presented to the regiment by the ladies of Pee Dee, fell dead within thirty yards of the enemy's works. All the color guard were either killed or wounded. Captain A.T. Harllee, commanding one of the color companies, seeing the flag fall, seized it and waving it aloft, called to the men to forward and take the breastworks. He, too, fell desperately wounded, shot through both thighs with a minnie ball. He then called to Colonel Henagan, he being near at hand, to take the colors. Snatching them from under Captain Harllee, Colonel Henagan shouted to the men to follow him, but had not gone far before he fell dangerously wounded. Some of the men lifted up their fallen Colonel and started to the rear; but just at this moment his regiment began to waver and break to the rear. The gallant Colonel seeing this ordered his men to put him down, and commanded in a loud, clear voice, "About face! Charge and take the works," which order was obeyed with promptness, and soon the flags of Kershaw's Regiments waved in triumph over the enemy's deserted works.

Walker had occupied Loudon Heights, on the Virginia side, and all were waiting now for Jackson to finish the work assigned to him and to occupy Bolivar Heights, thus finishing the cordon around the luckless garrison. The enemy's cavalry under the cover of the darkness crossed the river, hugged its banks close, and escaped. During the night a road was cut to the top of Maryland Heights by our engineer corps and several pieces of small cannon drawn up, mostly by hand,

and placed in such position as to sweep the garrison below. Some of Jackson's troops early in the night began climbing around the steep cliffs that overlook the Shenandoah, and by daylight took possession of the heights opposite to those occupied by Walker's Division. But all during the day, while we were awaiting the signal of Jackson's approach, we heard continually the deep, dull sound of cannonading in our rear. Peal after peal from heavy guns that fairly shook the mountain side told too plainly a desperate struggle was going on in the passes that protected our rear. General McLaws, taking Cobb's Georgia Brigade and some cavalry, hurried back over the rugged by-paths that had been just traversed, to find D.H. Hill and Longstreet in a hand-to-hand combat, defending the routes on South Mountain that led down on us by the mountain crests. The next day orders for storming the works by the troops beyond the river were given. McLaws and Walker had secured their position, and now were in readiness to assist Jackson. All the batteries were opened on Bolivar Heights, and from the three sides the artillery duel raged furiously for a time, while Jackson's infantry was pushed to the front and captured the works there. Soon thereafter the white flag was waving over Harper's Ferry, "the citadel had fallen." In the capitulation eleven thousand prisoners, seventy-two pieces of artillery, twelve thousand stands of small arms, horses, wagons, munitions, and supplies in abundance passed into the hands of the Confederates. Jackson's troops fairly swam in the delicacies, provisions, and "drinkables" constituting a part of the spoils taken, while Kershaw's and all of McLaw's and Walker's troops, who had done the hardest of the fighting, got none. Our men complained bitterly of this seeming injustice. It took all day to finish the capitulation, paroling prisoners, and dividing out the supplies; but we had but little time to rest, for Lee's Army was now in a critical condition. McClellan, having by accident captured Lee's orders specifying the routes to be taken by all the troops after the fall of Harper's Ferry, knew exactly where and when to strike. The Southern Army was at this time woefully divided, a part being between the Potomac and the Shenandoah, Jackson with three divisions across the Potomac in Virginia, McLaws with his own and a part of Anderson's Division on the heights of Maryland, with the enemy five miles in his rear at Crompton Pass cutting him off from retreat in that direction. Lee, with the rest of his army and reserve trains, was near Hagerstown.

On the 16th we descended the mountain, crossed the Potomac, fell in the rear of Jackson's moving army, and marched up the Potomac some distance, recrossed into Maryland, on our hunt for Lee and his army. The sun poured down its blistering rays with intense fierceness upon the already fatigued and fagged soldiers, while the dust along the pikes, that wound over and around the numerous hills, was almost stifling. We bivouaced for the night on the roadside, ten miles from Antietam Creek, where Lee was at the time concentrating his army, and where on the next day was to be fought the most stubbornly contested and bloody battle of modern times, if we take in consideration the number of troops engaged, its duration, and its casualties. After three days of incessant marching and fighting over mountain heights, rugged gorges, wading rivers—all on the shortest of rations, many of the men were content to fall upon the bare ground and snatch a few moments of rest without the time and trouble of a supper.

Battle of Sharpsburg (Antietam)

When Lee crossed the Potomac the Department at Washington, as well as the whole North, was thrown into consternation, and the wildest excitement prevailed, especially in Maryland and Pennsylvania. "Where was Lee?" "Where was he going?" were some of the questions that flitted over the wires to McClellan from Washington, Philadelphia, and Baltimore. But the personage about whose movements and whereabouts seemed to excite more anxiety and superstitious dread than any or all of Lee's Lieutenants was Jackson. The North regarded him as some mythical monster, acting in reality the parts assigned to fiction. But after it was learned that Lee had turned the head of his columns to the westward, their fears were somewhat allayed. Governor Curtis, of Pennsylvania, almost took spasms at the thought of the dreaded rebels invading his domain, and called upon the militia "to turn out and resist the invader." In less than three weeks after the battle of Manassas, the North, or more correctly, New York, Pennsylvania, New Jersey, Delaware, and Maryland, had out 250,000 State troops behind the Susquehanna River.

The great horde of negro cooks and servants that usually followed the army were allowed to roam at will over the surrounding country, just the same as down in Virginia. The negroes foraged for their masters wherever they went, and in times of short rations they were quite an adjunct to the Commissary Department, gathering chickens, butter, flour, etc. Even now, when so near the Free States, with nothing to prevent them from making their escape, the negroes showed no disposition to take advantage of their situation and conditions, their owners giving themselves no concern whatever for their safety. On more occasions than one their masters told them to go whenever they wished, that they would exercise no authority over them whatever, but I do not believe a single negro left of his own accord. Some few were lost, of course, but they were lost like many of the soldiers—captured by foraging parties or left broken down along the roadside. It is a fact, though, that during the whole war the negroes were as much afraid of the "Yankee" as the white soldier, and dreaded capture more.

It might be supposed that we fared sumptuously, being in an enemy's country at fruit and harvest time, with great waving fields of corn, trees bending under loads of choice ripe fruits, but such was far from being the case. Not an apple, peach, or plum was allowed to be taken without payment, or at the owner's consent. Fields, orchards, and farmhouses were strictly guarded against depredations. The citizens as a whole looked at us askance, rather passive than demonstrative. The young did not flock to our standards as was expected, and the old men looked on more in wonder than in pleasure, and opened their granaries with willingness, but not with cheerfulness. They accepted the Confederate money offered as pay for meals or provisions more as a respect to an overpowering foe than as a compensation for their wares. A good joke in this campaign was had at the expense of Captain Nance, of the Third. It must be remembered that the privates played many practical jokes upon their officers in camps, when at other times and on other occasions such would be no joke at all, but a bit of downright rascality and meanness—but in the army such was called fun. A nice chicken, but too old to fry, so it must be stewed. As the wagons were not up, cooking utensils were scarce—about one oven to twenty-five men. Captain Nance ordered Jess to bake the biscuit at night and put away till morning, when the chicken would be cooked and a fine breakfast spread. Now the Captain was overflowing in good humor and spirits, and being naturally generous-hearted, invited the Colonel and Lieutenant Colonel Rutherford, the latter his prospective brother-in-law, down to take breakfast with him. The biscuits were all baked nicely and piled high up on an old tin plate and put in the Captain's tent at his head for safe keeping during the night. Early next morning the fowl was "jumping in the pan," as the boys would say, while the Captain made merry with the others over their discomfiture at seeing him and his guests eating "chicken and flour bread," while they would be "chewing crackers." All things must come to an end, of course; so the chicken was at last "cooked to a turn," the Colonel and the future brother-in-law are seated expectantly upon the ground waiting the breakfast call. The Captain was assisting Jess in putting on the finishing touches to the tempting meal, as well as doing the honors to his distinguished guests. When all was ready he ordered Jess to bring out the biscuits. After an unusual long wait, as it may have appeared to Captain Nance under the condition of his appetite and the presence of his superiors, he called out, "Why in the thunder don't you bring out the biscuits, Jess?" Still blankets were overturned and turned again, knapsacks moved for the fourth or fifth time, yet Jess hunted faithfully in that little four by six tent for the plate of biscuits. "Why in the h——l don't you come on with the biscuits, Jess?" with a pronounced accent on the word "Jess." Meanwhile Jess poked his black, shaggy head through the tent door, the white of his eyes depicting the anguish of his mind, his voice the despair he felt, answered: "Well, Marse John, before God Almighty, ef somebody ain't tooken stole dem bisket." Tableaux!! Twenty-five years afterwards at a big revival meeting at Bethel Church, in Newberry County, a great many "hard cases," as they were called, were greatly impressed with the sermons, and one especially seemed on the point of "getting religion," as it is called. But he seemed to be burdened with a great weight. At the end of the service he took out Captain Nance and expressed a desire to make a confession. "Did you ever know who stole your biscuits that night at Frederick City?" "No." "Well, I and Bud Wilson—" But Captain Nance never allowed John Mathis to finish, for as the light of that far-off truth dawned upon him and seemed to bring back the recollection of that nice brown chicken and the missing biscuits he said: "No, I'll never forgive you; go home and don't try for religion any longer, for a crime as heinous as yours is beyond forgiveness. Oh, such depravity!" It appears since that two of his most intimate friends had robbed him just for the fun they would have over his disappointment in the morning and the chagrin the Captain would experience, but the biscuits were too tempting to keep.

On the morning of the 17th we were yet ten miles from Sharpsburg, where Lee had drawn up his army around that little hamlet and along Antietam Creek, to meet the shock of battle that McClellan was preparing to give. The battleground chosen was in a bend of the Potomac, Lee's left resting on the river above and around to the front to near the point where the Antietam enters the Potomac on the right. The little sluggish stream between the two armies, running at the base of the heights around and beyond Sharpsburg, was not fordable for some distance above the Potomac, and only crossed by stone bridges at the public roads. Up near Lee's left it could be crossed without bridges. The Confederate Army now lay in a small compass in this bend of the river, the Federal Army extending in his front from the river above to the Antietam below, just above its junction with the Potomac. That stream rolled in a deep, strong current in the rear of Lee.

Even before the sun had spread its rays over the heights of this quaint old Quaker town sufficient to distinguish objects a few feet away, the guns were booming along the crossings of Antietam. With a hurried breakfast Kershaw took up the line of march along the dusty roads in the direction of the firing, which had begun by daylight and continued to rage incessantly during the day and till after dark, making this the most bloody battle for the men engaged fought during the century. In its casualties—the actual dead upon the field and the wounded—for the time of action, it exceeded all others before or since. When we neared General Lee's headquarters, some distance in rear of the town, D.H. Hill and part of Jackson's forces were already in the doubtful toils of a raging conflict away to our left and front, where Hooker was endeavoring to break Lee's left or press it back upon the river. Barksdale's Brigade, of our division, was in front, and when near the battlefield formed in line of battle. Kershaw formed his lines with the Third, Colonel Nance, in front, nearly parallel with a body of woods, near the Dunker Church, and left of the road leading to it, the enemy being about five hundred yards in our front. The other regiments were formed in line on our left as they came up, Colonel Aiken, of the Seventh, Lieutenant Colonel Hoole, of the Eighth, and Colonel Kennedy, of the Second, in the order named, Barksdale moving in action before our last regiment came fairly in line. Sumner, of the Federal Army, was pushing his forces of the Second Army Corps forward at this point of the line in columns of brigades, having crossed the Antietam at the fords above. Sedgwick, of his leading division, had already formed in line of battle awaiting our assault. One of the Georgia Brigades of the division formed on Kershaw's left, while the other acted as reserve, and a general advance was ordered against the troops in the woods. The battle was in full blast now along the greater part of the line. General Longstreet, speaking of the time Kershaw came in action, says: "The fire spread along both lines from left to right, across the Antietam, and back again, and the thunder of the big guns became continuous and increased to a mighty volume. To this was presently added the sharper rattle of musketry, and the surge of mingling sound sweeping up and down the field was multiplied and confused by the reverberations from the rocks and hills. And in the great tumult of sound, which shook the air and seemed to shatter the cliffs and ledges above the Antietam, bodies of the facing foes were pushed forward to closer work, and soon added the clash of steel to the thunderous crash of cannon shot. Under this storm, now Kershaw advanced his men. Through the open, on through the woods, with a solid step these brave men went, while the battery on their left swept their ranks with grape and canister." In the woods the brigade was moved to the left to evade this storm of shot and shell. The Mississippians on the left were now reforming their broken ranks. Colonel Aiken, of the Seventh, had fallen badly wounded in the first charge, and the command was given to Captain White. This was the first battle in a fair field in which the new commanders of the regiments had had an opportunity to show their mettle and ability, and well did they sustain themselves. Savage Station and Maryland Heights were so crowded with underbrush and vision so obscured that they were almost battles in the dark. Colonel Kennedy, of the Second, and Lieutenant Colonel Hoole, of the Eighth, were handling their men in splendid style, the Seventh changing its commander three times while in battle. Colonel Nance changed his front in the lull of battle, and moved under the friendly cover of a hill, on which was posted the battery that had been graping the field so desperately during the first advance. The brigade had now passed through the field of waving corn, over the rail fence, and driven Sedgwick from his position. Barksdale, who had been staggered by the first impact, was now moving up in beautiful harmony; the steady, elastic step of his men, the waving banners, the officers marching in the rear, their bright blades glittering in the sunlight, made a most imposing spectacle. Up the slope, among the straggling oaks, they bent their steps, while the grape, shell, and canister thinned their ranks to such an extent that when the enemy's infantry was met, their galling fire forced Barksdale to retire in great disorder. The enemy's troops were being hurried ever the creek and forming in our front. Kershaw moved forward in line with those on the right to meet them, and swept everything from his front. The enemy had been massing along the whole line, and when Kershaw reached the farthest limit of the open field he was met by overwhelming numbers. Now the fight waged hot and fierce, but the line on the right having retired left the right flank of the Third Regiment entirely exposed both to the fire of the artillery and infantry, forcing the brigade to retire to its former ground, leaving, however, the second commander of the Seventh dead upon the field. It was here the famous scout and aide to General Stuart, Captain

W.D. Parley, killed at the Rappahannock, came to visit his brother, Lieutenant Parley, of the Third. He was made doubly famous by the fiction of Captain Estine Cooke.

McClellan was now growing desperate, his lines making no headway either on the left or centre. His forces were held at bay on our right across the Antietam, having failed to force a crossing at the bridges. Jackson and Hill, on the left, were being sorely pressed by the corps of Mansfield and Hooker, but still doggedly held their ground. Jackson had left the division of A.P. Hill at Harper's Ferry to settle the negotiations of surrender, and had but a comparative weak force to meet this overwhelming number of two army corps. Again and again the Confederate ranks were broken, but as often reformed. Stuart stood on the extreme left, with his body of cavalry, but the condition of the field was such as to prevent him from doing little more service than holding the flanks. General Toombs, with his Georgia Brigade, and some detached troops, with two batteries, held the lower fords all day against the whole of Burnside's corps, notwithstanding the imperative orders of his chief "to cross and strike the Confederates in the rear." Assaults by whole divisions were repeatedly made against the small force west of the stream, but were easily repulsed by Toombs and his Georgians. In all probability these unsuccessful attacks would have continued during the day, had not the Federals found a crossing, unknown to the Confederate Generals, between the bridges. When the crossing was found the whole slope on the western side of the stream was soon a perfect sheet of blue. So sure were they of victory that they called upon the Confederates to "throw down their arms and surrender." This was only answered by a volley and a charge with the bayonet point. But there was a factor in the day's battle not yet taken account of, and which was soon to come upon the field like a whirlwind and change the course of events. A.P. Hill, who had been left at Harper's Ferry, was speeding towards the bloody field with all the speed his tired troops could make. Gregg, Branch, and Archer, of Hill's Division, were thrown into the combat at this most critical moment, after the enemy had forced a crossing at all points and were pushing Lee backwards towards the Potomac. Short and decisive was the work. An advance of the whole right was made. The enemy first staggered, then reeled, and at last pressed off the field. The batteries lost in the early part of the day were retaken, and the enemy was glad to find shelter under his heavy guns on the other side of the Antietam. But the battle on the left was not so favorable. Jackson's, D.H.

Hill's, and McLaw's troops, jaded and fagged by the forced marches in the morning, their ranks woefully thinned by the day's continuous fighting, their ammunition sadly exhausted, could do no more than hold their ground for the remainder of the day. The enemy now being re-enforced by Porter's Corps, his batteries enfilading our ranks. McLaws was forced to move Kershaw and the troops on his right to the left and rear, nearly parallel to the line first formed during the day. There had been no material advantage on either side. On the right the enemy had crossed the Antietam, it is true, but to a position no better than the night before. Our left and centre were bent back in somewhat more acute angle than on the morning, but to an equally good position. Not many prisoners were taken on either side in proportion to the magnitude of the battle. The enemy's loss in killed and wounded was a little more than ours, but so far as the day's battle goes, the loss and gain were about equal. It is true Lee lost thousands of good and brave troops whose places could scarcely be filled; yet he inflicted such punishment upon the enemy that it took him months to recuperate. The moral effect was against us and in favor of the enemy. It had a decided bearing upon the coming elections at the North, and a corresponding depression upon the people at the South. The Southern Army, from its many successive victories in the past, had taught themselves to believe that they were simply invincible upon the field of battle, and the people of the South looked upon the strategy and military skill of Lee and Jackson as being far beyond the cope of any Generals the North could produce. But this battle taught the South a great lesson in many ways. It demonstrated the fact that it was possible to be matched in generalship, it was possible to meet men upon the field equal in courage and endurance to themselves. But it also proved to what point of forbearance and self-sacrifice the Southern soldier could go when the necessity arose, and how faithful and obedient they would remain to their leaders under the severest of tests. The Confederate soldier had been proven beyond cavil the equal in every respect to that of any on the globe. After fighting all day, without food and with little water, they had to remain on the field of battle, tired and hungry, until details returned to the wagons and cooked their rations. It may be easily imagined that both armies were glad enough to fall upon the ground and rest after such a day of blood and carnage, with the smoke, dust, and weltering heat of the day. Before the sound of the last gun had died away in the distance one hundred thousand men were stretched upon the ground fast asleep, while near a third of that number were sleeping their last sleep or suffering from the effects of fearful wounds. The ghouls of the battlefield are now at their wanton work. Stealthily and cautiously they creep and grope about in the dark to hunt the body of an enemy, or even a comrade, and strip or rob him of his little all. Prayers, groans, and curses mingle, but the robber of the battlefield continues his work. Friends seek lost comrades here and there, a brother looks, perhaps, in vain for a brother.

The loss in some of our regiments was appalling, especially the Seventh. Two regimental commanders, of that command had fallen, Colonel Aiken and Captain White, leaving Captain Hard, one of the junior Captains, in command. The regiment lost in the two battles of Maryland Heights and Sharpsburg, two hundred and fifty-three out of four hundred and forty-six.

General McClellan, in his testimony before the War Investigating Committee, says: "We fought pretty close upon one hundred thousand men. Our forces were, total in action, eighty-seven thousand one hundred and sixty-four." Deducting the cavalry division not in action of four thousand three hundred and twenty, gives McClellan eighty-two thousand eight hundred and forty-four, infantry and artillery.

General Lee says in his report: "The battle was fought by less than forty thousand men of all arms on our side." The actual numbers were:

Jackson, including A.P. Hill	10,000
Longstreet	12,000
D.H. Hill and Walker	7,000
Cavalry	8,000
	37,000

Deduct four thousand cavalry on detached service and not on the field from Lee's force, and we have of infantry, artillery, and cavalry, thirty-three thousand. Jackson only had four thousand on the left until the arrival of A.P. Hill, and withstood the assaults of forty thousand till noon; when re-enforced by Hill he pressed the enemy from the field.

The next day was employed in burying the dead and gathering up the wounded. Those who could travel were started off across the Potomac on foot, in wagons and ambulances, on the long one hundred miles march to the nearest railroad station, while those whose wounds would not admit of their removal were gathered in houses in the town and surgeons detailed to remain and treat them. On the morning of the 19th some hours before day the rumbling of the wagon trains told of our march backward. We crossed the Potomac, Longstreet leading, and Jackson bringing up the rear. A great many that had been broken down by the rapid marches and the sun's burning rays from the time of our crossing into Maryland till now, were not up at the battle of the 17th, thus weakening the ranks of Lee to nearly one-half their real strength, taking those on detached service into consideration also. But these had all come up and joined their ranks as we began crossing the Potomac. None wished to be left behind; even men so badly wounded that at home they would be confined to their beds marched one hundred miles in the killing heat. Hundreds of men with their arms amputated left the operating table to take up their long march. Some shot through the head, body, or limbs preferred to place the Potomac between themselves and the enemy.

Lee entered Maryland with sixty-one thousand men all told, counting Quartermaster and Commissary Departments, the teamsters, and those in the Medical and Engineer Department. Lee lost thirteen thousand six hundred and eighty-seven men killed and wounded on the field of battle, and several thousand in capture and broken down by the wayside, most of the latter, however, reporting for duty in a few days.

McClellan had of actual soldiers in the lines of battle and reserve eighty-seven thousand one hundred and sixty-four, his losses in battle being twelve thousand four hundred and ten, making his casualties one thousand two hundred and seventy-seven less than Lee's. The prisoners and cannon captured in action were about equal during the twelve days north of the Potomac, while at Harper's Ferry Lee captured sufficient ammunition to replenish that spent in battle, and horses and wagons enough to fully equip the whole army, thousands of improved small arms, seventy-two cannon and caissons, and eleven thousand prisoners. While the loss of prisoners, ammunition, horses, ordnance, etc., did not materially cripple the North, our losses in prisoners and killed and wounded could hardly be replaced at that time. So in summing up the results it is doubtful whether or not the South gained any lasting benefit from the campaign beyond the Potomac. But Lee was forced by circumstances after the enemy's disaster at Manassas to follow up his victories and be guided by the course of events, and in that direction they lead. McClellan offered the gauge of battle; Lee was bound to accept. The North claimed Sharpsburg or Antietam as a victory, and the world accepted it as such. This gave Lincoln the opportunity he had long waited for to write his famous Emancipation Proclamation. It was not promulgated, however, till the first of January following. Among military critics this battle would be given to Lee, even while the campaign is voted a failure. It is an axiom in war that when one army stands upon the defensive and is attacked by the other, if the latter fails to force the former from his position, then it is considered a victory for the army standing on the defensive. (See Lee at Gettysburg and Burnsides at Fredericksburg.) While Lee was the invader, he stood on the defensive at Sharpsburg or Antietam, and McClellan did no more than press his left and centre back. Lee held his battle line firmly, slept on the field, buried his dead the next day, then deliberately withdrew. What better evidence is wanting to prove Lee not defeated. McClellan claimed no more than a drawn fight.

On the 19th the enemy began pressing our rear near Sheperd-stown, and A.P. Hill was ordered to return and drive them off. A fierce and sanguinary battle took place at Bateler's Ford, between two portions of the armies, A.P. Hill gaining a complete victory, driving the enemy beyond the river. The army fell back to Martinsburg and rested a few days. Afterwards they were encamped at Winchester, where they remained until the opening of the next campaign.

Before closing the account of the First Maryland campaign, I wish to say a word in regard to the Commissary and Quartermaster's Departments. Much ridicule, and sometimes abuse, has been heaped upon the heads of those who composed the two Departments. I must say, in all justice, that much of this was ill timed and ill advised. It must be remembered that to the men who constituted these Departments belonged the duty of feeding, clothing, and furnishing the transportation for the whole army. Often without means or ways, they had to invent them. In an enemy's country, surrounded by many dangers, in a hostile and treacherous community, and mostly unprotected except by those of their own force, they had to toil night and day, through sunshine and rain, that the men who were in the battle ranks could be fed and clothed. They had no rest. When the men were hungry they must be fed; when others slept they had to be on the alert. When sick or unable to travel a means of transportation must be furnished. The Commissary and the Quartermaster must provide for the sustenance of the army. Kershaw's Brigade was doubly blessed in the persons of Captain, afterwards Major W.D. Peck and Captain Shell, of the Quartermaster Department, and Captain R.N. Lowrance, and Lieutenant J.N. Martin, of the Commissary. The troops never wanted or suffered while it was in the power of those officers to supply them.

Major Peck was a remarkable man in many respects. He certainly could be called one of nature's noblemen. Besides being a perfect high-toned gentleman of the old school, he was one of the most efficient officers in the army, and his popularity was universal His greatest service was in the Quartermaster's Department, but he served for awhile in the ranks in Captain Wm. Wallace's Company, Second Regiment, as Orderly Sergeant—served in that capacity at the bombardment of Fort Sumpter and the first battle of Manassas. On the death of Quartermaster W.S. Wood, Colonel Kershaw appointed him his Regimental Quartermaster to fill the place made vacant by Captain Wood, in July, 1861, with the rank of Captain. When Kershaw was made Brigadier General, on the resignation of General Bonham, he had him promoted to Brigade Quartermaster with the rank of Major. On the resignation of Major McLaws, Division Quartermaster, he was made Division Quartermaster in his stead, and held this position during the war. He received his last appointment only one month before his illustrious chief, J.B. Kershaw, was made Major General. It seems a strange coincidence in the rise of these two men, who entered the service together—each took different arms, but rose in parallel grades to the highest position in the division. Major Peck was seldom absent from duty, and a complaint against him was never heard. He was a bold, gallant officer, and when in the discharge of his duties he laid aside every other consideration. Major Peck had a very striking appearance, tall, erect, and dignified, and upon horseback he was a perfect cavalier. It might be truly said he was one of the handsomest men in the army. His commanding appearance attracted attention wherever he went, and he was often taken for a general officer. For cordiality, generosity, and unselfishness he was almost without a rival. It required no effort on his part to display the elegance of his character—his gentlemanly qualities and deportment were as natural to him as it is for the "sparks to fly upward." He was born in Columbia April 4th, 1833, and died there April 25th, 1870.

The mere fact of Captain G.W. Shell being appointed to such a responsible position as Quartermaster by so strict a disciplinarian as Colonel Nance is a sufficient guarantee of his qualifications. Captain Shell entered the army as a private in the "State Guards," from Laurens, served one year as such, then as Regimental Quartermaster with rank of Captain for a part of two years. Then that office in the army was abolished and put in charge of a non-commissioned officer. Appreciating his great services while serving his regiment, the officials were loath to dispense with his services, and gave him a position in the brigade department and then in the division as assistant to Major Peck, retaining his rank. All that has been said of Major Peck can be truly said of Captain Shell. He was an exceptional executive officer, kind and courteous to those under his orders, obedient and respectful to his superiors. He was ever vigilant and watchful of the wants of the troops, and while in the abandoned sections of Virginia, as well as in Maryland and Pennsylvania, he displayed the greatest activity in gathering supplies for the soldiers. He was universally loved and admired. He was of the same age of Captain Peck, born and reared in Laurens County, where he returned after the close of the war and still resides, enjoying all the comforts emanating from a well spent life. For several terms he filled the office of Clerk of the Court of his native county, and served two terms in the United States Congress. He was the leading spirit in the great reform movement that overspread the State several years ago, in which Ben Tillman was made Governor, and South Carolina's brightest light, both political and military, General Wade Hampton, was retired to private life.

As Colonel Aiken saw but little more service with the First Brigade, I will here give a short sketch of his life. I have made it a rule in this work, as far as practicable, to give a sketch at the end of the officer's service in the Brigade, but in this case I make an exception.

COLONEL AIKEN

Colonel Aiken was born in Winnsboro, Fairfield County, S.C., March 17th, 1828. He graduated at the South Carolina College in the class of 1849. Was professor at Mt. Zion College for two years, and married Miss Mattie Gaillard in 1852, settling at "Bellevue" Farm, near Winnsboro. He became county editor of Winnsboro News and Herald, and was married the second time to Miss Smith, of Abbeville, and removed to that county in 1858. Was fond of agriculture, and was editor of various periodicals devoted to that and kindred pursuits.

In 1861 he volunteered as a private in the Seventh South Carolina Volunteers, and was appointed Adjutant of that regiment. At the reorganization of the regiment in 1862 he was elected Colonel to

154

succeed Colonel Bacon, who declined re-election. At Sharpsburg he received a wound in the body, which for a long time was feared to be fatal. He, however, returned in June, 1863, and commanded his regiment in the Gettysburg battle, after which he was deemed unable for further active service in the field, and was appointed "commandant of the post" at Macon, Ga. This position he held for one year, and then discharged from the army as being unfit for further service.

After the war he was selected for three terms to the State Legislature. He was "Master of State Grange Patrons of Husbandry," and was twice President of the "State Agricultural and Mechanical Society of South Carolina." He was chosen Democratic standard bearer for Congress in the memorable campaign of 1876, and continually re-elected thereafter until his death, which occurred on April 6th, 1887.

Colonel Aiken was also one of nature's noblemen, bold, fearless, and incorruptible. He did as much, or perhaps more, than any of the many great and loyal men of that day to release South Carolina from the coils of the Republican ring that ruled the State during the dark days of Reconstruction.

CHAPTER 12
From Winchester to Fredericksburg

The brigade remained in camp in a beautiful grove, about four miles beyond Winchester, until the last of October. Here the regiments were thoroughly organized and put in good shape for the next campaign. Many officers and non-commissioned officers had been killed, or totally disabled in the various battles, and their places had to be filled by election and promotion. All officers, from Colonel down, went up by regular grades, leaving nothing but the Third Lieutenants to be elected. The non-commissioned officers generally went up by promotion also, where competent, or the Captains either promoted them by regular grade or left the selection to the men of the company. We had lost no field officer killed, except Lieutenant Colonel Garlington, of the Third, and Major Rutherford was promoted to that position, and Captain R.C. Maffett made Major. Several Lieutenants in all the regiments were made Captains, and many new Lieutenants were chosen from the ranks, so much so that the rolls of the various companies were very materially changed, since the reorganization in April last. Many of the wounded had returned, and large bodies of men had come in from the conscript camps since the reorganization. The Seventh Regiment had lost heavier, in officers and men, than any of the regiments. Colonel Aiken was wounded at Sharpsburg, and never returned only for a short time, but the regiment was commanded by Lieutenant Colonel Bland until the resignation of Colonel Aiken, except when the former was himself disabled by wounds.

Camp guards were kept up around the brigade, and regimental pickets, some two or three miles distant, about every two weeks. We had company and regimental drills about four times per week, and, in fact, we drilled almost every day, now that we were not on the actual march. The turn-pike road from Winchester to Staunton, ninety miles, for weeks was perfectly lined with soldiers returning at the expiration of their furloughs, or discharged from hospital, and our convalescent sick and wounded from the Maryland campaign going homeward.

On the 27th or 28th of October orders came to move. Longstreet took the lead, with McLaws' and Anderson's Divisions in front. General Lee had divided his army into two corps; the Department of Richmond having created the rank of Lieutenant General, raised Longstreet and Jackson to that grade in Lee's Army. Longstreet's Corps consisted of McLaws' Division, composed of Kershaw's, Barksdale's, Cobb's, and Semmes' Brigades, and Anderson's, Hood's, Pickett's, and Ransom's Divisions. Jackson's Corps consisted of D.H. Hill's, A.P. Hill's, Ewell's, and Taliaferro's Divisions. We marched by way of Chester Gap over the Blue Ridge, and came into camp near Culpepper on the 9th of November. The enemy had crossed the Potomac and was moving southward, by easy stages, on the east side of the mountain.

On the 5th of October General McClellan was removed from the command of the Army of the Potomac and Major General Burnsides, a corps commander, was made Commander-in-Chief in his stead. This change was universally regretted by both armies, for the Northern Army had great confidence in the little "Giant," while no officer in the Union Army was ever held in higher esteem by the Southern soldiers than little "Mack," as General McClellan was called. They admired him for his unsurpassed courage, generalship, and his kind and gentlemanly deportment, quite in contrast to the majority of Union commanders.

General Burnsides, who had succeeded McClellan, now divided his army by corps in three grand divisions—General Sumner, commanding the Right Grand Division, composed of the Second and Ninth Corps; General Hooker, the center, with the Third and Fifth Corps; and General Franklin, the left, with the First and Sixth Corps. So both armies had undergone considerable changes, and were now moving along on converging lines towards a meeting point to test the mettle of the new commanders and organizations.

We remained in camp around Culpepper until the morning of the 18th of November, when the march was resumed, by McLaws taking the road leading to Fredericksburg, headed by General Longstreet in person, and another division south along the line of the railroad in the direction of the North Anna River, the other divisions of the corps remaining stationary, awaiting developments. Jackson had not yet crossed the Blue Ridge, and General Lee was only waiting and watching the move of Burnsides before concentrating his army at any particular place. It was unknown at this time whether the Federal commander would take the route by way of Fredericksburg, or follow in a straight course and make the North Anna his base of operations. The cavalry, making a demonstration against the enemy's outposts, found the Union Army had left and gone in the direction of Fredericksburg. Then Lee began the concentration of his army by calling Jackson on the east side of the Blue Ridge and Longstreet down on the south side of the Rappahannock. We crossed the north fork of the Rappahannock at a rocky ford, two miles above the junction of the Rapidan and just below the railroad bridge, on a cold, blustery day, the water blue and cold as ice itself, coming from the mountain springs of the Blue Ridge, not many miles away. Some of the men took off their shoes and outer garments, while others plunged in just as they marched from the road. Men yelled, cursed, and laughed. Some climbed upon the rocks to allow their feet and legs to warm up in the sun's rays, others held up one foot for awhile, then the other, to allow the air to strike their naked shins and warm them. Oh! it was dreadfully cold, but such fun! The water being about three feet deep, we could easily see the rocks and sands in the bottom. The men who had pulled off their shoes and clothing suffered severely.

There was a man in my company who was as brave and as good a soldier as ever lived, but beyond question the most awkward man in the army. His comrades called him "mucus," as some one said that was the Latin for "calf." This man would fall down any time and anywhere. Standing in the road or resting on his rifle, he would fall—fall while marching, or standing in his tent. I saw him climb on top of a box car and then fall without the least provocation backwards into a ten-foot ditch. But in all his falling he was never known to hurt himself, but invariably blamed somebody for his fall. When he fell from the car, and it standing perfectly still, he only said: "I wish the d——n car would go on or stand still, one or the other." The road leading to the river makes a bend here, and between the bend and river bank an abutment of logs, filled in with stone to the height of fifteen feet, was built to prevent the water from encroaching upon the land. "Mucus," for no cause whatever that anyone could learn, quit the ranks and walked out on this abutment and along down its side, keeping near the edge of the water, but fifteen feet above, when, to the unaccountability of all, he fell headlong down into the river.

The water at this point was not more than three or four feet deep, but deep enough to drench him from head to foot. He rose up, and as usual, quick to place the blame, said:

"If I knew the d——n man who pushed me off in the water, I'd put a ball in him."

No one had been in twenty feet of him. All the consolation he got was "how deep was the water, 'Mucus'?" "Was the water cold?" But awkward as he was, he was quick-witted and good at repartee. He answered the question "how deep was the water?"

"Deep enough to drown a d——n fool, if you don't believe it, go down like I did and try it."

When we reached the other side we were told "no use to put on your shoes or clothing, another river one mile ahead," the Rapidan here joining the Rappahannock. Those who had partly disrobed put their clothing under their arms, shoes in their hands, and went hurrying along after the column in advance. These men, with their bare limbs, resembled the Scotch Highlanders in the British Army, but their modesty was put to the test; when about half-way to the other stream they passed a large, old-fashioned Virginia residence, with balconies above and below, and these filled with ladies of the surrounding country, visitors to see the soldiers pass. It was an amusing sight no less to the ladies of the house than to the men, to witness this long line of soldiers rushing by with their coat-tails beating a tattoo on their naked nether limbs. The other stream was not so wide, but equally as cold and deep.

General Kershaw, sitting on his horse at this point, amusing himself at the soldiers' plight, undertook to encourage and soothe their ruffled feelings by giving words of cheer. "Go ahead, boys," remarked the General, "and don't mind this; when I was in Mexico——" "But, General, it wasn't so cold in Mexico, nor did they fight war in winter, and a horse's legs are not so tender as a man's bare shins," were some of the answers given, and all took a merry laugh and went scudding away.

Passing over, we entered the famous Wilderness, soon to be made renowned by the clash of arms, where Lee and Hooker met and shook the surrounding country with the thunder of their guns a few months afterwards, and where Grant made the "echoes ring" and reverberate on the 5th and 6th of May, the year following. We found, too, the "Chancellor House," this lone, large, dismal-looking building standing alone in this Wilderness and surrounded on all sides by an almost impenetrable forest of scrubby oaks and tangled vines. The house was a large, old-fashioned hotel, situated on a cleared plateau, a piazza above and below, reaching around on three sides. It was called "Chancellorsville," but where the "ville" came in, or for what the structure was ever built, I am unable to tell. This place occupied a prominent place in the picture of the Battle of Chancellorsville, being for a time the headquarters of General Hooker, and around which the greater part of his cannon were placed. We took up camp in rear of Fredericksburg, about two miles south of the city.

While here we received into our brigade the Fifteenth South Carolina Regiment, commanded by Colonel DeSaussure, and the Third Battalion, composed of eight companies and commanded by Lieutenant Colonel Rice. As these are new additions, it will be necessary to give a brief sketch of their organization and movements prior to their connection with Kershaw's Brigade.

Soon after the battle of Bull Run or First Manassas, the Richmond Government made a call upon the different States for a new levy to meet the call of President Lincoln for three hundred thousand more troops to put down the Rebellion. The companies that were to compose the Fifteenth Regiment assembled at the old camping ground at Lightwood Knot Spring, three miles above Columbia. They were:

Company A	Captain Brown, Richland.
Company B	Captain Gist, Union.
Company C	Captain Lewie, Lexington.
Company D	Captain Warren, Kershaw.
Company E	Captain Davis, Fairfield.
Company F	Captain Boyd, Union.
Company G	Captain McKitchen, Williamsburg.
Company H	Captain Farr, Union.
Company I	Captain Koon, Lexington.
Company K	Captain Bird, ————

These names are given from the best information obtainable and may not be exactly correct, but as the fortunes of war soon made radical changes it is of little moment at this late date. These companies elected for their field officers:

Colonel	Wm. DeSaussure.
Lieutenant Colonel	Joseph Gist.
Major	————

The regiment remained in camp undergoing a thorough course of instruction until Hilton Head, on the coast of South Carolina, was threatened; then the Fifteenth was ordered in the field and hurried to that place, reaching it on the afternoon of the day before the battle of that name. The Fifteenth, with the Third Battalion and other State troops, was placed under the command of Brigadier General Drayton, also of South Carolina, and put in position. The next day, by some indiscretion of General Drayton, or so supposed at that time, the Fifteenth was placed in such position as to be greatly exposed to the heavy fire from the war vessels in the harbor. This caused the loss of some thirty or forty in killed and wounded. The slaughter would have been much greater had it not been for the courage and quick perception of Colonel DeSaussure in maneuvering them into a place of safety. After the battle the regiment lay for some time about Hardeesville and Bluffton doing guard and picket duty, still keeping up their course of daily drills. They were then sent to James Island, and were held in reserve at the battle of Secessionville. After the great Seven Days' Battles around Richmond it and the Third Battalion were ordered to Virginia and placed with a regiment from Alabama and one from Georgia in a brigade under General Drayton. They went into camp below Richmond as a part of a division commanded by Brigadier General D.R. Jones, in the corps commanded by Longstreet. When Lee began his march northward they broke camp on the 13th of August, and followed the lead of Longstreet to Gordonsville, and from thence on to Maryland. They were on the field during the bloody battle of Second Manassas, but not actually engaged, being held in the reserve line on the extreme right. At South Mountain they received their first baptism of fire in a battle with infantry. On the memorable 17th of September at Sharpsburg they were confirmed as veteran soldiers in an additional baptism of blood. However, as yet considered raw and undisciplined troops, they conducted themselves on each of these trying occasions like trained soldiers. Colonel DeSaussure was one of the most gallant and efficient officers that South Carolina ever produced. He was a Mexican War veteran and a born soldier. His attainments were such as fitted him for much higher position in the service than he had yet acquired. Had not the fortunes of war laid him low not many miles distant one year later, he would have shown, no doubt, as one of the brightest stars in the constellation of great Generals that South Carolina ever produced. After the return to Virginia Drayton's Brigade was broken up, and the Fifteenth and Third Battalion were assigned to the brigade of General J.B. Kershaw, and began its service in that organization on the heights of Fredericksburg.

The Third Battalion

I am indebted to Colonel W.G. Rice for a brief sketch of the Third Battalion, or as it was more generally known in the army, "James' Battalion," after its first commander, (who fell at South Mountain, Md.,) up to the time of joining the brigade:

"On the fall of Hilton Head and the occupation of Port Royal by the enemy, the Governor of South Carolina issued a call for volunteers for State service. Among the companies offering their services were four from Laurens County. Lieutenant Geo. S. James having resigned from the United States Army, and being personally known to several of the officers of said four companies, they united in forming a battalion and electing him Major. The companies became known thereafter as:

Company A	Captain W.G. Rice.
Company B	Captain J.G. Williams.
Company C	Captain J.M. Shumate.
Company D	Captain G.M. Gunnels.

"All of Laurens County, the organization being effected at Camp Hampton, near Columbia, November, 1861, and where Major James assumed command. In December the battalion was ordered to Charleston, and from thence to White Point, near the coast. Here the battalion was strengthened by three more companies, making it now a compound battalion and entitled to a Lieutenant Colonel and Major. The additional companies were:

Company E, from Laurens	Captain M.M. Hunter.
Company F, from Richland	Captain D.B. Miller.
Company G, from Fairfield	Captain A.P. Irby.

"Major James was promoted to Lieutenant Colonel, and Captain W.G. Rice, as senior Captain, made Major, while Lieutenant J.M. Townsend was raised to the grade of Captain in place of Major Rice.

"In April, 1862, a reorganization was ordered, and the troops enlisted in the Confederate States' service. Both Colonel James and Major Rice were elected to their former positions, with the following company commanders:

"J.M. Townsend Captain	Company A.
O.A. Watson Captain	Company B.
William Huggins Captain	Company C.
G.M. Gunnels Captain	Company D.
W.H. Fowler Captain	Company E.
D.B. Miller Captain	Company F.
B.M. Whitener Captain	Company G.

"Early in June the battalion was ordered to James' Island, arriving there two days before the battle of Secessionville, but not participating in it. A short while afterwards it was ordered to Richmond, and there remained until the great forward movement of General Lee's, which resulted in the Second Manassas Battle and the invasion of Maryland. The battalion was now brigaded with Philip's Georgia Legion, Fiftieth and Fifty-first Georgia, and Fifteenth South Carolina Regiments, and commanded by Brigadier General Drayton. The battalion was under fire at Waterloo Bridge and at Thoroughfare Gap, and the brigade held the extreme right of Lee's Army at the Second Manassas Battle, but was not seriously engaged. The topography of the country was such that while the incessant roar of artillery could be distinctly heard during the day, no infantry could be heard, and the extreme right did not hear of the result of the great battle until General Robert Toombs marched by and shouted to his fellow Georgians: 'Another great and glorious Bull Run.' After repeated marches and counter-marches during the day, night put an end to the bloody struggle, and the troops lay down to rest. A perfect tornado of shot and shell tore through the woods all around us until deep darkness fell and the enemy withdrew, leaving the entire field to the Confederates."

After resting for nearly a week at Frederick City, Md., the battalion, with the Fifteenth South Carolina and the Georgians of Drayton's Brigade, was ordered to re-enforce General D.H. Hill, who was guarding Lee's rear at Crompton's Gap, in South Mountain. Here the South Carolinians were for the first time thoroughly baptized with fire and blood, and in which the gallant Colonel James lost his life. Of this battle Colonel Rice says:

"Late in the evening of September 14th the brigade reached the battlefield and deployed in an old disused road that crossed the mountain some four hundred yards to the right of the turnpike. No enemy in sight. Failing to drive D.H. Hill from their front, the Federals made a detour and approached him by the flank. Two hundred yards from the road mentioned above was a belt of woods saddling the mountain, and at this point running parallel with the road. General Drayton, not seeing the enemy, ordered forward Captain Miller's Company as skirmishers to ascertain their whereabouts. Captain Miller had advanced but a short distance when he met the enemy in force. General Drayton ordered the command to forward and drive them from the woods. In the execution of this order some confusion arose, and a part of the brigade gave way, leaving the battalion in a very peculiar and isolated condition. There was a low rock fence running at right angles to the battle line, and behind this the battalion sought to protect itself, but it seemed and was in reality a deathtrap, for it presented its right flank to the enemy. It thus became only a question of a very short time when it must either leave the field or surrender. Right nobly did this little band of heroes hold their ground against overwhelming numbers, and their front was never successfully approached; but as both flanks were so mercilessly assailed, a short time was sufficient to almost annihilate them. Colonel James was twice admonished by his second in command of his untenable position, and that death or surrender was inevitable if he persisted in holding his ground, but without avail. The true soldier that he was preferred death to yielding. Just as night approached and firing began to cease, Colonel James was pierced through the breast with a minnie ball, from the effects of which he soon died."

Colonel Rice was dangerously wounded and left on the field for dead. But recovering consciousness, he found himself within the enemy's lines, that portion of his command nearest him having been withdrawn some distance in the rectifying of the lines. Colonel Rice escaped capture by crawling in a deep wash in the road, and was rescued by some skirmishers who were advancing to establish a new line. Colonel Rice gives this information in a foot-note:

> "The road in which the brigade was stationed was as all roads crossing hills, much washed and worn down, thus giving the troops therein stationed the advantage of first class breastworks. I do not know that the Fifteenth South Carolina and the other portion of the brigade were thus sheltered—have heard indeed that all were not—but within my vision the position was most admirable, now almost impregnable with good troops to defend it. To leave such a position was suicidal, especially when we were ordered to march through open ground and attack the enemy, sheltered behind trees and rocks. This is my estimate at least, and the result proved most disastrous to the brigade and General Drayton himself, as he was soon afterwards relieved of his command."

It has been the aim of the writer of this History not to criticize, condemn, nor make any comments upon the motives or acts of any of the officers whom he should have cause to mention, and he somewhat reluctantly gives space to Colonel Rice's stricture of General Drayton. It is difficult for officers in subaltern position to understand all that their superiors do and do not. The Generals, from their positions, can see differently from those in the line amid the smoke of battle, and they often give commands hard to comprehend from minor officers' point of view. General Drayton was an accomplished and gallant officer, and while he might have been rash and reckless at South Mountain, still it is hard to conceive his being relieved of his command through the charge of "rashness," especially when his brigade held up successfully for so long a time one of the most stubborn battles of the war.

At the Battle of Sharpsburg or Antietam, the little remnant of the battalion was again engaged. On Lee's return to Virginia, and during the last days of November or early in December, the Third Battalion and the Fifteenth Regiment were transferred to Kershaw's Brigade, and from thence on it will be treated as a part of the old First Brigade. At Fredericksburg, on the day of the great battle, the battalion held the railroad cut running from near the city to the right of Mayree's Hill, and was well protected by a bluff and the railroad, consequently did not suffer as great a loss as the other regiments of the brigade.

COLONEL GEORGE S. JAMES

The first commander of the Third Battalion, and who fell at South Mountain, was born in Laurens County, in 1829. He was the second son of John S. James, a prominent lawyer of Laurens, who, meeting with misfortune and losing a handsome fortune, attempted to retain it by moving to Columbia and engaging in mercantile pursuits. This he followed with success. Colonel George S. James received his early education in the academies of the up-country. While yet a youth some seventeen years of age, war with Mexico was declared, and his patriotic and chivalric spirit sent him at once to the ranks of the Palmetto Regiment, and he shared the triumphs and fortunes of that command to the close of the war.

After his return to his native State, he entered the South Carolina College, along with many others, who in after years made their State and themselves immortal by their fiery zeal in the War of Secession. At the college young James was a great favorite of all who knew him best, and while not a close student of text-books, he was an extensive reader, always delighting his friends with wit and humor. The student life, however, failed to satisfy his adventurous spirit, and wandering away to the far distant West, seeking adventure or congenial pursuits, he received a commission of Lieutenant in the United States Army.

The storm cloud of war, so long hovering over the land, was now about to burst, and Lieutenant James seeing separation and perhaps war inevitable, resigned his commission, and hastened to offer his sword to his native State. He commanded a battery at Fort Johnson, on James' Island, and shared with General Ruffin the honor of firing the first gun at Fort Sumter, a shot that was to electrify the world and put in motion two of the grandest and mightiest armies of all times.

CHAPTER 13

Battle of Fredericksburg

A portion of the Federal Army had preceded Lee, reaching the heights opposite Fredericksburg two days before the arrival of Kershaw's Brigade and the other parts of the division. The Federals had been met by a small body of Confederates doing outpost duty there and held at bay till the coming of Longstreet with his five divisions. General Lee was not long in determining the route Burnsides had selected and hurried Jackson on, and placed him some miles to our right, near Hamilton's Crossing, on the Richmond and Fredericksburg Railroad. When Burnsides became aware of the mighty obstacle of Lee's battalions between him and his goal, the deep, sluggish river separating the two armies, he realized the trouble that lay in his path. He began fortifying the ridges running parallel to and near the river, and built a great chain of forts along "Stafford Heights," opposite Fredericksburg. In these forts he mounted one hundred and thirty-seven guns, forty being siege pieces brought down from Washington by way of the Potomac and Acquia Creek, and lined the entire range of hills with his heaviest and long-distanced field batteries. These forts and batteries commanded the river and plain beyond, as well as every height and elevation on the Southern side. The range of hills on the opposite side were much higher and more commanding than those on the Southern side, still Lee began fortifying Taylor's, Mayree's, and Lee's Heights, and all the intervening hills also, by building forts and heavy redoubts, with protected embrasures on the flanks. Between these hills and along their crests the infantry threw up light earthworks. It could not be said that ours was a fortified position in any sense, only through natural barriers. There is a plain of a half to a mile in width between the river and the range to the South, commencing at Taylor's Hill, half a mile above the city, and widening as it diverges from the river below, terminating in a broken plateau down near Hamilton's Crossing. The highlands on the opposite side come rather precipitous to the water's edge. Along the banks, on either side, were rifle pits, in which were kept from three to five pickets, and on our side a brigade was stationed night and day in the city as a support to the videttes guarding the river front. These pickets were directed to prevent a crossing at all hazards until the troops at camp in the rear were all in position in front of Fredericksburg. Stuart, with the body of his cavalry, guarded the river and country on our right below Jackson, while Hampton kept a lookout at the crossings above on the left of Longstreet.

On the morning of the 11th, at 3 o'clock, when all was still and the soldiers fast asleep, they were rudely aroused from their slumbers by the deep boom of a cannon away to the front and across the river. Scarcely had the sound of the first gun died away than another report thundered out on the stillness of that December night, its echo reverberating from hill to hill and down along the river side. These sounds were too ominous to be mistaken; they were the signal guns that were to put in motion these two mighty armies. "Fall in" was the word given, and repeated from hill to hill and camp to camp. Drums beat the long roll at every camp, while far below and above the blast of the bugle called the troopers to "boots and saddle." Couriers dashed headlong in the sombre darkness from one General's headquarters to another's. Adjutants' and Colonels' orderlies were rushing from tent to tent, arousing the officers and men to arms, and giving instructions for the move.

I can remember well the sharp, distant voice of Adjutant Y.J. Pope on that morning, coming down the line of the officers' tents and calling out to each as he came opposite: "Captain ——, get your company ready to move at once."

Under such orders, companies have that same rivalry to be first on the parade ground as exists among fire companies in towns and cities when the fire bell rings. We were all soon in line and marching with a hasty step in the direction of the breastworks above the city, Kershaw taking position immediately to the right of the Telegraph Road. This is a public highway leading into the city, curving in a semi-circle around Mayree Hill on the left. From this road the hill rises on the west and north in a regular bluff—a stone wall of five feet in height bordering either side of the road. "Deep Run," a small ravine, runs between the hill on which Kershaw was stationed and that of Mayree's. Daylight was yet some hours off when we took position, but we could hear the rattle of the guns of Barksdale's Mississippians, whose turn it was to be on picket in the city, driving off the enemy's pontoon corps and bridge builders.

The city was almost deserted, General Lee advising the citizens to leave their homes as soon as it became apparent that a battle would be fought here. Still a few, loath to leave their all to the ravages of an army, decided to remain and trust to fate. But soon after the firing along the river began, we saw groups of women and children and a few old men in the glim twilight of the morning rushing along the roads out from the city as fast as their feeble limbs and tender feet could carry them, hunting a safe retreat in the backwoods until the cloud of war broke or passed over. Some were carrying babes in their arms, others dragging little children along by the hands, with a few articles of bedding or wearing apparel under their arms or thrown over their shoulders. The old men tottered along in the rear, giving words of comfort and cheer to the excited and frightened women and little ones. It was a sickening sight to see these helpless and inoffensive people hurrying away from the dangers of battle in the chilly morning of December, seeking some safe haunt in the backwoods, yet they bore it all without murmur or complaint.

Anderson's Division of Longstreet's Corps rested on the river on the extreme left, at Taylor's Hill; then Ransom's along the crest of the ridge between Taylor's and Mayree's, and McLaws' from his left across Deep Run Valley and along the ridge to Lee's Hill, where Pickett was posted; Hood extending from Pickett's right, touching the left of the troops of Jackson's Corps. Three of Cobb's regiments and one from North Carolina were posted behind the stone wall lining the sunken road, while two of Cooke's North Carolina regiments were on the crest of Mayree's Hill overlooking Cobb. Kershaw's Brigade, with the Third South Carolina on the left, was resting on the ridge running at right angles to the Telegraph Road, the left resting on the road, the Second South Carolina next, and so on to the left of Semmes' Brigade. Barksdale being in the city on picket, was relieved and placed in reserve.

As soon as the signal guns gave evidence of an impending battle, D.H. Hill, who had been sent on detached service down the river, was recalled and placed in line with the other portion of Jackson's Corps. Jackson had his entire force closely massed in the woodland around Hamilton's Crossing and along the Richmond and Fredericksburg Railroad, one mile from the river. The Light Division of A.P. Hill occupied the front line, with a heavy battery of fourteen guns on his right, supported by Archer's Brigade; then Lane's and Fender's in front, with Gregg's and Thomas' in reserve. Behind the Light Division lay Early on the right, Taliaferro on the left, with D.H. Hill in rear of all along the Mine Road, the right of these divisions resting on Hamilton's Crossing. Hood occupied the valley between Lee's Hill and the highland around Hamilton's Crossing; Pickett on the ridge between Hood and McLaws; Stuart's Cavalry ran at right angles to the infantry line from Hamilton's Crossing to the river, hemming the Federal Army in the plain between Hamilton's Crossing and Taylor's Hill above the city, a space three miles long by one wide.

Before day the enemy's pontoon corps came cautiously to the river and began operations at laying down the bridge, but the pickets in the rifle pits kept them off for a time by their steady fire. The manner of putting down army bridges is much more simple and rapid than the old country mode of building. Large boats are loaded on long-coupled wagons, the boats filled with plank for flooring and cross beams, with a large iron ring in the rear end of each boat, through which a stout rope is to run, holding them at equal distance when in the water. When all is ready the boats are launched at equal distance so that the beams can reach, then pushed out in the stream, and floated around in a semi-circle, until the opposite bank is reached, the rope fastened to trees on either bank, cross pieces are laid, the flooring put down, and the bridge is ready for crossing.

After making several ineffectual attempts in placing the bridge, the destructive fire of Barksdale's Riflemen forcing them back, the enemy attempted the bold project of filling the boats with armed soldiers, pushing out in the stream, and fighting their way across, under cover of their artillery fire. While the dense fog was yet hanging heavily over the waters, one hundred and forty guns, many siege pieces, were opened upon the deserted city and the men along the water front. The roar from the cannon-crowned battlements shook the very earth. Above and below us seemed to vibrate as from the effects of a mighty upheaval, while the shot and shell came whizzing and shrieking overhead, looking like a shower of falling meteors. For more than an hour did this seething volcano vomit iron like hail upon the city and the men in the rifle pits, the shells and shot from the siege guns tearing through the houses and plunging along the streets, and ricocheting to the hills above. Not a house nor room nor chimney escaped destruction. Walls were perforated, plastering and ceiling fell, chimneys tottering or spreading over yards and out into the streets. Not a place of safety, save the cellars and wells, and in the former some were forced to take refuge. Yet through all this, the brave Mississippians stood and bravely fought the bridge builders, beating them back till orders were given to retire. They had accomplished the purpose of delaying the enemy's crossing until our troops were in position. The Federals now hurried over in swarms, by thousands and tens of thousands, and made their way down the river, stationing a strong cordon of guards around the point of landing. The space between was soon a seething mass of humanity, the houses and streets crowded to overflowing. A second bridge was laid a mile below at the mouth of Deep Run, and here a continuous stream of all arms were soon pouring over. General Kershaw rode along our lines, encouraging the men, urging them to stand steadfast, assuring them that there was to be neither an advance nor retreat, that we were but to hold our ground, and one of the greatest victories of the war would be gained. How prophetic his words! All during the day and night the deep rumbling sound of the long wagon trains, artillery, and cavalry could be heard crossing the pontoon bridges above and below.

The next morning, the 12th, as the fog lifted, Stafford Heights and the inclines above the river were one field of blue. Great lines of infantry, with waving banners, their bright guns and bayonets glittering in the sunlight, all slowly marching down the steep inclines between the heights and the river on over the bridges, then down the river side at a double-quick to join their comrades of the night before. These long, swaying lines, surging in and out among the jutting of the hillsides beyond, down to the river, over and down among the trees and bushes near the water, resembled some monster serpent dragging its "weary length along." Light batteries of artillery came dashing at break-neck speed down the hillsides, their horses rearing and plunging as if wishing to take the river at a leap. Cavalry, too, with their heavy-bodied Norman horses, their spurs digging the flanks, sabres bright and glistening and dangling at their sides, came at a canter, all seeming anxious to get over and meet the death and desolation awaiting them. Long trains of ordnance wagons, with their black oilcloth covering, the supply trains and quartermaster departments all following in the wake of their division or corps headquarters, escorts, and trains. All spread out over the hills and in the gorges lay men by the thousands, awaiting their turn to move. Not a shot nor shell to mar or disturb "the even tenor of their way." Bands of music enlivened the scene by their inspiring strains, and when some national air, or specially martial piece, would be struck up, shouts and yells rended the air for miles, to be answered by counter yells from the throats of fifty thousand "Johnny Rebs," as the Southern soldiers were called. The Confederate bands were not idle, for as soon as a Federal band would cease playing, some of the Southern bands would take up the refrain, and as the notes, especially Dixie, would be wafted over the water and hills, the "blue coats" would shout, sing, and dance—hats and caps went up, flags waved in the breeze—so delighted were they at the sight and sound of Dixie. The whole presented more the spectacle of a holiday procession, or a gala day, rather than the prelude to the most sanguinary battle of modern times.

The night following was cold, and a biting wind was blowing. Only a few days before a heavy snow had fallen, and in some places it still remained banked up in shaded corners. To those who had to stand picket out in the plain between the armies the cold was fearful. The enemy had no fires outside of the city, and their sufferings from cold must have been severe. My company, from the Third, as well as one from each of the other regiments, were on picket duty, posted in an open cornfield in the plain close to the enemy, near enough, in fact, to hear voices in either camp—with no fire, and not allowed to speak above a whisper. The night became so intensely cold just before day that the men gathered cornstalks and kindled little fires along the beat, and at early dawn we were withdrawn.

All knew full well, as the day preceding had passed without any demonstrations, only maneuvering, this day, the 13th, would be a day of battle. A heavy fog, as usual, rose from the river and settled along the plains and hillsides, so much so that objects could not be distinguished twenty paces. However, the least noise could be heard at a great distance. Activity in the Federal camp was noticed early in the morning. Officers could be heard giving commands, wagons and artillery moving to positions. At half past ten the fog suddenly lifted, and away to our right and near the river great columns of men were moving, marching and counter-marching. These were in front of A.P. Hill, of Jackson's Corps. In front of us and in the town all was still and quiet as a city of the dead. The great siege guns from beyond the river on Stafford Heights opened the battle by a dozen or more shells screaming through the tree tops and falling in Jackson's camp. From every fort soon afterwards a white puff of smoke could be seen, then a vivid flash and a deafening report, telling us that the enemy was ready and waiting. From the many field batteries between Jackson and the river the smoke curled up around the tree tops, and shell went crashing through the timbers. Our batteries along the front of Longstreet's Corps opened their long-ranged guns on the redoubts beyond the river, and our two siege guns on Lee's Hill, just brought up from Richmond, paid special attention to the columns moving to the assault of A.P. Hill. For one hour the earth and air seemed to tremble and shake beneath the shock of three hundred guns, and the bursting of thousands of shells overhead, before and behind us, looked like bursting stars on a frolic. The activity suddenly ceases in front of Hill, and the enemy's infantry lines move to the front. First the skirmishers meet, and their regular firing tells the two armies that they are near together. Then the skirmish fire gives way to the deep, sullen roar of the line of battle. From our position, some three hundred yards in rear and to the right of Mayree's Hill, we could see the Union columns moving down the river, our batteries raking them with shot and shell. In crossing an old unfinished railroad cut the two siege guns played upon the flank with fearful effect. Huddling down behind the walls of the cut to avoid the fire in front, the batteries from Mayree's and in the fields to the right enfiladed the position, the men rushing hither and thither and falling in heaps from the deadly fire in front and flank. Jackson has been engaged in a heavy battle for nearly an hour, when suddenly in our front tens of thousands of "blue coats" seemed to spring up out of the earth and make for our lines. Near one-half of the army had concealed themselves in the city and along the river banks, close to the water's edge. The foliage of the trees and the declivity of the ground having hidden them thus far from view. From out of the streets and from behind walls and houses men poured, as if by some magical process or super-human agency, and formed lines of battle behind a little rise in the ground, near the canal. But in a few moments they emerged from their second place of protection and bore down upon the stone wall, behind which stood Cobb's Georgians and a Regiment of North Carolinians. When midway between the canal and stone fence, they met an obstruction—a plank fence—but this did not delay them long. It was soon dashed to the ground and out of their way, but their men were falling at every step from Cobb's infantry fire and grape and canister from the Washington Artillery of New Orleans on the hill. They never neared the wall nor did they take more time than to fire a volley or two before they fled the field. This retreating column of Franklin's met that of Hancock's, formed, and on its way to try issues with the troops behind the stone wall, Longstreet now saw what had never been considered before—that Burnsides was determined to possess himself of the key to Lee's position, "Mayree's Hill," in front of which was the stone wall. He ordered the two regiments of North Carolinians that were posted on the crest of the hill down behind the stone wall, to the left of Cobb and Kershaw, to reinforce the position with his brigade.

The Third Regiment being ordered to the top of Mayree's Hill, Colonel Nance, at the head of his regiment, entered the Telegraph Road, and down this the men rushed, followed by the Second, led by Colonel Kennedy, under one of the heaviest shellings the troops ever experienced. This two hundred yards' stretch of road was in full view and range of the heavy gun batteries on Stafford Heights, and as the men scattered out along and down the road, the shells passed, plowing in the road, bursting overhead, or striking the earth and ricocheting to the hills far in the rear. On reaching the ravine, at the lower end of the incline, the Third Regiment was turned to the left and up a by-road to the plateau in rear of the "Mayree Mansion." The house tops in the city were lined with sharpshooters, and from windows and doors and from behind houses the deadly missiles from the globe-sighted rifles made sad havoc in our ranks.

When the Third reached the top of the plateau it was in column of fours, and Colonel Nance formed line of battle by changing "front forward on first company." This pretty piece of tactics was executed while under the galling fire from the artillery and sharpshooters, but was as perfect as on dress parade. The regiment lined up, the right resting on the house and extending along a dull road to the next street leading into the city. We had scarcely gotten in position before Nance, Rutherford, and Maffett, the three field officers, had fallen. Colonel Kennedy, with the Second, passed over the left of the plateau and down the street on our left, and at right angles with our line, being in a position to give a sweeping fire to the flank of the columns of assault against the stone fence. From the preparation and determination made to break through the line here, Kershaw ordered Lieutenant Colonel Bland, with the Seventh, Colonel Henagan, with the Eighth, and Colonel DeSaussure, with the Fifteenth, to double-up with Cobb's men, and to hold their position "at the sacrifice of every man of their commands."

All of the different regiments, with the exception of the Third South Carolina, had good protection in the way of stone walls, this being the sole occasion that any of Kershaw's troops had been protected by breastworks of any kind during the whole war. The Second was in a sunken road leading to the city, walled on either side with granite, the earth on the outside being leveled up with the top. The maneuvering into position had taken place while Hancock was making the first assault upon the wall defended by Cobb. Howard was now preparing to make the doubtful attempt at taking the stronghold with the point of the bayonet, and without firing a gun. But with such men as the Georgians, South Carolinians, and North Carolinians in their front, the task proved too Herculean. Howard moved to the battle in beautiful style, their line almost solid and straight, their step in perfect unison with the long, moving columns, their guns carried at a trail, and the stars and stripes floating proudly above their heads. The shot and shell plunging through their ranks from the hills above, the two siege guns on Lee's Hill now in beautiful play, the brass pieces of the Washington Artillery firing with grape and shrapnel—but all this made no break nor halt in that long line of blue. The double column behind the stone wall and the Third South Carolina on the crest of the Hill met them in front with a cool and steady fire, while the Second South Carolina directed its attention to the flank. But the boldest and stoutest hearts could not withstand this withering blast of bullets and shells without returning the fire. The enemy opened upon us a terrific fire, both from the columns in front and from the sharpshooters in the housetops in the city. After giving us battle as long as human endurance could bear the ordeal, they, like their companions before them, fled in confusion.

Before making the direct attack, Howard attempted a diversion by endeavoring to turn Cobb's left. Passing out into the plain above the city, he was met by some of Cooke's North Carolinians, and there around the sacred tomb of Mary Washington was a hand to hand encounter between some New York and Massachusetts troops and those from the Pine Tree State. Sons of the same ancestry, sons of sires who fought with the "Father of his Country" in the struggle for the nation's independence, now fighting above the grave of the mother for its dissolution! Thrice were the Confederates driven from the position, but as often retaken, and at last held at the point of the bayonet by the hardy sons of North Carolina.

The battle, grand and awful in its sublimity, raged from the morning's opening till two o'clock, without the least abatement along the whole line. From the extreme right to our left at Taylor's Hill was a sea of fire. But Mayree's Hill was the center, around which all the other battles revolved. It was the key to Lee's position, and this had become the boon of contention. It was in the taking of Mayree's Hill and the defeat of the troops defending it that the North was pouring out its river of blood. Both commanders were still preparing to stake their all upon this hazard of the die—the discipline of the North against the valor of the South.

Our loss was heavy, both in officers and men. The brave, chivalric Cobb, of Georgia, had fallen. Of the Third South Carolina, Colonel Nance, Lieutenant Colonel Rutherford, and Major Maffett had all been severely wounded in the early part of the engagement. Captain Hance, while commanding, fell pierced through the heart. Then the next in command, Captain Summer, met a similar fate; then Captain Foster. Captain Nance, the junior Captain in the regiment, retained the command during the continuance of the fight, although painfully wounded. The dead of the Third Regiment lay in heaps, like hogs in a slaughter pen. The position of the Second Regiment gave it great advantage over the advancing column. From a piazza in rear of the sunken road, Colonel Kennedy posted himself, getting a better view, and to better direct the firing Lieutenant Colonel William Wallace remained with the men in the road, and as the column of assault reached the proper range, he ordered a telling fire on the enemy's flank. Men in the road would load the guns for those near the wall, thus keeping up a continual fire, and as the enemy scattered over the plain in their retreat, then was the opportunity for the Second and Third, from their elevated positions and better view, to give them such deadly parting salutes. The smoke in front of the stone wall became so dense that the troops behind it could only fire at the flashing of the enemy's guns. From the Third's position, it was more dangerous for its wounded to leave the field than remain on the battle line, the broad, level plateau in rear almost making it suicidal to raise even as high as a stooping posture.

From the constant, steady, and uninterrupted roll of musketry far to the right, we knew Jackson was engaged in a mighty struggle. From the early morning's opening the noise of his battle had been gradually bearing to the rear. He was being driven from position to position, and was meeting with defeat and possibly disaster. From the direction of his fire our situation was anything but assuring.

General Meade, of the Federal Army, had made the first morning attack upon the Light Brigade, under A.P. Hill, throwing that column in confusion and driving it back upon the second line. These troops were not expecting the advance, and some had their guns stacked. The heavy fog obscured the Federal lines until they were almost within pistol shot. When it was discovered that an enemy was in their front (in fact some thought them their friends), in this confusion of troops a retreat was ordered to the second line. In this surprise and disorder South Carolina lost one of her most gifted sons, and the South a brave and accomplished officer, Brigadier General Maxey Gregg.

General Hood, on Hill's left, failing to move in time to give him the support expected, the whole of Jackson's Corps was forced to retire. But the tide at length begins to turn. Meade is driven from the field. Division after division was rushed to the front to meet and check Jackson's steady advance. Cannon now boom as never before heard, even the clear ringing of Pelham's little howitzers, of Stuart's Cavalry, could be heard above the thunder of the big guns, telling us that Stuart was putting his horse artillery in the balance. His brave artillery leader was raking the enemy's flank as they fell back on the river. In our front new troops were being marshalled and put in readiness to swell the human holocaust before the fatal wall.

Franklin, Hancock, and Howard had made unsuccessful attempts upon this position, leaving their wounded and dead lying in heaps and wind rows from the old railroad cut to the suburbs. Now Sturgis, of the Ninth Corps, was steadily advancing. The Washington Artillery, from New Orleans, occupying the most conspicuous and favorable position on the right of the "Mayree House," had exhausted their shot and shell. The infantry in the road and behind the wall, Cobb's and part of Kershaw's, were nearly out of ammunition, and during the last charge had been using that of their dead and wounded. Calls were made on all sides for "more ammunition," both from the artillery and infantry. Orders and details had been sent to the ordnance trains to bring supplies to the front. But the orders had miscarried, or the trains were too far distant, for up to three o'clock no sign of replenishment was in sight. The hearts of the exhausted men began to fail them—the batteries silent, the infantry short of ammunition, while a long line of blue was making rapid strides towards us in front.

But now all hearts were made glad by the sudden rush of Alexander's Battery coming to the relief of the Washington Artillery. Down the Telegraph Road the battery came, their horses rearing and plunging, drivers burying the points of their spurs deep into the flanks of the foaming steeds; riders in front bending low upon the saddle bows to escape the shells that now filled the air, or plowing up the earth beneath the horses hoofs; the men on the caissons clinging with a death-like grip to retain their seats, the great heavy wheels spinning around like mad and bounding high in the air; while the officers riding at the side of this charging column of artillerists, shouted at the top of their voices, giving directions to the leaders. Down this open and exposed stretch of road, up over the plateau, then wheel to the right, they make a rush through the gauntlet that separates them from the fort in which stood the Washington Artillery. Over the dead and dying the horses leap and plunge, dragging the cannon and ammunition chests—they enter the fort at a gallop. Swinging into line, their brass pieces are now belching forth grape and canister into the ranks of the advancing columns. All this takes place in less time than it takes to record it. The bold dash and beautiful piece of evolution so excite the admiration of all who witnessed it, that a yell went up that drowns for a time the heavy baying of the siege guns on Stafford Heights.

About this time Jackson seems to have reached his limit of retreat, and was now forging steadily to the front, regaining every inch of the lost ground of the morning. The Federal Commander-in-Chief, seeing the stubborn resistance he is met with in front of the city, and Jackson's gray lines pressing his left back upon the river, began to feel the hopelessness of his battle, and sent orders to Franklin to attack Jackson with his entire force. Hooker was to reinforce Sumner on the right, the latter to take the stone wall and the heights beyond before night. Sturgis had met the fate of those who had assaulted before him. Now Getty and Griffin were making frantic efforts to reach the wall. Griffin had his men concealed and protected in the wet, marshy bed of the old canal. He now undertook to accomplish that which Howard had attempted in the morning, and failed—the feat of taking the stone walls with empty guns.

In this column of assault was the famous Meager's Irish Brigade, of New York,—all Irishmen, but undoubtedly the finest body of troops in the Federal Army. When the signal for advance was given, from out of their hiding places they sprang—from the canal, the bushes on the river bank, the side streets in the city, one compact row of glittering bayonets came—in long battle lines. General Kershaw, seeing the preparation made for this final and overwhelming assault upon our jaded troops, sent Captain Doby, of his staff, along our lines with orders to hold our position at all hazards, even at the point of the bayonet.

As the rifle balls from the housetops and shells from the batteries along the river banks sang their peculiar death notes overhead and around us, this brave and fearless officer made the entire length of the line, exhorting, entreating, and urging the men to redoubled efforts. How Captain Doby escaped death is little less than miraculous.

The casualties of battle among the officers and the doubling up process of the men behind the wall caused all order of organization to be lost sight of, and each man loaded and fired as he saw best. The men in the road, even the wounded, crowded out from the wall by force of number, loaded the guns for the more fortunate who had places, and in many instances three and four men loaded the guns for one, passing them to those who were firing from the top of the stone fence. Each seemed to fight on his own responsibility, and with the same determined spirit to hold the wall and the heights above. Each felt as if the safety of the army depended upon his exertions alone.

With a firm and elastic step this long, swaying line of Irishmen moved to the assault with as much indifference apparently to their fate as "sheep going to the shambles." Not a shot was fired from this advancing column, while the shells from our batteries cut swath after swath through their ranks, only to be closed again as if by some mechanical means; colors fall, but rise and float again, men bounding forward and eagerly grasping the fallen staff, indifferent of the fate that awaited them. Officers are in front, with drawn swords flashing in the gleam of the fading sunlight, urging on their men to still greater deeds of prowess, and by their individual courage set examples in heroism never before witnessed on this continent. The assault upon Mayree's Hill by the Irish Brigade and their compatriots will go down in history as only equalled by the famous ride of the "Six Hundred at Hohenlinden," and the "Charge of the Light Brigade at Balaclava." They forge their way forward over the heap of dead and dying that now strew the plain, nearer to the deadly wall than any of the troops before them. It began to look for the moment as if their undaunted courage would succeed, but the courage of the defenders of Mayree's Hill seemed to increase in ardour and determination in proportion to that of the enemy. The smoke and flame of their battle is now less than one hundred paces from the wall, but the odds are against them, and they, too, had to finally yield to the inevitable and leave the field in great disorder.

From both sides hopes and prayers had gone up that this charge would prove the last attempt to break our lines. But Humphries met the shattered columns with a fresh advance. Those who were marching to enter this maelstrom of carnage were entreated and prayed to by all of those who had just returned from the sickening scene not to enter this death trap, and begged them not to throw away their lives in the vain attempt to accomplish the impossible. But Humphries, anxious of glory for himself and men, urged on by the imperative orders from his Commander-in-Chief, soon had his men on the march to the "bloody wall." But as the sun dropped behind the hills in our rear, the scene that presented itself in the fading gloom of that December day was a plain filled with the dead and dying—a living stream of flying fugitives seeking shelter from the storm of shot and shell by plunging over the precipitous banks of the river, or along the streets and protecting walls of the city buildings.

Jackson had pressed all in his front back to the water's edge, while his batteries, with those of Stuart's, were still throwing shells into the huddled, panic-stricken, and now thoroughly vanquished army of the enemy.

That night the Federal Commander-in-Chief sat in his tent alone, and around him the groans of the wounded and the agonizing wails of the dying greet his ear—the gentle wind singing a requiem to his dead. He nursed alone the bitter consciousness of the total defeat of his army, now a scattered mass—a skeleton of its former greatness—while the flower of the Northern chivalry lie sleeping the sleep of death on the hills and plains round about. His country and posterity would charge him with all the responsibility of defeat, and he felt that his brief command of the once grand and mighty Army of the Potomac was now at an end. Sore and bitter recollections!

Burnsides had on the field one hundred and thirty-two thousand and seventeen men; of these one hundred and sixteen thousand six hundred and eighty-three were in line of battle. Lee had upon the field and ready for action sixty-nine thousand three hundred and ninety-one infantry and artillery, and about five thousand cavalry. Burnsides had three hundred and seventy pieces of field artillery and forty siege guns mounted on Stafford's Heights. Lee had three hundred and twelve pieces of field and heavy artillery, with two siege guns, both exploding, one in the early part of the day.

The enemy's loss was twelve thousand six hundred and fifty-three, of which at least eight thousand fell in front of the stone wall. It has been computed by returns made since that in the seven different charges there were engaged at least twenty-five thousand infantry alone in the assaults against the stone wall, defended by not more than four thousand men, exclusive of artillery. Lee's entire loss was five thousand three hundred and twenty-two killed, wounded, and missing; and one of the strangest features of this great battle, one in which so many men of all arms were engaged, the enormous loss of life on both sides, and the close proximity of such a large body of cavalry, the returns of the battle only give thirteen wounded and none killed of the entire cavalry force on the Confederate side.

The men who held the stone wall and Mayree's Hill were three regiments of Cooke's North Carolina Brigade; the Sixteenth Georgia, Colonel Bryan; the Eighteenth Georgia, Lieutenant Colonel Ruff; the Twenty-fourth Georgia, Colonel McMillan; the Cobb Legion and Philip Legion, Colonel Cook, of General T.R.R. Cobb's Brigade; the Second South Carolina, Colonel Kennedy; the Third South Carolina, Colonel Nance, Lieutenant Colonel Rutherford, Major Maffett, Captains Summer, Hance, Foster, and Nance; the Seventh South Carolina, Lieutenant Colonel Bland; the Eighth South Carolina, Colonel Henagan and Major Stackhouse; the Fifteenth South Carolina, Colonel DeSaussure; the Third Battalion, Major Rice, of Kershaw's Brigade; the Washington Battery, of New Orleans, and Alexander's Battery, from Virginia. The brigades from Hood's and Pickett's Divisions, Jenkins, of South Carolina, being from the latter, were sent to the support of McLaws, at Mayree's Hill, and only acted as reserve and not engaged.

The next day, as if by mutual consent, was a day of rest. The wounded were gathered in as far as we were able to reach them. The enemy's wounded lay within one hundred yards of the stone wall for two days and nights, and their piteous calls for help and water were simply heart-rending. Whenever one of our soldiers attempted to relieve the enemy lying close under our wall, he would be fired upon by the pickets and guards in the house tops.

On the night of the 15th, the Federal Army, like strolling Arabs, "folded their tents and silently stole away." The 16th was given up entirely to the burial of the dead. In the long line of pits, dug as protection for the enemy while preparing for a charge, these putrefying bodies were thrown headlong, pell mell, like the filling of blind ditches with timbers. One Confederate would get between the legs of the dead enemy, take a foot in either hand, then two others would each grasp an arm, and drag at a run the remains of the dead enemy and heave it over in the pit. In this way these pits or ditches were filled almost to a level of the surface, a little dirt thrown over them, there to remain until the great United States Government removed them to the beautiful park around Mayree's Heights. There to this day, and perhaps for all time, sleep the "blue and the gray," while the flag so disastrously beaten on that day now floats in triumph over all.

It must be said to the credit of General Burnsides, that the responsibility for this disastrous battle should not rest upon his shoulders. He felt his incapacity for handling so great a body of troops. Again and again he wrote the authorities in Washington protesting against the command being given him. "I am unable to handle so great an army." He wrote his chief, but in vain. The fiat had gone forth, "Go and crush Lee," and the result was to have been expected.

CHAPTER 14

Incidents of the Battle

The Battle of Fredericksburg was not the most desperate nor bloody of the war, nor was it so fruitful of events as others in its bearing on future results. Really neither side gained nor lost any great advantage; nor was the battle any more to the Confederate side than a great victory barren of ulterior results; the loss to the Federals no more than the loss of a number of men and the lowering of the morale among the troops. Within a day or two both armies occupied the same positions as before the battle. Not wishing to attempt any invidious comparisons or reflections upon troops in wars of other periods, but for the information of those who are not conversant with the magnitude of the Civil War, as compared with the Revolution and Mexican War, I will here give a few statistics. The reader then can draw his own conclusions as to the sanguinary effects and extent of some of our battles. Of course the different kinds of weapons used in the late war—their deadly effect, long range, better mode of firing—will have to be considered in comparison to the old.

As the Revolutionary War was more of a guerilla than actual war, I will speak more directly of the Mexican War. It will be noticed the difference in the killed to the wounded was far out of proportion in favor of the latter. This I attribute to the smallness of the gun's calibre, and in many instances buck-shot were used in connection with larger balls by the soldiers of the old wars, while the Mexicans used swords and lances, as well as pistols. During the three days' battle at Molino del Rey, Chapultepec, and the storming of the City of Mexico, considered the most bloody and sanguinary of that war, the four divisions of Scott's Army, of two thousand each, lost as follows: Pillow lost one officer killed and fourteen wounded, twenty-one privates killed and ninety-seven wounded. Worth lost two officers killed and nine wounded, twenty-three privates killed and ninety-five wounded. Quitman lost four officers killed and thirty wounded, thirty-seven privates killed and two hundred and thirty-seven wounded. Smith's Brigade, with Quitman, lost ten officers wounded and none killed, twenty-four privates killed and one hundred and twenty-six wounded. Twigg's Division lost three officers killed and twelve wounded, fifteen privates killed and seventy-seven wounded. This, with some few missing, making a grand total loss, out of Scott's Army of nine to ten thousand men, of between six hundred and fifty and seven hundred killed, wounded, and missing—a number that Kershaw's Brigade alone frequently lost in three or four hours.

The heaviest casualties in the three days' battle of Mexico in regiments were in the Palmetto Regiment and the Kentucky Rifles, where the former lost two officers killed and nine wounded, fourteen privates killed and seventy-five wounded; the latter lost six officers wounded and none killed, nine privates killed and sixty-four wounded. When it is remembered that the Third Regiment in the battle with about three hundred and fifty and four hundred men in line lost six regimental commanders killed and wounded, not less than three times that number of other officers killed and wounded, and more than one hundred and fifty men killed and wounded, some idea can be had of its bloody crisis and deadly struggle, in which our troops were engaged, in comparison to the patriots in Mexico.

But considering the close proximity of the troops engaged at Fredericksburg, the narrow compass in which they were massed, the number of elevated positions suitable for artillery on either side, and the number of troops on the field, the wonder is why the casualties were not even greater than the reports make them. Burnsides, from the nature of the ground, could not handle more than half his army, as by official returns not more than fifty thousand were in line of battle and in actual combat. There were only two points at which he could extend his line, and if at one he found a "Scylla," he was equally sure to find a "Charybdis" at the other. On his left flank Jackson's whole corps was massed, at Hamilton's Crossing; at his right was the stone wall and Mayree's Hill. To meet Hood and Pickett he would have had to advance between a quarter and half mile through a plain, where his army could be enfiladed by the guns of Longstreet and Jackson, and in front by the batteries of Hood and Pickett. It seems from reports since come to light that the authorities at Washington apprehended more danger in Burnsides crossing the river than in the battle that was to follow. Lincoln in giving him orders as to his movements instructed his Secretary of War, Stanton, to write Burnsides to be very careful in the crossing, to guard his flanks well, and not allow Lee to fall upon one part that had crossed and crush it before the other part could come to the rescue; nor allow that wing of the army yet remaining on the Northern side to be attacked and destroyed while the other had crossed to the Southern side. It is said Stanton wrote the order couched in the best of English, and phrased in elegant terms the instructions above, telling him to guard his flanks, etc., then read the order to Lincoln for his approval. Taking up the pen, the President endorsed it, and wrote underneath, in his own hand: "In crossing the river don't allow yourself to be caught in the fix of a cow, hurried by dogs, in jumping a fence, get hung in the middle, so that she can't either use her horns in front, nor her heels behind."

Many incidents of courage and pathos could be written of this, as well as many other battles, but one that I think the crowning act of courage and sympathy for an enemy in distress is due was that of a Georgian behind the wall. In one of the first charges made during the day a Federal had fallen, and to protect himself as much as possible from the bullets of his enemies, he had by sheer force of will pulled his body along until he had neared the wall. Then he failed through pure exhaustion. From loss of blood and the exposure of the sun's rays, he called loudly for water. "Oh, somebody bring me a drink of water!—water! water!!" was the piteous appeals heard by those behind the stone wall. To go to his rescue was to court certain death, as the housetops to the left were lined with sharpshooters, ready to fire upon anyone showing his head above the wall. But one brave soldier from Georgia dared all, and during the lull in the firing leaped the walls, rushed to the wounded soldier, and raising his head in his arms, gave him a drink of water, then made his way back and over the wall amid a hail of bullets knocking the dirt up all around him.

The soldier, like the sailor, is proverbial for his superstition. But at times certain incidents or coincidents take place in the life of the soldier that are inexplicable, to say the least. Now it is certain that every soldier going into battle has some dread of death. It is the nature of man to dread that long lost sleep at any time and in any place. He knows that death is a master of all, and all must yield to its inexorable summons, and that summons is more likely to come in battle than on ordinary occasions. That at certain times soldiers do have a premonition of their coming death, has been proven on many occasions. Not that I say all soldiers foretell their end by some kind of secret monitor, but that some do, or seem to do so.

Captain Summer, of my company, was an unusually good-humored and lively man, and while he was not what could be called profane, yet he had little predilection toward piety or the Church. In other battles he advanced to the front as light-hearted and free from care as if going on drill or inspection. When we were drawn up in line of battle at Fredericksburg the first morning an order came for the Captain. He was not present, and on enquiry, I was told that he had gone to a cluster of bushes in the rear. Thinking the order might be of importance, I hastened to the place, and there I found Captain Summer on his knees in prayer. I rallied him about his "sudden piety," and in a jesting manner accused him of "weakening." After rising from his kneeling posture, I saw he was calm, pale, and serious—so different from his former moods in going into battle. I began teasing him in a bantering way about being a coward.

"No," said he, "I am no coward, and will show I have as much nerve, if not more, than most men in the army, for all have doubts of death, but I have none. I will be killed in this battle. I feel it as plainly as I feel I am living, but I am no coward, and shall go in this battle and fight with the same spirit that I have always shown."

This was true. He acted bravely, and for the few moments that he commanded the regiment he exhibited all the daring a brave man could, but he fell shot through the brains with a minnie ball. He had given me messages to his young wife, to whom he had been married only about two months, before entering the services, as to the disposition of his effects, as well as his body after death.

Another instance was that of Lieutenant Hill, of Company G, Third South Carolina Regiment. The day before the battle he asked permission to return to camp that night, a distance perhaps of three miles. With a companion he returned to the camp, procured water, bathed himself, and changed his under-clothing. On being asked by his companion why he wished to walk three miles at night to simply bathe and change his clothing, with perfect unconcern he replied: "In the coming battle I feel that I will be killed, and such being the case, I could not bear the idea of dying and being buried in soiled clothes." He fell dead at the first volley. Was there ever such courage as this— to feel that death was so certain and that it could be prevented by absenting themselves from battle, but allowed their pride, patriotism, and moral courage to carry them on to sure death?

In the case of a private in Company C, Third Regiment, it was different. He did not have the moral courage to resist the "secret monitor," that silent whisperer of death. He had always asserted that he would be killed in the first battle, and so strong was this conviction upon him, that he failed to keep in line of battle on another occasion, and had been censured by his officers for cowardice. In this battle he was ordered in charge of a Sergeant, with instructions that he be carried in battle at the point of the bayonet. However, it required no force to make him keep his place in line, still he continued true to his convictions, that his death was certain. He went willingly, if not cheerfully, in line. As the column was moving to take position on Mayree's Hill, he gave instructions to his companions as he advanced what messages should be sent to his wife, and while giving those instructions and before the command reached its position he fell pierced through the heart.

Another instance that came under my own observation, that which some chose to call "presentiment," was of a member in my company in East Tennessee. He was an exceptionally good soldier and the very picture of an ideal hero, tall, erect, and physically well developed, over six feet in height, and always stood in the front rank at the head of the company. While Longstreet was moving upon Knoxville, the morning he crossed the Tennessee River before dawn and before there was any indication of a battle, this man said to me, with as much coolness and composure, as if on an ordinary subject, without a falter in his tone or any emotion whatever: "Captain, I will be killed to-day. I have, some money in my pocket which I want you to take and also to draw my four months' wages now due, and send by some trusty man to my wife. Tell her also—" but here I stopped him, told him it was childish to entertain such nonsense, to be a man as his conduct had so often in the past shown him to be. I joked and laughed at him, and in a good-natured way told him the East Tennessee climate gave him that disease known among soldiers as "crawfishing." This I did to withdraw his mind from this gloomy brooding. We had no real battle, but a continual skirmish with the enemy, with stray shots throughout the day. As we were moving along in line of battle, I heard that peculiar buzzing noise of a bullet, as if in ricochet, coming in our direction, but high in the air. As it neared the column it seemed to lower and come with a more hissing sound. It struck the man square in the breast, then reeling out of ranks he made a few strides towards where I was marching, his pocket-book in hand, and fell dead at my feet without a word or groan. He was the only man killed during the day in the brigade, and not even then on the firing line. Of course all will say these are only "coincidences," but be what they may, I give them as facts coming under my own eyes, and facts of the same nature came to the knowledge of hundreds and thousands of soldiers during every campaign, which none endeavor to explain, other than the facts themselves. But as the soldier is nothing more than a small fraction of the whole of a great machine, so much happens that he cannot fathom nor explain, that it naturally makes a great number of soldiers, like the sailor, somewhat superstitious. But when we speak of moral courage, where is there a courage more sublime than the soldier marching, as he thinks, to his certain death, while all his comrades are taking their chances at the hazard of war?

There are many unaccountable incidents and coincidents in a soldier's experience. Then, again, how differently men enter battle and how differently they act when wounded. Some men, on the eve of battle, the most trying time in a soldier's life, will stand calm and impassive, awaiting the command, "forward," while his next neighbor will tremble and shake, as with a great chill, praying, meditating, and almost in despair, awaiting the orders to advance. Then when in the heat of the conflict both men seem metamorphosed. The former, almost frightened out of his wits, loses his head and is just as apt to fire backwards as forwards; while the latter seems to have lost all fear, reckless of his life, and fights like a hero. I have known men who at home were perfect cowards, whom a schoolboy could run away with a walking cane, become fearless and brave as lions in battle; while on the other hand men who were called "game cocks" at home and great "crossroads bullies," were abject cowards in battle. As to being wounded, some men will look on a mortal wound, feel his life ebbing away, perfectly calm and without concern, and give his dying messages with the composure of an every day occurrence; while others, if the tip of the finger is touched, or his shin-bone grazed, will "yell like a hyena or holler like a loon," and raise such a rumpus as to alarm the whole army. I saw a man running out of battle once (an officer) at such a gait as only fright could give, and when I asked him if he was wounded, he replied, "Yes, my leg is broken in two places," when, as a matter of fact, he had only a slight flesh wound. These incidents the reader may think merely fiction, but they are real facts. A man in Company E, Third South Carolina Regiment, having a minnie ball lodged between the two bones of his arm, made such a racket when the surgeons undertook to push it out, that they had to turn him loose; while a private in Company G, of the same regiment, being shot in the chest, when the surgeon was probing for the ball with his finger, looked on with unconcern, only remarking, "Make the hole a little larger, doctor, and put your whole hand in it." In a few days he was dead. I could give the names of all these parties, but for obvious reasons omit them. I merely single out these cases to show how differently men's nervous systems are constructed. And I might add, too, an instance of a member of my company at the third day of the battle of Gettysburg. Lying under the heavy cannonading while Pickett was making his famous charge, and most of the men asleep, this man had his foot in the fork of a little bush, to better rest himself. In this position a shot struck him above the ankle; he looked at the wound a moment, then said: "Boys, I'll be——if that ain't a thirty days' furlough." Next day his foot had to be amputated, and to this day he wears a cork. Such is the difference in soldiers, and you cannot judge them by outward appearance.

I here insert a few paragraphs from the pen of Adjutant Y.J. Pope, of the Third, to show that there was mirth in the camps, notwithstanding the cold and hardships:

Playing "Anthony Over"

At Headquarters on 7th December, 1862

There was one thing that always attracted my attention during the war and that was the warm fellowship which existed amongst the soldiers. If a man got a trunk or box laden with good things from home, there was no selfishness about it; the comrades were expected and did share in the feast. While out on picket on the banks of the Rappahannock River, when we were told that another regiment had come to relieve ours, at the same time we were told that Colonel Rutherford had come back to us; he had been absent since September, and we were all very anxious to see him, for he was a charming fellow—whole-souled, witty, and always an addition to any party. We knew, too, that he would bring something good to eat from home. My feathers fell, though, when Colonel Nance said to me, "Go yourself and see that every company is relieved from picket duty, and bring them to the regiment." I knew what this meant. It was at night, the ground was covered with snow, and the companies would take a long time to march back to camp. A soldier is made to obey orders, whether pleasant or unpleasant, so I rode at the head of the battalion; I was chilled through; my ears felt—well I rubbed a little feeling into them. At last we reached camp. Before I did so I could hear the merry laughter of the group about our regimental headquarter fire. Rutherford greeted me with the utmost cordiality, and had my supper served, having had the servants to keep it hot. But I could not forget my having to ride three miles at the head of the four companies, and how cold I had got in doing so. Therefore, I was in a bad humor, and refusing to join the merry group around the fire, went to bed at once. About twelve o'clock that night I heard the voices in the game of "Anthony over," and was obliged to laugh. Of course the merry cup had circulated. We lived in a Sibley tent that had a cap to fit over the top. And that night, as it was very cold, it had been determined to put the cap on the tent. So the merry-makers formed themselves into two groups, and pitched the cap to the top, and when it failed to lodge the other side would try its hand. One side would call out, "Anthony," to which call the other party would reply, "over." Then the first crowd would sing out, "Here she comes," throwing the cap with the uttering of those words. The peals of laughter from both sides, when the effort to lodge the cap would fail and the teasing of each side, made me laugh whether I wished to do so or not. After awhile it lodged alright, then "good-nights" were exchanged, and then to bed.

I need not add that on the next day all was good humor at headquarters, and in six days afterwards Colonel Nance, Colonel Rutherford, and Major Maffett were all painfully wounded in battle.

DECEMBER, 1862

While Longstreet's troops occupied the City of Fredericksburg in the winter of 1862, I had learned that at night one of the quartermasters of McLaws' Division was in the habit of going across to an island in the Rappahannock River, just above the city, to obtain hay and corn, and to come down to the main incentive, that there was a very charming old Virginia family who lived there, and that a bright-eyed daughter was of that family. I set about getting a sight of this "Island enchantress," and at last Captain Franks, who was Quartermaster of the Seventeenth Regiment of Barksdale's Brigade, agreed to take me with him one night. Here I was, the Adjutant of a Regiment, going over to an island without leave, with the enemy in strong force just across the river, and therefore liable to be captured. Nevertheless, the hope of a peep at bright eyes has got many a man into dangerous ventures, and my case was not different from the rest. So I went. I saw the fair maid. She was not only beautiful, but very interesting.

After it was all over prudence whispered to me not to tempt my fate again—especially as a fair lady in another State would have had a right to except to such conduct on my part. I never regretted my visit to the island, though!

AN ACT OF HEROIC FIDELITY OF A
NEGRO SLAVE IN THE WAR

In looking back at the incidents of the War Between the States, it is with great pleasure that an incident highly honorable to the African slave race* is recalled.

It was on the 13th of December, 1862, when the Third South Carolina Regiment of Infantry was ordered from the position at the foot of Lee's Hill, at Fredericksburg, Va., to Mayree's House, near but to the right of the sunken road protected by the rock fence, that in going down the Telegraph Road the regiment was for a time exposed to the fire of the Federal batteries on the Stafford Heights. A shell from those batteries was so accurately directed that it burst near by Company C, of that regiment, and one of the results was that Lieutenant James Spencer Piester, of that company, was instantly killed. His body lay in that road and his faithful body servant, Simpson Piester, went to the body of his master and tenderly taking it into his arms, bore it to the rear, so that it might be sent to his relatives in Newberry, South Carolina. Anyone who had occasion to go upon the Telegraph Road in that day must appreciate the courage and fidelity involved in the act performed by Simpson Piester.

*PUBLISHER'S NOTE: We would ask readers to remember that this book necessarily reflects the attitudes of the time. We in no way endorse this view of African Americans and in re-publishing this book we had to decide whether to amend this reference and others in this book expressing similar sentiments. Our final decision was to leave them as originally published for the sake of historical veracity. We hope this decision does not cause offence.

The Leonaur Editors

CHAPTER 15
Reminiscences

After the smoke of the great battle had cleared away and the enemy settled permanently in their old quarters north of the Rappahannock, Lee moved his army some miles south of Fredericksburg, on the wooded highlands, and prepared for winter quarters. This was not a very laborious undertaking, nor of long duration, for all that was necessary was to pitch our old wornout, slanting-roof tents, occupied by six or eight men each. The troops had become too well acquainted with the uncertainty of their duration in camp to go into any very laborious or elaborate preparations. Kershaw had a very desirable location among the wooded hills, but this was soon denuded of every vestige of fuel of every kind, for it must be understood the army had no wagons or teams to haul their fire wood, but each had to carry his share of the wood required for the daily use, and often a mile or mile and a half distant. At the close of the year the Eastern Army found itself in quite easy circumstances and well pleased with the year's campaign, but the fruits of our victory were more in brilliant achievements than material results.

In the Western Army it was not so successful. On the first of the year General Albert Sidney Johnston had his army at Bowling Green, Ky. But disaster after disaster befell him, until two states were lost to the Confederacy, as well as that great commander himself, who fell at the moment of victory on the fatal field of Shiloh. Commencing with the fall of Fort Henry on the Tennessee, then Fort Donaldson on the Cumberland, which necessitated the evacuation of the lines of defense at Bowling Green, and the withdrawal of the army from Kentucky. At Pittsburg Landing Grant was overwhelmingly defeated by the army under Beauregard, but by the division of the army under the two Confederate leaders, and the overpowering numbers of the enemy under some of the greatest Generals in the Union Army, Beauregard was forced to withdraw to Shiloh. Here the two combined armies of Beauregard and Johnston attacked the Union Army under Grant, Sherman, Buell, Lew Wallace, and other military geniuses, with over one hundred and sixteen thousand men, as against an army of forty-eight thousand Confederates. After one of the most stubborn, as well as bloodiest battles of the war, the Confederates gained a complete victory on the first day, but through a combined train of circumstances, they were forced to withdraw the second. After other battles, with varied results, the end of the year found the Western Army in Northern Mississippi and Southern Tennessee.

The Eastern Army, on the other hand, had hurled the enemy from the very gates of the Capital of the Confederacy, after seven days fighting, doubling it up in an indefinable mass, and had driven it northward in haste; on the plains of Manassas it was overtaken, beaten, and almost annihilated, only failing in a repetition of the same, ending as the first battle of that name and place; by the same causes, viz., Sykes' Regulars, the enemy pushed across the Potomac, putting the Capitol, as well as the whole North, in a perfect state of panic; the Confederates entered the enemy's own country, capturing one of their strongholds, with eleven thousand prisoners and munitions of war, enough to equip an army; fought one of the most sanguinary battles of modern times almost within sight of the Capitol itself, if not to a successful finish to a very creditable draw; returned South, unmolested, with its prisoners and untold booty; fought the great battle of Fredericksburg, with the results just enumerated. Could Napoleon, Frederick the Great, or the "Madman of the North" have done better with the forces at hand and against an enemy with odds of two and three to one? So Lee's Army had nothing of which to complain, only the loss of so many great and chivalrous comrades.

We had little picketing to do, once perhaps a month, then in the deserted houses of Fredericksburg. Guard duty around camp was abolished for the winter; so was drilling, only on nice, warm days; the latter, however, was rarely seen during that season. The troops abandoned themselves to base ball, snow fights, writing letters, and receiving as guests in their camps friends and relatives, who never failed to bring with them great boxes of the good things from home, as well as clothing and shoes for the needy soldiers. Furloughs were granted in limited numbers. Recruits and now the thoroughly healed of the wounded from the many engagements flocked to our ranks, making all put on a cheerful face.

That winter in Virginia was one of the most severe known in

many years, but the soldiers had become accustomed to the cold of the North, and rather liked it than otherwise, especially when snow fell to the depth of twelve to sixteen inches, and remained for two or three weeks. So the reader can see that the soldier's life has its sunny side, as well as its dark. The troops delight in "snow balling," and revelled in the sport for days at a time. Many hard battles were fought, won, and lost; sometimes company against company, then regiment against regiment, and sometimes brigades would be pitted against rival brigades. When the South Carolinians were against the Georgians, or the two Georgia brigades against Kershaw's and the Mississippi brigades, then the blows would fall fast and furious. The fiercest fight and the hardest run of my life was when Kershaw's Brigade, under Colonel Rutherford, of the Third, challenged and fought Cobb's Georgians. Colonel Rutherford was a great lover of the sport, and wherever a contest was going on he would be sure to take a hand. On the day alluded to Colonel Rutherford martialed his men by the beating of drums and the bugle's blast; officers headed their companies, regiments formed, with flags flying, then when all was ready the troops were marched to the brow of a hill, or rather half way down the hill, and formed line of battle, there to await the coming of the Georgians. They were at that moment advancing across the plain that separated the two camps. The men built great pyramids of snow balls in their rear, and awaited the assault of the fast approaching enemy. Officers cheered the men and urged them to stand fast and uphold the "honor of their State," while the officers on the other side besought their men to sweep all before them off the field.

The men stood trembling with cold and emotion, and the officers with fear, for the officer who was luckless enough to fall into the hands of a set of "snow revelers," found to his sorrow that his bed was not one of roses. When the Georgians were within one hundred feet the order was given to "fire." Then shower after shower of the fleecy balls filled the air. Cheer after cheer went up from the assaulters and the assaultant—now pressed back by the flying balls, then to the assault again. Officers shouted to the men, and they answered with a "yell." When some, more bold than the rest, ventured too near, he was caught and dragged through the lines, while his comrades made frantic efforts to rescue him. The poor prisoner, now safely behind the lines, his fate problematical, as down in the snow he was pulled, now on his face, next on his back, then swung round and round by his heels—all the while snow being pushed down his back or in his bosom, his eyes, ears, and hair thoroughly filled with the "beautiful snow." After a fifteen minutes' struggle, our lines gave way. The fierce looks of a tall, muscular, wild-eyed Georgian, who stood directly in my front, seemed to have singled me out for sacrifice. The stampede began. I tried to lead the command in the rout by placing myself in the front of the boldest and stoutest squad in the ranks, all the while shouting to the men to "turn boys turn." But they continued to charge to the rear, and in the nearest cut to our camp, then a mile off, I saw the only chance to save myself from the clutches of that wild-eyed Georgian was in continual and rapid flight. The idea of a boy seventeen years old, and never yet tipped the beam at one hundred, in the grasp of that monster, as he now began to look to me, gave me the horrors. One by one the men began to pass me, and while the distance between us and the camp grew less at each step, yet the distance between me and my pursuer grew less as we proceeded in our mad race. The broad expanse that lay between the men and camp was one flying, surging mass, while the earth, or rather the snow, all around was filled with men who had fallen or been overtaken, and now in the last throes of a desperate snow battle. I dared not look behind, but kept bravely on. My breath grew fast and thick, and the camp seemed a perfect mirage, now near at hand then far in the distance. The men who had not yet fallen in the hands of the reckless Georgians had distanced me, and the only energy that kept me to the race was the hope that some mishap might befall the wild-eyed man in my rear, otherwise I was gone. No one would have the temerity to tackle the giant in his rage. But all things must come to an end, and my race ended by falling in my tent, more dead than alive, just as I felt the warm breath of my pursuer blowing on my neck. I heard, as I lay panting, the wild-eyed man say, "I would rather have caught that d——n little Captain than to have killed the biggest man in the Yankee Army."

CHAPTER 16
Battle of Chancellorsville

On the morning of April 29th the soldiers were aroused from their slumbers by the beating of the long roll. What an ominous sound is the long roll to the soldier wrapped in his blanket and enjoying the sweets of sleep. It is like a fire bell at night. It denotes battle. It tells the soldier the enemy is moving; it means haste and active preparation. A battle is imminent. The soldiers thus roused, as if from their long sleep since Fredericksburg, feel in a touchous mood. The frightful scenes of Fredericksburg and Mayree's Hill rise up before them as a spectre. Soldiers rush out of their tents, asking questions and making suppositions. Others are busily engaged folding blankets, tearing down tents, and making preparations to move; companies formed into regiments and regiments into brigades. The distant boom of cannon beyond the Rappahannock tells us that the enemy is to cross the river again and try conclusions with the soldiers of Lee. All expected a bloody engagement, for the Federal Army had been greatly recruited, under excellent discipline, and headed by Fighting Joe Hooker. He was one of the best officers in that army, and he himself had boasted that his was the "finest army that had ever been organized upon the planet." It numbered one hundred and thirty-one thousand men of all arms, while Lee had barely sixty thousand. We moved rapidly in the direction of Fredericksburg. I never saw Kershaw look so well. Riding his iron-gray at the head of his columns, one could not but be impressed with his soldierly appearance. He seemed a veritable knight of old. Leading his brigade above the city, he took position in the old entrenchments.

Before reaching the battle line, the enemy had already placed pontoons near the old place of landing, crossed over a portion of their army, and was now picketing on the south side of the river. One company from each regiment was thrown out as sharpshooters or skirmishers, under Captain Goggans, of the Seventh, and deployed in the valley below, where we could watch the enemy. My company was of the number. Nothing was done during the day but a continual change of positions. We remained on the skirmish line during the night without fire or without any relief, expecting an advance next morning, or to be relieved at least. The sun was obscured by the densest fog the following morning I had almost ever witnessed. When it cleared up, about 10 o'clock, what was our astonishment?—to find no enemy in our front, nor friends in our rear. There were, however, some Federals opposite and below the city, but they belonged to another division. We could hear occasional cannonading some miles up the Rappahannock. By some staff officers passing, we ascertained that Hooker had withdrawn during the night in our front, recrossed the river at Ely's and Raccoon fords, or some of the fords opposite the Wilderness. This was on Friday, May the first. After a consultation with the officers of our detachment, it was agreed to evacuate our position and join our regiments wherever we could find them. We had no rations, and this was one of the incentives to move. But had the men been supplied with provisions, and the matter left to them alone, I doubt very much whether they would have chosen to leave the ground now occupied, as we were in comparative safety and no enemy in sight, while to join our commands would add largely to the chances of getting in battle. I am sorry to say a majority of the officers were of that opinion, too. Some brought to bear one of Napoleon's maxims I had heard when a boy, "When a soldier is in doubt where to go, always go to the place you hear the heaviest firing," and we could indistinctly hear occasional booming of cannon high up the river, indicating that a part of the army at least was in that direction.

So we moved back and over the breastworks, on to the plank road leading to Orange Court House. Making our way, keeping together as a battalion, up that road in the direction of the Wilderness, near noon we could hear the deep bay of cannon, now distant and indistinct, then again more rapidly and quite distinguishable, showing plainly that Lee was having a running fight. Later in the day we passed dead horses and a few dead and wounded soldiers. On every hand were indications of the effects of shot and shell. Trees were shattered along the road side, fences torn down and rude breastworks made here and there, the evidence of heavy skirmishing in our front. Lee was pressing the advance guard that had crossed at one of the lower fords back on the main army, crossing then at fords opposite and above the Chancellor's House. Near sundown

197

the firing was conspicuously heavy, especially the artillery. The men of most of the companies evinced a desire to frequently rest, and in every way delay our march as much as possible. Some of the officers, too, joined with the men and offered objections to rushing headlong into battle without orders. I knew that our brigade was somewhere in our front, and from the firing I was thoroughly convinced a battle was imminent, and in that case our duty called us to our command. Not through any cowardice, however, did the men hesitate, for all this fiction written about men's eagerness for battle, their ungovernable desire to throw themselves upon the enemy, their great love of hearing the bursting of shells over their heads, the whizzing of minnie balls through their ranks is all very well for romance and on paper, but a soldier left free to himself, unless he seeks notoriety or honors, will not often rush voluntarily into battle, and if he can escape it honorably, he will do it nine times out of ten. There are times, however, when officers, whose keen sense of duty and honorable appreciation of the position they occupy, will lead their commands into battle unauthorized, when they see the necessity, but a private who owes no obedience nor allegiance only to his superiors, and has no responsibility, seldom ever goes voluntarily into battle; if so, once is enough.

Under these circumstances, as the sun was near setting, we learned from some wounded soldier that Kershaw was moving in line of battle to the left of the plank road. Another Captain and myself deserted our companions and made our way to our regiments with our companies. As we came upon it, it was just moving out from a thicket into an open field under a heavy skirmish fire and a fierce fire from a battery in our front. We marched at a double-quick to rejoin the regiment, and the proudest moments of my life, and the sweetest words to hear, was as the other portion of the regiment saw us coming they gave a cheer of welcome and shouted, "Hurrah! for the Dutch; the Dutch has come; make way to the left for the Dutch," and such terms of gladness and welcome, that I thought, even while the "Dutch" and its youthful commander were but a mere speck of the great army, still some had missed us, and I was glad to feel the touch of their elbow on the right and left when a battle was in progress.

Companies in the army, like school boys, almost all have "nicknames." Mine was called the "Dutch" from the fact of its having been raised in that section of the country between Saluda River and the Broad, known as "Dutch Fork." A century or more before, this country, just above Columbia and in the fork of the two rivers, was settled by German refugees, hence the name "Dutch Fork."

After joining the regiment, we only advanced a little further and halted for the night, sleeping with guns in arms, lest a night attack might find the troops illy prepared were the guns in stack. We were so near the enemy that fires were not allowed, and none permitted to speak above a whisper. Two men from each company were detailed to go to the rear and cook rations. It is not an easy task for two men, who had been marching and fighting all day, to be up all night cooking three meals each for thirty or forty men, having to gather their own fuel, and often going half mile for water. A whole day's ration is always cooked at one time on marches, as night is the only time for cooking. The decrees of an order for a detail are inexorable. A soldier must take it as it comes, for none ever know but what the next duties may be even worse than the present. As a general rule, soldiers rarely ever grumble at any detail on the eve of an engagement, for sometimes it excuses them from a battle, and the old experienced veteran never refuses that.

At daylight a battery some two hundred yards in our front opened a furious fire upon us, the shells coming uncomfortably near our heads. If there were any infantry between the battery and our troops, they must have laid low to escape the shots over their heads. But after a few rounds they limbered up and scampered away. We moved slowly along with heavy skirmishing in our front all the morning of the second. When near the Chancellor's House, we formed line of battle in a kind of semi-circle, our right resting on the river and extending over the plank road, Kershaw being some distance to the left of this road, the Fifteenth Regiment occupying the right. Here we remained for the remainder of the day. We heard the word coming up the line, "No cheering, no cheering." In a few moments General Lee came riding along the lines, going to the left. He had with him quite a number of his staff and one or two couriers. He looked straight to the front and thoughtful, noticing none of the soldiers who rushed to the line to see him pass. He no doubt was then forming the masterful move, and one, too, in opposition to all rules or order of military science or strategy, "the division of his army in the face of the enemy," a movement that has caused many armies, before, destruction and the downfall of its commander. But nothing succeeds like success. The great disparity in numbers was so great that Lee could only watch and hope for some mistake or blunder of his adversary, or by some extraordinary strategic manoeuver on his own part, gain the advantage by which his opponent would be ruined. Hooker had one hundred and thirty thousand men, while Lee had only sixty thousand. With this number it seemed an easy task for Hooker to threaten Lee at Fredericksburg, then fall upon him with his entire force at Chancellorsville and crush him before Lee could extricate himself from the meshes that were surrounding him, and retreat to Richmond. The dense Wilderness seemed providential for the movement upon which Lee had now determined to stake the fate of his army and the fortunes of the Confederacy. Its heavy, thick undergrowth entirely obstructed the view and hid the movements to be made. Jackson, with Rhodes, Colston's, and A.P. Hill's Divisions, were to make a detour around the enemy's right, march by dull roads and bridle paths through the tangled forest, and fall upon the enemy's rear, while McLaws, Anderson's, and Early's Divisions were to hold him in check in front. Pickett's Division had, before this time, been sent to Wilmington, N.C., while Ransom's Division, with Barksdale's Mississippi Brigade, of McLaws' Division, were to keep watch of the enemy at Fredericksburg. The Federal General, Stoneman, with his cavalry, was then on his famous but disastrous raid to Richmond. Jackson commenced his march early in the morning, and kept it up all day, turning back towards the rear of the enemy when sufficiently distant that his movement could not be detected. By marching eighteen or twenty miles he was then within three miles of his starting point. But Hooker's Army stood between him and Lee. Near night Jackson struck the enemy a terrific blow, near the plank road, just opposite to where we lay, and the cannonading was simply deafening. The shots fired from some of the rifled guns of Jackson passed far overhead of the enemy and fell in our rear. Hooker, bewildered and lost in the meshes of the Wilderness, had formed his divisions in line of battle in echelon, and moved out from the river. Great gaps would intervene between the division in front and the one in rear. Little did he think an enemy was marching rapidly for his rear, another watching every movement in front, and those enemies, Jackson and Lee, unknown to Hooker, his flank stood exposed and the distance between the columns gave an ordinary enemy an advantage seldom offered by an astute General, but to such an enemy as Jackson it was more than he had hoped or even dared to expect. As he sat watching the broken columns of the enemy struggling through the dense undergrowth, the favorable moment came. Seizing it with promptness and daring, so characteristic of the man, he, like Napoleon at Austerlitz, when he saw the Russians passing by his front with their flanks exposed, rushed upon them like a wild beast upon its prey, turning the exposed column back upon its rear. Colston, commanding Jackson's old Division, led the attack, followed by A.P. Hill. Rhodes then fell like an avalanche upon the unexpectant and now thoroughly disorganized divisions of the retreating enemy. Volley after volley was poured into the seething mass of advancing and receding columns. Not much use could be made of artillery at close range, so that arm of the service was mainly occupied in shelling their trains and the woods in rear. Until late in the night did the battle rage in all its fury. Darkness only added to its intensity, and the fire was kept up until a shot through mistake lay the great Chieftain, Stonewall Jackson, low. General A.P. Hill now took command of the corps, and every preparation was made for the desperate onslaught of to-morrow. By some strange intuition peculiar to the soldier, and his ability to gather news, the word that Jackson had fallen burst through the camp like an explosion, and cast a gloom of sorrow over all.

As our brother South Carolinians, of McGowan's Brigade, were on the opposite side of us, and in the heat of the fray, while we remained idle, I take the liberty of quoting from "Caldwell's History" of that brigade a description of the terrible scenes being enacted on that memorable night in the Wilderness in which Jackson fell:

"Now it is night. The moon a day or two past full, rose in cloudless sky and lighted our way. We were fronted, and then advanced on the right of the road into a thick growth of pines. Soon a firing of small arms sprang up before us, and directly afterwards the enemy's artillery opened furiously, bearing upon us. The scene was terrible. Volley after volley of musketry was poured by the Confederate line in front of us upon the enemy. The enemy replied with equal rapidity; cheer, wild and fierce, rang over the whole woods; officers shouted at the top of their voices, to make themselves heard; cannon roared and shells burst continuously. We knew nothing, could see nothing, hedged in by the matted mass of trees. Night engagements are always dreadful, but this was the worst I ever knew. To see your danger is bad enough, but to hear shells whizzing and bursting over you, to hear shrapnell and iron fragments slapping the trees and cracking off limbs, and not know from whence death comes to you, is trying beyond all things. And here it looked so incongruous—below raged, thunder, shout, shriek, slaughter—above soft, silent, smiling moonlight, peace!"

The next morning A.P. Hill was moving early, but was himself wounded, and General Jeb. Stuart, of the cavalry, took command. The fighting of Jackson's Corps to-day surpassed that of the night before, and after overcoming almost insurmountable obstacles, they succeeded in dislodging Hooker from his well fortified position.

Kershaw remained in his line of battle, keeping up a constant fire with his skirmishers. An advance upon the Chancellor's House was momentarily expected. The long delay between the commencement of Jackson's movement until we heard the thunder of his guns immediately in our front and in rear of the enemy, was taken up in conjecturing, "what move was next." All felt that it was to be no retreat, and as we failed to advance, the mystery of our inactivity was more confounding.

Early next morning, however, the battle began in earnest. Hooker had occupied the night in straightening out his lines and establishing a basis of battle, with the hope of retrieving the blunder of the day before. Stuart (or rather A.P. Hill, until wounded,) began pressing him from the very start. We could hear the wild yells of our troops as line after line of Hooker's were reformed, to be brushed away by the heroism of the Southern troops. Our skirmishers began their desultory firing of the day before. The battle seemed to near us as it progressed, and the opening around Chancellor's House appeared to be alive with the enemy's artillery. About two o'clock our lines were ordered forward, and we made our way through the tangled morass, in direction of our skirmish line. Here one of the bravest men in our regiment was killed, private John Davis, of the "Quitman Rifles." He was reckless beyond all reason. He loved danger for danger's sake. Stepping behind a tree to load (he was on skirmish line) he would pass out from this cover in plain view, take deliberate aim, and fire. Again and again he was entreated and urged by his comrades to shield himself, but in vain. A bullet from the enemy's sharpshooters killed him instantly.

A singular and touching incident of this family is here recorded. Davis had an only brother, who was equally as brave as John and younger, James, the two being the only children of an aged but wealthy couple, of Newberry County. After the death of John, his

202

mother exerted herself and hired a substitute for her baby boy, and came on in a week after the battle for the body of her oldest son and to take James home with her, as the only hope and solace of the declining years of this aged father and mother. Much against his will and wishes, but by mother's entreaties and friends' solicitations, the young man consented to accompany his mother home. But fate seemed to follow them here and play them false, for in less than two weeks this brave, bright, and promising boy lay dead from a malignant disease.

As our brigade was moving through the thicket in the interval between our main line and the skirmishers, and under a heavy fire, we came upon a lone stranger sitting quietly upon a log. At first he was thought an enemy, who in the denseness of the undergrowth had passed our lines on a tour of observation. He was closely questioned, and it turned out to be Rev. Boushell, a methodist minister belonging to one of McGowan's South Carolina regiments, who became lost from his command in the great flank movement of Jackson (McGowan's Brigade belonged to Jackson's Corps), and said he came down "to see how the battle was going and to lend aid and comfort to any wounded soldier should he chance to find one in need of his services."

The batteries in our front were now raking the matted brush all around and overhead, and their infantry soon became aware of our presence, and they, too, began pouring volleys into our advancing column. The ranks became confused, for in this wilderness we could not see twenty paces in front. Still we moved forward with such order as was under the conditions permissible. When near the turn-pike road General Kershaw gave the command to "charge." The Fifteenth raised the yell; then the Third dashed forward; the Seventh was somewhat late on account of the almost impassable condition of the ground, but still it and the Third Battalion, with the Second on the left, made a mad rush for the public road, and entered it soon after the Fifteenth and Third. A perfect sea of fire was in our faces from the many cannon parked around the Chancellor House and graping in all directions but the rear. Lee on the one side and Stuart on the other had closed upon the enemy, their wings joining just in front of the house. Some of the pieces of the enemy's artillery were not more than fifty yards in our front, and the discharges seemed to blaze fire in our very ranks. Infantry, too, was there massed all over the yard, and in rear of this one vast, mingling, moving body of humanity, dead horses lay in all directions, while the dead and wounded soldiers lay heaped and strewn with the living. But a few volleys from our troops in the road soon silenced all opposition from the infantry, while cannoneers were hitching up their horses to fly away. Some were trying to drag away their caissons and light pieces by hand, while thousands of "blue coats," with and without arms, were running for cover to the rear. In less than twenty minutes the firing ceased in our front, and men were ordered to prepare breastworks. Our soldiers, like the beaver in water, by this time had become accustomed to burrow in the ground as soon as a "halt" was made. A shovel and a spade were carried at all times by each company to guard against emergencies. The bursting of a shell near my company caused a fragment to strike one of my own men on the shoulder. He claimed to be desperately wounded, and wished to go to the hospital. I examined him hastily to see if I could give him any assistance. He claimed his shoulder was broken. Just then the order was given to "commence to fortify." "G.," the wounded man, was the first to grasp the shovel, and threw dirt with an energy that caused my Orderly Sergeant, a brave and faithful soldier, but who never allowed the comic side of any transaction to pass him, to say: "Captain, look at the 'wild pigeon;' see how he scratches dirt." All soldiers carried a "nick-name," a name given by some physical disability or some error he had made, or from any circumstance in his life out of the usual order. Hardly had we taken possession of the turn-pike road and began fortifying, than the sound of shells down the river was heard, and we were hurriedly marched down the road. McLaws' and Andersen's Divisions were doubled-quicked down the turn-pike road and away from the battle to meet Sedgwick, who had crossed the Rappahannock at Fredericksburg, stormed Mayree's Heights, routed and captured the most of Barksdale's Mississippi Brigade, and was making his way rapidly upon Lee's rear.

This Battle of Chancellorsville certainly had its many sides, with its rapid marching, changing of positions, and generalship of the highest order. On the day before Jackson had gone around the right flank of Hooker and fell upon his rear, while to-day we had the novel spectacle of Sedgwick in the rear of Lee and Stuart in rear of Hooker. No one can foretell the result of the battle, had Hooker held his position until Sedgwick came up. But Lee's great mind ran quick and fast. He knew the country and was well posted by his scouts of every move and turn of the enemy on the chessboard of battle. Anderson, with his division, being on our right, led the advance down the road to meet Sedgwick. We passed great parks of wagons (ordnance and commissary) on either side of the road. Here and there were the field infirmaries where their wounded were being attended to and where all the surplus baggage had been stacked before the battle.

On reaching Zoar Church, some five miles in rear, we encountered Sedgwick's advance line of skirmishers, and a heavy fusilade began. Anderson formed line of battle on extreme right, and on right of plank road, with the purpose of sweeping round on the enemy's left. McLaws formed on left of the corps, his extreme left reaching out toward the river and across the road; Kershaw being immediately on right of the road, with the Second resting on it, then the Fifteenth, the Third Battalion, the Eighth, the Third, and the Seventh on the right. On the left of the road leading to Fredericksburg was a large open field extending to the bluff near the river; on the right was a dense thicket of pines and undergrowth. In this we had to form. The Seventh experienced some trouble in getting into line, and many camp rumors were afloat a few days afterwards of an uncomplimentary nature of the Seventh's action. But this was all false, for no more gallant regiment nor better officered, both in courage and ability, was in the Confederate service than the "Bloody Seventh." But it was the unfavorable nature of the ground, the difficulties experienced in forming a line, and the crowding and lapping of the men that caused the confusion.

Soon after our line of battle was formed and Kershaw awaiting orders from McLaws to advance, a line of support came up in our rear, and mistaking us for the enemy, commenced firing upon us. Handkerchiefs went up, calls of "friends," "friends," but still the firing continued. One Colonel seeing the danger—the enemy just in front, and our friends firing on us in the rear—called out:

"Who will volunteer to carry our colors back to our friends in rear?"

Up sprang the handsome and gallant young Sergeant, Copeland, of the "Clinton Divers," (one of the most magnificent and finest looking companies in his service, having at its enlistment forty men over six feet tall), and said:

"Colonel, send me." Grasping the colors in his hand, he carried them, waving and jesticulating in a friendly manner, until he convinced the troops that they were friends in their front.

While thus waiting for Anderson to swing around the left of the enemy, a desperate charge was made upon us. The cannonading was exceedingly heavy and accurate. Great trees all around fell, snapped in twain by the shell and solid shot, and many men were killed and wounded by the falling timber. Trees, a foot in diameter, snapped in two like pipe stems, and fell upon the men. It was growing dark before Anderson could get in position, and during that time the troops never experienced a heavier shelling. It was enough to make the stoutest hearts quake. One of my very bravest men, one who had never failed before, called to me as I passed, "Captain, if I am not here when the roll is called, you may know where I am. I don't believe I can stand this." But he did, and like the man he was, withstood it. Another, a young recruit, and under his first fire, almost became insane, jumping upon me and begging "for God's sake" let him go to the rear. I could not stand this piteous appeal, and knowing he could not be of any service to us in that condition, told him "to go." It is needless to say he obeyed my orders. Dr. Evans, our surgeon, told me afterwards that he came to his quarters and remained three days, perfectly crazy.

At last the order came after night to advance. In a semi-circle we swept through the thicket; turning, we came into the road, and over it into the opening in front. The enemy was pushed back into the breastworks on the bluff at the river. These breastworks had been built by our troops during the Fredericksburg battle, and afterwards to guard and protect Raccoon and Ely's fords, just in rear. As night was upon us, and the enemy huddled before us at the ford, we were halted and lay on the field all night. This was the ending of the battle of Chancellorsville.

Next morning the sun was perfectly hidden by a heavy fog, so much so that one could not see a man twenty yards distant. Skirmishers were thrown out and our advance made to the river, but nothing was found on this side of the river but the wounded and the discarded rifles and munitions of war. The wounded lay in all directions, calling for help and heaping curses upon their friends, who had abandoned them in their distress. Guns, tent flies, and cartridge boxes were packed up by the wagon loads. Hooker's Army was thoroughly beaten, disheartened, and disorganized. Met and defeated at every turn and move, they were only too glad to place themselves across the river and under the protection of their siege guns on Stafford's Heights. Hooker's losses were never correctly given, but roughly computed at twenty-five thousand, while those of Lee's were ten thousand two hundred and eighty-one. But the Confederates counted it a dear victory in the loss of the intrepid but silent Stonewall Jackson. There was a magic in his name that gave enthusiasm and confidence to the whole army. To the enemy his name was a terror and himself an apparition. He had frightened and beaten Banks out of the Shennandoah Valley, had routed Fremont, and so entangled and out-generaled Seigle that he was glad to put the Potomac between himself and this silent, mysterious, and indefatigable chieftain, who often prayed before battle and fought with a Bible in one hand and a sword in the other. He came like a whirlwind upon the flank of McClellan at Mechanicsville, and began those series of battles and victories that terminated with the "Little Giant" being hemmed in at Drury's Bluff and Malvern Hill. While Pope, the "Braggart," was sweeping the fields before him in Northern Virginia, and whose boast was he "saw only the enemy's back," and his "headquarters were in the saddle," Jackson appeared before him like a lion in his path. He swings around Pope's right, over the mountains, back through Thoroughfare Gap; he sweeps through the country like a comet through space, and falls on Pope's rear on the plains of Manassas, and sent him flying across the Potomac like McDowell was beaten two years before. While pursuing the enemy across the river and into Maryland, he turns suddenly, recrosses the river, and stands before Harper's Ferry, and captures that stronghold with scarcely a struggle. All this was enough to give him the sobriquet of the "Silent Man," the man of "mystery," and it is not too much to say that Jackson to the South was worth ten thousand soldiers, while the terror of his name wrought consternation in the ranks of the enemy.

CHAPTER 17
From Chancellorsville to Gettysburg

Again we are in our old quarters. Details were sent out every day to gather up the broken and captured guns, to be shipped to Richmond for repairs. The soldiers had gathered a great amount of camp supplies, such as oil cloths, tents, blankets, etc. When a soldier captured more than a sufficiency for his own wants, he would either sell to his comrades or to the brigade sutler. This was a unique personage with the soldiers. He kept for sale such articles as the soldier mostly needed, and always made great profits on his goods. Being excused from military duty, he could come and go at will. But the great danger was of his being captured or his tent raided by his own men, the risk therefore being so great that he had to ask exorbitant prices for his goods. He kept crackers, cards, oysters and sardines, paper and envelopes, etc., and often a bottle; would purchase all the plunder brought him and peddle the same to citizens in the rear. After the battle of Chancellorsville a member of Company D, from Spartanburg, took the sutler an oil cloth to buy. After the trade was effected, the sutler was seen to throw the cloth behind a box in the tent. Gathering some of his friends, to keep the man of trade engaged in front, the oil cloth man would go in the rear, raise the tent, extract the oil cloth, take it around, and sell it again. Paying over the money, the sutler would throw the cloth behind the box, and continue his trade with those in front. Another would go behind the tent, get the cloth, bring it to the front, throw it upon the counter, and demand his dollar. This was kept up till everyone had sold the oil cloth once, and sometimes twice, but at last the old sutler began to think oil cloths were coming in too regularly, so he looked behind the box, and behold he had been buying the same oil cloth all night. The office was abolished on our next campaign.

Lee began putting his army in splendid trim. All furloughs were discontinued and drills (six per week) were now begun. To an outsider this seemed nonsensical and an useless burden upon the soldiers, but to a soldier nothing is more requisite to the discipline and morale of an army than regular drills, and the army given a good share of what is called "red tape." By the last of May, or the first of June, Lee had recruited his army, by the non-extension of all furloughs and the return of the slightly wounded, to sixty-eight thousand. It is astonishing what a very slight wound will cause a soldier to seek a furlough. He naturally thinks that after the marches, danger, and dread of battle, a little blood drawn entitles him to at least a thirty days' furlough. It became a custom in the army for a man to compute the length of his furlough by the extent of his wound. The very least was thirty days, so when a soldier was asked the nature of his wound he would reply, "only a thirty days'," or "got this time a sixty days;" while with an arm or foot off he would say, "I got my discharge" at such battle.

On the 27th of June Hooker was superseded by General Geo. B. Meade, and he bent all his energies to the discipline of his great army.

General Kershaw, on his promotion to Brigadier, surrounded himself with a staff of young men of unequalled ability, tireless, watchful, and brave to a fault. Captain C.R. Holmes, as Assistant Adjutant General, was promoted to that position from one of the Charleston companies. I fear no contradiction when I say he was one of the very best staff officers in the army, and had he been in line of promotion his merits would have demanded recognition and a much higher position given him. Captain W.M. Dwight, as Adjutant and Inspector General, was also an officer of rare attainments. Cool and collected in battle, his presence always gave encouragement and confidence to the men under fire. He was captured at the Wilderness the 6th of May, 1864. Captain D.A. Doby was Kershaw's Aide-de-Camp, or personal aid, and a braver, more daring, and reckless soldier I never saw. Wherever the battle raged fiercest, Captain Doby was sure to be in the storm center. Riding along the line where shells were plowing up great furrows, or the air filled with flying fragments, and bullets following like hail from a summer cloud, Doby would give words of cheer and encouragement to the men. It seemed at times that he lived a charmed life, so perilous was his situation in times of battle. But the fatal volley that laid the lamented Jenkins low, and unhorsed Longstreet at the Wilderness, gave Doby his last long furlough, felling from his horse dead at the feet of his illustrious chieftain. Lieutenant John Myers was Brigade Ordnance officer, but his duties did not call him to the firing line, thus he was debarred from sharing with his companions their triumphs, their dangers, and their glories, the halo that will ever surround those who followed the plume of the knightly Kershaw.

The Colonels of the different regiments were also fortunate in their selection of Adjutants. This is one of the most important and responsible offices in the regimental organization. The duties are manifold, and often thankless and unappreciated. He shares more dangers (having to go from point to point during battle to give orders) than most of the officers, still he is cut off, by army regulation, from promotion, the ambition and goal of all officers. Colonel Kennedy, of the Second, appointed as his Adjutant E.E. Sill, of Camden, while Colonel Nance, of the Third, gave the position to his former Orderly Sergeant, Y.J. Pope, of Newberry. Colonel Aiken, of the Seventh, appointed as Adjutant Thomas M. Childs, who was killed at Sharpsburg. Colonel Elbert Bland then had Lieutenant John R. Carwile, of Edgefield, to fill the position during the remainder of the service, or until the latter was placed upon the brigade staff. Colonel Henagan made Lieutenant Colin M. Weatherly, of Bennettsville, S.C., Adjutant of the Eighth. All were young men of splendid physique, energetic, courteous, and brave. They had the love and confidence of the entire command. W.C. Hariss, Adjutant of the Third Battalion, was from Laurens. Of the Fifteenth, both were good officers, but as they were not with the brigade all the while, I am not able to do them justice.

The troops of Lee were now at the zenith of their perfection and glory. They looked upon themselves as invincible, and that no General the North could put in the field could match our Lee. The cavalry of Stuart and Hampton had done some remarkably good fighting, and they were now looked upon as an indispensable arm of the service. The cavalry of the West were considered more as raiders than fighters, but our dismounted cavalry was depended upon with almost as much confidence as our infantry. This was new tactics of Lee's, never before practiced in any army of the world. In other times, where the cavalry could not charge and strike with their sabres, they remained simply spectators. But Lee, in time of battle, dismounted them, and they, with their long-ranged carbines, did good and effective service.

Grant had been foiled and defeated at Vicksburg. At Holly Springs, Chickasaw Bayou, Yazo Pass, and Millikin's Bend he had been successfully met and defeated. The people of West Virginia, that mountainous region of the old commonwealth, had ever been loyal to the

Union, and now formed a new State and was admitted into the Union on the 20th of April, 1863, under the name of "West Virginia." Here it is well to notice a strange condition of facts that prevailed over the whole South, and that is the loyalty to the Union of all mountainous regions. In the mountains of North Carolina, where men are noted for their hardihood and courage, and who, once in the field, made the very best and bravest of soldiers, they held to the Union, and looked with suspicion upon the heresy of Secession. The same can be said of South Carolina, Tennessee, Georgia, and Alabama. These men would often go into hiding in the caves and gorges of the mountains, and defy all the tact and strategy of the conscript officers for months, and sometimes for years. It was not for want of courage, for they had that in abundance, but born and reared in an atmosphere of personal independence, they felt as free as the mountains they inhabited, and they scorned a law that forced them to do that which was repugnant to their ideas of personal liberty. Living in the dark recesses of the mountains, far from the changing sentiments of their more enlightened neighbors of the lowland, they drank in, as by inspiration with their mother's milk, a loyalty to the general government as it had come down to them from the days of their forefathers of the Revolution. As to the question of slavery, they had neither kith nor kin in interest or sentiment with that institution. As to State's rights, as long as they were allowed to roam at will over the mountain sides, distill the product of their valleys and mountain patches, and live undisturbed in their glens and mountain homes, they looked upon any changes that would effect their surroundings as innovations to be resisted to the death. So the part that West Virginia and the mountainous regions of the South took in the war was neither surprising to nor resented by the people of the Confederacy.

By the middle of June Lee began to turn his eyes again to the tempting fields of grain and army supplies of Pennsylvania and Maryland. The Valley had been laid waste, West Virginia given up, the South was now put to her utmost resources to furnish supplies for her vast armies. All heavy baggage was sent to the rear, and Lee's troops began moving by various routes up and across the river in the direction of Culpepper Court House. But before the march began, General Lee renewed the whole of Longstreet's Corps, and the sight of this magnificent body of troops was both inspiring and encouraging. The corps was formed in two columns, in a very large and level old field. The artillery was formed on the right, and as General Lee with his staff rode into the opening thirteen guns were fired as a salute to the Chief. Certain officers have certain salutes. The President has, I think, twenty-one guns, while the Commander-in-Chief has thirteen, and so on. Wofford's Georgia regiment was on the right, then Barksdale's Mississippi, Kershaw's South Carolina and Cobb's Georgia constituted McLaws' division. The column wheeled by companies into line and took up the march of review. The bands headed each brigade, and played National airs as the troops marched by.

Barksdale had a magnificent brass band, while Kershaw had only a fife corps headed by that prince of players, Sam Simmonds, who could get more real music out of a fife or flute than some musicians could out of a whole band. The music of the fife and drum, while it may not be so accomplished, gives out more inspiring strains for the marching soldier than any brass band. The cornet, with its accompanying pieces, makes fine music on the stillness of the night, when soldiers are preparing for their night's rest, but nothing gives the soldier on the march more spirit than the fife and drum. When a company nears the reviewing officer they give the salute by bringing their pieces from "right shoulder" to "carry," while on the march, and from "carry" to "present arms" when stationary. The officers raise the hilt of the sword, grasped firmly in the right hand, till the hilt is opposite the chin, the point of the blade extending outward about eighteen inches from the eyes, then, with a quick movement, to the side, the point downward and forward, and kept in this position till the reviewing officer has passed about eighteen paces.

The army had been placed under three Lieutenant Generals: Longstreet, with McLaw's, Hoole's and Pickett's first corps; General Ewell, with Early's, Rhodes' and Trimble's constituting the 2d; while General A.P. Hill commanded Anderson's, Heath's and Pendar's, the 3d. Colonel James D. Nance commanded the 3d South Carolina, Colonel John D. Kennedy the 2d, Lieutenant Colonel Bland the 7th, Colonel Henagan the 8th. Colonel Dessausure the 15th, and Lieutenant Colonel W. C.G. Rice the 3d battalion, which had now been recruited by one man from each company in the brigade, forming two new companies, and formed a battalion of sharpshooters and skirmishers.

The great army was now ready for the ever memorable second invasion of Maryland and Pennsylvania, which culminated in Gettysburg. The army was never before nor afterwards under better discipline nor in better fighting trim.

I will say here, that Colonel Aiken soon joined the brigade and took command of his regiment until after the great battle, and then retired permanently from active service.

On the 3d of June McLaws led off, Hood following on the 4th. Pickett followed Hood. On the 4th and 5th Ewell broke camp and followed in the wake of Longstreet. A.P. Hill, with 3d corps, was left at Fredericksburg to watch the movements of the enemy. After some delay, the enemy threatening a crossing, the 3d corps followed the other troops, all congregating near Culpepper Court House. Reaching the Blue Ridge mountains at Ashby's Gap on the 12th of June, at the western base of which runs the Shenandoah, we forded the stream, it being somewhat swollen, so much so, indeed, that men had to link hands as a protection. The water came up under the armpits, and four men marched abreast, holding each other by the hands. Some caught hold of horses belonging to officers of the regimental staff. In this way we crossed over, and took up camp in the woods beyond. The wagon trains were in advance, and the march was slow and much impeded. Very few of the men had divested themselves of their clothing in crossing, and consequently when we went into quarters it was a very wet army. The soldiers had built fires and were rinsing out their clothes, when an order came to "fall in ranks at once." The men hastily drew on their now thoroughly wet clothes, with all haste got into line and took up the march back towards the river. A rumor was started "the cavalry was pressing our rear." Kershaw's Brigade was marched back over the river, much to their disgust, and posted on the right and left of the road on top of the mountain. Here we were stationed all night, and being on the watch for the enemy, no fires were allowed. Towards day a cold mountain wind set in, and the troops suffered no little from the chilly wind and wet clothing. At sun-up we were marched for the third time across the river, and prepared our meals for the morning in the quarters of the evening before. Up to this time no intimation was given us of our destination, but while preparing our breakfast Adjutant Pope came around with orders stating we were on our way to Hagerstown, Md. At first some seemed to regard this as a joke, but as Adjutant Pope was so noted for his truthfulness and lack of jesting in business matters, we were compelled to take the matter seriously. Of all the officers in the 3d South Carolina, Adjutant Pope, I believe, was the most beloved. His position kept him in close contact with the officers and men, and all had the utmost confidence in his honor and integrity and none doubted his impartiality. He had to keep the list of companies, to do picket duty, and detail, and he was never accused of showing preferment to any company. He was kind and courteous to all, and while he mingled and caroused with the men, he never forgot his dignity nor the respect due to his superiors. Whenever a favor was wanted, or a "friend at court" desired, he never failed to relieve and assist the poorest private the same as the highest officer. While a strict disciplinarian, he was indulgent to almost a fault, and was often seen to dismount and walk with the troops and allow some tired or sick soldier to ride his horse. Adjutant Pope and old "Doc," the name of his horse, were indispensable to the 3d South Carolina regiment. The trusty old horse, like his master, survived the war and did good service after its close.

The next day, the 13th, we took up our march in earnest. No straggling under any circumstances was allowed. The greatest respect was to be paid to all property, no pilfering of hen roosts, no robbery of orchards nor burning of palings or fences along the march. Some miles in front we struck the Staunton and Winchester turn-pike, and at regular intervals the troops were halted for a few minutes' rest. Occasionally the bands struck up a march and the soldiers were ordered into line and to take up the step.

So away down the valley we marched with banners flying, bands playing and the soldiers with a swinging step. Our march was regulated to about eighteen miles a day. But with all the orders and strict discipline, a great many of the soldiers who were given the name of "Foragers" could leave camp at night and often cross the mountain into the Luray valley, a valley, strictly speaking, laden with "milk and honey." It had never suffered the ravages of the Shenandoah, and there everything enticing to the appetite of the soldier was found. Before day the forager would return with butter, bread, and often canteens filled with pure old "Mountain Corn" or "Apple Jack." How men, after an all day's straggling march, which is far more tiresome than an ordinary walk, could go from ten to fifteen miles over the mountains at night in search of something to eat or drink, is more than I could understand.

In a day or two we heard the news of Ewell capturing Milroy at Winchester, with 500 prisoners, and on the way a part of their troops passed us in high glee on their way to Richmond prison. I always noticed that the Federals, on their march to Richmond, were generally in better spirits when being escorted by Confederates than when commanded by their own officers with the Confederates between them and the Southern Capital.

On the fifth day of our march we passed through Winchester, with A.P. Hill marching parallel to us, some eight or ten miles to our right. Ewell had pushed on to the Potomac, and was turning Washington wild and frantic at the sight of the "Rebels" so close to their capital. As we neared the border we could discover Union sentiment taking the place of that of the South. Those who ever sympathized with us had to be very cautious and circumspect. Now and then we would see a window slowly raise in a house by the roadside, or on a hill in the distance, and the feeble flutter of a white handkerchief told of their Confederate proclivities. Generally the doors of all dwellings in the extreme northern portion of Virginia, and in Maryland and Pennsylvania, were mostly closed.

On the morning of the 25th of June we crossed the Potomac at Williamsport. Here was shouting and yelling. Hats went into the air, flags dipped and swayed, the bands played "Maryland, My Maryland," while the men sang "All Quiet on the Potomac To-night." We were now in the enemy's country, and scarcely a shot was fired. We had lost Stuart. "Where was he?" "Stuart has left us." These and like expressions were heard on all sides. That bold and audacious cavalier, in a sudden fit of adventure, or hardihood unequalled, had crossed the Potomac in sight of the spires of Washington, almost under its very guns, and had frightened the authorities out of their wits. Every citizen that could possibly get out of the place was grabbing his valuables and fleeing the city on every train. The Cabinet officers were running hither and thither, not able to form a sensible or rational idea. Had it been possible to have evacuated the city, that would have been done. A Confederate prison or a hasty gibbet stared Staunton in the face, and he was sending telegrams like lightning over the land. Lincoln was the only one who seemingly had not lost his head. But Stuart pushed on toward York and Carlisle, while Ewell had carried fear and trembling to Philadelphia and Baltimore. Mead was marching with the energy of despair to head off Lee and his victorious troops. Longstreet halted at Chambersburg and awaited developments. The troops lived in clover. The best of everything generally was given freely and willingly to them. Great herds of the finest and fattest beeves were continually being gathered together. Our broken down artillery horses and wagon mules were replaced by Pennsylvania's best. But in all, duly paid for in Confederate notes given by our Commissaries and Quartermasters.

At Hagerstown, Hill's troops came up with those of Longstreet, both moving on to Chambersburg, and there remained until the 27th.

General Lee had issued an address to the people of Maryland setting forth the reasons and causes of his army invading their country, offering peace and protection, and calling upon them to repair to his standard and throw off the tyranny and oppression that were bearing them down. He claimed to come, not as a conqueror, nor as one in pursuit of conquest, but as a liberator. But the people seemed to be in a state of lethargy, and to take little interest in the contest one way or the other. Guards were placed at all homes where such protection was asked for, and their fields of grain and orchards, as well as their domestic possessions, were sacredly guarded.

It was the general plan of Lee not to fight an aggressive battle in the enemy's country, but to draw the army of the North away from his lines of communities, and fight him on the defensive at favorable points.

Ewell had been sent on towards Carlisle and York, both those places being promptly delivered to the Confederates by the civil authorities.

In passing through Pennsylvania, many curious characters were found among the quaint old Quaker settlers, who viewed the army of Lee not with "fear" or "trembling," but more in wonder and Christian abhorrence. When the front of the column came to the line dividing Pennsylvania and Maryland, it was met by a delegation of those rigorously righteous old Quakers who, stepping in the middle of the road, commanded, as in the name of God, "So far thou canst go, but no farther." After performing this seemingly command of God, and in accordance with their faith, a perfect abhorrence to war and bloodshed, they returned to their homes perfectly satisfied. It is needless to say the commander of Lee's 2nd corps paid little heed to the command of the pious Quakers.

After remaining near Chambersburg Kershaw, with the other portion of the division, marched on to a little hamlet called Greenwood, leaving a part of Pickett's division at Chambersburg to guard our trains.

On the 29th the troops in advance began gradually to concentrate in the direction of Cashtown, some eight or ten miles west of Gettysburg. Ewell was bearing down from Carlisle, A.P. Hill was moving east, while Longstreet was moved up to Greenwood.

On the first of July A.P. Hill had met the enemy near Gettysburg, and fought the first day's battle of that name, driving the enemy back and through that city, part of his lines occupying the streets of Gettysburg and extending north and around the city. The distance intervening and the mountainous condition of the country prevented us from hearing the roar of the guns, and little did any of us think, while enjoying the rest in our tents, one portion of our army was in the throes of a desperate battle. Up to this time not a word had been heard from Stuart and his cavalry, and this seriously disturbed the mind of our great commander. The positions of the enemy, moving against our rear and flank, necessitated a battle or a withdrawal, and to fight a great battle without the aid of cavalry simply seemed preposterous. General Stuart has been greatly censured for his conduct during these stirring times, just on the eve of this, the greatest battle fought in modern times.

Near sundown, June 1st, we got orders to move along a dull road over hills, mountains and valleys. We marched with elastic step, every one feeling the time had come for active work. Early on our march we encountered General J.E. Johnston's brigade of Early's division, that had been left at Chambersburg, together with all of Ewell's wagon trains. This delayed our march until it was thought all were well out of the way. But before midnight it was overtaken again, and then the march became slow and tedious. To walk two or three steps, and then halt for that length of time, was anything but restful and assuring to troops who had marched all night without sleep or rest. About three o'clock at night, when we had reached the summit of an eminence, we saw in the plain before us a great sea of white tents, silent and still, with here and there a groan, or a surgeon passing from one tent to another relieving the pain of some poor mortal who had fallen in battle on the morning of the day before. We had come upon the field hospital of Hill, where he had his wounded of the day before encamped. Here we first heard of the fight in which so many brave men had fallen, without any decided results. As we had friends and relatives in A.P. Hill's corps, all began to make inquiries for Gregg's old brigade. We heard with delight and animation of the grand conduct of the banner brigade of South Carolina, "Gregg's" or McGowan's, and listened with no little pride to the report of their desperate struggle through the streets of Gettysburg, and to learn that the flag in the hands of a member of a Palmetto regiment first waved over the city. I heard here of the desperate wounding of an old friend and school-mate, Lieutenant W.L. Leitsey, and left the ranks long enough to hunt him up in one of the many tents to the left. I found him severely wounded, so much so that I never met him afterwards. While marching along at a "snail's gait" among the wagons and artillery trains, with a long row of tents to the left, tired and worn out and so dark that you could not distinguish objects a few feet distant, a lone man was standing by the road side viewing, as well as he could in the dark, the passing troops. The slowness of our march enabled me to have a few words of conversation with him. At its end, and just as I was passing him, I heard, or thought I heard him say, "I have a drink in here," pointing to a tent, "if you feel like it." Reader, you may have heard of angel's voices in times of great distress, but if ever an angel spoke, it was at that particular moment, and to me. I was so tired, sleepy and worn out I could scarcely stand, and a drink would certainly be invigorating, but for fear I had not heard or understood him clearly I had him to repeat it. In fact, so timely was it that I felt as if I could have listened all night, so much like the voice of a syren was it at that moment. I said "Yes! Yes!!" But just then I thought of my friend and companion, my next Color Captain, John W. Watts, who was just ahead of me and marching under the same difficulties as myself. I told the man I had a friend in front who wanted a drink worse than I did. He answered "there is enough for two," and we went in. It was Egyptian darkness, but we found a jug and tin cup on the table, and helped ourselves. It may have been that in the darkness we helped ourselves too bountifully, for that morning Watts found himself in an ambulance going to the rear. Overcome by weariness and the potion swallowed in the dark perhaps, he lay down by the roadside to snatch a few moments sleep, and was picked up by the driver of the ambulance as one desperately wounded, and the driver was playing the Good Samaritan. Just before we went into action that day, I saw coming through an old field my lost friend, and right royally glad was I to see him, for I was always glad when I had Watts on my right of the colors. Our brigade lay down by the roadside to rest and recuperate for a few hours, near Willoughby's Run, four miles from Gettysburg.

CHAPTER 18

Battle of Gettysburg—July 2nd

When the troops were aroused from their slumbers on that beautiful clear morning of the 2nd of July, the sun had long since shot its rays over the quaint old, now historic, town of Gettysburg, sleeping down among the hills and spurs of the Blue Ridge. After an all-night's march, and a hard day's work before them, the troops were allowed all the rest and repose possible. I will here state that Longstreet had with him only two divisions of his corps, with four brigades to a division. Pickett was left near Chambersburg to protect the numerous supply trains. Jenkins' South Carolina brigade of his division had been left in Virginia to guard the mountain passes against a possible cavalry raid, and thus had not the opportunity of sharing with the other South Carolinians in the glories that will forever cluster around Gettysburg. They would, too, had they been present, have enjoyed and deserved the halo that will for all time surround the "charge of Pickett," a charge that will go down in history with Balaclava and Hohenlinden.

A.P. Hill, aided by part of Ewell's corps, had fought a winning fight the day before, and had driven the enemy from the field through the streets of the sleepy old town of Gettysburg to the high ground on the east. But this was only the advance guard of General Meade, thrown forward to gain time in order to bring up his main army. He was now concentrating it with all haste, and forming in rear of the rugged ridge running south of Gettysburg and culminating in the promontories at the Round Top. Behind this ridge was soon to assemble an army, if not the largest, yet the grandest, best disciplined, best equipped of all time, with an incentive to do successful battle as seldom falls to the lot of an army, and on its success or defeat depended the fate of two nations.

There was a kind of intuition, an apparent settled fact, among the soldiers of Longstreet's corps, that after all the other troops had made their long marches, tugged at the flanks of the enemy, threatened his rear, and all the display of strategy and generalship had been exhausted in the dislodgement of the foe, and all these failed, then when the hard, stubborn, decisive blow was to be struck, the troops of the first corps were called upon to strike it. Longstreet had informed Lee at the outset, "My corps is as solid as a rock—a great rock. I will strike the blow, and win, if the other troops gather the fruits of victory." How confident the old "War Horse," as General Lee called him, was in the solidity and courage of his troops. Little did he know when he made the assertion that so soon his seventeen thousand men were to be pitted against the whole army of the Potomac. Still, no battle was ever considered decisive until Longstreet, with his cool, steady head, his heart of steel and troops who acknowledged no superior, or scarcely equal, in ancient or modern times, in endurance and courage, had measured strength with the enemy. This I give, not as a personal view, but as the feelings, the confidence and pardonable pride of the troops of the 1st corps.

As A.P. Hill and Ewell had had their bout the day before, it was a foregone conclusion that Longstreet's time to measure strength was near at hand, and the men braced themselves accordingly for the ordeal.

A ridge running parallel with that behind which the enemy stood, but not near so precipitous or rugged, and about a mile distant, with a gentle decline towards the base of the opposite ridge, was to be the base of the battle ground of the day. This plain or gentle slope between the two armies, a mile in extent, was mostly open fields covered with grain or other crops, with here and there a farm house, orchard and garden. It seems from reports since made that Lee had not matured his plan of battle until late in the forenoon. He called a council of war of his principal Lieutenant to discuss plans and feasibilities. It was a long time undecided whether Ewell should lead the battle on the right, or allow Longstreet to throw his whole corps on the Round Top and break away these strongholds, the very citadel to Meade's whole line. The latter was agreed upon, much against the judgment of General Longstreet but Lee's orders were imperative, and obeyed with alacrity. At ten o'clock the movement began for the formation of the columns of assault. Along and in rear of the ridge we marched at a slow and halting gait. The Washington artillery had preceded us, and soon afterwards Alexander's battery passed to select positions. We marched and countermarched, first to the right, then to the left. As we thus marched we had little opportunity as yet to view the strongholds of the enemy on the opposite ridge, nor the incline between, which was soon to be strewn with the dead and dying. Occasionally a General would ride to the crest and take a survey of the surroundings. No cannon had yet been fired on either side, and everything was quiet and still save the tread of the thousands in motion, as if preparing for a great review.

Longstreet passed us once or twice, but he had his eyes cast to the ground, as if in a deep study, his mind disturbed, and had more the look of gloom than I had ever noticed before. Well might the great chieftain look cast down with the weight of this great responsibility resting upon him. There seemed to be an air of heaviness hanging around all. The soldiers trod with a firm but seeming heavy tread. Not that there was any want of confidence or doubt of ultimate success, but each felt within himself that this was to be the decisive battle of the war, and as a consequence it would be stubborn and bloody. Soldiers looked in the faces of their fellow-soldiers with a silent sympathy that spoke more eloquently than words an exhibition of brotherly love never before witnessed in the 1st corps. They felt a sympathy for those whom they knew, before the setting of the sun, would feel touch of the elbow for the last time, and who must fall upon this distant field and in an enemy's country.

About noon we were moved over the crest and halted behind a stone wall that ran parallel to a county road, our center being near a gateway in the wall. As soon as the halt was made the soldiers fell down, and soon the most of them were fast asleep. While here, it was necessary for some troops of Hill's to pass over up and through the gate. The head of the column was lead by a doughty General clad in a brilliant new uniform, a crimson sash encircling his waist, its deep, heavy hanging down to his sword scabbard, while great golden curls hung in maiden ringlets to his very shoulders. His movement was superb and he sat his horse in true Knightly manner. On the whole, such a turn-out was a sight seldom witnessed by the staid soldiers of the First Corps. As he was passing a man in Company D, 3d South Carolina, roused up from his broken sleep, saw for the first time the soldier wonder with the long curls. He called out to him, not knowing he was an officer of such rank, "Say, Mister, come right down out of that hair," a foolish and unnecessary expression that was common throughout the army when anything unusual hove in sight.

This hail roused all the ire in the flashy General, he became as "mad as a March hare," and wheeling his horse, dashed up to where the challenge appeared to have come from and demanded in an angry tone:

"Who was that spoke? Who commands this company?" And as no reply was given he turned away, saying, "D——d if I only knew who it was that insulted me, I would put a ball in him." But as he rode off the soldier gave him a Parthian shot by calling after him:

"Say, Mister, don't get so mad about it, I thought you were some d——n wagon master."

Slowly again our column began moving to the right. The center of the division was halted in front of little Round Top. Kershaw was then on the right, Barksdale with his Mississippians on his left, Wofford and Semmes with their Georgians in rear as support. Everything was quiet in our front, as if the enemy had put his house in order and awaited our coming. Kershaw took position behind a tumbled down wall to await Hood's movements on our right, and who was to open the battle by the assault on Round Top. The country on our right, through which Hood had to manoeuver, was very much broken and thickly studded with trees and mountain undergrowth, which delayed that General in getting in battle line. Anderson's Georgians, with Hood's old Texas Brigade under Robertson, was on McLaws' immediate right, next to Kershaw. Law's Alabama Brigade was on the extreme right, and made the first advance. On McLaws' left was Wilcox, of General "Tige" Anderson's Division of the 3d Corps, with Posey and other troops to his left, these to act more as a brace to Longstreet as he advanced to the assault; however, most of them were drawn into the vortex of battle before the close of the day. In Kershaw's Brigade, the 2d under Colonel John D. Kennedy and Lieutenant Colonel Frank Gilliard, the 15th under Colonel W.D. Dessausure and Major Wm. Gist, the 3d under Colonel James D. Nance and Major R.C. Maffett, the 7th under Colonel D. Wyatt Aiken and Lieutenant Colonel Elbert Bland, the 3d Battallion under Lieutenant Colonel W.G. Rice, the 8th under Colonel John W. Henagan, Lieutenant Colonel Hool and Major McLeod, went into battle in the order named, as far as I remember. Major Wm. Wallace of the 2d commanded the brigade skirmish line or sharpshooters, now some distance in our front. A battery of ten guns was immediately in our rear, in a grove of oaks, and drew on us a heavy fire when the artillery duel began. All troops in line, the batteries in position, nothing was wanting but the signal gun to put these mighty forces in motion.

Ewell had been engaged during the morning in a desultory battle far to our left and beyond the town, but had now quieted down. A blue puff of smoke, a deafening report from one of the guns of the Washington Artillery of New Orleans, followed in quick succession by others, gave the signal to both armies—the battle was now on.

It was the plan of action for Hood to move forward first and engage the enemy, and when once the combat was well under way on the right, McLaws to press his columns to the front. Law, with his Alabamians, was closing around the southern base of greater Round Top, while Robertson, with his three Texas regiments and one Arkansas, and Anderson with his Georgians, were pushing their way through thickets and over boulders to the front base of the Round Tops and the gorges between the two. We could easily determine their progress by the "rebel yell" as it rang out in triumph along the mountain sides.

The battery in our rear was drawing a fearful fire upon us, as we lay behind the stone fence, and all were but too anxious to be ordered forward. Barksdale, on our left, moved out first, just in front of the famous Peach Orchard. A heavy battery was posted there, supported by McCandless' and Willard's Divisions, and began raking Barksdale from the start. The brave old Mississippian, who was so soon to lose his life, asked permission to charge and take the battery, but was refused. Kershaw next gave the command, "forward," and the men sprang to their work with a will and determination and spread their steps to the right and left as they advanced. Kershaw was on foot, prepared to follow the line of battle immediately in rear, looking cool, composed and grand, his steel-gray eyes flashing the fire he felt in his soul.

The shelling from the enemy on the ridge in front had, up to this time, been mostly confined to replying to our batteries, but as soon as this long array of bristling bayonets moved over the crest and burst out suddenly in the open, in full view of the cannon-crowned battlements, all guns were turned upon us. The shelling from Round Top was terrific enough to make the stoutest hearts quake, while the battery down at the base of the ridge, in the orchard, was raking Barksdale and Kershaw right and left with grape and shrapnell. Semmes' Georgians soon moved up on our right and between Kershaw and Hood's left, but its brave commander fell mortally wounded at the very commencement of the attack. Kershaw advanced directly against little Round Top, the strongest point in the enemy's line, and defended by Ayer's Regulars, the best disciplined and most stubborn fighters in the Federal army. The battery in the orchard began grapeing Kershaw's left as soon as it came in range, the right being protected by a depression in the ground over which they marched. Not a gun was allowed to be fired either at sharpshooters that were firing on our front from behind boulders and trees in a grove we were nearing, or at the cannoneers who were raking our flank on the left. Men fell here and there from the deadly minnie-balls, while great gaps or swaths were swept away in our ranks by shells from the batteries on the hills, or by the destructive grape and canister from the orchard. On marched the determined men across this open expanse, closing together as their comrades fell out. Barksdale had fallen, but his troops were still moving to the front and over the battery that was making such havoc in their ranks. Semmes, too, had fallen, but his Georgians never wavered nor faltered, but moved like a huge machine in the face of these myriads of death-dealing missiles. Just as we entered the woods the infantry opened upon us a withering fire, especially from up the gorge that ran in the direction of Round Top. Firing now became general along the whole line on both sides. The Fifteenth Regiment met a heavy obstruction, a mock-orange hedge, and it was just after passing this obstacle that Colonel Dessausure fell. The center of the Third Regiment and some parts of the other regiments, were partially protected by boulders and large trees, but the greater part fought in the open field or in sparsely timbered groves of small trees. The fight now waged fast and furious.

Captain Malloy writes thus of the 8th:

"We occupied the extreme left of the brigade, just fronting the celebrated 'Peach Orchard.' The order was given. We began the fatal charge, and soon had driven the enemy from their guns in the orchard, when a command was given to 'move to the right,' which fatal order was obeyed under a terrible fire, this leaving the 'Peach Orchard' partly uncovered. The enemy soon rallied to their guns and turned them on the flank of our brigade. Amid a storm of shot and shell from flank and front, our gallant old brigade pushed towards the Round Top, driving all before them, till night put an end to the awful slaughter. The regiment went in action with 215 in ranks, and lost more than half its number. We lost many gallant officers, among whom were Major McLeod, Captain Thomas E. Powe, Captain John McIver, and others."

The move to the right was to let Wofford in between Barksdale and Kershaw.

Barksdale was pressing up the gorge that lay between little Round Top and the ridge, was making successful battle and in all likelihood would have succeeded had it not been for General Warren. General Meade's Chief Engineer being on the ground and seeing the danger, grasped the situation at once, called up all the available force and lined the stone walls that led along the gorge with infantry. Brigade after brigade of Federal infantry was now rushed to this citadel, while the crown of little Round Top was literally covered with artillery. Ayer's Regulars were found to be a stubborn set by Kershaw's troops. The Federal volunteers on our right and left gave way to Southern valor, but the regulars stood firm, protected as they were by the great boulders along their lines. Barksdale had passed beyond us as the enemy's line bent backward at this point, and was receiving the whole shock of battle in his front, while a terrific fire was coming from down the gorge and from behind hedges on the hillside. But the Mississippians held on like grim death till Wofford, with his Georgians, who was moving in majestic style across the open field in the rear, came to his support.

General Wofford was a splendid officer, and equally as hard a fighter. He advanced his brigade through the deadly hail of bullets and took position on Bardsdale's right and Kershaw's left, and soon the roar of his guns were mingling with those of their comrades. The whole division was now in action. The enemy began to give way and scamper up the hillside. But Meade, by this time, had the bulk of his army around and in rear of the Round Top, and fresh troops were continually being rushed in to take the places of or reinforce those already in action. Hood's whole force was now also engaged, as well as a part of A.P. Hill's on our left. The smoke became so dense, the noise of small arms and the tumult raised by the "Rebel Yell," so great that the voices of officers attempting to give commands were hushed in the pandemonium. Along to the right of the 3d, especially up the little ravine, the fire was concentrated on those who held this position and was terrific beyond description, forcing a part of the line back to the stone house. This fearful shock of battle was kept up along the whole line without intermission till night threw her sable curtains over the scene of carnage and blood-shed and put an end to the strife. Wofford and Barksdale had none to reinforce them at the gorge, and had to fight it out single-handed and alone, while the Regulars, with their backs to the base of little Round Top, protected by natural formations, were too strong to be dislodged by Kershaw. As soon as the firing ceased the troops were withdrawn to near our position of the forenoon.

The work of gathering up the wounded lasted till late at night. Our loss in regimental and line officers was very great. Scarcely a regiment but what had lost one of its staff, nor a company some of its officers. Dr. Salmond, the Brigade Surgeon, came early upon the field and directed in person the movements of his assistants in their work of gathering up the wounded. "The dead were left to take care of the dead" until next day.

When the brigade was near the woodland in its advance, a most deadly fire was directed towards the center of the 3rd both by the battery to our left, and sharpshooting in the front. It was thought by some that it was our flag that was drawing the fire, four color guards having gone down, some one called out:

"Lower the colors, down with the flag."

Sergeant Lamb, color bearer, waved the flag aloft, and moving to the front where all could see, called out in loud tones, "This flag never goes down until I am down."

Then the word went up and down the line "Shoot that officer, down him, shoot him," but still he continued to give those commands, "Ready, aim, fire," and the grape shot would come plunging into our very faces. The sharpshooters, who had joined our ranks, as we advanced, now commenced to blaze away, and the cannoneers scattered to cover in the rear. This officer finding himself deserted by his men, waved his sword defiantly over his head and walked away as deliberately as on dress parade, while the sharpshooters were plowing up the dirt all around him, but all failed to bring him down. We bivouaced during the night just in rear of the battle ground.

CHAPTER 19

Gettysburg Continued—Pickett's Charge

The next morning, July the 3rd, the sun rose bright and clear. Rations were brought to the men by details, who, after marching and fighting all day, had to hunt up the supply train, draw rations and cook for their companies for the next day—certainly a heavy burden on two men, the usual detail from each company.

No one could conjecture what the next move would be, but the army felt a certainty that Lee would not yield to a drawn battle without, at least, another attempt to break Meade's front. Either the enemy would attempt to take an advantage of our yesterday's repulse and endeavor to break our lines, crush Lee by doubling him back on the Potomac, or that Lee would undertake the accomplishment of the work of the day before. After the heavy battle of yesterday and the all night's march preceding, the soldiers felt little like renewing the fight of to-day, still there was no despondency, no lack of ardor, or morale, each and every soldier feeling, while he had done his best the day before, still he was equal to that before him for to-day.

In the First Corps all was still and quiet, scarcely a shot from either side, a picket shot occasionally was the only reminder that the enemy was near.

Away to our left, and beyond the city, the Federals had assaulted Ewell's lines, and a considerable battle was raging from daylight till 10 o'clock.

The enemy were endeavoring to regain some of the trenches they had lost two days before.

General Pickett, who had been left at Chambersburg, had now come up with his three Virginia Brigades, Garnett's, Kemper's, and Armstead's, (Jenkins being left in Virginia) and was putting them in position for his famous charge.

While this has no real connection with the work in hand, still, since the "Charge of Pickett," has gone in song and story, as the most gallant, dashing, and bloody of modern times, I am tempted here to digress somewhat, and give, as far as I am able, an impartial account of this memorable combat, being an eye witness. While Pickett led the storming party, in person, still the planning and details were entrusted to another head, namely, General Longstreet. In justice to him I will say he was opposed to this useless sacrifice of life and limb. In his memoirs he tells how he pleaded with Lee, to relieve him from the responsibility of command, and when the carnage was at its zenith, riding through the hail from three hundred cannons and shells bursting under and over him, the Old Chieftain says, "I raised my eyes heavenward and prayed that one of these shots might lay me low and relieve me from this awful responsibility." While I would, by no word, or intimation detract one iota from the justly earned fame of the great Virginian, nor the brave men under him, still it is but equal justice to remember and record that there were other Generals and troops from other States as justly meritorious and deserving of honor as participants in the great charge, as Pickett and his Virginians. On the day before, Kershaw, in the battle before little "Round Top," Semmes to the right, Wofford and Barksdale in front of the peach orchard and up the deadly gorge around Little Round Top to say nothing of Hood at Round Top, charged and held in close battle, two thirds of the Army of the Potomac, without any support whatever. See now how Pickett was braced and supported. Cemetery Ridge was a long ridge of considerable elevation, on which, and behind it the enemy was marshalled in mass; opposite this ridge was another of less eminence, and one mile, or near so, distant, behind which the Confederates were concentrating for the assault. Longstreet moved McLaws up near to the right of the assaulting columns in two lines, Semmes and Wofford in the front and Barksdale and Kershaw in the rear lines as support. I continue to retain the names of the Brigade Commanders to designate the troops, although Barksdale and Semmes had fallen the day before.

Kemper and Garnett were on the right of the assaulting column, with Armstead as support, all Virginians and of Pickett's Division. Wilcox, with his Alabama Brigade was to move some distance in rear of Pickett's right to take any advantage of the break in the line, and to protect Pickett's flank. On the left of Pickett, and on the line of attack was Heath's Division, commanded by General Pettigrew, composed of Archer's Brigade, of Alabama and Tennesseeans, Pettigrew's, North Carolina, Brockenborro's, Virginia, and Davis' Brigade, composed of three Mississippi Regiments and one North Carolina, with Scales' and Lanes' North Carolina Brigade in support. Hood and McLaws guarding the right and A.P. Hill the left. I repeat it, was there ever an assaulting column better braced or supported?

General Alexander had charge of the artillery at this point, and the gunners along the whole line were standing to their pieces, ready to draw the lanyards that were to set the opposite hills ablaze with shot and shell, the moment the signal was given.

Every man, I dare say, in both armies held his breath in anxious and feverish suspense, awaiting the awful crash. The enemy had been apprised of the Confederate movements, and were prepared for the shock.

When all was ready the signal gun was fired, and almost simultaneously one hundred and fifty guns belched forth upon the enemy's works, which challenge was readily accepted by Meade's cannoneers, and two hundred shrieking shells made answer to the Confederate's salute. Round after round were fired in rapid succession from both sides, the air above seemed filled with shrieking, screaming, bursting shells. For a time it looked as if the Heavens above had opened her vaults of thunder bolts, and was letting them fall in showers upon the heads of mortals below. Some would burst overhead, while others would go whizzing over us and explode far in the rear. It was the intention of Lee to so silence the enemy's batteries that the assaulting column would be rid of this dangerous annoyance. Longstreet says of the opening of the battle: "The signal guns broke the silence, the blaze of the second gun, mingling in the smoke of the first, and salvos rolled to the left and repeating themselves along the ridges the enemy's fine metal spreading its fire to the converging lines of the Confederates, plowing the trembling ground, plunging through the line of batteries and clouding the heavy air. Two or three hundred guns seemed proud of their undivided honors of organized confusion. The Confederates had the benefit of converging fire into the enemy's massed position, but the superior metal of the enemy neutralized the advantages of position. The brave and steady work progressed."

After almost exhausting his ammunition, General Alexander sent a message to General Pickett, "If you are coming, come at once, or I cannot give you proper support. Ammunition nearly exhausted; eighteen guns yet firing from the cemetery." This speaks volumes for our artillerist, who had silenced over one hundred and fifty guns, only eighteen yet in action, but these eighteen directly in front of Pickett.

Under this deadly cannonade, Pickett sprang to the assault. Kemper and Garnett advanced over the crest, closely followed by Armstead. Wilcox, with his Alabamians, took up the step and marched a short distance in rear of the right. The Alabamians, Tennesseeans, North Carolinians, and Virginians under Pettigrew lined up on Pickett's left, followed by Trimble, with his two North Carolina Brigades and the columns were off. The batteries on the ridges in front now turned all their attention to this dreaded column of gray, as soon as they had passed over the crest that up to this time had concealed them. To the enemy even this grand moving body of the best material in the world must have looked imposing as it passed in solid phalanx over this broad expanse without scarcely a bush or tree to screen it. And what must have been the feelings of the troops that were to receive this mighty shock of battle? The men marched with firm step, with banners flying, the thunder of our guns in rear roaring and echoing to cheer them on, while those of the enemy were sweeping wind rows through their ranks. McLaws was moved up nearer the enemy's lines to be ready to reap the benefit of the least signs of success. Brockenborro and Davis were keeping an easy step with Kemper and Garnett, but their ranks were being thinned at every advance. Great gaps were mown out by the bursting of shells while the grape and canister caused the soldiers to drop by ones, twos and sections along the whole line. Men who were spectators of this carnage, held their breath in horror, while others turned away from the sickening scene, in pitying silence. General Trimble was ordered to close up and fill the depleted ranks, which was done in splendid style, and on the assaulting columns sped.

Trimble had fallen, Garnett was killed, with Kemper and Gibbon being borne from the field more dead than alive. At last the expected crash came, when infantry met infantry. Pickett's right strikes Hancock's center, then a dull, sullen roar told too well that Greek had met Greek. Next came Davis, then Brockenborro, followed on the left by Archer's and Pettigrew's Brigade, and soon all was engulfed in the smoke of battle and lost to sight. Such a struggle could not last long for the tension was too great. The Confederates had driven in the first line, but Meade's whole army was near, and fresh battalions were being momentarily ordered to the front. The enemy now moved out against Pickett's right, but Semmes and Wofford of McLaws' Division were there to repulse them.

For some cause, no one could or ever will explain, Pickett's Brigades wavered at a critical moment, halted, hesitated, then the battle was lost. Now began a scene that is as unpleasant to record as it is sickening to contemplate. When Pickett saw his ruin, he ordered a retreat and then for a mile or more these brave men, who had dared to march up to the cannon's mouth with twenty thousand infantry lying alongside, had to race across this long distance with Meade's united artillery playing upon them, while the twenty thousand rifles were firing upon their rear as they ran.

Pettigrew's Division, which was clinging close to the battle, saw the disaster that had befallen the gallant Virginians, then in turn they, too, fled the field and doubling up on Lane and Scales, North Carolinians, made "confusion worse confounded." This flying mass of humanity only added another target for the enemy's guns and an additional number to the death roll.

Alexander's batteries, both of position, and the line now turned loose with redoubled energy on those of the enemy's to relieve, as far as possible, our defeated, flying, and demoralized troops. For a few moments (which seemed like days to the defeated) it looked as if all nature's power and strength were turned into one mighty upheaval; Vessuvius, Etna, and Popocatepetl were emptying their mighty torrents upon the heads of the unfortunate Confederates. Men fell by the hundreds, officers ceased to rally them until the cover of the ridge was reached. The hills in front were ablaze from the flashes of near two hundred guns, while the smoke from almost as many on our lines slowly lifted from the ridge behind us, showing one continued sheet of flames, the cannoneers working their guns as never before. The earth seemed to vibrate and tremble under the recoil of these hundreds of guns, while the air overhead was filled with flying shells. Not a twinkling of the eye intervened between the passing of shots or shells. The men who were not actively engaged became numbed and a dull heavy sleep overcame them as they lay under this mighty unnatural storm, shells falling short came plowing through the ground, or bursting prematurely overhead, with little or no effect upon the slumberers, only a cry of pain as one and another received a wound or a death shot from the flying fragments. The charge of Pickett is over, the day is lost, and men fall prone upon the earth to catch breath and think of the dreadful ordeal just passed and of the many hundreds lying between them and the enemy's line bleeding, dying without hope or succor.

Farnsworth, of Kilpatrick's Cavalry, had been watching the fray from our extreme right, where Hood had stationed scattered troops to watch his flank, and when the Union General saw through the mountain gorges and passes the destruction of Pickett he thought his time for action had come. The battle-scarred war horses snuffed the blood and smoke of battle from afar, and champed their bits in anxious impatience. The troopers looked down the line and met the stern faces of their comrades adjusting themselves to their saddles and awaiting the signal for the charge. Farnsworth awaits no orders, and when he saw the wave of Pickett's recede he gave the command to "Charge," and his five hundred troopers came thundering down upon our detachments on the extreme right. But Farnsworth had to ride over and between the Fourth, Fourteenth, and Fifteenth Alabama Regiments, the Eleventh Georgia and the First Texas, and it is needless to add, his ride was a rough and disastrous one. Farnsworth, after repeated summons to surrender, fell, pierced with five wounds, and died in a few moments. His troopers who had escaped death or capture fled to the gorges and passes of the mountains through which they had so recently ridden in high expectation.

The enemy, as well as the Confederates, had lost heavily in general officers. Hancock had fallen from his horse, shot through the side with a minnie ball, disabling him for a long time. General Dan Sickles, afterwards military Governor of South Carolina, lost a leg. General Willard was killed. Generals Newton, Gibbon, Reynolds, Barlow were either killed or wounded, with many other officers of note in the Federal Army.

The soldier is not the cold unfeeling, immovable animal that some people seem to think he is. On the contrary, and paradoxical as it may appear, he is warm-hearted, sympathetic, and generous spirited and his mind often reverts to home, kindred, and friends, when least expected. His love and sympathy for his fellow-soldier is proverbial in the army. In the lull, of battle, or on its eve, men with bold hearts and strong nerves look each other in the face with grim reliance. With set teeth and nerve's strung to extreme tension, the thoughts of the soldier often wander to his distant home. The panorama of his whole life passes before him in vivid colors. His first thoughts are of the great beyond—all soldiers, whatever their beliefs or dogmas, think of this. It is natural, it is right, it is just to himself. He sees in his imagination the aged father or mother or the wife and little ones with outstretched arms awaiting the coming of him who perhaps will never come. These are some of the sensations and feelings of a soldier on the eve of, or in battle, or at its close. It is no use denying it, all soldiers feel as other people do, and when a soldier tells as a fact that he "went into battle without fear," he simply tells "what George Washington never told." It is human, and "self-preservation is the first law of nature." No one wants to die. Of course ambition, love of glory, the plaudits of your comrades and countrymen, will cause many a blade to flash where otherwise it would not. But every soldier who reads this will say that this is honest and the whole truth. I am writing a truthful history of the past and honesty forces me to this confession. "All men are cowards" in the face of death. Pride, ambition, a keen sense of duty, will make differences outwardly, but the heart is a coward still when death stares the possessor in the face. Men throw away their lives for their country's sake, or for honor or duty like a cast off garment and laugh at death, but this is only a sentiment, for all men want to live. I write so much to controvert the rot written in history and fiction of soldiers anxious to rush headlong into eternity on the bayonets of the enemy.

Historians of all time will admit the fact that at Gettysburg was fought a battle, not a skirmish, but it was not what Northern writers like to call it, "Lee's Waterloo." The Wilderness, Spottsylvania, and Petersburg were yet to come.

CHAPTER 20
Gettysburg—Fourth Day

A flag of truce now waves over both armies, granting a respite to bury the dead and care for the wounded. The burial of the dead killed in battle is the most trying of all duties of the soldier. Not that he objects to paying these last sad rites to his fallen comrades, but it is the manner in which he must leave them with his last farewell.

A detail from each company is formed into a squad, and armed with spades or shovels they search the field for the dead. When found a shallow pit is dug, just deep enough to cover the body, the blanket is taken from around the person, his body being wrapped therein, laid in the pit, and sufficient dirt thrown upon it to protect it from the vultures. There is no systematic work, time being too precious, and the dead are buried where they fell. Where the battle was fierce and furious, and the dead lay thick, they were buried in groups. Sometimes friendly hands cut the name and the company of the deceased upon the flap of a cartridge box, nail it to a piece of board and place at, the head, but this was soon knocked down, and at the end of a short time all traces of the dead are obliterated.

The wounded were gathered in the various farm houses, and in the city of Gettysburg. Those who were too badly wounded to be moved were left in charge of Surgeons, detailed by the Medical Directors to remain with the wounded. Surgeons in the discharge of their duties are never made prisoners, and the yellow flag flies as much protection as the white. A guard is placed around the hospitals to prevent those who may convalesce while there from escaping, but notwithstanding this vigilance many made their escape and came south, as the soldiers had a horror of the Federal prison pen. Ambulances and empty wagons were loaded to their full capacity with the wounded, unable to walk, while hundreds with arms off, or otherwise wounded as not to prevent locomotion, "hit the dust," as the soldiers used to say, on their long march of one hundred and fifty miles to Staunton, Va.

The Confederate forces numbered in the battles around Gettysburg on May 31st, 75,000, including Pickett's Division. The Federals had 100,000 ready and equipped for action, divided in seven army corps, under General Doubleday commanding First Corps, General Hancock Second Corps, General Sickles Third Corps, General Sykes Fifth Corps, General Sedgwick Sixth Corps, General Howard Eleventh Corps, General Slocum Twelfth Corps, and three divisions of cavalry under Pleasanton. The Confederate losses were: Longstreet, 7,539; Ewell, 5,973; A.P. Hill, 6,735; Cavalry under Stuart, 1,426; in all 21,643. Enemy's loss, 23,049.

I herewith give sketches of Colonel Dessausure and Major McLeod, killed in action, and of Doctor Salmond, Brigade Surgeon. As the latter acted so gallantly, and showed such generous impulses during and after the engagement, I think it a fitting moment to give here a brief sketch of his life.

COLONEL WILLIAM DAVIE DESSAUSURE

OF THE THIRTEENTH

Colonel Dessausure was certainly the Bayard of South Carolina, having served during his entire manhood, with little exception, amid the exciting, bustling scenes of army life. He was a hero of both the Mexican and Civil wars, and served in the Old Army for many years on the great Western Plains. A friend of his, an officer in his command who was very close to the Colonel, writes me a letter, of which I extract the following:

"In my judgment, he was the superior of Kershaw's fine set of Colonels, having, from nature, those rare qualities that go to make up the successful war commander, being reticent, observant, far-seeing, quick, decided, of iron will, inspiring confidence in his leadership, cheerful, self-possessed, unaffected by danger, and delighting like a game cock in battle. He was singularly truth loving and truth speaking, and you could rely with confidence on the accuracy of his every statement. He understood men, was clear sighted, quick and sound of judgment, and seemed never to be at a loss what to do in emergencies. He exposed himself with reckless courage, but protected his men with untiring concern and skill. He was rather a small man, physically, but his appearance and bearing were extremely martial, and had a stentorian voice that could be heard above the din of battle."

Colonel Dessausure was born in Columbia, S.C., December 12th, 1819, was reared and educated there, graduated at the South Carolina

College, and studied law in the office of his father, Hon. Wm. F. Dessausure. He raised a company in Columbia for the Mexican war, and served through that war as Captain of Company H, Palmetto Regiment. After that he was commissioned Captain of Cavalry, and assigned to General (then Colonel) Joseph K. Johnston's Regiment in the United States Army, and served on the Plains until the Civil war commenced, when he resigned, returned to his native State and organized the Fifteenth Regiment, and was assigned to Drayton's Brigade, then on the coast.

After the Seven Days' Battle around Richmond he went with his Regiment, as a part of Drayton's Brigade, in the first Maryland campaign. On Lee's return to Virginia, just before the Fredericksburg battle, his regiment was assigned to Kershaw.

The papers promoting him to the rank of Brigadier General were in the hands of the Secretary of War at the time he was killed. He was buried in a private cemetery near Breane's Tavern, in Pennsylvania, and his body removed to the family burying ground after the war.

He was married to Miss Ravenel of Charleston, who survived him some years.

Major Donald McDiarmid McLeod

Donald McDiarmid McLeod was descended from Scotch ancestors who immigrated to this country about 1775 and settled in Marlboro District, near Hunt's Bluff, on Big Pee Dee River. He was son of Daniel McLeod and Catherine Evans McLeod. He graduated from the South Carolina College about 1853, and for some time engaged in teaching school in his native county; then married Miss Margaret C. Alford and engaged in planting near where he was born. He was then quietly leading a happy and contented life when South Carolina seceded. When the toscin of war sounded he raised the first company of volunteers in Marlboro and was elected Captain of it. This company, with another from Marlboro organized about the same time under Captain J.W. Hamington, formed part of the Eighth Regiment, of Kershaw's Brigade. Capt. McLeod was of commanding presence, being six feet four inches tall, erect, active, and alert, beloved by his company, and when the test came proved himself worthy of their love and confidence. On the field of battle his gallantry was conspicuous, and he exhibited undaunted courage, and was faithful to every trust.

At the reorganization of the Regiment he was elected Major and served as such through the battles of Savage Station, Malvern Hill, Sharpsburg, Fredericksburg, Chancellorsville, and Gettysburg. In the last named he was killed while gallantly leading the Regiment in the desperate charge on the enemy's twenty pieces of artillery, in the celebrated peach orchard, where in a few minutes the Eighth Regiment, being on the left of the Brigade, without support, assailed in front and flanked, lost one hundred and eleven of the one hundred and seventy who were engaged in the battle. Of this number twenty-eight were killed and buried on the field of battle. Notwithstanding this slaughter the Old Eighth never faltered, but with the other regiments drove the enemy from the field, pursuing them upon the rugged slopes of Round Top Hill. Thus ended the life of one of the noblest and most devoted of Carolina's sons.

DR. T.W. SALMOND

T. W. Salmond was born in Camden, S.C., on 31st of August, 1825. Received his diploma from the Medical College, in Charleston, S.C., in 1849. Practiced medicine in Camden till the war came on. Married first, Miss Mary Whitaker, afterwards Miss Isabel Scota Whitaker. He had two daughters, one by each marriage. When the troops were ordered to Charleston, he left with General Kershaw as Surgeon of his regiment. General Kershaw was Colonel of the Second South Carolina Regiment. His regiment was at the bombardment of Sumter. His staff consisted of Dr. T.W. Salmond, Surgeon; Fraser, Quarter-Master; J.I. Villipigue, Commissary; A.D. Goodwyn, Adjutant.

At the reorganization of the Brigade, Dr. Salmond was promoted to Brigade Surgeon and was in all of the battles in Virginia. He went with General Kershaw to Tennessee and came home when General Kershaw went back to Virginia, owing to ill health in the spring of 1864.

He resumed his practice after the war and continued till his death, August 31st, 1869.

I give below a short sketch concerning the Brigade Surgeon, copied from a local paper, as showing the kind of metal of which Dr. Salmond was made:

To the Editor of The Kershaw Gazette:

I never look upon a maimed soldier of the "Lost Cause," who fought manfully for the cause which he deemed to be right, without being drawn towards him with I may say brotherly love, commingled with the profoundest respect. And I beg space in your valuable columns to relate an incident in connection with the battle of Gettysburg, which, I think, will equal the one between General Hagood and the Federal officer, Daley.

In that memorable battle, whilst we were charging a battery of sixteen pieces of artillery, when great gaps were being made in the lines by the rapid discharge of grape and canister, when the very grass beneath our feet was being cut to pieces by these missiles of death, and it looked as if mortal men could not possibly live there; Capt. W.Z. Leitner of our town was shot in the midst of this deadly shower at the head of his company. When his comrades were about to remove him from the field he said, "Men I am ruined but never give up the battle. I was shot down at the head of my company, and I would to God that I was there yet." He refused to let them carry him off the field. Dr. Salmond, then Brigade Surgeon of Kershaw's Brigade, learning that his friend Captain Leitner was seriously wounded, abandoned his post at the infirmary, mounted his horse and went to the field where Captain Leitner lay, amid the storm of lead and iron, regardless of the dangers which encompassed him on every hand. He placed Captain Leitner on his horse, and brought him off the field. The writer of this was wounded severely in this charge, and while he was making his way as best he could to the rear, he met the Brigade Surgeon on his mission of mercy to his fallen friend, ordering those to the front who were not wounded, as he went along. Brave man, he is now dead. Peace to his ashes. As long as I live, I shall cherish his memory and think of this circumstance.

A Member of the Old Brigade
from Kershaw Gazette of February 26, 1880

Judge Pope gives me several instances of devotion and courage during the Gettysburg campaign, which I take pleasure in inserting.

Did the Negroes Wish Freedom?

I have listened to much which has been said and written as to the aspiration of the negroes for freedom while they were slaves, but much that I saw myself makes me doubt that this aspiration was general.

Let me relate an instance that fell under my immediate observation. An officer had lost his bodyservant in May, 1863, when he mentioned the fact to some of the gentlemen of the and regiment, the reply was made: "There is a mess in Company A or I of the Third Regiment who have an excellent free negro boy in their employment, but they must give him up and no doubt you can get him." I saw the soldiers they referred to and they assured me that they would be glad if I would take the servant off their hands. The result was the servant came to me and I hired him. Soon afterwards we began the march to the Valley of Virginia, then to Maryland and Pennsylvania. The servant took care of my horse, amongst his other duties. Having been wounded at Gettysburg and placed in a wagon to be transported to Virginia this boy would ride the horse near by the wagon, procuring water and something to eat. As the caravan of wagons laden with wounded soldiers was drawing near to Hagerstown, Maryland, a flurry was discovered and we were told the Yankees were capturing our train. At this time the servant came up and asked me what he should do. I replied, "Put the Potomac River between you and the Yankees." He dashed off in a run. When I reached the Potomac River I found William there with my horse. The Yankees were about to attack us there. I was to be found across the river. I said to William, "What can you do?" He replied that he was going to swim the horse across the Potomac River, but said he himself could not swim. I saw him plunge into the river and swim across. The soldiers who were with me were sent from Winchester to Staunton, Virginia. While in Staunton, I was assured that I would receive a furlough at Richmond, Virginia, so William was asked if he wished to accompany me to South Carolina. This seemed to delight him. Before leaving Staunton, the boy was arrested as a runaway slave, being owned by a widow lady in Abbeville County. The servant admitted to me, when arrested, that he was a slave. A message was sent to his mistress how he had behaved while in my employment—especially how he had fled from the Yankees in Pennsylvania and Maryland. This was the last time I ever saw him. Surely a desire for freedom did not operate very seriously in this case, when the slave actually ran from it.

In parting I may add that, left to themselves negroes are very kindhearted, and even now I recall with lively pleasure the many kindnesses while I was wounded, from this servant, who was a slave.

HE WOULD FIGHT

Why is it that memory takes us away back into our past experiences without as much saying, "With your leave, sir"? Thirty-six years ago I knew a fine fellow just about eighteen years old and today he comes back to us so distinctly! He was a native of Newberry and when the war first broke out he left Newberry College to enlist as a private in Company E of the Third South Carolina Infantry. With his fine qualities of head and heart, it was natural that he should become a general favorite—witty, very ready, and always kind. His was a brave heart, too. Still he was rather girlish in appearance, for physically he was not strong. This latter condition may explain why he was called to act as Orderly at Regimental Headquarters when J.E. Brown gave up that position for that of courier with General Longstreet early in the year 1863. Just before the Third Regiment went into action at Gettysburg, Pennsylvania, and while preparing for that event, it became necessary, under general orders, that the field and staff of the regiment should dismount. It was the habit during battles to commit the horses to the control of the Regimental Orderly. On this occasion the Adjutant said to young Sligh: "Now, Tom, get behind some hill and the moment we call you, bring up the horses; time is often of importance." To the Adjutant's surprise Sligh burst into tears and besought that officer not to require him to stay behind, but on the contrary, to allow him to join his company and go into battle. At first this was denied, but so persistent was he in his request that the Adjutant, who was very fond of him, said: "Well Tom, for this one time you may go, but don't ask it again." Away he went with a smile instead of a tear. Poor fellow! The Orderly, Thomas W. Sligh, was killed in that battle while assisting to drive back General Sickles from the "Peach Orchard" on the 2d day of July, 1863.

RETURN TO VIRGINIA

At daylight on the morning of the 5th the remnant of that once grand army turned its face southward. I say remnant, for with the loss of near one-third its number in killed, wounded, and prisoners the pride, prestige of victory, the feelings of invincibility, were lost to the remainder, and the army was in rather ill condition when it took up the retreat. Lee has been severely criticised for fighting the battle of Gettysburg, especially the last charge of Pickett; but there are circumstances of minor import sometimes that surround a commander which force him to undertake or attempt that which his better judgment might dictate as a false step. The world judges by results the successes and achievements of a General, not by his motives or intentions. Battles, however, are in a great measure but series of accidents at best. Some unforeseen event or circumstance in the battles of Napoleon might have changed some of his most brilliant victories to utter defeats and his grandest triumphs into disastrous routs. Had not General Warren seen the open gap at little Round Top, and had it been possible for Federal troops to fill it up, or that Hancock had been one hour later, or that our troops had pushed through the gorge of little Round Top before seen by Warren and gained Meade's rear—suppose these, and many other things, and then reflect what momentous results depended upon such trivial circumstances, and we will then fail to criticise Lee. His chances were as good as Meade's. The combination of so many little circumstances, and the absence of his cavalry, all conduced to our defeat.

Hill took the lead, Longstreet followed, while Ewell brought up the rear. Our wagon trains had gone on, some of them the day before, towards Williamsport. Kilpatrick made a dash and captured and destroyed a goodly number of them, but the teamsters, non-combatants and the wounded succeeded in driving them off after some little damage.

Along down the mountain sides, through gorges and over hills, the army slowly made its way. No haste, no confusion. The enemy's cavalry harassed over rear, but did little more. Meade had had too severe a lesson to hover dangerously close on the heels of Lee, not knowing what moment the wily Confederate Chieftain might turn and strike him a blow he would not be able to receive. The rain fell in torrents, night and day. The roads were soon greatly cut up, which in a measure was to Lee's advantage, preventing the enemy from following him too closely, it being almost impossible to follow with his artillery and wagons after our trains had passed. We passed through Fairfield and Hagerstown and on to Williamsport. Near Funkstown we had some excitement by being called upon to help some of Stuart's Cavalry, who were being hard pressed at Antietam Creek.

After remaining in line of battle for several hours, on a rocky hillside, near the crossing of a sluggish stream, and our pickets exchanging a few shots with those of the enemy, we continued our march. On the night of the 6th and day of the 7th our army took up a line of battle in a kind of semi-circle, from Williamsport to Falling Waters. The Potomac was too much swollen from the continuous rains to ford, and the enemy having destroyed the bridge at Falling Waters we were compelled to entrench ourselves and defend our numerous trains of wagons and artillery until a bridge could be built. In the enclosure of several miles the whole of Lee's army, with the exception of some of his cavalry, were packed. Here Lee must have been in the most critical condition of the war, outside of Appomattox. Behind him was the raging Potomac, with a continual down-pour of rain, in front was the entire Federal army. There were but few heights from which to plant our batteries, and had the enemy pressed sufficiently near to have reached our vast camp with shells, our whole trains of ordnance would have been at his mercy. We had no bread stuff of consequence in the wagons, and only few beef cattle in the enclosure. For two days our bread supply had been cut off. Now had such conditions continued for several days longer, and a regular siege set in, Lee would have had to fight his way out. Lumber was difficult to obtain, so some houses were demolished, and such planks as could be used in the construction of boats were utilized, and a pontoon bridge was soon under way.

In this dilemma and strait an accident in the way of a "wind fall" (or I might more appropriately say, "bread fall") came to our regiment's relief. Jim George, a rather eccentric and "short-witted fellow," of Company C, while plundering around in some old outbuildings in our rear, conceived the idea to investigate a straw stack, or an old house filled with straw. After burrowing for some time away down in the tightly packed straw, his comrades heard his voice as he faintly called that he had struck "ile." Bounding out from beneath the straw stack, he came rushing into camp with the news of his find. He informed the Colonel that he had discovered a lot of flour in barrels hidden beneath the straw. The news was too good to be true, and knowing Jim's fund of imagination, few lent ear to the story, and most of the men shook their heads credulously. "What would a man want to put flour down in a straw stack for when no one knew of 'Lee's coming?'" and, moreover, "if they did, they did not know at which point he would cross." Many were the views expressed for and against the idea of investigating further, until "Old Uncle" Joe Culbreath, a veteran of the Mexican War, and a lieutenant in Jim George's company, said: "Boys, war is a trying thing; it puts people to thinking, and these d——n Yankees are the sharpest rascals in the world. No doubt they heard of our coming, and fearing a raid on their smoke houses, they did not do like us Southern people would have done—waited until the flour was gone before we thought of saving it—so this old fellow, no doubt, put his flour there for safety." That settled it. "Investigate" was the word, and away went a crowd. The straw was soon torn away, and there, snugly hidden, were eight or ten barrels of flour. The Colonel ordered an equal division among the regiment, giving Jim an extra portion for himself.

By the 13th the bridge was completed, and the waters had so far subsided that the river was fordable in places. An hour after dark we took up the line of march, and from our camp to the river, a distance of one mile or less, beat anything in the way of marching that human nature ever experienced. The dust that had accumulated by the armies passing over on their march to Gettysburg was now a perfect bog, while the horses and vehicles sinking in the soft earth made the road appear bottomless. We would march two or three steps, then halt for a moment or two; then a few steps more, and again the few minutes' wait. The men had to keep their hands on the backs of their file leaders to tell when to move and when to halt. The night being so dark and rainy, we could not see farther than "the noses on our faces," while at every step we went nearly up to our knees in slash and mud. Men would stand and sleep—would march (if this could be called marching) and sleep. The soldiers could not fall out of ranks for fear of being hopelessly lost, as troops of different corps and divisions would at times be mingled together. Thus we would be for one hour moving the distance of a hundred paces, and any soldier who has ever had to undergo such marching, can well understand its laboriousness. At daybreak we could see in the gloomy twilight our former camp, almost in hollering distance. Just as the sun began to peep up from over the eastern hills, we came in sight of the rude pontoon bridge, lined from one end to the other with hurrying wagons and artillery—the troops at opened ranks on either side. If it had been fatiguing on the troops, what must it have been on the poor horses and mules that had fasted for days and now drawing great trains, with roads almost bottomless? It was with a mingled feeling of delight and relief that the soldiers reached the Virginia side of the river—but not a murmur or harsh word for our beloved commander—all felt that he had done what was best for our country, and it was more in sorrow and sympathy that we beheld his bowed head and grief-stricken face as he rode at times past the moving troops.

General Pettigrew had the post of rear guard. He, with his brave troops, beat back the charge after charge of Kirkpatrick's Cavalry as they attempted to destroy our rear forces. It was a trying time to the retreating soldiers, who had passed over the river to hear their comrades fighting, single-handed and alone, for our safety and their very existence, without any hope of aid or succor. They knew they were left to be lost, and could have easily laid down their arms and surrendered, thus saving their lives; but this would have endangered Lee's army, so they fought and died like men. The roar of their howitzers and the rattle of their musketry were like the blasts of the horn of Roland when calling Charlemagne to his aid along the mountain pass of Roncesvalles, but, unlike the latter, we could not answer our comrades' call, and had only to leave them alone to "die in their glory." The brave Pettigrew fell while heading his troops in a charge to beat back some of the furious onslaughts of the enemy. The others were taken prisoners, with the exception of a few who made their escape by plunging in the stream and swimming across.

At first our march was by easy stages, but when Lee discovered the enemy's design of occupying the mountain passes along the Blue Ridge to our left, no time was lost. We hastened along through Martinsburg and Winchester, across the Shenandoah to Chester Gap, on the Blue Ridge. We camped at night on the top of the mountain.

Here an amusing, as well as ludicrous, scene was enacted, but not so amusing to the participants however. Orders had been given when on the eve of our entrance into Maryland, that "no private property of whatever description should be molested." As the fields in places were enclosed by rail fences, it was strictly against orders to disturb any of the fences. This order had been religiously obeyed all the while, until this night on the top of the Blue Ridge. A shambling, tumble-down rail fence was near the camp of the Third South Carolina, not around any field, however, but apparently to prevent stock from passing on the western side of the mountain. At night while the troops lay in the open air, without any protection whatever, only what the scrawny trees afforded, a light rain came up. Some of the men ran to get a few rails to make a hurried bivouac, while others who had gotten somewhat damp by the rain took a few to build a fire. As the regiment was formed in line next morning, ready for the march, Adjutant Pope came around for company commanders to report to Colonel Nance's headquarters. Thinking this was only to receive some instructions as to the line of march, nothing was thought of it until met by those cold, penetrating, steel-gray eyes of Colonel Nance. Then all began to wonder "what was up." He commenced to ask, after repeating the instructions as to private property, whose men had taken the rails. He commenced with Captain Richardson, of Company A.

"Did your men take any rails?"

"Yes, sir."

"Did you have them put back?"

"Yes, sir."

"Captain Gary, did your men use any rails?"

"Yes, sir."

"Did you have them replaced?"

"No, sir."

And so on down to Company K. All admitted that their men had taken rails and had not put them back, except Captain Richardson. Then such a lecture as those nine company commanders received was seldom heard. To have heard Colonel Nance dilate upon the enormity of the crime of "disobedience to orders," was enough to make one think he had "deserted his colors in the face of the enemy," or lost a battle through his cowardice. "Now, gentlemen, let this never occur again. For the present you will deliver your swords to Adjutant Pope, turn your companies over to your next officer in command, and march in rear of the regiment until further orders." Had a thunder bolt fallen, or a three hundred-pound Columbiad exploded in our midst, no greater consternation would they have caused. Captain Richardson was exhonorated, but the other nine Captains had to march in rear of the regiment during the day, subject to the jeers and ridicule of all the troops that passed, as well as the negro cooks. "Great Scott, what a company of officers!" "Where are your men?" "Has there been a stampede?" "Got furloughs?" "Lost your swords in a fight?" were some of the pleasantries we were forced to hear and endure. Captain Nance, of Company G, had a negro cook, who undertook the command of the officers and as the word from the front would come down the line to "halt" or "forward" or "rest," he would very gravely repeat it, much to the merriment of the troops next in front and those in our rear. Near night, however, we got into a brush with the enemy, who were forcing their way down along the eastern side of the mountain, and Adjutant Pope came with our swords and orders to relieve us from arrest. Lieutenant Dan Maffett had not taken the matter in such good humor, and on taking command of his company, gave this laconic order, "Ya hoo!" (That was the name given to Company C.) "If you ever touch another rail during the whole continuance of the war, G——d d——n you, I'll have you shot at the stake."

"How are we to get over a fence," inquired someone.

"Jump it, creep it, or go around it, but death is your portion, if you ever touch a rail again."

On the 13th of August the whole army was encamped on the south side of the Rapidan. We were commencing to settle down for several months of rest and enjoy a season of furloughs, as it was evident neither side would begin active operations until the armies were recruited up and the wounded returned for duty. This would take at least several months. But, alas! for our expectations—a blast to our fondest dreams—heavy fighting and hard marching was in store for our corps. Bragg was being slowly driven out of Tennessee and needed help; the "Bull Dog of the Confederacy" was the one most likely to stay the advancing tide of Rosecrans' Army.

CHAPTER 21

Transferred to Georgia

While in camp great stress was laid on drills. The brigade drill was the most important. Every day at 3 o'clock the whole brigade was marched to a large old field, and all the evolutions of the brigade drill were gone through with. Crowds of citizens from the surrounding country came to witness our maneuvers, especially did the ladies grace the occasions with their presence. The troops were in the very best of spirits—no murmurs nor complaints. Clothing and provision boxes began coming in from home. A grand corps review took place soon after our encampment was established, in which Generals Lee and Longstreet reviewed the troops.

All expected a good, long rest after their many marches and bloody battles in Maryland and Pennsylvania, but we were soon to be called upon for work in other fields. General Bragg had been driven out of Tennessee to the confines of Georgia, and it seemed that, without succor from the Army of the East to aid in fighting their battles, and to add to the morale of the Western Army, Bragg would soon be forced through Georgia. It had long been the prevailing opinion of General Longstreet that the most strategic movement for the South was to reinforce General Bragg with all the available troops of the East (Lee standing on the defensive), crush Rosecrans, and, if possible, drive him back and across the Ohio. With this end in view, General Longstreet wrote, in August, to General Lee, as well as to the Secretary of War, giving these opinions as being the only solution to the question of checking the continual advance of Rosecrans—renewing the morale of the Western Army and reviving the waning spirits of the Confederacy, thus putting the enemy on the defensive and regaining lost territory.

It should be remembered that our last stronghold on the Mississippi, Vicksburg, had capitulated about the time of the disastrous battle of Gettysburg, with thirty thousand prisoners. That great waterway was opened to the enemy's gun boats and transports, thus cutting the South, with a part of her army, in twain.

This suggestion of General Longstreet was accepted, so far as sending him, with a part of his corps, to Georgia, by his receiving orders early in September to prepare his troops for transportation.

The most direct route by railroad to Chattanooga, through Southwest Virginia and East Tennessee, had for some time been in the hands of the enemy at Knoxville. We were, therefore, forced to take the circuitous route by way of the two Carolinas and Georgia. There were two roads open to transportation, one by Wilmington and one by Charlotte, N.C., as far as Augusta, Ga., but from thence on there was but a single line, and as such our transit was greatly impeded.

On the morning of the 15th or 16th of September Kershaw's Brigade was put aboard the trains at White Oak Station, and commenced the long ride to North Georgia. Hood's Division was already on the way. Jenkins' (S.C.) Brigade had been assigned to that division, but it and one of the other of Hood's brigades failed to reach the battleground in time to participate in the glories of that event. General McLaws, also, with two of his brigades, Bryan's and Wofford' (Georgians), missed the fight, the former awaiting the movements of his last troops, as well as that of the artillery.

Long trains of box cars had been ordered up from Richmond and the troops were loaded by one company being put inside and the next on top, so one-half of the corps made the long four days' journey on the top of box cars. The cars on all railroads in which troops were transported were little more than skeleton cars; the weather being warm, the troops cut all but the frame work loose with knives and axes. They furthermore wished to see outside and witness the fine country and delightful scenery that lay along the route; nor could those Inside bear the idea of being shut up in a box car while their comrades on top were cheering and yelling themselves hoarse at the waving of handkerchiefs and flags in the hands of the pretty women and the hats thrown in the air by the old men and boys along the roadside as the trains sped through the towns, villages, and hamlets of the Carolinas and Georgia, No, no; the exuberant spirits of the Southern soldier were too great to allow him to hear yelling going on and not yell himself. He yelled at everything he saw, from an ox-cart to a pretty woman, a downfall of a luckless cavalryman to a charge in battle.

The news of our coming had preceded us, and at every station and road-crossing the people of the surrounding country, without regard to sex or age, crowded to see us pass, and gave us their blessings and God speed as we swept by with lightning speed. Our whole trip was one grand ovation. Old men slapped their hands in praise, boys threw up their hats in joy, while the ladies fanned the breeze with their flags and handkerchiefs; yet many a mother dropped a silent tear or felt a heart-ache as she saw her long absent soldier boy flying pass without a word or a kiss.

At the towns which we were forced to stop for a short time great tables were stretched, filled with the bounties of the land, while the fairest and the best women on earth stood by and ministered to every wish or want. Was there ever a purer devotion, a more passionate patriotism, a more sincere loyalty, than that displayed by the women of the South towards the soldier boys and the cause for which they fought? Was there ever elsewhere on earth such women? Will there ever again exist circumstances and conditions that will require such heroism, fortitude, and suffering? Perhaps so, perhaps not.

In passing through Richmond we left behind us two very efficient officers on a very pleasant mission, Dr. James Evans, Surgeon of the Third, who was to be married to one of Virginia's fair daughters, and Captain T.W. Gary, of same regiment, who was to act as best man. Dr. Evans was a native South Carolinian and a brother of Brigadier General N.G. Evans, of Manassas fame. While still a young man, he was considered one of the finest surgeons and practitioners in the army. He was kind and considerate to his patients, punctual and faithful in his duties, and withal a dignified, refined gentleman. Such confidence had the soldiers in his skill and competency, that none felt uneasy when their lives or limbs, were left to his careful handling. Both officers rejoined us in a few days.

We reached Ringold on the evening of the 19th of September, and marched during the night in the direction of the day's battle-field. About midnight we crossed over the sluggish stream of Chickamauga, at Alexander's Bridge, and bivouaced near Hood's Division, already encamped. Chickamauga! how little known of before, but what memories its name is to awaken for centuries afterwards! What a death struggle was to take place along its borders between the blue and the gray, where brother was to meet brother—where the soldiers of the South were to meet their kinsmen of the Northwest! In the long, long ago, before the days of fiction and romance of the white man in the New World, in the golden days of legend of the forest dwellers, when the red man chanted the glorious deeds of his ancestors during his death song to the ears of his children, this touching story has come down from generation to generation, until it reached the ears of their destroyers, the pale faces of today:

Away in the dim distant past a tribe of Indians, driven from their ancestral hunting grounds in the far North, came South and pitched their wigwams along the banks of the "river of the great bend," the Tennessee. They prospered, multiplied, and expanded, until their tents covered the mountain sides and plains below. The braves of the hill men hunted and sported with their brethren of the valley. Their children fished, hunted, played, fought, and gamboled in mimic warfare as brothers along the sparkling streamlets that rise in the mountain ridges, their sparkling waters leaping and jumping through the gorges and glens and flowing away to the "great river." All was peace and happiness; the tomahawk of war had long since been buried, and the pipe of peace smoked around their camp fires after every successful hunting expedition. But dissentions arose—distrust and embittered feelings took the place of brotherly love. The men of the mountains became arrayed against their brethren of the plains, and they in turn became the sworn enemies of the dwellers of the cliffs. The war hatchet was dug up and the pipe of peace no longer passed in brotherly love at the council meeting. Their bodies were decked in the paint of war, and the once peaceful and happy people forsook their hunting grounds and entered upon, the war path.

Early on an autumn day, when the mountains and valleys were clothed in golden yellow, the warriors of the dissenting factions met along the banks of the little stream, and across its turbid waters waged a bitter battle from early morn until the "sun was dipping behind the palisades of Look-Out Mountain"—no quarters given and none asked. It was a war of extermination. The blood of friend and foe mingled in the stream until its waters were said to be red with the lifeblood of the struggling combatants. At the close of the fierce combat the few that survived made a peace and covenant, and then and there declared that for all time the sluggish stream should be called Chickamauga, the "river of blood." Such is the legend of the great battleground and the river from whence it takes its name.

General Buckner had come down from East Tennessee with his three divisions, Stewart's, Hindman's, and Preston's, and had joined General Bragg some time before our arrival, making General Bragg's organized army forty-three thousand eight hundred and sixty-six strong. He was further reinforced by eleven thousand five hundred from General Joseph E. Johnston's army in Mississippi and five thousand under General Longstreet, making a total of sixty thousand three hundred and thirty-six, less casualties of the 18th and 19th of one thousand one hundred and twenty-four; so as to numbers on the morning of the 20th, Bragg had of all arms fifty-nine thousand two hundred and forty-two; while the Federal commander claimed only sixty thousand three hundred and sixty six, but at least five thousand more on detached duty and non-combatants, such as surgeons, commissaries, quartermasters, teamsters, guards, etc. Bragg's rolls covered all men in his army. Rosecrans was far superior in artillery and cavalry, as all of the batteries belonging to Longstreet's corps, or that were to attend him in the campaign of the West, were far back in South Carolina, making what speed possible on the clumsy and cumbersome railroads of that day. So it was with Wofford's and Bryan's Brigades, of McLaw's Division, Jenkins' and one of Hood's, as well as all of the subsistence and ordnance trains. The artillery assigned to General Longstreet by General Lee consisted of Ashland's and Bedford's (Virginia), Brooks' (South Carolina), and Madison's (Louisiana) batteries of light artillery, and two Virginia batteries of position, all under the command of Colonel Alexander.

As for transportation, the soldiers carried all they possessed on their backs, with four days of cooked rations all the time. Generally one or two pieces of light utensils were carried by each company, in which all the bread and meat were cooked during the night.

Our quartermasters gathered up what they could of teams and wagons from the refuse of Bragg's trains to make a semblance of subsistence transportation barely sufficient to gather in the supplies. It was here that the abilities of our chiefs of quartermaster and commissary departments were tested to the utmost. Captains Peck and Shell, of our brigade, showed themselves equal to the occasion, and Captain Lowrance, of the Subsistence Department, could always be able to furnish us with plenty of corn meal from the surrounding country.

The sun, on the morning of the 20th, rose in unusual splendor, and cast its rays and shadows in sparkling brilliancy over the mountains and plains of North Georgia. The leaves of the trees and shrubbery, in their golden garb of yellow, shown out bright and beautiful in their early autumnal dress—quite in contrast with the bloody scenes to be enacted before the close of day. My older brother, a private in my company, spoke warmly of the beautiful Indian summer morning and the sublime scenery round about, and wondered if all of us would ever see the golden orb of day rise again in its magnificence. Little did he think that even then the hour hand on the dial plate of destiny was pointing to the minute of "high noon," when fate was to take him by the hand and lead him away. It was his turn in the detail to go to the rear during the night to cook rations for the company, and had he done so, he would have missed the battle, as the details did not return in time to become participants in the engagement that commenced early in the morning. He had asked permission to exchange duties with a comrade, as he wished to be near me should a battle ensue during the time. Contrary to regulations, I granted the request. Now the question naturally arises, had he gone on his regular duties would the circumstances have been different? The soldier is generally a believer in the doctrine of predestination in the abstract, and it is well he is so, for otherwise many soldiers would run away from battle. But as it is, he consoles himself with the theories of the old doggerel quartet, which reads something like this:—

> He who fights and runs away,
> May live to fight another day;
> But he who is in battle slain,
> Will ne'er live to fight again.

Longstreet's troops had recently been newly uniformed, consisting of a dark-blue round jacket, closely fitting, with light-blue trousers, which made a line of Confederates resemble that of the enemy, the only difference being the "cut" of the garments—the Federals wearing a loose blouse instead of a tight-fitting jacket. The uniforms of the Eastern troops made quite a contrast with the tattered and torn homemade jeans of their Western brethren.

General Bragg had divided his army into two wings—the right commanded by Lieutenant General Leonidas Polk (a Bishop of the M.E. Church, and afterwards killed in the battles around Atlanta.) and the left commanded by that grand chieftain (Lee's "Old War Horse" and commander of his right), Lieutenant General James Longstreet. Under his guidance were Preston's Division on extreme left, Hindman's next, with Stewart's on extreme right of left wing, all of Major General Buckner's corps. Between Hindman and Stewart was Bushrod Johnson's new formed division. In reserve were Hood's three brigades, with Kershaw's and Humphries', all under Major General Hood, standing near the center and in rear of the wing.

The right wing stood as follows: General Pat Cleburn's Division on right of Stewart, with Breckenridge's on the extreme right of the infantry, under the command of Lieutenant General D.H. Hill, with Cheatham's Division of Folk's Corps to the left and rear of Cleburn as support, with General Walker's Corps acting as reserve. Two divisions of Forrest's Cavalry, one dismounted, were on the right of Breckenridge, to guard that flank, while far out to the left of Longstreet were two brigades of Wheeler's Cavalry. The extreme left of the army, Preston's Division, rested on Chickamauga Creek, the right thrown well forward towards the foot hills of Mission Ridge.

In the alignment of the two wings it was found that Longstreet's right overlapped Folk's left, and fully one-half mile in front, so it became necessary to bend Stewart's Division back to join to Cleburn's left, thereby leaving space between Bushrod Johnson and Stewart for Hood to place his three brigades on the firing line.

Longstreet having no artillery, he was forced to engage all of the thirty pieces of Buckner's. In front of Longstreet lay a part of the Twentieth Corps, Davis' and Sheridan's Divisions, under Major General McCook, and part of the Twenty-first Corps, under the command of General Walker. On our right, facing Polk, was the distinguished Union General, George H. Thomas, with four divisions of his own corps, the Fourteenth, Johnson's Division of the Twentieth, and Van Cleve's of the Twenty-first Corps.

General Thomas was a native Virginian, but being an officer in the United States Army at the time of the secession of his State, he preferred to remain and follow the flag of subjugation, rather than, like the most of his brother officers of Southern birth, enter into the service of his native land and battle for justice, liberty, and States Rights. He and General Hunt, of South Carolina, who so ably commanded the artillery of General Meade at Gettysburg, were two of the most illustrious of Southern renegades.

In the center of Rosecrans' Army were two divisions, Woods' and Palmer's, under Major General Crittenden, posted along the eastern slope of Mission Ridge, with orders to support either or both wings of the army, as occasions demanded.

General Gordon Granger, with three brigades of infantry and one division of cavalry, guarded the Union left and rear and the gaps leading to Chattanooga, and was to act as general reserve for the army and lay well back and to the left of Brannan's Division that was supporting the front line of General Thomas.

The bulk of the Union cavalry, under General Mitchell, was two miles distant on our left, guarding the ford over Chickamauga at Crawfish Springs. The enemy's artillery, consisting of two hundred and forty-six pieces, was posted along the ridges in our front, giving exceptional positions to shell and grape an advancing column.

Bragg had only two hundred pieces, but as his battle line occupied lower ground than that of the enemy, there was little opportunity to do effective work with his cannon.

The ground was well adapted by nature for a battlefield, and as the attacking party always has the advantage of maneuver and assault in an open field, each commander was anxious to get his blow in first. So had not Bragg commenced the battle as early as he did, we would most assuredly have had the whole Federal Army upon our hands before the day was much older. Kershaw's Brigade, commanded by General Kershaw, stood from right to left in the following order: Fifteenth Regiment on the right, commanded by Lieutenant Colonel Joseph Gist; Second Regiment, Colonel James D. Kennedy; Third, Colonel James D. Nance; Third Battalion, by Captain Robert H. Jennings; Eighth, Colonel John W. Henagan; Seventh, Colonel Elbert Bland.

The Battle of Chickamauga

As I have already said, this was a lovely country—a picturesque valley nestling down among the spurs of the mountain, with the now classic Chickamauga winding its serpentine way along with a sluggish flow. It was also a lovely day; nature was at her best, with the fields and woods autumn tinged—the whole country rimmed in the golden hue of the Southern summer. The battling ground chosen, or rather say selected by fate, on which the fierce passions of men were to decide the fortunes of armies and the destiny of a nation, was rolling, undulating, with fields of growing grain or brown stubble, broken by woods and ravines, while in our front rose the blue tinted sides of Mission Ridge.

Both commanders were early in the saddle, their armies more evenly matched in numbers and able Lieutenants than ever before, each willing and anxious to try conclusions with the other—both confident of success and watchful of the mistakes and blunders of their opponent, ready to take advantage of the least opportunity that in any way would lead to success. The armies on either side were equally determined and confident, feeling their invincibility and the superiority of their respective commanders. Those of the North felt that it was impossible for the beaten Confederates to stand for a moment, with any hope of triumph, before that mighty machine of armed force that had been successfully rolling from the Ohio to the confines of Georgia. On the other hand, the Army of Tennessee felt that, with the aid from Joe Johnston, with Buckner, and the flower of Lee's Army to strengthen their ranks, no army on earth could stay them on the battlefield.

The plan of battle was to swing the whole army forward in a wheel, Preston's Division on Longstreet's extreme left being the pivot, the right wing to break the enemy's lines and uncover the McFarland and Rossville Gaps, thus capturing the enemy's lines of communication to Chattanooga.

The Union Army was well protected by two lines of earthworks and log obstructions, with field batteries at every salient, or scattered along the front lines at every elevation, supported by the pieces of position on the ridges in rear.

The Confederate commander made no secret of his plan of battle, for it had been formulated three days before, and his manoeuvers on the 18th and 19th indicated his plan of operations. Early in the morning Bragg saluted his adversary with thirty pieces of artillery from his right wing, and the Federal Commander was not slow in acknowledging the salutation. The thunder of these guns echoed along the mountain sides and up and down the valleys with thrilling effect. Soon the ridges in our front were one blaze of fire as the infantry began their movements for attack, and the smoke from the enemy's guns was a signal for our batteries along the whole line.

The attack on the right was not as prompt as the commander in chief had expected, so he rode in that direction and gave positive orders for the battle to begin. General D.H. Hill now ordered up that paladin of State craft, the gallant Kentuckian and opponent of Lincoln for the Presidency, General John C. Breckenridge, and put him to the assault on the enemy's extreme left. But one of his brigade commanders being killed early in the engagement, and the other brigades becoming somewhat disorganized by the tangled underbrush, they made but little headway against the enemy's works. Then the fighting Irishman, the Wild Hun of the South, General Pat Cleburn, came in with his division on Breckenridge's left, and with whoop and yell he fell with reckless ferocity upon the enemy's entrenchments. The four-gun battery of the Washington (Louisiana) Artillery following the column of Assault, contended successfully with the superior metal of the three batteries of the enemy. The attack was so stubborn and relentless that the enemy was forced back on his second line, and caused General Thomas to call up Negley's Division from his reserves to support his left against the furious assaults of Breckenridge and Cleburn. But after somewhat expending their strength in the first charge against the enemy's works, and Federal reinforcements of infantry and artillery coming up, both Confederate divisions were gradually being forced back to their original positions. Deshler's Brigade, under that prince of Southern statesmen, Roger Q. Mills, supported by a part of Cheatham's Division, took up Cleburn's battle, while the division under General States R. Gist (of South Carolina), with Liddell's, of Walker's Corps, went to the relief of Breckenridge.

Gist's old Brigade (South Carolina) struck the angle of the enemy's breastworks, and received a galling fire from enfilading lines. But the other brigades of Gist's coming up and Liddell's Division pushing its way through the shattered and disorganized ranks of Breckenridge, they made successful advance, pressing the enemy back and beyond the Chattanooga Road.

Thomas was again reduced to the necessity of calling for reinforcements, and so important was it thought that this ground should be held, that the Union commander promised support, even to the extent of the whole army, if necessary.

But eleven o'clock had come and no material advantage had been gained on the right. The reinforcements of Thomas having succeeded in checking the advance of Gist and Liddell, the Old Warhorse on the left became impatient, and sent word to Bragg, "My troops can break the lines, if you care to have them broken." What sublime confidence did Lee's old commander of the First Corps have in the powers of his faithful troops! But General Bragg, it seems, against all military rules or precedent, and in violation of the first principles of army ethics, had already sent orders to Longstreet's subalterns, directly and not through the Lieutenant General's headquarters, as it should have been done, to commence the attack. General Stewart, with his division of Longstreet's right, was at that moment making successful battle against the left of the Twentieth and right of Twenty-first Corps. This attack so near to Thomas' right, caused that astute commander to begin to be as apprehensive of his right as he had been of his left flank, and asked for support in that quarter. Longstreet now ordered up the gallant Texan, General Hood, with his three brigades, with Kershaw's and Humphreys in close support. Hood unmercifully assailed the column in his front, but was as unmercifully slaughtered, himself falling desperately wounded. Benning's Brigade was thrown in confusion, but at this juncture Kershaw and Humphreys moved their brigades upon the firing line end commenced the advance. In front of these two brigades was a broad expanse of cultivated ground, now in stubble. Beyond this field was a wooded declivity rising still farther away to a ridge called Pea Ridge, on which the enemy was posted. Our columns were under a terrific fire of shells as they advanced through the open field, and as they neared the timbered ridge they were met by a galling tempest of grape and canister. The woods and underbrush shielded the enemy from view.

Law now commanding Hood's Division, reformed his lines and

assaulted and took the enemy's first lines of entrenchments. Kershaw marched in rear of the brigade, giving commands in that clear, metallic sound that inspired confidence in his troops. At the foot of the declivity, or where the ground begun to rise towards the enemy's lines, was a rail fence, and at this obstruction and clearing of it away, Kershaw met a galling fire from the Federal sharpshooters, but not a gun had been fired as yet by our brigade. But Humphreys was in it hot and heavy. As we began our advance up the gentle slope, the enemy poured volley after volley into us from its line of battle posted behind the log breastworks. Now the battle with us raged in earnest.

Bushrod Johnson entered the lists with his division, and routed the enemy in his front, taking the first line of breastworks without much difficulty. Hindman's Division followed Johnson, but his left and rear was assailed by a formidable force of mounted infantry which threw Manigault's (South Carolina) Brigade on his extreme left in disorder, the brigade being seriously rattled. But Twigg's Brigade, from Preston's pivotal Division, came to the succor of Manigault and succeeded in restoring the line, and the advance continued. Kershaw had advanced to within forty paces of the enemy's line, and it seemed for a time that his troops would be annihilated. Colonel Bland, then Major Hard, commanding the Seventh, were killed. Lieutenant Colonel Hoole, of the Eighth, was killed. Colonel Gist, commanding the Fifteenth, and Captain Jennings, commanding the Third Battalion, were dangerously wounded, while many others of the line officers had fallen, and men were being mown down like grain before a sickle.

General Kershaw ordered his men to fall back to the little ravine a hundred paces in rear, and here they made a temporary breastwork of the torn down fence and posted themselves behind it. They had not long to wait before a long line of blue was seen advancing from the crest of the hill. The enemy, no doubt, took our backward movement as a retreat, and advanced with a confident mien, all unconscious of our presence behind the rail obstruction. Kershaw, with his steel-gray eyes glancing up and down his lines, and then at the advancing line of blue, gave the command repeatedly to "Hold your fire." When within a very short distance of our column the startling command rang out above the din of battle on our right and left, "Fire!" Then a deafening volley rolled out along the whole line. The enemy halted and wavered, their men falling in groups, then fled to their entrenchments, Kershaw closely pursuing.

From the firing of the first gun away to the right the battle became one of extreme bitterness, the Federals standing with unusual gallantry by their guns in the vain hope that as the day wore on they could successfully withstand, if not entirely repel, the desperate assaults of Bragg until night would give them cover to withdraw.

The left wing was successful, and had driven the Federal lines back at right angles on Thomas' right. The Federal General, Gordon Granger, rests his title to fame by the bold movement he now made. Thomas was holding Polk in steady battle on our right, when General Granger noticed the Twentieth Corps was being forced back, and the firing becoming dangerously near in the Federal's rear. General Granger, without any orders whatever, left his position in rear of Thomas and marched to the rescue of McCook, now seeking shelter along the slopes of Mission Ridge, but too late to retrieve losses—only soon enough to save the Federal Army from rout and total disaster.

But the turning point came when Longstreet ordered up a battalion of heavy field pieces, near the angle made by the bending back of the enemy's right, and began infilading the lines of Thomas, as well as Crittenden's and McCook's. Before this tornado of shot and shell nothing could stand. But with extraordinary tenacity of Thomas and the valor of his men he held his own for a while longer.

Kershaw was clinging to his enemy like grim death from eleven o'clock until late in the evening—his men worn and fagged, hungry and almost dying of thirst, while the ammunition was being gradually exhausted and no relief in sight. Hindman (Johnson on the left) had driven the enemy back on Snodgrass Hill, where Granger's reserves were aiding them in making the last grand struggle. Snodgrass Hill was thought to be the key to the situation on our left, as was Horse Shoe Bend on the right, but both were rough and hard keys to handle. Kershaw had driven all before him from the first line of works, and only a weak fire was coming from the second line. All that was needed now to complete the advance was a concentrated push along the whole line, but the density of the smoke settling in the woods, the roar of battle drowning all commands, and the exhaustion and deflection of the rank and file made this move impossible.

But just before the sun began dipping behind the mountains on our left, a long line of gray, with glittering bayonets, was seen coming down the slope in our rear. It was General Grade, with his Alabama Brigade of Preston's Division, coming to reinforce our broken ranks and push the battle forward. This gallant brigade was one thousand one hundred strong and it was said this was their first baptism of fire and blood. General Gracie was a fine specimen of physical manhood and a finished looking officer, and rode at the head of his column. Reaching Kershaw, he dismounted, placed the reins of his horse over his arm, and ordered his men to the battle. The enemy could not withstand the onslaught of these fresh troops, and gave way, pursued down the little dell in rear by the Alabamians. The broken lines formed on the reserves that were holding Snodgrass Hill, and made an aggressive attack upon Gracie, forcing him back on the opposite hill.

Twigg's Brigade, of the same division, came in on the left and gave him such support as to enable him to hold his new line.

The fire of Longstreet's batteries from the angle down Thomas' lines, forced that General to begin withdrawing his troops from their entrenchments, preparatory to retreat. This movement being noticed by the commanding General, Liddell's Division on the extreme right was again ordered to the attack, but with no better success than in the morning. The enemy had for some time been withdrawing his trains and broken ranks through the gaps of the mountain in the direction of Chattanooga, leaving nothing in front of the left wing but the reserves of Granger and those of Crittenden. These held their ground gallantly around Snodgrass Hill, but it was a self-evident fact to all the officers, as well as the troops, that the battle was irretrievably lost, and they were only fighting for time, the time that retreat could be safely made under cover of darkness. But before the sun was fairly set, that great army was in full retreat. But long before this it was known to the brilliant Union commander that fate had played him false—that destiny was pointing to his everlasting overthrow. He knew, too, that the latter part of the battle, while brief and desperate, the lurid cloud of battle settling all around his dead and dying, a spectre had even then arisen as from the earth, and pointing his bony fingers at the field of carnage, whispering in his ear that dreaded word, "Lost!"

As night closed in upon the bloody scenes of the day, the Federal Army, that in the morning had stood proud and defiant along the crests and gorges of the mountain ridges, was now a struggling mass of beaten and fleeing fugitives, or groups groping their way through the darkness towards the passes that led to Chattanooga.

Of all the great Captains of that day, Longstreet was the guiding genius of Chickamauga. It was his masterful mind that rose equal to the emergency, grasped and directed the storm of battle. It was by the unparalleled courage of the troops of Hood, Humphreys, and Kershaw, and the temporary command under Longstreet, throwing themselves athwart the path of the great colossus of the North, that checked him and drove him back over the mountains to the strongholds around Chattanooga. And it is no violent assumption to say that had the troops on the right under Polk supported the battle with as fiery zeal as those on the left under Longstreet, the Union Army would have been utterly destroyed and a possible different ending to the campaign, if not in final, results might have been confidently expected.

The work of the soldier was not done with the coming of night. The woods along the slopes where the battle had raged fiercest had caught fire and the flames were nearing the wounded and the dead. Their calls and piteous wails demanded immediate assistance. Soldiers in groups and by ones and twos scoured the battlefield in front and rear, gathering up first the wounded then the dead. The former were removed to the field infirmaries, the latter to the new city to be built for them—the city of the dead. The builders were already at work on their last dwelling places, scooping out shallow graves with bayonets, knives, and such tools that were at hand. Many pathetic spectacles were witnessed of brother burying brother. My brother and five other members of the company were laid side by side, wrapped only in their blankets, in the manner of the Red Men in the legend who fought and died here in the long, long ago. Here we left them "in all their glory" amid the sacred stillness that now reigned over the once stormy battlefield, where but a short while before the tread of struggling legions, the thunder of cannon, and the roar of infantry mingled in systematic confusion. But now the awful silence and quietude that pervades the field after battle—where lay the dreamless sleepers of friend and foe, victor and vanquished, the blue and the gray, with none to sing their requiems—nothing heard save the plaintive notes of the night bird or the faint murmurs of grief of the comrades who are placing the sleepers in their shallow beds! But what is death to the soldier? It is the passing of a comrade perhaps one day or hour in advance to the river with the Pole Ferryman.

Bragg, out of a total of fifty-nine thousand two hundred and forty-two, lost seventeen thousand eight hundred. Rosecran's total was sixty thousand eight hundred and sixty-seven (exclusive of the losses on the 18th and 19th). His loss on the 20th was sixteen thousand five hundred and fifty. The greater loss of the Confederates can be accounted for when it is remembered that they were the assaulting party—the enemy's superior position, formidable entrenchments, and greater amount of artillery.

The Battle of Chickamauga was one of the most sanguinary of the war, when the number of troops engaged and the time in actual combat are taken into consideration. In the matter of losses it stands as the fifth greatest battle of the war. History gives no authentic record of greater casualties in battle in the different organizations, many of the regiments losing from fifty to fifty-seven per cent, of their numbers, while some reached as high as sixty-eight per cent. When it's remembered that usually one is killed out right to every five that are wounded, some idea of the dreadful mortality on the field can be formed.

CHAPTER 23
Notes of the Battle

The Seventh Regiment was particularly unfortunate in the loss of her brilliant officers. Colonel Bland and Lieutenant Colonel Hood both being killed, that regiment was left without a field officer. Lieutenant Colonel Joseph Gist, of the Fifteenth, being permanently disabled, and Major William Gist being soon afterwards killed, the Fifteenth was almost in the same condition of the Seventh. So also was the Third Battalion. Captain Robert Jennings, commanding the battalion as senior Captain, lost his arm here, and was permanently retired, leaving Captain Whitner in command. Major Dan Miller had received a disabling wound in some of the former battles and never returned. Colonel Rice returning soon after this battle, he likewise received a wound from which he never sufficiently recovered for active service, so the Third Battalion was thereafter commanded by a Captain, Captain Whitner commanding until his death one year later. The Eighth Regiment met an irreparable loss in the death of Lieutenant Colonel Hoole. No officer in the brigade had a more soldierly bearing, high attainments, and knightly qualities than Colonel Hoole, and not only the regiment, but the whole brigade felt his loss. He was one of those officers whose fine appearance caused men to stop and look at him twice before passing. The many fine officers, Captains as well as Lieutenants, that were killed or wounded here made a death and disabled roll, from the effects of which the brigade never fully recovered. Then the whole army mourned the supposed death of the gallant and dashing Texan, General Hood, but he lived to yet write his name in indelible letters on the roll-of fame among the many officers of distinction in the Army of Tennessee.

In our first general advance in the morning, as the regiment reached the brow of the hill, just before striking the enemy's breastworks, my company and the other color company, being crowded together by the pressure of the flanks on either side, became for the moment a tangled, disorganized mass. A sudden discharge of grape from the enemy's batteries, as well as from their sharpshooters posted behind trees, threw us in greater confusion, and many men were shot down unexpectedly. A Sergeant in my company, T.C. Nunnamaker, received a fearful wound in the abdomen. Catching my hand while falling, he begged to be carried off. "Oh! for God's sake, don't leave me here to bleed to death or have my life trampled out! Do have me carried off!" But the laws of war are inexorable, and none could leave the ranks to care for the wounded, and those whose duty it was to attend to such matters were unfortunately too often far in the rear, seeking places of safety for themselves, to give much thought or concern to the bleeding soldiers. Before our lines were properly adjusted, the gallant Sergeant was beyond the aid of anyone. He had died from internal hemorrhage. The searchers of the battlefield, those gatherers of the wounded and dead, witness many novel and pathetic scenes.

Louis Spillers, a private in my company, a poor, quiet, and unassuming fellow, who had left a wife and little children at home when he donned the uniform of gray, had his thigh broken, just to the left of where the Sergeant fell. Spillers was as "brave as the bravest," and made no noise when he received the fatal wound. As the command swept forward down the little dell, he was of course left behind. Dragging himself along to the shade of a small tree, he sought shelter behind its trunk, protecting his person as well as he could from the bullets of the enemy posted on the ridge in front, and waited developments. When the litter-bearers found him late at night, he was leaning against the tree, calmly puffing away at his clay pipe. When asked why he did not call for assistance, he replied: "Oh, no; I thought my turn would come after awhile to be cared for, so I just concluded to quietly wait and try and smoke away some of my misery." Before morning he was dead. One might ask the question. What did such men of the South have to fight for—no negroes, no property, not even a home that they could call their own? What was it that caused them to make such sacrifices—to even give their lives to the cause? It was a principle, and as dear to the poorest of the poor as to him who counted his broad acres by the thousands and his slaves by the hundreds. Of such mettle were made the soldiers of the South—unyielding, unconquerable, invincible!

An old man in Captain Watts' Company, from Laurens, Uncle Johny Owens, a veteran of the Florida War, and one who gave much merriment to the soldiers by his frequent comparisons of war, "fighting Indians" and the one "fighting Yankees," was found on the slope, just in front of the enemy's breastworks, leaning against a tree, resting on his left knee, his loaded rifle across the other. In his right hand, between his forefinger and thumb, in the act of being placed upon the nipple of the gun, was a percussion cap. His frame was rigid, cold, and stiff, while his glossy eyes seemed to be peering in the front as looking for a lurking foe. He was stone dead, a bullet having pierced his heart, not leaving the least sign of the twitching of a muscle to tell of the shock he had received. He had fought his last battle, fired his last gun, and was now waiting for the last great drum-beat.

A story is told at the expense of Major Stackhouse, afterwards the Colonel of the Eighth, during this battle. I cannot vouch for its truthfulness, but give it as it was given to me by Captain Harllee, of the same regiment. The Eighth was being particularly hard-pressed, and had it not been for the unflinching stoicism of the officers and the valor of the men, the ranks not yet recruited from the results of the battle at Gettysburg, the little band would have been forced to yield. Major Stackhouse was in command of the right wing of the regiment, and all who knew the old farmer soldier knew him to be one of the most stubborn fighters in the army, and at the same time a "Methodist of the Methodists." He was moreover a pure Christian gentleman and a churchman of the straightest sect. There was no cant superstitions or affectation in his make-up, and what he said he meant. It was doubtful if he ever had an evil thought, and while his manners might have been at times blunt, he was always sincere and his language chosen and chaste, with the possible exception during battle. The time of which I speak, the enemy was making a furious assault on the right wing of the Eighth, and as the Major would gently rise to his knees and see the enemy so stubbornly contesting the ground, he would call out to the men, "There they are, boys, give them hell!" Then in an under tone he would say, "May God, forgive me for that!" Still the Yankees did not yield, and again and again he shouted louder and louder, "Boys, give it to them; give them hell!" with his usual undertone, "May God, forgive me for that," etc. But they began closing on the right and the center, and his left was about to give way; the old soldier could stand it no longer. Springing to his feet, his tall form towering above all around him, he shouted at the top of his voice, "Give them hell; give them hell, I tell you, boys; give them hell, G—— souls" The Eighth must have given them what was wanting, or they received it from somewhere, for after this outburst they scampered back behind the ridge.

Years after this, while Major Stackhouse was in Congress, and much discussion going on about the old Bible version of hell and the new version hades, some of his colleagues twitted the Major about the matter and asked him whether he was wanting the Eighth to give the Union soldiers the new version, or the old. With a twinkle in his eye, the Major answered "Well, boys, on all ordinary occasions the new version will answer the purposes, but to drive a wagon out of a stall or the Yankees from your front, the old version is the best."

Major Hard, who was killed here, was one of the finest officers in the brigade and the youngest, at that time, of all the field officers. He was handsome, brilliant, and brave. He was one of the original officers of the Seventh; was re-elected at the reorganization in May, 1862, and rose, by promotion, to Major, and at the resignation of Colonel Aiken would have been, according to seniority, Lieutenant Colonel. Whether he ever received this rank or not, I cannot remember. I regret my inability to get a sketch of his life.

But the Rupert of the brigade was Colonel Bland, of the Seventh. I do not think he ever received his commission as full Colonel, but commanded the regiment as Lieutenant Colonel, with few exceptions, from the battle of Sharpsburg until his death. Colonel Aiken received a wound at Sharpsburg from which he never fully recovered until after the war. Colonel Aiken was a moulder of the minds of men; could hold them together and guide them as few men could in Kershaw's Brigade, but Bland was the ideal soldier and a fighter "par excellence." He had the gift of inspiring in his men that lofty courage that he himself possessed. His form was faultless—tall, erect, and well developed, his eyes penetrating rather than piercing, his voice strong and commanding. His was a noble, generous soul, cool and brave almost to rashness. He was idolized by his troops and beloved as a comrade and commander. Under the guise of apparent sternness, there was a gentle flow of humor. To illustrate this, I will relate a little circumstance that occurred after the battle of Chancellorsville to show the direction his humor at times took. Colonel Bland was a bearer of orders to General Hooker across the Rappahannock, under a flag of truce. At the opposite bank he was met by officers and a crowd of curious onlookers, who plied the Colonel with irrelevant questions. On his coat collar he wore the two stars of his rank, Lieutenant Colonel. One of the young Federal officers made some remark about Eland's stars, and said, "I can't understand your Confederate ranks; some officers have bars and some stars. I see you have two stars; are you a Brigadier General?"

"No, sir," said Bland, straightening himself up to his full height; "but I ought to be. If I was in your army I would have been a Major General, and in command of your army." Then with a merry chuckle added, "Perhaps then you would not have gotten such a d—n bad whipping at Chancellorsville." Then all hands laughed.

COLONEL ELBERT BLAND

SEVENTH REGIMENT

Elbert Bland was born in Edgefield County, S.C., and attended the common schools until early manhood, when choosing medicine as a profession, he attended the Medical College of New York, where he graduated with distinction. Ardently ambitious, he remained sometime after graduation, in order to perfect himself in his chosen profession. Shortly after his graduation, war broke out between the States and Mexico, and he was offered and accepted the position of Assistant Surgeon of the Palmetto Regiment, Colonel P.M. Butler commanding. By this fortunate occurrence he was enabled to greatly enlarge his knowledge of surgery. At the close of the war he came home, well equipped for the future. Shortly after his return from the war he was happily married to Miss Rebecca Griffin, a daughter of Hon. N.L. Griffin, of Edgefield. Settling in his native county, he entered at once into a lucrative practice, and at the beginning of the late war was enjoying one of the largest country practices in the State. When the mutterings of war began he was one of the first to show signs of activity, and when Gregg's Regiment went to the coast in defense of his native State, he was appointed Surgeon of that Regiment. Having had some experience already as a Surgeon in the Mexican War, he determined to enter the more active service, and in connection with Thos. G. Bacon, raised the Ninety-Six Riflemen, which afterwards formed part of the Seventh South Carolina Regiment. Bacon was elected Captain and Bland First Lieutenant. Upon organizing the regiment, Bacon was elected Colonel of the regiment and Bland was to be Captain.

Whilst very little active service was seen during the first year of the war, still sufficient evidence was given of Eland's ability as a commander of the men, and upon the reorganization of the regiment, Captain Bland was elected Lieutenant Colonel. From this time until September 20th, 1863, his fortunes were those of the Seventh Regiment. He was conspicuous on nearly every battlefield in Virginia, and was twice wounded—at Savage Station, seriously in the arm, from which he never recovered, and painfully in the thigh at Gettysburg. At the sanguinary battle of Chickamauga, on September 20th, 1863, whilst in command of his regiment, and in the moment of victory, he fell mortally wounded, living only about two hours.

No knightlier soul than his ever flashed a sabre in the cause he loved so well, and like Marshall Nay, he was one of the bravest of the brave. He sleeps quietly in the little cemetery of his native town, and a few years ago, upon the death-bed of his wife, her request was that his grave and coffin should be opened at her death, and that she should be placed upon his bosom, which was done, and there they sleep. May they rest in peace.

Lieutenant Colonel Hoole

Eighth Regiment

Axalla John Hoole was of English decent, his grandfather, Joseph Hoole, having emigrated from York, England, about the close of the Revolutionary War, and settled at Georgetown, S.C.

James C. Hoole, the father of A.J. Hoole, was a soldier of the war of 1812. He removed to Darlington District and married Elizabeth Stanley, by whom he had five children, the third being the subject of this sketch.

Axalla John Hoole was born near Darlington Court House, S.C., October 12th, 1822. His father died when he was quite small, leaving a large family and but little property, but his mother was a woman of great energy, and succeeded in giving him as good an education as could be obtained at St. John's Academy, Darlington Court House. Upon the completion of the academic course, at the age of eighteen, he taught school for twelve years, after which he followed the occupation of farming.

While a young man he joined the Darlington Riflemen, and after serving in various capacities, he was elected Captain about 1854 or 1855. He was an enthusiastic advocate of States Rights, and during the excitement attending the admission of Kansas as a State, he went out there to oppose the Abolitionists. He married Elizabeth G. Brunson, March 20th, 1856, and left the same day for Kansas. Taking an active part in Kansas politics and the "Kansas War," he was elected Probate Judge of Douglas County by the pro-slavery party, under the regime of Governor Walker.

He returned to Darlington December 5th, 1857, and shortly afterwards was re-elected Captain of the Darlington Riflemen. At a meeting of the Riflemen, held in April, 1861, on the Academy green, he called for volunteers, and every man in the company volunteered, except one. The company went to Charleston April 15th, 1861, and after remaining a short while, returned as far as Florence, where they were mustered in as Company A, Eighth S.C.V.

The Eighth Regiment left Florence for Virginia June 2d, 1861. At the expiration of the period of enlistment, the regiment was reorganized, and Captain Hoole was elected Lieutenant Colonel, in which capacity he served until he was killed at the battle of Chickamauga, September 20th, 1863. He was buried at the Brunson graveyard, near Darlington.

Colonel E. T. Stackhouse

Eighth Regiment

As I have made some mention of Major Stackhouse, he being promoted to Lieutenant Colonel, and afterwards Colonel of the Eighth, I will take this opportunity of giving the readers a very brief sketch of the life of this sterling farmer, patriot, soldier, and statesman, who, I am glad to say, survived the war for many years.

Colonel E.T. Stackhouse was born in Marion County, of this State, the 27th of March, 1824, and died in the City of Washington, D.C., June 14th, 1892. He was educated in the country schools, having never enjoyed the advantages of a collegiate course. He married Miss Anna Fore, who preceded him to the grave by only a few months. Seven children was the result of this union. In youth and early manhood Colonel Stackhouse was noted for his strict integrity and sterling qualities, his love of truth and right being his predominating trait. As he grew in manhood he grew in moral worth—the better known, the more beloved.

His chosen occupation was that of farming, and he was ever proud of the distinction of being called one of the "horny-handed sons of toil." In the neighborhood in which he was born and bred he was an exemplar of all that was progressive and enobling.

In April, 1861, Colonel Stackhouse was among the very first to answer the call of his country, and entered the service as Captain in the Eighth South Carolina Regiment. By the casualties of war, he was promoted to Major, Lieutenant Colonel, and Colonel, and led the old Eighth, the regiment he loved so well, in some of the most sanguinary engagements of the war. All that Colonel Stackhouse was in civil life he was that, and more if possible, in the life of a soldier. In battle he was calm, collected, and brave; in camp or on the march he was sociable, moral—a Christian gentleman. As a tactician and disciplinarian, Colonel Stackhouse could not be called an exemplar soldier, as viewed in the light of the regular army; but as an officer of volunteers he had those elements in him to cause men to take on that same unflinching courage, indomitable spirit, and bold daring that actuated him in danger and battle. He had not that sternness of command nor niceties nor notion of superiority that made machines of men, but he had that peculiar faculty of endowing his soldiers with confidence and a willingness to follow where he led.

He represented his county for three terms in the State Legislature, and was President of the State Alliance. He was among the first to advocate college agricultural training for the youth of the land, and was largely instrumental in the establishment of Clemson College, and became one of its first trustees.

He was elected, without opposition, to the Fifty-first Congress, and died while in the discharge of his duties at Washington.

CHAPTER 24

In Front of Chattanooga

Early on the morning of the 22d we were ordered forward towards Chattanooga, the right wing having gone the day before. On nearing the city, we were shelled by batteries posted on the heights along the way and from the breastworks and forts around the city. It was during one of the heavy engagements between our advanced skirmish lines and the rear guard of the enemy that one of the negro cooks, by some means, got lost between the lines, and as a heavy firing began, bullets flying by him in every direction, he rushed towards the rear, and raising his hands in an entreating position, cried out, "Stop, white folks, stop! In the name of God Almighty, stop and argy!"

In moving along, near the city we came to a great sink in the ground, caused by nature's upheaval at some remote period, covering an acre or two of space. It seemed to have been a feeding place for hogs from time immemorial, for corn cobs covered the earth for a foot or more in depth. In this place some of our troops were posted to avoid the shells, the enemy having an exact range of this position. They began throwing shells right and left and bursting them just over our heads, the fragments flying in every direction. At every discharge, and before the shell reached us, the men would cling to the sides of the sloping sink, or burrow deeper in the cobs, until they had their bodies almost covered. A little man of my company, while a good soldier, had a perfect aversion to cannon shot, and as a shell would burst just overhead, his body was seen to scringe, tremble, and go still deeper among the cobs. Some mischievous comrade took advantage of his position, seized a good sound cob, then just as a shell bursted overhead, the trembling little fellow all flattened out, he struck him a stunning blow on the back. Such a yell as he set up was scarcely ever heard. Throwing the cobs in every direction, he cried out, "Oh! I am killed; I am killed! Ambulance corps! Ambulance corps!" But the laugh of the men soon convinced

271

him his wound was more imaginary than real so he turned over and commenced to burrow again like a mole.

Rosecrans having withdrawn his entire force within the fortifications around Chattanooga, our troops were placed in camp, surrounding the enemy in a semi-circle, and began to fortify. Kershaw's Brigade was stationed around a large dwelling in a grove, just in front of Chattanooga, and something over a mile distant from the city, but in plain view. We had very pleasant quarters in the large grove surrounding the house, and, in fact, some took possession of the porches and outhouses. This, I think, is the point Grant stormed a few months afterwards, and broke through the lines of Bragg. We had built very substantial breastworks, and our troops would have thought themselves safe and secure against the charge of Grant's whole army behind such works.

If those who are unfamiliar with the life of the soldier imagines it is one long funeral procession, without any breaks of humor, they are away off from the real facts. The soldier is much the same as the schoolboy. He must have some vent through which the ebullition of good feelings can blow off, else the machinery bursts.

While encamped around this house, a cruel joke was played upon Captain—well we will call him Jones; that was not his name, however, but near enough to it to answer our purpose. Now this Captain Jones, as we call him, was engaged to be married to one of the fairest flowers in the Palmetto State, a perfect queen among beauties—cultured, vivacious, and belonging to one of the oldest families in that Commonwealth of Blue Bloods. The many moves and changes during the last month or two considerably interrupted our communications and mail facilities, and Jones had not received the expected letters. He became restless, petulant, and cross, and to use the homely phrase, "he was all torn up." Instead of the "human sympathy" and the "one touch of nature," making the whole world akin, that philosophers and sentimentalists talk about, it should be "one sight of man's misery"—makes the whole world "wish him more miserable." It was through such feelings that induced Captain I.N. Martin, our commissary, with Mack Blair and others, to enter into a conspiracy to torture Jones with all he could stand. Blair had a lady cousin living near the home of Jones' fiancee, with whom he corresponded, and it was through this channel that the train was laid to blow up Jones while said Jones was in the piazza engaged in a deeply interesting game of chess. Martin was to be in the piazza watching the game, when Blair was to enter reading a letter. Then something like the following colloquy took place:

"Well, Mack, what is the news from home?"

"Nothing very interesting," replies Blair. Then, as a sudden recollection strikes him, "Oh, yes, there is to be a big wedding at Old Dr. Blanks."

"You don't say so?" (The game of chess stands still.) "And who is to be married, pray?" innocently enquires Martin.

"Why it will surprise you as much as it did me, I suppose, and I would not believe it, only Cousin Sallie says she is to be bride's maid." (Jones ceases to play and listens intently.) "It is nobody else than Mr. —— and Miss 'Blank.'"

Now, this Miss "Blank" is Jones' intended. Jones is paralyzed. His face turns livid, then pale, now green! He is motionless, his eyes staring vacantly on the chessboard. Then with a mighty exertion Jones kicked the board aside and sprang to his feet. Shaking his trembling finger in the face of Blair, his whole frame convulsed with emotion, his very soul on fire, he hissed between his teeth: "That's an infernal lie, I don't care whose Cousin Sallie wrote it."

Jones was nearly crazed for the balance of the day. He whistled and sang strange melodies while walking aimlessly about. He read and re-read the many love missives received long ago. Some he tore into fragments; others he carefully replaced in his knapsack.

But those evil geniuses were still at work for further torture, or at least to gloat over Jones' misery. It was arranged to formally bury him, allegorically. At night, while Jones was asleep, or trying to sleep on the piazza, a procession was formed, headed by Major Maffett, who was to act as the priest, and I must say he acted the part like a cardinal. We had a little rehearsal of the part each was to play, and those who "couldn't hold in" from laughing were ruled out, for it was expected that Jones would cut some frightful antics as the ceremony proceeded. I was not allowed to accompany the procession, as it was decided I could not "hold in," and under no condition was there to be a laugh or even a smile; but I took up position behind the balusters and watched events as the shadows were cast before. Major Maffett was dressed in a long dark overcoat, to represent the priestly gown, with a miter on his head, carrying Hardee's Tactics, from which to read the burial service. All had in their hands a bayonet, from which burned a tallow candle, in place of tapers. The procession marched up the steps in single file, all bearing themselves with the greatest solemnity and sombre dignity, followed by the sexton, with a frying-pan as a shovel, and took their places around the supposed corpse. Maffett began the duties by alluding to that part of the service where "it is allotted that all men shall die," etc., waving his hand in due form to the sexton as he repeated the words, "Earth to earth and dust to dust," the sexton following the motions with the frying pan.

I must say, in all truthfulness, that in all my life I never saw a graver or more solemn set of faces than those of the would-be mourning procession. Captain Wright appeared as if he was looking into his own grave, and the others appeared equally as sorrowful. Major Maffett gave out in clear, distinct tones the familiar lines of—

> Solemn strikes the funeral chime,
> Notes of our departing time.

Well, such grotesque antics as Jones did cut up was perfectly dreadful. He laughed, he mimicked the priest, kicked at the mourners, and once tried to grab the tactics. The Major and his assistants pitched the tune on a high key. Captain Wright braced it with loud, strong bass, while Martin and Sim Pratt came in on the home stretch with tenor and alto that shook the rafters in the house. Then all dispersed as silently and sorrowfully as they had come.

In a few days Jones got a letter setting all things straight. Martin and Blair confessed their conspiracy against his peace of mind, and matters progressed favorably thereafter between Jones and Miss "Blank," but Jones confessed afterwards that he carried for a long time "bad, wicked blood in his heart."

But soldiers have their tragedies as well as their comedies in camp. It was here we lost our old friend, Jim George, the shallow-pated wit—the man who found us the flour on the Potomac, and who floundered about in the river "for three hours," as he said, on that bitter cold night at Yorktown. It was also told of Jim, that during the first battle he was loading and shooting at the wounded enemy for all his gun was worth, and when remonstrated with by his Captain, Chesley Herbert, telling Jim he "should not kill them," Jim indignantly asked, "What in the hell did we come to the war for, if not to kill Yankees?" But this, I think, is only a joke at Jim's expense. Nevertheless, he was a good solider, of the harmless kind, and a good, jolly fellow withal, taking it as a pleasure to do a friend a kindness.

As I have said, however, Jim was a great boaster and blusterer, glorying in the marvelous and dangerous. Had he lived in the heroic age,

I have no doubt he would have regaled the ears of his listeners with blood curdling stories of his battles with giants, his fights with dragons and winged serpents. He claimed to possess a charm. He wore an amulet around his neck to protect him against the "bullets of lead, of copper, or of brass" of his enemies, through which, he said, nothing could penetrate but the mystic "balls of silver," the same with which "witch rabbits" are killed. He would fill his pockets, after battle, with spent and battered bullets, and exhibit them as specimens of his art in the catching of bullets on "the fly."

He professed to be a very dangerous and blood-thirsty individual, but his comrades only laughed at his idiosyncrasies, knowing him as they did as being one of the best and most harmless soldiers in the army. He often boasted, "No Yankee will ever kill me, but our own men will," his companions little dreaming how prophetic his words would prove.

One night while Jim, in company with some companions, were on a "foraging expedition," they came to a farm house on Missionary Ridge and ordered supper. A cavalryman was there, also, waiting to be served. A negro servant attending to the table gave some real or imaginary affront, and the soldiers, in a spirit of jest, pretended as if they were going to take the negro out and flog him. Now Jim, as well as the cavalryman, thought the midnight revelers were in earnest, and Jim was in high glee at the prospect of a little adventure. But nothing was further from the thoughts of the soldiers than doing harm to the negro. When they had him in the yard the cavalryman came on the porch, and in an authoritative manner, ordered the negro turned loose.

This was a time Jim thought that he could get in some of his bullying, so going up on the steps where the cavalryman stood, jesticulating with his finger, said, "When we get through with the negro we will give you some of the same."

In an instant the strange soldier's pistol was whipped out—a flash, a report, and Jim George fell dead at his feet, a victim to his own swagger and an innocent jest of his companions. So dumbfounded were the innocent "foragers," that they allowed the cavalryman to ride away unmolested and unquestioned.

The bones of the unfortunate Jim lie buried on the top of Missionary Ridge, and the name of his slayer remains a mystery to this day.

While in Tennessee our diet was somewhat changed. In the East, flour, with beef and bacon, was issued to the troops; but here we got nothing but corn meal, with a little beef and half ration of bacon.

The troops were required to keep four days' rations cooked on hand all the time. Of the meal we made "cart wheels," "dog heads," "ash cakes," and last, but not least, we had "cush." Now corn bread is not a very great delicacy at best, but when four days' old, and green with mold, it is anything but palatable. But the soldiers got around this in the way "cush" was manipulated. Now it has been said "if you want soldiers to fight well, you must feed them well;" but this is still a mooted question, and I have known some of the soldiers of the South to give pretty strong battle when rather underfed than overfed.

For the benefit of those Spanish-American soldiers of the late war, who had nothing to vary their diet of ham and eggs, steak, pork, and potatoes, biscuits, light bread, coffee, and iced teas, but only such light goods as canned tomatoes, green corn, beans, salmon, and fresh fish, I will tell them how to make "cush." You will not find this word in the dictionaries of the day, but it was in the soldier's vocabulary, now obsolete. Chip up bacon in fine particles, place in an oven and fry to a crisp. Fill the oven one-third or one-half full of branch water, then take the stale corn bread, the more moldy the better, rub into fine crumbs, mix and bring the whole to a boil, gently stirring with a forked stick. When cold, eat with fingers and to prevent waste or to avoid carrying it on the march, eat the four days' rations at one sitting. This dish will aid in getting clear of all gestion of meat, and prevent bread from getting old. A pot of "cush" is a dish "fit for a king," and men who will not fight on it would not fight if penned.

The forest and farms around abounded in sheep and hogs. In fact, Tennessee and North Georgia were not the worst places in the South in which to live through a campaign. We had strict orders to protect all private property and molest nothing outside of camp requirements, but the men would forage at night, bring in a sheep or hog, divide up, and by the immutable law of camps it was always proper to hang a choice piece of mutton or pork at the door of the officers' tent. This helped to soothe the conscience of the men and pave the way to immunity from punishment. The stereotyped orders were issued every night for "Captains to keep their men in camp," but the orders were as often disregarded as obeyed. It was one of those cases where orders are more regarded "in the breach than in the observance." Officers winked at it, if not actually countenancing the practice, of "foraging for something to eat." Then again the old argument presented itself, "If we don't take it the Yankees will," so there you were.

Most of the soldiers took the opportunity of visiting Lookout

Mountain and feasting their eyes upon the finest scenery of the South. While they had crossed and recrossed the Blue Ridge and the many ranges of lesser note in Virginia, Maryland, and Pennsylvania—had gazed with wonder and admiration at the windings of the Potomac and Shenandoah from the Heights of Maryland overlooking Harper's Ferry—yet all these were nothing as compared to the view from Lookout Mountain. Standing on its brow, we could see the beautiful blue waters of the Tennessee flowing apparently at our feet, but in reality a mile or two distant. Beyond lay the city of Chattanooga, nestling down in the bend of the river, while away in the distance occasional glimpses of the stream could be had as it wound in and out around the hills and mountains that lined its either side, until the great river looked no larger than a mountain brooklet. From the highest peak of Lookout Mountain we catch faint streaks of far away Alabama; on the right, North Carolina; to the north, Tennessee; and to the south and east were Georgia and our own dear South Carolina. From this place many of our soldiers cast the last lingering look at the land they loved so well. On the plateau of the mountain was a beautiful lake of several acres in extent, surrounded by lovely little villas and summer houses, these all hurriedly deserted by the necessities of war—the furniture and fixtures left all in place as the owners took their hastened departure. In one house we visited was left a handsome piano, on which those who could perform gave the soldiers delightful music.

There was a roadway winding around the base of the mountain and gradually up its slopes to the plateau above, where wagons and other vehicles passed to the top. Most of the soldiers who wished to visit this beautiful and historic place passed up this road way, but there was another route—just a foot-path—up its precipitous sides, which had to be climbed hundreds of feet, perpendicularly, by means of ladders fastened to its sides. After going up one ladder, say fifty or seventy-five feet, we would come to a little offset in the mountain side, just wide enough to get a foot-hold, before taking another ladder. Some of the boldest climbers took this route to reach the summit, but after climbing the first ladder and looking back towards the gorge below, I concluded it was safer and more pleasant to take the "longer way round." It certainly takes a man of stout heart and strong nerves to climb those ladders up to the "lands of the sky."

The scenery in and around Chattanooga and Lookout Mountain is grand, far beyond pen picturing. The surroundings had a kind of buoyancy even to the spirits of the badly clad and badly fed soldiers, which caused their stale bread and "cush" to be eaten with a relish. The mountain homes seemed veritable "castles in the air." Looking from the top of Lookout Mountain—its position, its surroundings, its natural fortresses—this would have made an old Feudal lord die of envy. Autumn is now at hand, with its glorious sunsets, its gorgeous coloring of the leaves and bushes away to the right on Missionary Ridge, the magnificent purple draperies along the river sides that rise and fall to our right and left, its blue waters dwindling away until they meet the deeper blue of the sky—are all beautiful beyond description. Lovely though this scenery may be in autumn, and its deeper coloring of green in the summer, how dazzled must be the looker on in beholding it in its tender, blushing mantle of spring?

For quite a time rumors came of Burnside's advance through East Tennessee and of Longstreet's detachment from the army to meet him. The troops were kept in constant expectation, with the regulation "four days" cooked rations on hand. It is not our purpose to criticise the acts of Generals, or the schemes and plans of the Southern Government, but future historical critics will not differ as to the ultimate results of the East Tennessee move. That Longstreet's advance to East Tennessee was without results, if not totally disastrous, all will agree. To divide an army in the face of an enemy, is dangerous at best, and, with few exceptions, has been avoided by Generals and commanders of all time. Lee could afford it, because he was *Lee* and had a *Jackson* to execute the movements, but on occasions when the enemy in front are more numerous and commanded by the most able and astute Generals of the time, the movement is hazardous in the extreme. Lee and his Lieutenants had already "robbed the cradle and the grave" to replenish their ranks, and what real benefit would accrue to the South had Longstreet captured the whole of Burnside's Army, when the North had many armies to replace it? The critics of the future will judge the movement as ill-timed and fraught with little good and much ill to the Confederacy. However, it was so ordered, and no alternate was left the officers and soldiers but to obey.

On the 9th of October President Davis came out to Chattanooga to give matters his personal attention and seek, if possible, some "scape-grace" upon which to saddle the blame for not reaping greater fruits of the battle, and to vindicate the conduct of his commander in chief.

General Bragg had already preferred charges against Lieutenant

General Polk, commander of the right wing of the army, for his tardiness in opening the battle of the 20th, and General Hindman was relieved of the command of his division for alleged misconduct prior to that time. Many changes were proposed and made in the corps and division commanders, as well as plans discussed for the future operations of the army. All agreed that it should be aggressive.

Major General Cheatham was temporarily placed in command of Folk's Corps after the downfall of that General, and he himself soon afterwards superseded by lieutenant General Hardee. President Davis had thought of placing Pemberton, who had capitulated to Grant at Vicksburg, but who had been exchanged, in command of the corps; but the officers and troops demurred at this, and public opinion was so outspoken, that Mr. Davis was forced to abandon the idea. It was, therefore, given to Hardee. For some offense given by Major General D.H. Hill, who commanded the right of the right wing on the 20th, he was relieved of his command and his connection with the Army of Tennessee. Major General Buckner, commanding the divisions on the left of Longstreet's wing, also came under the ban of official displeasure and was given an indefinite leave of absence. There was wrangling, too, among the Brigadiers in Hood's Division, Jenkins, Law, and Robertson. Jenkins being a new addition to the division, was senior officer, and commanded the division in Hood's absence by virtue of his rank. Law had been in the division since its formation, and after Hood's disabilities from wounds, commanded very acceptably the balance of the days at Gettysburg. For this and other meritorious conduct, he thought the command should be given to him as senior in point of service with the division. Robertson had some personal difficulty with General Longstreet, which afterwards resulted in a call for a courtmartial. The advanced ideas and undisguised views of Longstreet himself were considered with suspicion by both the President and the General commanding the army, and had it not been for the high prestige and his brilliant achievements in the East, the unbounded love and devotion of his troops, the loyalty and confidence of General Lee in the high military ability of the old War Horse, his commander of the First Corps, in all probability his official head would have fallen in the basket. But President Davis was strong in his prejudices and convictions, and as usual, tenacious in his friendship and confidence towards his favorites. Bragg, in President Davis' estimation at least, was vindicated, but at the expense of his subalterns, and was, therefore, retained in command in the face of overwhelming discontent among the Generals and the pressing demands of public opinion for his recall from the command of the army.

General Lee in the meantime had sought to relieve the pressure against Bragg as much as possible by making a demonstration in force against Meade, forcing the Federal Army back behind Bull Run, thereby preventing a further reinforcement of Rosecrans from the Army of the Potomac.

I digress thus far from the thread of my story, that the reader may better understand the conditions confronting our army—the morale, and esprit de corps of the officers and troops composing it.

On the 19th of October General Rosecrans was superseded by Major General George B. Thomas, in command of the Union Army, with Grant, who was rapidly climbing to the zenith of this renown, marching to his relief as commander of the department.

A considerable commotion was caused in camp about the last of October by the news of a large body of Union soldiers making a demonstration against our left flank and rear. It seems that a body of troops had embarked on board pontoon and flat boats in Chattanooga, and during the night had floated eight miles down the river and there were joined by a similar body marching over land on the north side. This formidable array was crossed over to the south side and moved in the direction of our rear and our line of communication under cover of the hills and mountain ridges. Jenkins' and McLaw's Divisions were ordered to intercept them and drive them off. A night attack was ordered, but by some misunderstanding or disobedience of orders, this movement on the part of the Confederates miscarried, and was abandoned; not, however, until General Bratton, of Jenkins' old Brigade, came up and attacked the rear guard with such vigor that the enemy was glad enough to get away, leaving their wounded and dead upon the field. No further movements were made against the army until after our removal to East Tennessee.

About the first of November orders were issued for the transfer of Longstreet to begin, and on the 5th and 6th the greater part of his army was embarked on hastily constructed trains at Tyner's Station, some five or six miles out on the E.T. & K.R.R. The horses, artillery, and wagon trains took the dirt road to Sweetwater, in the Sweetwater Valley, one of the most fertile regions in East Tennessee.

Longstreet's command consisted of Kershaw's (South Carolina), Bryan's and Wofford's (Georgia), and Humphreys' (Mississippi) Brigades, under Major General McLaws; Anderson's (Georgia), Jenkins'

(South Carolina), Law's (Alabama), Robertson's (Arkansas and Texas), and Benning's (Georgia) Brigades, under Brigadier General M. Jenkins, commanding division; two batteries of artillery, under General Alexander; and four brigades of cavalry, under Major General Wheeler.

General Hood had been so desperately wounded at Chickamauga, that it was thought he could never return to the army; but he had won a glorious name, the prestige of which the war department thought of too much value to be lost, but to be used afterwards so disastrously in the campaign through Middle Tennessee. General Hood was, no doubt, an able, resolute, and indefatigable commander, although meteoric, something on the order of Charles, the "Madman of the North;" but his experience did not warrant the department in placing him in the command of an expedition to undertake the impossible—the defeat of an overwhelming army, behind breastworks, in the heart of its own country.

The movement of Longstreet to East Tennessee and Hood through Middle Tennessee was but the commencement of a series of blunders on the part of our war department that culminated eventually in the South's downfall. But it is not our province to speculate in the rosy fields of "might-have-been," but to record facts.

General Longstreet had of all arms fifteen thousand men, including teamsters, guards, medical and ambulance corps. General Burnside had an army of twenty-five thousand men and one hundred pieces of artillery, and this was the army Longstreet was expected to capture or destroy.

General Grant was marching from Mississippi with a large portion of his victorious troops of the Vicksburg campaign to reinforce Rosecrans, Sherman coming down through Tennessee, and Meade was sending reinforcements from the East, all to swell the defeated ranks of Rosecrans. With the knowledge of all these facts, the department was preparing to further reduce the forces of Bragg by sending Longstreet up in East Tennessee, with soldiers badly clad, worse equipped, and with the poorest apology of camp equipage, for an active and progressive campaign.

Both governments were greatly displeased with the results of the battle of Chickamauga—the Federals at their army failing to come up to their expectations and gaining a victory, instead of a disastrous defeat; the Confederates at their commanders in not following up their success and reaping greater results. Under such circumstances, there must be some one on whom to place the blame. General Rosecrans censured General McCook and General Crittenden, commanders of the Twentieth and Twenty-first Corps, and these two able soldiers were relieved of their commands, while General Rosecrans himself was severely censured by the department in Washington, and soon afterwards relieved of his command.

The regiments of the brigade were now all short of field officers— the Seventh and Battalion with none, and the Eighth and Fifteenth in charge of Majors. However, Colonel W.G. Rice joined us on the way to East Tennessee and took command of his battalion.

After a stay of a week in the beautiful Valley of Sweetwater, we were moved to Loudon, the railroad crossing of the Tennessee River, the railroad bridge having been burned by the enemy. The country in East Tennessee was greatly divided in sentiment, some for the Union cause and some for the Confederate cause. Rumors of outrages and doings of desperadoes were rife, and the soldiers were somewhat dubious in going far into the country, for fear of running up against bushwhackers, of which the country was said to be full.

While one train with the Third was being pulled over the East Tennessee Railroad towards Sweetwater by a strange engineer over a track long unused, and cars out of repair, an occurrence took place which might have ended more seriously than it did under the circumstances. The train, composed of box cars, one company inside and one on top, was running along at a good, lively rate. A stampede took place among the troops on top, who began jumping right and left down a steep embankment and running with all their speed to the woods in the distance. It was just after daylight, and those inside the cars not knowing what the trouble was, and a great many on the top being roused from their slumbers and seeing the others leaping in great disorder, and hearing the word "bushwhackers" being called out, threw their blankets aside and jumped likewise. Soon the cars were almost empty, those above and within all thinking danger was somewhere, but invisible. Just then a train of passenger cars, containing General McLaws, General Kershaw, their staffs, and others, rounded the cut in our rear, and was running at break-neck speed into the freight train in front. Those in the passenger cars seeing those from the train in front running for dear life's sake for the woods, began to climb through windows and off of the platforms, the engineers and firemen on both trains leaping like the men. So we had the spectacle of one train running into another and neither under control, although the levers had been reversed. In a moment the rear train plunged into the front one, piling up three or four cars on their ends. Fortunately, only one or two were hurt by jumping and none by the collision. It seems almost miraculous to think of two car loads of soldiers jumping from trains at full speed and on a high embankment and a great many from top, and so few getting hurt.

General Longstreet's plan of campaign was to move up the east side of the Holston, or, as it is now called, the Tennessee River, pass through Marysville, cross the river in the vicinity of Knoxville with his infantry, the cavalry to take possession of the heights above and opposite the city, thus cutting off the retreat of the Federals in front of Loudon, and capture the garrison in the city of Knoxville. But he had no trains to move his pontoon bridge, nor horses to pull it. So he was forced to make a virtue of necessity and cross the river just above the little hamlet of Loudon in the face of the enemy. On the night of the 12th the boats and bridge equipment were carried to the river, the boats launched and manned by a detachment of Jenkins' South Carolina Brigade, under the command of the gallant Captain Foster. This small band of men pushed their boats across the river under a heavy fire of the enemy's pickets, succeeded in driving off the enemy, and took possession of the opposite side. The boats were soon joined together and the bridge laid. The troops then began to cross rapidly and push their way out far in advance. By morning the greater part of the army was on the west side of the river.

General Wheeler, with his cavalry, started simultaneously with the infantry, but on the east side, with the view of taking possession of the heights around Knoxville, which he partly accomplished after several severe engagements with the Union cavalry, in which the young Confederate cavalier came off victorious.

The next morning after our crossing the enemy showed some disposition to attack our lines, but did no more than drive in our skirmishers, and then began to fall slowly back. Longstreet remained near the river constructing some defensive earthworks to protect the bridge, and to allow the supply train, which had been out on a foraging expedition, time to come up. By his not making as rapid advance as was expected, the enemy again, on the 14th, returned to feel our lines and to learn the whereabouts of his foe.

On the morning of the 15th, just at daylight, we took up our line of march through a blinding mist or fog, our skirmishers not being able to see an object fifty paces in front. Our line of advance was along the dirt road, on the west side of the little mountain range, a spur of the clinch, while the main body of the enemy kept close to the railroad, on the east side, and between the mountain range and the river, traversing a narrow valley, which gave him strong positions for defensive battle. The mountain was crossed in several places by dull roads and bridle paths, and it was the intention of the commanding General to take possession of these passes and turn the enemy's flank, or to move around the head of the mountain, where the two roads followed by the armies came together on converging lines, then to either close him in between the mountain and the river and give battle, or fall upon his rear and crush him. Some few miles out Jenkins' skirmishers came upon those of the enemy and a running fight took place, the Federals retreating through the mountain gap to the east side.

Jenkins kept up his advance (not following the enemy, however, over the mountain), with Alexander's Battalion of Artillery, while McLaws followed closely, with Leydon's Battery as a support. Thus the march was continued all day, taking up camp at night far in advance of the enemy on the other side of the mountain. Jenkins was ordered at midnight, with a part of his command, to take possession of a gap in the mountain, and at daylight throw himself across the line of the enemy's retreat. But for some unforeseen circumstance, or treachery or ignorance in Jenkins' guide, he failed in his undertaking, and the enemy passed in safety during the night beyond our lines to a place of comparative security.

Early next morning the army was in motion, but instead of an enemy in our front we found a park of eighty wagons, well laden with supplies of provisions, camp equipage, tools, etc., deserted by the retreating column. The horses had been cut loose, still this capture was a very serviceable acquisition to the outfit of the army, especially in entrenching tools. Jenkins followed close on the heels of the retreating army, occasionally coming to a severe brush with the enemy's rear guard, using every exertion to force Burnside to battle until McLaws, with Hart's Brigade of Cavalry, could reach Cambell's Station, the point where the two converging roads meet. McLaws marched nearly all day in full line of battle, Kershaw being on the left of the main thoroughfare and under a continual skirmish fire. But all too late. The wily foe had escaped the net once more and passed over and beyond the road crossing, and formed line of battle on high ground in rear. Longstreet still had hopes of striking the enemy a crushing blow before reaching Knoxville, and all he desired and all that was necessary to that end was that he should stand and give battle. The attitude of the Union Army looked favorable towards the consummation of the Confederate leader's plan. Our troops had been marching all the forenoon in one long line of battle, near a mile in length, over ditches, gullies, and fences; through briars, brambles, and undergrowth; then again through wide expanse of cultivated fields, all the while under a galling fire from the enemy's batteries and sharpshooters, and they felt somewhat jaded and worn out when they came upon their bristling bayonets, ready for combat. A great number of our men were barefooted, some with shoes partly worn out, clothes ragged and torn, not an overcoat or extra garment among the line officers or men throughout the army, as all surplus baggage had been left in Virginia. But when the battle was about to show up the soldiers were on hand, ready and willing as of old, to plunge headlong into the fray. McLaws was on the left wing and Jenkins on the right.

Preparation for a general engagement was made. McLaws was ordered to throw forward, Wofford on his extreme left, supported by cavalry, while Jenkins was to send two of his brigades, under General Law, far to the right, on the flank and rear of the enemy's left. Law was first to make the attack on the enemy's flank, then the columns in front were to advance and make direct assault. But the "best laid plans of mice and men oft' gang aglee." Law missed his line of direction—failed to come upon the enemy's flank, night was upon us, and it must be remembered that all these movements took time, thus giving the Union Army an opportunity, under the sable curtains of night, to "fold their tents and gently steal away."

General Longstreet, in his book written nearly thirty years after the occurrence of Cambell's Station, severely criticises General Law, who commanded the two flanking brigades, and in withering and scathing terms directly charges him with the loss of a great victory. He quotes one of his staff officers as saying that it was the common camp rumor that General Law had made the remark "that he could have made a successful attack, but that Jenkins would have reaped the credit of it, hence he delayed until the enemy got out of the way." This is unjust and ungenerous to a gallant and faithful officer, one, too, who had, by his many and heavy blows in battle, added largely to the immortal fame of Longstreet himself. That there was a laudable ambition and rivalry among all officers and men in the Confederate Army, there can be no question—an ambition to outstrip all others in heroic actions, noble deeds, and self-sacrificing, but jealously never. As for treachery, as General Longstreet clearly intimates in the case of General Law, why the poorest, ragged, starved, or maimed soldier in the South would not have sold his country or companions for the wealth of the Indies, nor would he have unnecessarily sacrificed a life of a comrade for the greatest place on this continent, or the fairest crown of Europe. It must be remembered in this connection that there were personal differences between the corps commander and General Law at times, and with one of his division commanders, all during our Western campaign. That General Law was obstinate, petulant, and chafed under restraint, is true, but this is only natural in a volunteer army, and must be expected. And had General Longstreet, so rigid a disciplinarian as he was, but a breath of suspicion at the time of disobedience, lack of courage, or unfaithfulness in his subaltern, General Law would have been put under immediate arrest, and a courtmartial ordered. The old General, in several places in his memoirs, makes uncomplimentary remarks and insinuations against some of his old compatriots in arms, but these should not be taken seriously. It will be remembered by all the old Confederates in this connection that during the period just succeeding the war mighty social convulsions took place in the South—political upheavals, whereby one party was as bitter against the other as during the mighty struggle of the North against the South, and that General Longstreet, unfortunately for his name as a civilian, aligned himself along with the party whom the whites of the South acknowledged as antagonistic to their welfare and interest. This roused the ire of all his old army associates, and many of his former friends now began to hurl poisoned and fiery shafts at the old "War Horse" of the South, and no place so vulnerable as his army record. This, of course, was resented by him, and a deadly feud of long standing sprang up between Generals Longstreet, Mahone, and a few others, who joined him on the one side, and the whole army of "Confederate Brigadiers" on the other. This accounts, in a large measure, for many of Longstreet's strictures upon the conduct of officers of the army, and, no doubt, a mere after thought or the weird imaginations of an old and disappointed politico-persecuted man.

No, No! The officers and men of the Confederate Army were patriots of diamond purity, and all would have willingly died a martyr's death that the Confederacy might live.

CHAPTER 25
The Siege and Storming of Fort Sanders

After the fiasco at Cambell's Station, the enemy retired behind his entrenched position in the suburbs of Knoxville. Longstreet followed rapidly, with McLaws in front, in line of battle, but all hopes of encountering the enemy before he reached his fortified position around the city had vanished. We reached the rolling hillsides just outside of the city limits about noon on the 17th, and found the enemy's dismounted cavalry, acting as sharpshooters, posted on the heights in front and between the railroad and the river, well protected by rail piles along the crest of the hill.

Colonel Nance was ordered with the Third South Carolina Regiment to dislodge those on the hill, near the railroad, by marching over and beyond the road and taking them in flank, which was successfully done by making a sudden dash from a piece of woodland over an open field and gaining the embankment of the railroad immediately on the right flank of the enemy's sharpshooters. But scarcely had the Third got in position than it found itself assailed on its left and rear by an unseen enemy concealed in the woods. Here Colonel Nance was forced to sacrifice one of his most gallant officers, Lieutenant Allen, of Company D. Seeing his critical and untenable position, he ordered the Lieutenant, who was standing near him, to report his condition to General Kershaw and ask for instruction. This was a hazardous undertaking in the extreme, but Lieutenant Allen undertook it with rare courage and promptness. Back across the open field he sped, while the whole fire of the sharpshooters was directed towards him instead of to our troops behind the embankment. All saw and felt that the brave officer was lost as soon as he got beyond the cover of the railroad, and turned their heads from the sickening scene. But Allen did not hesitate or falter, but kept on to the fulfilment of his desperate mission, while hundreds of bullets flew around him in every direction—over his head, under his feet, before, and behind—until at last the fatal messenger laid him low, a heroic martyr to the stern duties of war. Colonel Nance seeing the hopelessness of his attack, ordered a retreat. Then the whole regiment had to run the same gauntlet in which young Allen lost his life. Away across the open corn field the troops fled in one wild pell mell, every man for Himself, while the bullets hummed and whistled through our scattered ranks, but luckily only a few were shot. Jenkins' Division came up late in the day and took position on McLaws' left, then with the cavalry commenced the investment of the city on the west side of the Holston or Tennessee River. To advance McLaws' lines to a favorable position, it was first necessary to dislodge the sharpshooters on the hill tops between the river and the railroad. General Kershaw was ordered to take the works in front by direct assault. The Third was on the extreme left of the brigade, next to the railroad, while the Second, Seventh, Eighth, and Third Battalion were in the center, with the Fifteenth, under Major Gist, between the dirt road on which we had traveled and the river on extreme right. The Third had to assault the same troops and position that they had failed to dislodge some hours before.

Major William Wallace was in command of the skirmishers. The heavy siege pieces at Fort Sanders had been hammering away at us all day, as well as the many field batteries that bristled along the epaulments around Knoxville. The skirmishers were ordered forward, the battle line to closely follow; but as Colonel Wallace was in front and could see the whole field, I will allow him to give his version of the engagement.

"We were stationed on a high hill," says Colonel Wallace, "west of said town, which descended gradually some two hundred yards, then rose to a smaller hill nearer to Knoxville. Between these two hills was a smooth valley, the middle of which was distinctly marked by a line running north and south by different crops which had been planted on opposite sides of it. Brigade skirmishers were ordered to advance towards Knoxville and drive in the enemy's pickets. I was in command of the left wing, and drove the enemy from my front, across the creek, which was beyond the smaller hill. On reaching the creek and finding our skirmishers on my right, did not advance over the hill. I returned to my original position where I found them. Soon afterwards the skirmish line was again ordered forward to the line in the valley above described, and to lie down. Just then I heard a yell behind me and saw the Third South Carolina advancing rapidly towards the smaller hill. I did not order my skirmishers to lie down, but as soon as the regiment was abreast of me I advanced and drove the enemy again across the creek. On hearing firing on the west of the hill, I closed up my skirmishers and advanced south towards the crest of the hill. I found a regiment of Union sharpshooters lying behind a breastwork of rails and firing on the Third, which was within forty yards of them. As soon as the enemy saw us on their flank, they threw up their hands and surrendered. The Third had lost forty men up to this time."

Colonel Wallace tells also of how a Federal soldier, who had surrendered, was in the act of shooting him, but was prevented from doing so by the muzzle of a rifle being thrust in his face by a member of Company E.W.W. Riser, afterwards Sheriff of Newberry County. Colonel Nance was much gratified at the able assistance rendered him by Colonel Wallace, and made special and favorable mention of him in his report.

The Second, Seventh, Eighth, and Third Battalion swept across the plain like a hurricane, driving everything before them right in the teeth of the deadly fire of Fort Sanders, but the Third and Fifteenth Regiments were unusually unfortunate in their positions, owing to the strength of the works in their front. The Fifteenth got, in some way, hedged in between the road and river, and could make little progress in the face of the many obstacles that confronted them. Their young commander, Major William Gist, son of ex-Governor Gist, becoming somewhat nettled at the progress his troops were making, threw aside all prudence and care, recklessly dashed in front of his column, determined to ride at its head in the assault that was coming, but fell dead at the very moment of victory. How many hundreds, nay thousands, of brave and useful officers and men of the South wantonly threw away their lives in the attempt to rouse their companions to extra exertions and greater deeds of valor.

The Third fought for a few moments almost muzzle to muzzle, with nothing but a few rails, hastily piled, between assailants and the assailed. At this juncture another gallant act was performed by Captain Winthrop, of Alexander's Battery. Sitting on his horse in our rear, watching the battle as it ebbed and flowed, and seeing the deadly throes in which the Third was writhing, only a few feet separating them from the enemy, by some sudden impulse or emotion put spurs to his horse and dashed headlong through our ranks, over the breastworks, and fell desperately wounded in the ranks of the Federals, just as their lines gave way or surrendered. This was only one of the many heroic and nerve-straining acts witnessed by the soldiers that followed the flag of Kershaw, McLaws, and Longstreet.

Colonel Rice, of the Battalion, was so seriously wounded that he never returned to active duty in the field. Major Miller, in a former battle, had been permanently disabled, but no other field promotions were ever made, so the gallant little Battalion was commanded in future by senior Captains.

By morning of the 19th of November the enemy had retired within the walls of Knoxville, and the investment of the city completed. During the nights our sharpshooters were advanced a little distance at a time until they were under the very walls of the city, and there entrenched themselves in rifle pits. The troops began building works to protect against attacks, and laying parallels, so that every few nights we advanced a little nearer the city.

Jenkins, with three brigades and a part of the cavalry, stretched around the city on the north and to the river on the opposite side of us. A pontoon bridge was laid across the river below the city, and Law, with two brigades of Jenkins' Division and a battery of our best artillery, crossed the Holston River and took possession of some heights that were thought to command the city on the south side. Burnside had also some strong works on the south of the Holston, strongly guarded by infantry, dismounted cavalry, and some of their best rifled pieces of artillery. This force was just opposite the city, having easy access thereto by a military bridge and a pontoon bridge. Burnside had twelve thousand regular troops in his outer trenches, several thousand recent volunteers from Tennessee in his inner lines, with fifty-one pieces of artillery in place, ready for action, in Knoxville alone. Longstreet had between fifteen and seventeen thousand, after some reinforcements had reached him, and three battalions of artillery, inclusive of the horse artillery.

Night and day the work of entrenchment went bravely on in both armies, each working in plain view of the other; without any disposition to disturb the operations of either by shelling from the forts in our front or from our works in the rear. Each commander seemed willing and disposed to give his opponent an open field and a fair fight. No advantage was asked and none taken on either side, and the coming contest appeared to be one between the hot blood of the South in assault and the dogged determination of the North in resistance—valor, impetuosity, dash, impulsive courage against cool, calculating, determined resistance. Greeks of the South were preparing to meet Greeks of the North—the passionate Ionian was about to measure swords with the stern Dorian, then of a necessity "comes the tug of war."

On the 22d, McLaws reporting as being ready for the assault, he was ordered to prepare for it on the night of the 23d. But a report coming to the commanding General that a large body of the enemy's cavalry was moving upon our rear from near Kinston, General Wheeler, with his troopers, was detached from the army to look after them, and did not return until the 26th, having frightened the enemy away in the meantime. The officers of McLaws' assaulting column protested against the night attack, preferring daylight for such important work, which in the end was granted.

The night of the 24th the enemy made a sally, attacking Wofford's front; but was soon repulsed and driven back within his lines. Longstreet now awaited the reinforcement that was approaching with all speed. Jones' Brigade of Cavalry, from Southwest Virginia, came up on the 28th, while Bushrod Johnston, with his own Brigade of Tennessee Infantry and Gracie's Brigade of Alabamians, was near at hand and moving with all haste. The infantry and artillery promised from Virginia were more than one hundred miles away, and could not reach us in time to take part in the pending attack. General Bragg, commanding the Army of Tennessee after his disastrous defeat at Missionary Ridge, in front of Chattanooga, was at the head of the war department, and ordered Longstreet to assault Knoxville at once.

Orders were given and preparations made to commence the attack on Fort Sanders at early dawn on the 29th by the brigades of McLaws. Fort Sanders, the key to Burnside's position, was a formidable fortress, covering several acres of ground, built by the Confederates when in possession of Knoxville, and called by them "Fort London," but named "Fort Sanders" by the Federals, in honor of the brave commander who fell in wresting it from the Confederates. The enemy had greatly strengthened it after Longstreet's advent in East Tennessee. It was surrounded by a deep and wide moat, from the bottom of which to the top of the fort was from eighteen to twenty feet. In front of the moat for several hundred yards was felled timber, which formed an almost impassable abattis, while wire netting was stretched from stump to stump and around the fort. The creek that ran between our lines and the enemy's had been dammed in several places, forcing the water back to the depth of four to five feet. The fort was lined on three sides with the heaviest of field and siege pieces, and crowded to its utmost capacity with infantry. This fort was on an acute angle of the line of entrenchments. From the right and left ran the outer or first line of breastworks, manned by infantry, and at every salient position cannons were mounted, completely encircling the entire city.

In the early gray of the morning Longstreet had marshalled his forces for the combat, while the troops in Fort Sanders slept all unconscious of the near approaching storm cloud, which was to burst over their heads. The artillery was all in position, the gunners standing by their guns, lanyard in hand, awaiting the final order to begin the attack. The armies were separated by a long, shallow vale—that to our left, in front of Jenkins, was pierced by a small stream, but obstructed by dams at intervals, until the water was in places waist deep. But the men floundered through the water to the opposite side and stood shivering in their wet garments, while the cool air of the November morning chilled their whole frames. All along the whole line the men stood silent and motionless, awaiting the sound of the signal gun.

Wofford, with his Georgians, and Humphrey, with his Mississippians, were to lead the forlorn hope in the assault on Fort Sanders, supported by Bryan's (Georgia) Brigade and one regiment of Mississippians. Kershaw stood to the right of the fort and Anderson, of Jenkins' Division, on the left, supported by the other two brigades then present of Jenkins'. The battle was to focus around the fort until that was taken or silenced, then Kershaw was to storm the works on the right, carry them, charge the second line of entrenchment, in which were posted the reserves and recent Tennessee recruits. Jenkins, with Anderson's Brigade on his right and next to McLaws, was to act as a brace to the assaulting column until the fort was taken, then by a sudden dash take the entrenchments to the left of the fort, wheel and sweep the line towards the north, and clear the way for Jenkins' other brigades.

The expectant calm before the great storm was now at hand. The men stood silent, grim, and determined, awaiting the coming crash! The crash came with the thunder of the signal gun from Alexander's Battery. Longstreet then saluted his enemy with the roar of twenty guns, the shells shrieking and crashing in and around Fort Sanders. Burnside answered the salutation with a welcome of fifty guns from the fort and angles along the entrenchments. Salvos after salvos sounded deep and loud from the cannon's mouth, and echoed and re-echoed up and down the valleys of the Holston. After the early morning compliments had continued ten or fifteen minutes, the infantry began to make ready for the bloody fray. Wofford commenced the advance on the northwest angle of the fort, Humphrey the South. Not a yell was to be given, not a gun to be fired, save only those by the sharpshooters. The dread fortress was to be taken by cold steel alone. Not a gun was loaded in the three brigades. As the mist of the morning and the smoke of the enemy's guns lifted for a moment the slow and steady steps of the "forlorn hope" could be seen marching towards the death trap—over fallen trees and spreading branches, through the cold waters of the creek, the brave men marched in the face of the belching cannon, raking the field right and left. Our sharpshooters gave the cannoneers a telling fire, and as the enemy's infantry in the fort rose above the parapets to deliver their volley, they were met by volleys from our sharpshooters in the pits, now in rear of the assaulting columns, and firing over their heads. When near the fort the troops found yet a more serious obstruction in the way of stout wires stretched across their line of approach. This, however, was overcome and passed, and the assailants soon found themselves on the crest of the twelve foot abyss that surrounded Fort Sanders. Some jumped into the moat and began climbing up upon the shoulders of their companions. The enemy threw hand bombs over the wall to burst in the ditch. Still the men struggled to reach the top, some succeeding only to fall in the fort. Scaling ladders were now called for, but none were at hand. Anderson had moved up on Wofford's left, but finding the fort yet uncovered, instead of charging the entrenchment, as ordered, he changed his direction towards the fort, and soon his brigade was tangled in wild confusion with those of Worfford and Humphrey, gazing at the helpless mass of struggling humanity in the great gulf below.

Kershaw's men stood at extreme tension watching and waiting the result of the struggle around the fort. Never perhaps were their nerves so strung up as the few moments they awaited in suspense the success or reverse of the assaulting column, bending every effort to catch the first command of "forward." All but a handful of the enemy had left the fort, and victory here seemed assured, and in that event the result of Kershaw's onslaught on the right and Jenkins' South Carolinians and Benning's Georgians on the left would have been beyond the range of conjecture. Just at this supreme moment Major Goggans, of McLaws' staff, who had been at the fort and took in the worst phases of the situation, rode to General Longstreet and reported the fortress impregnable without axes and scaling ladders. Under this misapprehension, General Longstreet gave the fatal order for the assaulting columns to retire, and all the support back to their entrenchments. Thus was one of the most glorious victories of the war lost by the ill judgment of one man. General Longstreet bitterly regretted giving this order so hastily, but pleads in extinuation his utmost confidence in Major Goggans, his class-mate at West Point.

In the twenty minutes of the assault Longstreet lost in his three brigades, Wofford's, Humphrey's, and Anderson's, eight hundred and twenty-two; Burnside, six hundred and seventy-three. During the campaign Longstreet lost twelve hundred and ninety-six. During the campaign Burnside lost fourteen hundred and eighty-one.

Kershaw's Brigade lost many gallant officers and men during the sanguinary struggles around Knoxville, and it must be confessed in sorrow and regret, all to no purpose. Not that the commanding general was wanting in ability, military training, or tactical knowledge; nor the soldiers in courage, daring, and self-denials. None of these were lacking, for the officers and men of the line performed deeds of prowess that have never been excelled by any soldiers on the planet, while in skill or fearlessness the regimental brigade and division commanders were equal to Ney, Murat, St. Cyr, or any of the host of great commanders of the Napoleonic era. But in the first place the Confederate forces were too weak, poorly equipped in all those essentials that are so requisite to an invading army.

Major William M. Gist

Major William M. Gist was a son of Governor W.H. Gist, the Governor just preceding Secession, and Mrs. Mary E. Gist; born in Union County in 1840. He was educated in the common schools of Union and York Counties and by private tutors, until January, 1854. He then went to school at Glenn Springs to Rev. C.S. Beard for six months. His health failing, he returned to his home, and in January, 1855, entered the Mt. Zion College, at Winnsboro, Fairfield County, taught by Hon. J.W. Hudson, and spent one year at that institution. He next entered the South Carolina College, in January, 1856, and graduated in the class of '59. The class which Major Gist was in at the time, the Junior, did not participate in the great "college rebellion" of March 28th, 1858. Through that rebellion one hundred and eleven of the students were suspended for six months.

When the first alarm of war was sounded, Major Gist responded promptly, with the same chivalric spirit that was so characteristic of his whole life. He joined, as a private, Captain Gadberry's Company, from Union, and left for Charleston on January 12, 1861, the company forming a part of Colonel Maxey Gregg's First Six Months' Volunteers, and remained with the command until their term of service expired. A vacancy occurring, Colonel Gregg appointed him his Sergeant Major.

After the fall of Sumter a part of Colonel Gregg's Regiment was disbanded, and Major Gist returned to Union and began at once organizing a company for the Confederate States Army. He was elected Captain of the company and was joined to the Fifteenth Regiment, then collecting at camp near Columbia for drill and instruction. He served as Captain until the death of Colonel DeSaussure, then was promoted to Major. There being no officer senior to him, his way was open to the Colonelcy of his regiment at the time of his death.

Major Gist was a young man of rare qualities—open, frank, generous, and brave. He commanded the respect and esteem of all. Just verging into mature manhood as the toscin of war sounded, he had no opportunity to display his great qualities as a civilian, but as a soldier he was all that the most exacting could desire. He was beloved by his men, and they appreciated his worth. He was kind and affectionate to all, and showed favoritism or privileges to none. It was through that ungovernable impulse that permeates the body and flows through the hot Southern blood that he so recklessly threw his life away, leading his men to the charge. In a moment of hesitancy among his troops, he felt the supreme responsibility of Leadership, placed himself where danger was greatest, bullets falling thick and fast; thus by the inspiration of his own individual courage, he hoped to carry his men with him to success, or to meet a fate like his own.

LIEUTENANT COLONEL W. G. RICE.

Lieutenant Colonel W.G. Rice was born in Union County, S.C., on December 9th, 1831. He was the fourth son of R.S. Rice and Agnes B. Rice, nee Morgan, and resided in the upper portion of the county, near Broad River. His family removed to the lower section of the county, near Goshen Hill, when the son was ten years old, and he attended the schools of the surrounding country until fourteen years of age, when he was sent to the Methodist Conference School, at Cokesbury. He remained a pupil here until October, 1848, then he entered the South Carolina College, graduating from that institution with the class of '51. He engaged in planting for one year at his original home, then began the study of law in the office of Judge T.N. Dawkins, but did not prosecute the study to graduation.

In March following he married Miss Sarah E. Sims, of Broad River, of which union eleven children were born, seven of whom are living. The year of his marriage he moved to Laurens County, near Waterloo, where we find him surrounded by "peace and plenty" until the outbreak of the Civil War. In October, 1861, he raised a volunteer company, and later, together with three other companies from Laurens County, formed a battalion, and tendered the command to George S. James, who had resigned from the United States Army. Major James assumed command at Camp Hampton in December. During the early months of 1862 three other companies united with the battalion, and Major James was promoted to Lieutenant Colonel, and Captain W.G. Rice being senior Captain, was made Major.

During the month of April following, a reorganization took place, and Lieutenant Colonel James and Major Rice were re-elected to their former positions by exactly the same vote. Major Rice being detailed on court martial on James' Island, did not accompany his battalion to Virginia, but joined it soon thereafter, near Richmond.

The battalion marched with the brigade (Drayton's) from Gordonsville to second battle of Manassas, but was not actively engaged. At the battle of Crompton's Gap, Md., Colonel Rice was severely wounded, Colonel James killed, and the battalion almost torn to pieces. Colonel Rice was left for dead upon the field, and when he gained consciousness he was within the enemy's line, and only by exercising the greatest caution, he regained the Confederate camp. By Colonel Rice's prudence at this battle in ordering a retreat to a more sheltered position, the battalion was saved from utter destruction, but suffering himself almost a fatal wound. He was sent across the Potomac, and next day to Shepherdstown. Returning from leave of absence occasioned by the desperate nature of his wound, he found that he had been promoted to Lieutenant Colonel, and that his battalion and the Fifteenth Regiment made a part of Kershaw's Brigade, this being in December, 1862. Colonel Rice led his command through the battles of Fredericksburg and Chancellorsville without incident of special interest (wide sketch of battalion).

Returning from an enjoyable leave of absence, he found his command at Chambersburg, Pa. Three days later he commanded the battalion at the bloody battle of Gettysburg. Again Colonel Rice is absent on sick leave, and regains the army just as Longstreet was crossing the Holston. Four days afterwards he was given one company from each of the five regiments to reinforce his battalion, and ordered to feel for and drive the enemy from the position which they held. This proved to be a fortified camp and the enemy in strong line of battle. In the engagement that followed, Colonel Rice was again so severely wounded as to render him unfit for service thereafter.

After this he returned home to the prosecution of his life-work, farming. He removed to Abbeville, now Greenwood County, December, 1869, where he may now be found, as he says, "in the enjoyment of a reasonable degree of health and strength, surrounded by friends and relatives."

JULIUS ZOBEL

To show with what devotion and fidelity the private soldier of the Southland served the cause he espoused, I will relate as an example the act of Julius Zobel, who fell so dangerously wounded before Knoxville. This is not an isolated case, for hundreds and thousands were tempted like Zobel, but turned away with scorn and contempt. But Julius Zobel was an exception in that he was not a native born, but a blue-eyed, fair-haired son of the "Fatherland." He had not been in this "Land of the free and home of the brave" long enough to comprehend all its blessings, he being under twenty-one years of age, and not yet naturalized. He was a mechanic in the railroad shops, near Newberry, when the first call for volunteers was made. He laid aside his tools and promptly joined Company E (Captain Nance), of the Third South Carolina, called "Quitman Rifles."

He had a smooth, pleasant face, a good eye, and the yellow hair of his countrymen. His nature was all sunshine, geniality, and many a joke he practiced upon his comrades, taking all in good humor those passed upon him. One day, as a comrade had been "indulging" too freely, another accosted him with—

"Turn away your head, your breath is awful. What is the matter with you?"

Zobel, in his broad German brogue, answered for his companion. "Led 'em alone, dare been nodden to madder mid Mattis, only somding crawled in him and died."

He lost his leg at Knoxville and fell in the enemy's hands after Longstreet withdrew, and was sent North with the other wounded. While in the loathsome prison pen, enduring all the sufferings, hardships, and horrors of the Federal "Bastile," he was visited by the German Consul, and on learning that he had not been naturalized, the Consul offered him his liberty if he would take the oath of allegiance to the North.

Zobel flashed up as with a powder burst, and spoke like the true soldier that he was. "What! Desert my comrades; betray the country I have sworn to defend; leave the flag under whose folds I have lost all but life? No, no! Let me die a thousand deaths in this hell hole first!"

He is living to-day in Columbia, an expert mechanic in the service of the Southern Railroad, earning an honest living by the sweat of his brow, with a clear conscience, a faithful heart, and surrounded by a devoted family.

That the campaign against Knoxville was a failure, cannot be wondered at under the circumstances. In the first place Longstreet's forces were too weak—the two thousand reinforcements to come from Virginia dwindled down to a few regiments of cavalry and a battery or two. The men were badly furnished and equipped—a great number being barefoot and thinly clad. Hundreds would gather at the slaughter pens daily and cut from the warm beef hides strips large enough to make into moccasins, and thus shod, marched miles upon miles in the blinding snow and sleet. All overcoats and heavy clothing had been left in Virginia, and it is a fact too well known to be denied among the soldiers of the South that baggage once left or sent to the rear never came to the front again.

Longstreet did not have the support he had the right to expect from his superiors and those in authority at Richmond. He had barely sufficient transportation to convey the actual necessaries of camp equippage, and this had to be used daily in gathering supplies from the surrounding country for man and beast. He had no tools for entrenching purposes, only such as he captured from the enemy, and expected to cross deep and unfordable rivers without a pontoon train. With the dead of winter now upon him, his troops had no shelter to protect them from the biting winds of the mountains or the blinding snow storms from overhead save only much-worn blankets and thin tent flys five by six feet square, one to the man. This was the condition in which the commanding General found himself and troops, in a strange and hostile country, completely cut off from railroad connection with the outside world. Did the men murmur or complain? Not a bit of it. Had they grown disheartened and demoralized by their defeat at Knoxville, or had they lost their old-time confidence in themselves and their General? On the contrary, as difficulties and dangers gathered around their old chieftain, they clung to him, if possible, with greater tenacity and a more determined zeal. It seemed as if every soldier in the old First Corps was proud of the opportunity to suffer for his country—never a groan or pang, but that he felt compensated with the thought that he was doing his all in the service of his country—and to suffer for his native land, his home, and family, was a duty and a pleasure.

The soldiers of the whole South had long since learned by experience on the fields of Virginia, Maryland, and Pennsylvania, along the valleys of Kentucky, the mountains and gorges of Tennessee, and the swamps of the Mississippi, that war was only "civilized barbarism," and to endure uncomplaining was the highest attributes of a soldier. Civilization during the long centuries yet to come may witness, perhaps, as brave, unselfish, unyielding, and patriotic bands of heroes as those who constituted the Confederate Army, but God in His wisdom has never yet created their equals, and, perhaps, never will create their superiors.

CHAPTER 26
Battle of Bean Station

On the night of the 4th of December preparations were made to raise the siege around Knoxville and vacate the fortifications built around the city after a fortnight's stay in the trenches. The wagons had begun moving the day before, with part of the artillery, and early in the night the troops north and west of the city took up the line of march towards Rutledge, followed by McLaws on the right.

Kershaw being on the extreme right of the army and next to the river on the South, could not move until the troops on the left were well underway, thus leaving us in position until near midnight. Lieutenant Colonel Rutherford commanded the rear guard of skirmishers, deployed several hundred yards on either side of the road. Our march was extremely fatiguing, the roads being muddy and badly cut up by the trains in our front. The weather was cold and bleaky; the night so dark that the troops could scarcely see their way, but all night long they floundered through the mud and slough—over passes and along narrow defiles, between the mountain and the river to their right—the troops trudged along, the greater portion of whom were thinly clad, some with shoes badly worn, others with none. Two brigades of cavalry were left near the city until daylight to watch the movements of the enemy. The next day we met General Ranson with his infantry division and some artillery on his long march from Virginia to reinforce Longstreet, but too late to be of any material service to the commanding General. Bragg's orders had been imperative, "to assault Knoxville and not to await the reinforcement."

Burnside did not attempt to follow us closely, as he was rather skeptical about leaving his strong positions around Knoxville with the chances of meeting Longstreet in open field. But strong Federal forces were on a rapid march to relieve the pressure against Knoxville—one column from the West and ten thousand men un-

300

der Sherman were coming up from Chattanooga, and were now at Loudon, on the Tennessee.

Longstreet continued the march to Rodgersville, some fifty or sixty miles northeast of Knoxville, on the west bank of the Holston, and here rested for several days. It was the impression of the troops that they would remain here for a length of time, and they began building winter quarters. But Burnside feeling the brace of strong reinforcements nearing him, moved out from Knoxville a large detachment in our rear to near Bean Station (or Cross Roads), the one leading from Knoxville by way of Rutledge, the other from the eastern side of the Holston and over the mountain on the western side at Bean's Gap. Longstreet determined to retrace his steps, strike Burnside a stunning blow, and, if possible, to capture his advance forces at Bean Station.

Here I will digress a few moments from my narrative to relate an incident that took place while encamped near Rodgersville, an incident that will ever remain fresh in the memory of all of the old First Division who witnessed it. It is with feelings of sorrow at this distant day to even recall it to mind, and it is with pain that I record it. But as I have undertaken to give a faithful and true story of the army life of the First Brigade, this harrowing scene becomes a part of its history. It was near the middle of the month. The sun had long since dropped out of sight behind the blue peaks of the distant Cumberland. All is still in camp; the soldiers, after their many hardships and fatiguing marches, rest, and soon all in sound slumber. Even the very voices of nature seemed hushed and frozen in the gloomy silence of the night. All is quiet, save in one lonely tent, apart some distance from the rest, before which walks a silent sentinel, as if he, too, feels the chilling effects of the sombre stillness. Murmurings soft and low in the one lighted tent are all that break the oppressive death-like silence. In the back ground the great forest trees of the mountain stand mute and motionless, not even a nod of their stately heads to a passing breeze, while far away to the south could be seen an occasional picket fire, making the surrounding objects appear like moving, grotesque phantoms. The heavens above were all bedecked with shimmering stars, pouring down upon the sleeping Valley of the Holston a cold and trembling light.

In the lonely tent sits a soldier, who is spending his last night on earth; by his side sits his little son, who has come far away over the mountains to spend the last moments with his father and see him die—not to die like a soldier wishes for death, but as a felon and out-

301

cast, the ignominious death at the stake. An occasional sob escapes the lips of the lad, but no sigh or tears of grief from the condemned. He is holding converse with his Maker, for to His throne alone must he now appeal for pardon. Hope on earth had gone. He had no friend at court, no one to plead his cause before those who had power to order a reprieve. He must die. The doomed man was an ignorant mountaineer, belonging to one of the regiments from North Georgia or Tennessee, and in an ill-fated moment he allowed his longings for home to overcome his sense of duty, and deserted his colors—fled to his mountain home and sought to shelter himself near his wife and little ones in the dark recesses and gorges thereabout. He was followed, caught, returned to his command, courtmartialed, and sentenced to death—time, to-morrow.

During the days and nights that passed since the dread sentence had been read to him, he lay upon his rude couch in the guard tent all indifferent to his environments, and on the march he moved along with the guard in silence, gazing abstractedly at the blue vaults of heaven or the star-strewn, limitless space. That far away future now to him so near—that future which no vision can contemplate nor mortal mind comprehend—is soon to be unfolded. Little heed was paid to the comforting words of his sympathetic comrades in arms, who bid him hope, for the condemned man felt inwardly and was keenly conscious of the fact that he had been caught upon the crest of a great wave of destiny, soon to be swept away by its receding force to darkness, despair, death. "Fate had played him falsely."

To witness death, to see the torn and mangled remains of friends and comrades, are but incidents in the life of a soldier. While all dread it, few fear it. Yet it is upon the field of battle that it is expected—amid the din and smoke, the shouts of his comrades, the rattle of musketry, and the cannon's roar. There is the soldier's glory, his haven, his expected end; and of all deaths, that upon the battlefield, surrounded by victorious companions and waving banners, the triumphant shouts of comrades, is the least painful.

The grounds selected for the carrying out of the court's sentence were on a broad plateau, gently sloping towards the center on three sides. So well were the grounds and surroundings adapted to the end in view, that it seemed as if nature had anticipated the purposes of man.

By 9 o'clock the troops of the division were in motion, all under the command of Colonel James D. Nance, of the Third South Carolina, marching for the field of death. Kershaw's Brigade took the lead, and formed on the left of the hollow square. Wofford's on the right, with Bryan's doubling on the two, while Humphrey's closed the space at the west end of the square.

A detail of thirty men were made to do the firing, fifteen guns being loaded with powder and ball, the others with powder alone, this arrangement being made, perhaps, with a view to ease the qualms of conscience, should any of the guards have scruples of shedding the blood of a former comrade in arms. None could know positively who held the death-dealing guns. An opening was made at the lower end and the first platoon of guards entered with arms reversed, then the band playing the "Dead March," followed by the condemned and his son, the second platoon bringing up the rear. The cortege marched around the whole front of the lined-up troops, keeping step to the slow and dismal sounds of the "Dead March." The prisoner walked with the firm and steady step of a Sagamore, or an Indian brave marching and singing his death chants, to the place of his execution. His son was equally as courageous and self-possessed, not a tremor or faltering in either. At times the father and son would speak in low, soft tones to each other, giving and receiving, perhaps, the last messages, the last farewells on earth, the soldier-outcast being now under the very shadow of death.

After making the entire circuit of the square, the condemned was conducted to the open space at the eastern side, where a rude stake had been driven in the ground. To this he boldly walked, calmly kneeling in front, allowing himself to be bandaged and pinioned thereto. The guards had formed in double ranks, fifteen paces in front, his faithful son standing some distance to his right, calm, unmoved, and defiant, even in the face of all the terrors going on before him. The officer in charge gives the command, "ready," thirty hammers spring back; "aim," the pieces rise to the shoulders; then, and then only, the tension broke, and the unfortunate man, instead of the officer, cried out in a loud, metallic voice, "fire." The report of the thirty rifles rang out On the stillness of the morning; the man at the stake gives a convulsive shudder, his head tails listlessly on his breast, blood gushes out in streams, and in a moment all is still. The deserter has escaped.

The authorities at Washington had grown tired of Burnside's failure to either crush Longstreet or drive him out of East Tennessee, and had sent General Foster to relieve him, the latter General bringing with him the standing orders, "Crush or drive out Longstreet." How well General Foster succeeded will be related further on. In obedience to the department's special orders, General Longstreet had, several days previous, sent Wheeler's Cavalry back to General Johnston, now commanding Bragg's Army. Our troops had heard the confirmation of the report of General Bragg's desperate battle at Missionary Ridge—his disastrous defeat his withdrawal to Dalton, and his subsequent relinquishment of command of the Army of Tennessee. This had no effect upon our troops, no more so than the news of the fall of Vicksburg just after Lee's bloody repulse at Gettysburg. The soldiers of the eastern Army had unbounded confidence in themselves and their commander, and felt that so long as they stood together they were invincible.

The enemy had fortified a position at Bean's Station, in a narrow valley between the Holston River and the Clinch Mountains, the valley being about two miles in breadth. This force Longstreet determined to capture, and his plans were admirably adapted to bring about the result. To the right of the enemy was the river; to their left, a rugged mountain spur; passable at only a few points. Part of our cavalry was to pass down the western side of the mountain, close the gaps in rear, the infantry to engage the enemy in front until the other portion of the cavalry could move down the east bank of the river, cross over, and get in the enemy's rear, thus cutting off all retreat. This part of the Valley of the Holston had been pretty well ravaged to supply the Federal Army, and our troops, with never more than a day's rations on hand at a time, had to be put on short rations, until our subsistence trains could gather in a supply and the neighborhood mills could grind a few days' rations ahead. Old soldiers know what "short rations" mean—next to no rations at all.

General Longstreet says of the morale of his army at this time: "The men were brave, steady, patient. Occasionally they called pretty loudly for parched corn, but always in a bright, merry mood. There was never a time we did not have corn enough, and plenty of wood with which to keep us warm and parch our corn. At this distance it seems as almost incredible that we got along as we did, but all were then so healthy and strong that we did not feel severely our really great hardship. Our serious trouble was in the matter of shoes and clothing."

Early on the morning of the 14th the troops were put in motion and marched rapidly down the almost impassable thoroughfare. Bushrod Johnston's Division being in the front, followed by McLaws'—Kershaw's Brigade in the lead. Part of Jenkins' Division was acting as escort for supply trains in the surrounding country, and that Division did not join the army for several days. Late in the day of the 15th we came in sight of the enemy's breastworks. The Federal artillery opened a furious fusilade upon the troops, coming down the road with their rifled guns and field mortars. Bushrod Johnston had filed to the left of the road and gotten out of range, but the screaming shells kept up a continual whiz through the ranks of Kershaw. The men hurried along the road to seek shelter under a bluff in our front, along the base of which ran a small streamlet. The greater portion of the brigade was here huddled together in a jam, to avoid the shells flying overhead. The enemy must have had presage of our position, for they began throwing shells up in the air from their mortars and dropping them down upon us, but most fell beyond, while a great many exploded in the air. We could see the shells on their downward flight, and the men pushed still closer together and nearer the cliff. Here the soldier witnessed one of those incidents so often seen in army life that makes him feel that at times his life is protected by a hand of some hidden, unseen power. His escape from death so often appears miraculous that the soldier feels from first to last that he is but "in the hollow of His hand," and learns to trust all to chance and Providence.

As a shell from a mortar came tumbling over and over, just above the heads of this mass of humanity, a shout went up from those farther back, "Look out! Look out! There comes a shell." Lower and lower it came, all feeling their hopelessness of escape, should the shell explode in their midst. Some tried to push backwards; others, forward, while a great many crowded around and under an ambulance, to which was hitched an old broken down horse, standing perfectly still and indifferent, and all oblivious to his surroundings. The men gritted their teeth, shrugged their shoulders, and waited in death-like suspense the falling of the fatal messenger—that peculiar, whirling, hissing sound growing nearer and more distinct every second. But instead of falling among the men, it fell directly upon the head of the old horse, severing it almost from the body, but failed to explode. The jam was so great that some had difficulty in clearing themselves from the falling horse. Who of us are prepared to say whether this was mere chance, or that the bolt was guided and directed by an invisible hand?

Bushrod Johnston had formed on the left of the road; Kershaw marching over the crest of the hill in our front, and putting his brigade in line of battle on a broad plateau and along the foot hills of the mountains on the right. Here the troops were halted, to wait the coming up of the rest of the division and Jenkins' two brigades. The cannonading of the enemy was especially severe during our halt, and General Kershaw had to frequently shift his regiments to avoid the terrific force of the enemy's shells. It was not the intention of the commanding General to bring on a general engagement here until he heard from his cavalry beyond the river and those to the west of the mountain. The cavalry had been sent to cut off retreat and close the mountain passes, and the infantry was to press moderately in front, in order to hold the enemy in position.

Just before sunset, however, a general advance was made. One of Kershaw's regiments was climbing along the mountain side, endeavoring to gain the enemy's left, and as our skirmishers became hotly engaged, the movements of the regiment on the side of the mountain were discovered, and the enemy began to retire. Now orders were given to press them hard. The rattle of Bushrod Johnston's rifles on our left told of a pretty stiff fight he was having. As the long row of bristling bayonets of Kershaw's men debouched upon the plain in front of the enemy's works, nothing could be seen but one mass of blue, making way to the rear in great confusion. Our artillery was now brought up and put in action, our infantry continuing to press forward, sometimes at double-quick.

We passed over the enemy's entrenchments without firing a gun. Night having set in, and General Longstreet hearing from his cavalry that all in the enemy's rear was safe, ordered a halt for the night, thinking the game would keep until morning. During the night, however, by some misunderstanding of orders, the commander of the cavalry withdrew from the mountain passes, and the enemy taking advantage of this outlet so unexpectedly offered, made his escape under cover of darkness. Here we had another truthful verification of the oft' quoted aphorism of Burns, about "the best laid plans of mice and men."

This last attempt of Longstreet to bring the enemy to an engagement outside of Knoxville proving abortive, the commanding General determined to close the campaign for the season, and to put his troops in as comfortable winter quarters as possible. This was found on the right or east bank of the Holston, near Morristown and the little hamlet of Russellville. The brigade crossed the Holston about the 17th of December, in a little flat boat, holding about two companies at a time, the boat being put backwards and forwards by means of a stout rope, the men pulling with their hands. A blinding sleet was falling, covering the rope continually with a sheet of ice, almost freezing the hands of the thinly clad and barefooted soldiers. But there was no murmuring nor complaint—all were as jolly and good-natured as if on a picnic excursion. Hardship had become a pleasure and sufferings, patriotism. There were no sickness, no straggling, nor feelings of self-constraint.

General Longstreet speaks thus of his army after he had established his camps and the subsistence trains began to forage in the rich valleys of the French Broad and Chucky Rivers and along the banks of Mossy Creek:

"With all the plentitude of provisions, and many things, which, at the time, seemed luxuries, we were not quite happy. Tattered blankets, garments, shoes (the later going—some gone) opened ways on all sides for piercing winter blasts. There were some hand looms in the country from which we occasionally picked up a piece of cloth, and here and there we received other comforts—some from kind, some from unwilling hands, which could nevertheless spare them. For shoes, we were obliged to resort to raw-hides, from beef cattle, as temporary protection from the frozen ground. Then we found soldiers who could tan the hides of our beeves, some who could make shoes, some who could make shoe pegs, some who could make shoe lasts, so that it came about that the hides passed rapidly from the beeves to the feet of the soldiers in the form of comfortable shoes."

We took up very comfortable quarters, in the way that comfort goes with a soldier—cut off from the outside world. Only a few officers had the old army fly tents; the soldiers were each supplied, or rather had supplied themselves upon the battlefield of the enemy with small tent flies, about five by six feet, so arranged with buttons and button holes that two being buttoned together and stretched over a pole would make the sides or roof and the third would close the end, making a tent about six feet long, five feet wide, and four feet high, in which three or four men could sleep very comfortably. In the bitter weather great roaring fires were built in front during the night, and to which the soldier, by long habit, or a kind of intuition, would stretch his feet, when the cold would become unbearable under his threadbare blanket.

But notwithstanding all these disadvantages, the men of Kershaw's Brigade were bent on having a good time in East Tennessee. They foraged during the day for apples, chickens, butter, or whatever they could find to eat. Some of sporting proclivities would purchase a lot of chicken roosters and then fight, regiment against regiment, and seemed to enjoy as much seeing a fight between a shanghai and a dunghill, as a match between gaved Spanish games.

Many formed the acquaintance of ladies in the surrounding country, and they, too, Union as well as Southern, being cut off like ourselves—their husbands and brothers being either in the Northern or Southern Army—seemed determined on having a good time also. Dancing parties were frequent, and the ladies of Southern sympathies gave the officers and soldiers royal dinners.

In this connection, I will relate an anecdote told on our gallant Lieutenant Colonel Rutherford, of the Third, by a friend of his.

When the Third South Carolina Regiment of Infantry was in East Tennessee, in the month of January, 1864, not only did the soldiers find it difficult to get enough to eat, but their supply of shoes and clothing ran pretty low. Those who had extra pants or jackets helped their needy friends. Lieutenant Colonel Rutherford had turned over his extra pair of pants to some one, which left him the pair he wore each day as his only stock on hand in the pants line. Heavy snows fell. The regiment was encamped very near a pleasant residence, where a bevy of pretty girls lived. After an acquaintance of sometime, a snow-balling was indulged in. It was observed that Colonel Rutherford used his every endeavor to constantly face the girls, who were pelting him pretty liberally on all sides. After awhile he slipped up and fell, but in his fall his face was downward, when lo! the girls discovered that he had a hole in his pants. Too good-natured to appear to see his predicament, no notice was seemingly taken of his misfortune; but as the officers were about going off to bed that night, the married lady said to him:

"Colonel, lay your pants on the chair at your room door tonight, and you will find them there again in the morning. We hope you won't mind a patch."

The Colonel, who was always so gallant in actual battle, and could not bear to turn his back to the Federal soldiers, was just as unwilling to turn his back to snow-balls, who happened to be Confederate lasses, and the reason therefor, although never told, was discovered by them.

The weather had gotten down to two degrees below zero, the ground frozen as hard as brick-bats, and the winds whistled gaily through our tattered tents, our teeth beating tattoo and our limbs shivering from the effects of our scanty clothing and shoes. But our wagons were gathering in supplies from the rich valleys of the French Broad and the Nolachucky, and while we suffered from cold, we generally had provisions sufficient for our want. By the middle of January we had to temporarily break up camp to meet the enemy, who had left Knoxville with the greater part of the army, and was marching up on the right banks of the French Broad to near Dandridge. General Foster seeing the penalty put upon General Burnside for not driving out Longstreet from East Tennessee, the former undertook to accomplish in this bitter weather what the latter had failed to do in comparative good season. Our cavalry, with Jenkins' Division, headed direct towards the moving column of the enemy, while McLaws' Division marched in the direction of Strawberry Plains, with a view to cutting off the enemy and forcing him to battle in an open field. But General Granger, in command of the Federal column, was too glad to cross the French Broad and beat a hasty retreat to Knoxville. We returned to our old camps, and waited, like Micawber, "for something to turn up."

By some disagreement or want of confidence in General McLaws by the commanding General, he was relieved of his command, and General Kershaw being the senior Brigadier General of the division, was placed in command. What the differences were between General Longstreet and his Major General were never exactly understood by the soldiers. While General McLaws may have been a brave soldier and was well beloved by officers and men, still he was wanting in those elements to make a successful General of volunteer troops— dash, discipline, and promptness in action.

General Longstreet had bent all his energies to the repairing of the railroad through East Tennessee and Virginia, and as soon as this was accomplished, a limited number of soldiers were furloughed for twenty-one days. A large lot of shoes and clothing was sent us from Richmond, and this helped to make camp life more enjoyable. Not all the men by any means could be spared by furlough even for this brief period, for we had an active and vigilant foe in our front. Most of the men drew their furloughs by lot, those who had been from home the longest taking their chances by drawing from a hat, "furlough" or "no furlough."

While in winter quarters, during the spasm of chicken fighting, a difficulty occurred between Lieutenant A and Private B, of the Third, both good friends, and no better soldiers were ever upon a battlefield. These are not the initials of their names, but will answer the purpose at hand, and that purpose is to show the far-reaching results of the courtmartial that followed, and a decision reached under difficulties, that the most learned jurist might feel proud of.

I will say for the benefit of those not learned in the law of army regulations, that for an officer to strike a private he is cashiered, and for a private to strike an officer the penalty is either death or long imprisonment with ball and chain attachments.

Now it appeared to the officers who composed the courtmartial, Captain Herbert, Lieutenant Garlington, and the writer of this (all parties of the Third), that Lieutenant A had knocked Private B down. The officer appeared in his own defense, and gave in extenuation of his crime, that Private B had hit his (Lieutenant A's) chicken a stunning blow on the head while they were "petting" them between rounds. Now that decision of the courtmartial astonished our Colonel as much as the men who were parties to the combat themselves. Now it read something like this—time, dress parade:

"Whereas, Lieutenant A, of Company ——, Third South Carolina, did strike Private B, of same company and regiment, with his fist in the face, that he should receive the severest of punishment; but, whereas, Private B did strike the game chicken in the hands of Lieutenant A, without cause or provocation, therefore both are equally guilty of a crime and misdemeanor, and should be privately reprimanded by the Colonel commanding."

Such a laugh as was set up, notwithstanding the grave countenance of the Colonel, was never heard on ordinary occasions.

LEONAUR

This concludes Volume 1 of

Kershaw's Brigade

Volume 2 continues with:

The Battle of the Wilderness
Cold Harbor
Petersburg
The Shenandoah Valley Campaign
Cedar Creek
& the Conclusion of the War

Comprehensive Regimental Rolls are
also included in Volume 2

Available in hardcover and softcover
from Leonaur

ISBN (10 digit): 1-84677-105-6 (hardcover)

ISBN (13 digit): 978-1-84677-105-7 (hardcover)

ISBN (10 digit): 1-84677-104-8 (softcover)

ISBN (13 digit): 978-1-84677-104-0 (softcover)

LEONAUR

ALSO FROM LEONAUR
AVAILABLE IN SOFTCOVER OR HARDCOVER WITH DUST JACKET

LEONAUR

ALSO FROM LEONAUR
AVAILABLE IN SOFTCOVER OR HARDCOVER WITH DUST JACKET

LEONAUR

CLASSIC SF FROM LEONAUR

AVAILABLE IN SOFTCOVER OR HARDCOVER WITH DUST JACKET

SF1 CLASSIC SCIENCE FICTION SERIES
BEFORE ADAM & Other Stories
by Jack London

Volume 1 of The Collected Science Fiction & Fantasy of Jack London.

SOFTCOVER : **ISBN 1-84677-008-4**
HARDCOVER : **ISBN 1-84677-015-7**

Contains the complete novel Before Adam plus shorter works: The Scarlet Plague, A Relic of the Pliocene, When the World Was Young, The Red One, Planchette, A Thousand Deaths, Goliah, A Curious Fragment and The Rejuvenation of Major Rathbone

SF2 CLASSIC SCIENCE FICTION SERIES
THE IRON HEEL & Other Stories
by Jack London

Volume 2 of The Collected Science Fiction & Fantasy of Jack London.

SOFTCOVER : **ISBN 1-84677-004-1**
HARDCOVER : **ISBN 1-84677-011-4**

Contains the complete novel The Iron Heel plus shorter works: The Enemy of All the World, The Shadow and the Flash, The Strength of the Strong, The Unparalleled Invasion and The Dream of Debs

SF3 CLASSIC SCIENCE FICTION SERIES
THE STAR ROVER & Other Stories
by Jack London

Volume 3 of The Collected Science Fiction & Fantasy of Jack London.

SOFTCOVER : **ISBN 1-84677-006-8**
HARDCOVER : **ISBN 1-84677-013-0**

Contains the complete novel The Star Rover plus shorter works: The Minions of Midas, The Eternity of Forms and The Man With the Gash

Lightning Source UK Ltd.
Milton Keynes UK
UKOW04f1051150216

268388UK00001B/237/P